CW01023007

The Voice of Judith in 300 Years of Oratorio and Opera

The Voice of Judith in 300 Years of Oratorio and Opera

Helen Leneman

LONDON • NEW YORK • OXFORD • NEW DELHI • SYDNEY

T&T CLARK
Bloomsbury Publishing Plc
50 Bedford Square, London, WC1B 3DP, UK
1385 Broadway, New York, NY 10018, USA
29 Earlsfort Terrace, Dublin 2, Ireland

BLOOMSBURY, T&T CLARK and the T&T Clark logo are trademarks of
Bloomsbury Publishing Plc

First published in Great Britain 2021
This paperback edition published 2023

Copyright © Helen Leneman, 2021

Helen Leneman has asserted her right under the Copyright, Designs and
Patents Act, 1988, to be identified as Author of this work.

For legal purposes the Acknowledgments on p. vii constitute an extension
of this copyright page.

Cover design: Charlotte James
Cover image © Irina Koren

All rights reserved. No part of this publication may be reproduced or
transmitted in any form or by any means, electronic or mechanical, including
photocopying, recording, or any information storage or retrieval system,
without prior permission in writing from the publishers.

Bloomsbury Publishing Plc does not have any control over, or responsibility for, any
third-party websites referred to or in this book. All internet addresses given in this
book were correct at the time of going to press. The author and publisher regret any
inconvenience caused if addresses have changed or sites have ceased to exist, but can
accept no responsibility for any such changes.

A catalogue record for this book is available from the British Library.

Library of Congress Cataloging-in-Publication Data
Names: Leneman, Helen, author.
Title: The voice of Judith in 300 years of oratorio and opera / Helen Leneman.
Description: London ; New York : T&T Clark, [2021] |
Includes bibliographical references and index. | Summary: "This volume focuses on the
story of Judith as presented by composers, librettists and playwrights over four centuries.
Helen Leneman analyzes numerous examples of music, librettos and the librettists' views
of Judith - strongly influenced by societal attitudes of their time - and how these librettos
in turn suggest unexpected ways of understanding biblical women and their stories"–
Provided by publisher.
Identifiers: LCCN 2020052694 (print) | LCCN 2020052695 (ebook) |
ISBN 9780567687302 (hardback) | ISBN 9780567687319 (pdf)
Subjects: LCSH: Bible. Judith–Drama. | Bible. Judith–Criticism, interpretation, etc. |
Bible in music. | Operas–Analysis, appreciation. | Oratorios–Analysis, appreciation.
Classification: LCC BS1735.52 .L46 2021 (print) |
LCC BS1735.52 (ebook) | DDC 782.1–dc23
LC record available at https://lccn.loc.gov/2020052694
LC ebook record available at https://lccn.loc.gov/2020052695

ISBN: HB: 978-0-5676-8730-2
PB: 978-0-5676-9993-0
ePDF: 978-0-5676-8731-9

Typeset by Newgen KnowledgeWorks Pvt. Ltd., Chennai, India

To find out more about our authors and books visit www.bloomsbury.com
and sign up for our newsletters.

Contents

Acknowledgments

As with all my books, I received invaluable help with my research from several people and organizations. I was able to study the score of Achille Peri's very rare 1860 opera only through the generous help of my London friend and colleague Reverend Dr. Ann Jeffers. The score is in the British Library, and she spent many hours there scanning this large score and sending it to me electronically. I obtained hard-to-find librettos and two crucial recordings from a friend in New York, a serious collector of rare recordings. He copied the original LP of Goossens's work onto a CD for me, as well as a recording of the radio broadcast of Reznicek's opera. I also thank my friend and colleague Jack M. Sasson, emeritus at Vanderbilt University, a brilliant and insightful scholar with a sense of humor welcome in this field. He gave me several research tips and provided support and encouragement. I also thank Dartmouth College and the Arnold Bennett Society for generously providing me with important reference materials from their archives.

My mentor, friend, and PhD advisor Prof. Athalya Brenner continues to offer encouragement and support, fifteen years after I completed my PhD under her expert guidance. I have never forgotten her frequent question at the end of many discussions— "So what?"—forcing me to focus on the meaning and significance of every idea I was developing. She is still sitting on my shoulder asking that question, never letting me coast through without a good closing explanation. I also thank Dominic Mattos, my editor, for his enthusiasm about my work. It is a real pleasure to be working with a fellow singer and music enthusiast. I also wish to thank Irina Koren, a wonderful local artist I was lucky to find. She listened carefully to my ideas and vision for a cover and produced numerous sketches, repeatedly going back to produce the perfect image— and she did!

My spouse, Sima, patiently read every word of this book and provided invaluable insights and comments, pushing me to dig deeper and think outside the box. My thanks to her for her continual loving support.

Links to Audio, Scores, and Librettos
where Available

Alessandro Scarlatti (1660–1725): *La Giuditta* (two versions: 1693, 1697)

Naples version: the Italian libretto is here: https://issuu.com/klassiek.nl/docs/ digital_booklet_scarlatti_la_giudit.

On YouTube: https://www.youtube.com/watch?v=RJXVVapmuCw.

Cambridge version: on YouTube: https://www.youtube.com/watch?v=5cB35 U5BYXg.

A fine recording on the Albany Record label, featuring The Queen's Chamber Band (2007).

Antonio Vivaldi (1675–1741): *Juditha Triumphans* (1716)

On YouTube: https://www.youtube.com/watch?v=6mTEpicRFwM.

There are numerous recordings, with widely varied casting choices.

The full libretto with translation is here: https://static1.squarespace.com/ static/530098fbe4b03a0d7dde4700/t/53204b88e4b0db5158a58f7b/1394625416813/ Juditha+Triumphans+program+Pinchgut+Opera.pdf.

Thomas Arne (1710–1778): *Judith* (1761, 1764)

The only recording is stored at the British Library and can only be accessed there.

The full libretto, by Isaac Bickerstaffe, can be found here: https://quod.lib.umich. edu/e/ecco/004799605.0001.000/1:11?rgn=div1;view=fulltext.

A full score is available online, but it includes only solos, no recitatives or choruses; and solos are identified by the name of the singer who sang them, not by the character being portrayed: http://ks4.imslp.info/files/imglnks/usimg/f/ff/IMSLP341885-PMLP 551471-arne_judith.pdf.

A plot outline can be found at https://www.revolvy.com/page/Judith-%28oratorio %29.

Wolfgang Amadeus Mozart (1756–1791: *Betulia Liberata* (1771)

The full libretto is here: https://dsd-files.s3.amazonaws.com/challenge/CC72590/ CC72590/CC72590.pdf.

There are two recordings on YouTube; the shorter one without recitatives is here: https://www.youtube.com/watch?v=sBHvp8wN8R0.

I recommend listening to the full work, as there is masterful, subtle music even in the recitatives: https://www.youtube.com/watch?v=vPHdeM2STPQ.

Henry David Leslie (1822–1896): *Judith* (1858)
Never recorded; score available in some libraries.

C. H. H. Parry (1848–1918): *Judith, or The Regeneration of Manasseh* (1888)
On YouTube: https://www.youtube.com/watch?v=qNH8NpEMvAQ.
The full libretto and piano-vocal score is here: http://conquest.imslp.info/files/
imglnks/usimg/f/f4/IMSLP108864-SIBLEY1802.15027.48cc-39087011304260score.
pdf.

Paul Hillemacher (1852–1933): *Judith, Scène Lyrique* (1876)
The full score online is here: https://babel.hathitrust.org/cgi/pt?id=uc1.c2821777;
view=2up;seq=74;size=175.

Arthur Honegger (1892–1955): *Judith, Drame Biblique* (1925)
The oratorio version is on YouTube here: https://www.youtube.com/watch?v=
bTSF-CIQXq.
The score is available in some libraries.

Achille Peri (1812–1880): *Giuditta* (1860)
The Italian libretto is here: https://ia801808.us.archive.org/13/items/giudittamelo
dram00peri2/giudittamelodram00peri2.pdf.
A translated libretto is here: https://babel.hathitrust.org/cgi/pt?id=hvd.320440443
00440;view=1up;seq=17.
The score is available in very few libraries: The British Library in London and the
University of California at Berkeley are two.

Domenico Silveri (1818–1900): *Giuditta* (1885)
The score is not available online but is in some libraries.

Charles Lefebvre (1843–1917): *Judith, drame lyrique en 3 acts 4 scenes* (1877)
The score is here: http://ks.imslp.info/files/imglnks/usimg/7/7b/IMSLP256693-
PMLP416052-Lefebvre_-_Judith_VS.pdf.

Alexandre Serov (1820–1871): *Iudif* (1863)
The score is here: https://imslp.org/wiki/Judith_(Serov%2C_Aleksandr).
There is a fine recording, widely available: Brilliant Opera Collection, 2011, Bolshoi
Theater Orchestra.

George Whitefield Chadwick (1854–1931): *Judith* (1901)
The score can be found in some libraries.

Emil von Reznicek (1854–1931): *Judith* (1901)
The German libretto is here: http://ks.imslp.info/files/imglnks/usimg/1/1a/IMSLP
215110-PMLP357933-Tr_473_Judith_und_Holofernes.

The score is also available online: https://imslp.org/wiki/Judith_und_Holofernes_ (Reznicek%2C_Emil_von).

Eugene Goossens (1893–1962): *Judith* (1927)

A sound recording is stored at the National Library of Australia.
The score is available in some libraries.

Siegfried Matthus (1934–): *Judith* (1984)

The original 1985 production can be seen here: https://www.youtube.com/watch?v =GJMvTvIFn1g.

The audio only is here: https://www.youtube.com/watch?v=pPdS4ZNnBSQ.

Musical Illustrations

Introduction

This introduction will begin (1) with a summary of trends found in the seventeen musical works discussed in this book. That will be followed by (2) a discussion of Judith's story reimagined in the arts in different eras, (3) a synopsis and brief overview of the origins of the book of Judith, (4) portrayals of the three main characters (Judith, her servant, or Abra, and Holofernes) in the biblical book and in later interpretations, and (5) highlights of the major themes found in the book of Judith.

This book features in-depth analyses of the librettos and music to seventeen operas and oratorios based on the book of Judith spanning three hundred years (1694–1984). Two influential plays of the nineteenth century will also be discussed, since they inspired several librettos. Composers represented are Italian, English, Austrian, French, Swiss, Russian, and American. No extensive study of musical settings of the book of Judith has ever been done, and therefore this book is an important contribution to the field of Reception History. A cultural history of Judith's story can be found in Margarita Stocker's *Judith: Sexual Warrior*, which offers many valuable insights, though it does not include music. An in-depth study of the book of Judith from historical and cultural perspectives, a contributed volume that includes several chapters on musical settings, is *The Sword of Judith: Judith Studies across the Disciplines*.[1]

The book is organized both chronologically and by genre. Since opera did not become a popular genre until the nineteenth century, the first two chapters deal with oratorios. Two works straddled the divide between these genres but were included in the oratorio section. Each chapter includes biographical notes on the composers and then a scene-by-scene discussion of their works. The librettos (texts for the musical works) became increasingly more creative after the nineteenth century, since biblical oratorios tended to stick to mostly original biblical texts. Other than introducing many largely unknown works to readers, the ultimate goal of this book is to demonstrate what music adds to a text. Music is like a subtext, and in this role it can suggest humor, passion, desperation, and suspense, among other moods. The discussion will repeatedly highlight when and how music is utilized to create extra layers of meaning to the story.

---

[1] Kevin R. Brine, ed. *The Sword of Judith: Judith Studies across the Disciplines* (Cambridge: Open Book, 2010). This highly recommended volume is available on the internet: http://books.openedition.org/obp/972 (ISBN: 9781906924171).

1. The Music

Key: this is the major or minor scale upon which a musical piece is built. Examples are C major, Bb minor, etc. A key is always capitalized.

Note: a single note is also capitalized. For example, "a loud B is heard in the basses."

Pitch: this refers to how high or how low a note is played or sung—in what range. Notes in the first octave above Middle C are marked *d'*, *a'*, *etc*. Notes in the next octave are notated as *c"*, *d"*, *etc*. Notes below middle C have no additional symbol: just b, a, etc.

Certain trends can be noted in many of these works. These are as follows:

- Almost all works open in Bethulia, with a chorus of Hebrews singing of their suffering. Only a few works open in the Assyrian camp, skipping the first seven chapters. Those works focus more on Holofernes than on the Hebrews' suffering.
- Most works end with a victory chorus, with notable exceptions.
- The lengthy prayers of Judith in the original book do not appear in their entirety in any work. Oratorios, particularly British ones of the nineteenth century, use mostly text from the original book and therefore set many verses of Judith's prayers to music. Judith does pray in all the works, however—but for other things. For example, she sometimes prays not to be attracted to or seduced by Holofernes. This adds another dimension to the story.
- Holofernes's feelings for Judith are greatly amplified. He uses the word "love" repeatedly in many of the earlier works, which is not found in the original story. It is hard to separate his feelings of love from lust, since his soaring and passionate music can depict both. His singing can almost convince the listener that he truly has feelings for Judith. And what if he did? That would make Judith's violent act even more abhorrent, seeming almost like a betrayal. Yet interestingly, even where Holofernes is portrayed sympathetically, Judith is not in any way censured for her act.
- In many works of every period, Holofernes does not completely fall asleep when he is drunk. He can be heard mumbling, which makes Judith hesitate and doubt herself. This very dramatic device creates heightened suspense in that pivotal scene.
- Virtually every work elaborates on the banquet scene, including lengthy choruses, solos, and dances to create a milieu barely described in the original book. Readers of earlier periods might have assumed this background. In the operatic orgy scenes, a sense of intimacy is missing. But when eventually the revelers are dismissed, the intimacy between only Judith and Holofernes is more striking in contrast.

Many gaps, as well as ambiguities and uncertainties in the original story, are filled creatively and dramatically in oratorios and operas of every era. The broadest changes from the biblical story of Judith in the seventeen musical settings of Judith's story presented in this book are as follows:

- Judith's servant is given a key role in works where she is included, including a back story and suggesting various degrees of closeness to Judith. The relationship between the two women has many more dimensions. This can in part be attributed to the fact that the two women communicate, whereas in the original story, the servant's words are never recorded.

- New qualities of Judith's character are highlighted, such as confidence or the lack thereof, assertion of her power, and cleverness, demonstrated through strategic planning and often manipulative speech.
- Holofernes also has new dimensions, sometimes coming across as an almost sympathetic, even appealing character, through seductive music and fervent declarations of love. The complete opposite is also found, where he is sometimes portrayed as evil incarnate, a megalomaniac and narcissistic personality.
- An expansion and elaboration of the murder scene is found in some works, while in a few works, it is not represented but only recounted after the fact. Holofernes does not always die quickly or quietly, adding an element of suspense and terror to Judith's action. The account of the killing is sometimes much bloodier than in the original story, for example, including the presence of blood-stained clothes or a dripping sword.

In common to almost all oratorios, of any era, is the extensive praise given to God more than to Judith, a more or less obligatory point of view in a biblical oratorio. This became less of a requirement by the later nineteenth century. Operas in general take more liberties with the story, being based on librettos or plays that strayed from the original story more than oratorios. Characters are invented to create roles for tenors and opportunities for duets and ensembles that are de rigueur in nineteenth-century operas. The twentieth-century works stray even further from the original story and create some fascinating responses to the ever-present question in explorations of retellings: *What if ….* The responses to that question, throughout this book, lead to nuanced, unexpected, and fascinating retellings of the book of Judith.

2. The Book of Judith in the Arts

Artists, composers, and writers have been attracted to the story of Judith for centuries. Each genre that retells her story provides another way of seeing Judith. In many ways, dramatic music was the perfect medium to explore the "binary oppositions" found in Judith's story: two peoples—the Hebrews against the Assyrians; two religions: Judaism versus paganism; and the weak versus the strong, humble versus proud, chaste versus lustful, all found in female and male characters.[2] An addition and key advantage of musical settings of Judith's story is the prominence of the voice. Deception in Judith's discourse is a crucial element, which is highlighted by the use of the voice and musical techniques to tell Judith's story. This is true for choruses as well, which amplify the voice of the people, both in their suffering and triumphs. To portray a Judith that was mature but also heroic, some composers wrote the role for a mezzo-soprano. In actual fact, Judith would have most likely been a very young woman (which would be

[2] Jann Pasler, "Politics, Biblical Debates, and French Dramatic Music on Judith after 1870," chap. 24 in *The Sword of Judith*, p. 434.

represented by a soprano voice), since she had been married only three years (probably at age 15) and never bore children. The evolution in perceptions and interpretations of Judith through the centuries, moving from individualistic to nationalistic, was reflected in music. Changes in the ideology of a society in different eras often run parallel to developments in music.

The story became less visible in cultural representations after the late nineteenth century, when it was first omitted from English Bibles. At that time, it was considered literature rather than Bible. In an ironic twist, Judith's noncanonical status liberated her for more secular activity. Prior to this era, Judith is celebrated in two Jewish *piyyutim* (liturgical poems) for Hanukah, dating to the twelfth century and recited in some Jewish communities on the first and second Shabbat of Hanukah.[3] Judith is also found in Latin church hymns from the sixteenth century up to the present day. There are English epics and a medieval High German poem based on Judith, both dating to the thirteenth century. The French epic poem *Judit* (1574), by a popular Protestant poet, Guillame de Salluste du Bartas, transposed the story into an allegory of the French Protestants' struggle against the monarchy. The poem was translated and popular everywhere in Europe, possibly becoming "the most important single catalyst of Judith's symbolic centrality for Protestantism," in Stocker's opinion.[4] In early Christianity, Judith was praised as a model of chastity, as well as a symbol of God's power working through the weak and humble. A more or less positive view of Judith continued through the Middle Ages, when at least 150 plays were written about her.

The development in the late Middle Ages of illustrated short versions of Judith's story probably contributed to the newer iconography of Judith as a seductress and eventually femme fatale. Judith has even appeared on playing cards as the queen of hearts since the nineteenth century. There has been more ambivalence about Judith in the modern era. In addition to operas and oratorios written in the past three hundred years, there is a ballet commissioned by Martha Graham in 1963 by Israeli composer Mordechai Seter.[5] According to one writer, 220 librettos on Judith's story (written to be set to music) were written in Italy between 1621 and 1934.[6]

In the Romantic era, different views of Judith prevailed. A disturbing example is Friedrich Hebbel's 1840 play *Judith* (on which at least two operas were based). This play was apparently so popular that when Germans thought of Judith they thought of this play rather than the Bible.[7] In Hebbel's view, Judith epitomized Judaism. This idea, combined with Hebbel's misogyny, motivated him to depict Holofernes as the "bombastic Romantic hero, an historical superman." In addition, in this version, Judith, though a widow, is a hysterical virgin because her husband could never overcome her resistance. Holofernes, superman here, is virility personified and though Judith wants to resist and kill him, she cannot overcome her desire

---

[3]   Deborah Levine Gera, "The Jewish Textual Traditions," chap. 2 in *The Sword of Judith*, p. 34.
[4]   Margarita Stocker, *Judith: Sexual Warrior* (New Haven: Yale University Press, 1998), p. 89.
[5]   Nira Stone in James Vanderkam, *No One Spoke Ill of Her* (Atlanta, GA: Scholars Press, 1992), p.73. Stone mistakenly labels his Judith an opera.
[6]   Giorgio Mangini in David Marsh, "Judith in Baroque Oratorio," chap. 21 in *The Sword of Judith*, p. 385.
[7]   Stocker, p. 130.

for him. She therefore sleeps with him before killing him, and then to her horror discovers she is pregnant. "Judith pregnant is Judith overcome," in Stocker's words.[8] The full play can be found online (and will be discussed in Chapter 3).[9] In Hebbel's disturbing retelling, Judith's chief motivation is "penis envy," rather than patriotism. Modern writers have often portrayed Judith as an antiheroine, with Holofernes as the hero. Throughout this book, I will be noting the appearance of these motifs in musical representations.

Dominant in artistic representations, according to Nira Stone, are the aspect of self-sacrifice when Judith dared to enter the enemy camp and the courage it took to decapitate Holofernes. She has been presented in both a patriotic and religious way, and in modern art, in a more emotional and feminine way.[10] Many artists of the last two hundred years painted Judith as a courtesan (e.g., Jean Giraudoux in 1931) or worse: Rubens's Judith is a lewd and provocative whore. There was a trend in Renaissance art of portraying biblical women involved in any sexual activity as courtesans or prostitutes. Judith was sometimes converted by artists into an amalgam of Susanna and Bathsheba, an excuse to portray her with full frontal nudity. These paintings in that era were usually intended to be hung in luxury bathrooms.[11] The countless modern artistic depictions of a nude Judith run counter to biblical descriptions, as Athalya Brenner points out. In the Bible, including Judith, it is clothing that signifies sexual temptation, not outright nudity. This is one example of countless others of a tendency to visually sexualize biblical female figures.[12]

Another genre that attempted to justify nude portraits of Judith was the *Vanitas*, warnings to women against the "sin of self-love." Judith's deliberate and lengthy toilette preparations were a pretext to transform the hair-shirt-wearing pious widow into an image of what was supposed to be women's invariable weakness, represented here by vanity. In a patriarchal society, of course, women's only power was usually sexual attraction (and cleverness, I would add); but the Vanity genre portrayed that power as "morally culpable."[13] In the Renaissance, newly married couples in wealthy circles in Italy often received richly decorated chests (*cassoni*) intended for the bedroom. Decorations often were intended to be instructional narratives. Ironically, an illustration of Petrarca's fourteenth-century poem *The Triumph of Love* portrayed Judith as an exemplar of sublime beauty and idealized passion. In this way, the Renaissance theme of Love's Triumph ironically converted a man-killer into an object of desire that brides were meant to emulate. As Stocker wryly comments, "Husbands with an aptitude for iconography … were probably given pause by this idea."[14]

The period of the Reformation, the sixteenth to seventeenth centuries, saw the greatest profusion of representations of Judith in all artistic media (music as well as

---

[8] Stocker, p. 130.
[9] https://quod.lib.umich.edu/g/genpub/AJD8469.0025.001?rgn=main;view=fulltext (Hebbel's play is found there on pp. 257–321, in an English translation).
[10] Stone in Vanderkam, p. 74.
[11] Stocker, p. 29.
[12] Athalya Brenner, "Clothing Seduces," in *A Feminist Companion to Tobit and Judith*, ed. Athalya Brenner-Idan (London: Bloomsbury T&T Clark, 2015), p. 223.
[13] Stocker, pp. 32–3.
[14] Stocker, pp. 41–2.

art). In addition to paintings, depictions of Judith's story often overlooked were those found on very popular German pottery of the late sixteenth century, for both the upper and lower classes. These objects testify to the popularity of this story for Protestants. In this period, "Judith belonged to the people," in Stocker's words.[15] All of these trends had an influence on composers in that era.

The movement of Renaissance humanism had a spirit of enquiry, and one of its primary interests was women: what they were like, and what their purpose was. They did not see women as activists, and therefore they viewed Judith not only as a "paradigm of woman as man's conqueror but … one who damaged patriarchal stereotypes of authority."[16] This obviously was a measure of the high degree of misogyny in that society. Images of strong women were very popular between 1500 and 1700, and Judith was the most popular figure for artistic depictions: the Renaissance's "primary image of the strong woman" in Stocker's words.[17] It is likely that the popularity of these images led to the great interest in portraying Judith in musical settings in the same period. Judith could represent that era's fears and hopes at the same time. Her fascination in the Renaissance (and possibly other eras) was due to her being frightening, strong, and sensual all at once.[18] Many of these ideas changed in the eighteenth century.

Transformations in the cultural mythology of Judith reflected major changes in attitudes to marriage, sexuality, and feminism. Judith's changing images in different eras reflected contemporary ideas about male-female relations. Judith's prominence in visual art began to diminish in the eighteenth century and into the nineteenth.

In literature, in the early part of the twentieth century, Judith was very popular. A 1904 play was later turned into a film by D. W. Griffith (*Judith of Bethulia*, 1914). There were also films based on Judith in Italy and France in this time period. Another shift of perception occurred throughout the nineteenth century in Italy, when Judith moved from being an "individual" to a 'national' hero.[19]

3. Synopsis of the Book of Judith, and Origins of the Book

The book could be divided from a narratological point of view into three parts: chapters 1–3, 4–7, and 8–16. But this does not take into consideration the very large number of verses dedicated to speeches and prayers, which take up more than a third of the narrative.[20] These speeches and prayers are the parts of the book most frequently set to music, as will be seen.

[15] Stocker, p. 57.
[16] Stocker, p. 49.
[17] Stocker, p. 51.
[18] Stocker, p. 54.
[19] Paolo Bernardini, "Judith in the Italian Unification Process," chap. 22 in *The Sword of Judith*, p. 397.
[20] Barbara Schmitz, "The Function of the Speeches and Prayers in the Book of Judith," chap. 9 in *Feminist Companion to Tobit*, p. 166.

Synopsis of the Book of Judith

The ruler Nebuchadnezzar "was so incensed" (1:12; p. 3)[21] with those who did not accept his rule that he swore revenge on all the rebellious territories, which included Judea. He summoned Holofernes and commanded him to occupy all the rebel territories. Led by Holofernes, a great Assyrian army advanced from Mesopotamia to Syria and Lebanon, toward Israel. Every nation surrenders and "sues for peace" (p. 6), but the Israelites "humbled themselves with much fasting … and put on sackcloth" (4:9–10; p. 7). The (fictional) town of Bethulia is crucial to Holofernes, "as access into Judea was through them" (4:7; p. 7) (chapters 1–4).

Holofernes is amazed and furious that the Israelites are resisting him. He asks: "Who is this people that lives in the hill country? … And why have they … refused to come and meet me?" (5:3–4; p. 8). Achior, leader of the Ammonites now serving under Holofernes, summarizes Israel's history for Holofernes (5:6–19) and explains that Israel can be defeated only "if they are sinning against their god" (5:20; p. 9). Holofernes's response is: "What God is there besides Nebuchadnezzar?" (6:2). He is so offended that he tells Achior: "My servants will now deliver you to the hill country and leave you at one of the towns in the passes" (6:7; p. 10). Holofernes says to Achior (6:5): "You shall not see my face again," an interesting echo of Pharaoh's words to Moses in Exod 10:28: "The day you see my face, you will die," creating a subtle parallel between two of the greatest oppressors of the Israelites. When the Bethulians find Achior, "they reassured him and commended him highly" (6:20; p. 11).

Meanwhile, Holofernes prepares his troops for battle, but his generals convince him to remain in camp with his men while his servants "take possession of the spring which flows from the foot of the water. So thirst will destroy them" (7:12–13; p. 12). The siege has now been going on for over a month, and the people are prepared to surrender. But Uzziah, an elder, convinces them they should "hold out for five more days" (6:30; p. 13). If God has not delivered them by the fifth day, he vows he will allow the town to surrender to Holofernes's forces (chapters 5–7; most musical settings open with chapter 7).

Only now, in chapter 8, does Judith, known as a pious widow, appear on the scene. She criticizes her people for questioning and testing God (8:12). She also warns them that if they are captured, it would lead to the capture of all of Judea and the plunder of the sanctuary in Jerusalem, for which God would punish them (8:21). She announces that "the Lord will deliver Israel by [her] hand" (8:33; p. 15). Prostrating herself, Judith recites one of the longest prayers in the Bible (9:2–14). She begs God to give her hand the strength she needs (9:9) and, most unusually, begs God to grant her "a beguiling tongue" (9:13; p. 17). She then sheds her sackcloth and widow's clothes and dresses glamorously. She hands her maid various food items, a skin of wine, and dishes, which the maid carries in a bag. As the two approach the town gate, the town elders are "struck by her beauty" (10:7; p. 17). On Judith's orders, the elders open the town gate for the two women, who then leave. As they approach the entrance to the Assyrian

---

[21] All biblical quotes and their page references are from Carey A. Moore, *Judith: A New Translation*, The Anchor Bible, vol. 40 (New York: Doubleday, 1985).

camp, Judith is stopped by an Assyrian patrol, who are "much struck by her beauty" (10:14; p. 18). Judith persuades them that she has reliable information for Holofernes and is then taken to him amid general excitement about her beauty (chapters 8–10).

Holofernes reassures Judith that he has never hurt anyone who chose to serve Nebuchadnezzar, "king of the whole world" (11:1, p. 19). She confirms what Achior told him about the Israelites' invincibility. However, she adds that the people of Bethulia have exhausted both their food supply and water and are therefore about to sin by consuming sacred food items dedicated to God (11:12). She tells Holofernes that it was this dire situation that convinced her to escape Bethulia, to avoid sharing the Israelites' now certain doom. She promises to act as Holofernes's agent, telling him when God informs her that the Israelites have committed these sins. Then, Holofernes can attack without resistance. Judith's words "delighted Holofernes" (11:20; p. 20), and he and his attendants were all "struck by her wisdom" (11:20; p, 20). Holofernes also promises Judith numerous rewards (11.23). He offers her a meal of delicacies, but Judith declines to eat the non-kosher food, which would be "an offense to God" (12:2; p. 21). Judith informs Holofernes that she has brought her own food in a bag and that there is enough for the length of their stay. She and her servant are granted permission to leave their tent nightly to pray, supposedly for God's revelation about the best time for Assyria to attack. On the fourth day, Holofernes gives a party for his retinue and orders his eunuch, Bagoas, to persuade Judith to eat and drink with them. He says they will be disgraced if they let such a woman go without "having" her (12:11–12; p. 21; this phrase has been translated various ways, but the sexual innuendo is unmistakable). Judith now accepts his offer to eat with him (though she eats only what her servant prepared: 12:19), and she reclines before him. Holofernes, "beside himself with desire" (12:16; p. 22), consumes a great deal of wine at dinner in anticipation of having sex with Judith (chapters 11–12).

When the servants leave, Bagoas closes the tent and dismisses all the attendants, leaving Holofernes alone with Judith. Holofernes "is sprawled on his bed, dead drunk" (13:2; p. 22). Judith prays to God to help her carry out her plan. She takes Holofernes's sword from where it hangs above his bed. After praying to God for strength, she decapitates him with two strokes. She summons her servant to place Holofernes's head in Judith's food bag and they escape, unnoticed because of their approved nightly prayer vigils outside the camp. Returning to Bethulia, Judith displays Holofernes's head to the people, proclaiming that God "struck him down by the hand of a female" (14:15; p. 23). The people, amazed, bow down and worship God (14:17). Judith instructs the people to hang Holofernes's head from the walls and to descend on the Assyrians after daybreak, when they will have discovered the fate of their commander (15:1–3). Achior is summoned to confirm the identity of the head. At first, he collapses, then blesses and praises Judith and her God. He is so impressed by God's miraculous work through Judith that he is circumcised and becomes an Israelite (15:6–7, 10). The Assyrians, meanwhile, have discovered Holofernes's headless corpse and flee in panic. Following Judith's advice, the men of Bethulia attack, encouraging their fellow Israelites to join in attacking the enemy. The Bethulians loot the Assyrian camp for a month. At the end, Judith sings a hymn of thanksgiving, and the people add a hymn of praise (15:13–16).

In a brief Epilogue, Judith retires to her home and lives the rest of her life as a widow, despite many offers of marriage. She dies at the age of 105 (chapters 13–16).

The opening chapters make it clear, most scholars agree, that the story is a fantasy, using illusions in the historical and geographical details. Even the name of the town, Bethulia, is made up. Because Judith first appears only in chapter 8, commentators until recently virtually ignored the previous seven chapters. Scholars now focus on the unity of the entire book. The first chapters are set in communities where men have all the leading roles. Acts of military aggression and religious compromise are described, giving no inkling of what is to come. Toni Craven notes that it is precisely because of chapters 1–7 that the book as a whole succeeds. The reader understands Israel's struggle to survive and its attempts to cope with hardship.[22]

In the first half of the book, the opposing parties are presented: Assyria and its god Nebuchadnezzar, counterpoised against Israel and the Hebrew God. (Though Nebuchadnezzar is identified as the king, he is sometimes referred to as a god, as when Holofernes claims "What god is there except Nebuchadnezzar?" in 5:2). The two parts vary primarily in that various subjects and characters appear in chapters 1–7, while Judith completely dominates chapters 8–16. In addition, the second half of the book is more appealing to readers because there is far greater use of direct address. A higher percentage of the text is direct speech in the second half—in Carey Moore's calculation, roughly 59 percent versus only 36 percent in chapters 1–7. Direct address gives an immediacy to the action, but is less common in biblical literature than in Greek tragedy.[23] Extensive speech, of course, is very well suited to musical treatment.

Origins of the Book

The book of Judith is widely believed to have originally been written in Hebrew, probably sometime in the second (some say first) century BCE. Scholars, such as Deborah Levine Gera, maintain that the book is "undoubtedly a Jewish work, written by and intended for Jews … though Judith seems to have disappeared from Jewish tradition for well over a millennium."[24] The Hebrew text was the basis for the Greek translation, which in turn was the basis for the later Aramaic, Hebrew, Old Latin, Syriac, and other translations.[25] These are conjectures by respected scholars, but there is no unanimous agreement on the text's origins. Judith is a deuterocanonical book, meaning it was included in the Septuagint and the Catholic and Eastern Orthodox Christian Bibles but assigned by Protestants and Jews to the Apocrypha. There is a certain irony in the fact that this book, whose hero is a pious, devout, practicing Jewish woman, was not included in the canon by the Jews but rather was by the Christians. Craven believes this book "represents one of the best examples of Jewish story-telling" and she cites several scholars who support that claim.[26]

---

[22] Toni Craven, *Artistry and Faith in the Book of Judith*, SBL Dissertation Series 70 (Chico, CA: Scholars Press, 1983), p. 5. Scholars are generally in agreement with Craven.
[23] Moore, p. 237.
[24] Gera, p. 23.
[25] Craven, p. 5.
[26] Craven, p. 6.

There is some consensus that the book's background seems to be historical events in Hasmonean times. Judith's defeat of Holofernes, in fact, bears some resemblance to the encounter between Judah the Maccabee and Nicanor, the Seleucid commander (1 Macc 7:26–50; 2 Macc 15:1–36). Both Judith and Judah are pious figures who overturn a threat to the temple in Jerusalem, and both behead the chief military commander. This tenuous link explains the popularity of Chanukah menorahs that include Judith imagery.

4. The Portrayals of Judith, "Abra," and Holofernes

Judith

Significantly, Judith's is the longest genealogy attached to her name of any woman in the Bible—sixteen names. And her late husband Manasseh derives his identity from his wife, the reverse of the patriarchal norm. He is given no genealogy at all and is introduced only in reference to Judith's family. This is unconventional both in the Bible and in Hellenistic Jewish literature. Judith is the only woman named in the book and also the only one with whom male characters interact. She is unusual as a woman who makes her own decisions in a patriarchal world. There are very few such women in the Bible: some examples are Ruth and Naomi, Jezebel, and Abigail and Jael. Judith and Ruth also are bound with other women: Ruth with Naomi, Judith with her servant (who, however, never speaks in the biblical text). Only Jael worked completely alone.

Though she is politically shrewd and militarily effective, Judith lives a life of simple piety and temperance. She is described as wealthy, beautiful, and respected, in the text. Even though she seems modeled on female figures such as Miriam and Jael, the reader could just as well be reminded of Moses, Samson, and David, and even particularly Ehud who assassinates King Eglon of Moab (Judg 3:12–30; this narrative is actually recounted in one musical work). Judith shares attributes with all of these men. Judith triumphs through deceit, which puts her in the company of numerous biblical women whose deceits have positive national and personal consequences (Rebecca, Tamar, the midwives Shifrah and Puah in Exod 1, Miriam, Rahab, etc.). Yet Judith is notably the only biblical woman who actually asks God to make her a good liar. The ease with which she played the part of a seductress "implies a more flexible personality," in the words of D. N. Freedman.[27] Delilah's case is similar in that she uses Samson's strength against him; but she was not a hero in biblical tradition, since she worked against Israel. She also seduced Samson deliberately, whereas how actively Judith "seduced" Holofernes is left ambiguous in the text.

Other unique aspects of Judith are the fact that she has another woman ("Abra" or "handmaiden") who is so loyal that she follows Judith into the enemy camp. Of course, if she was a slave, she did not have a choice. Judith also leaves Abra in charge of her estate. And though Judith remains childless, she still refuses to marry again up until

---

[27] David Noel Freedman as quoted in Moore, p. 186.

her death at age 105. Also significant is that Judith makes the decision on her own to go to the enemy camp and kill Holofernes. She does not share her plan with the men of the city, and she is clearly powerful enough to convince them to simply let her go. She virtually usurps (or embodies) God's voice in this exchange.

Judith's story was read and used in different eras with widely different connotations, in Kevin Brine's words: "misogynistic, erotic, anti-Semitic, patriotic, nationalistic, and feminist."[28] Judith's positive traits—faith, courage, determination—are sometimes overshadowed by her use of deceit and sexual wiles to kill a man. These negative attributes sometimes minimize the importance of the motive and result: saving her people. Judith, in Moore's view, combines the beauty and brains of Esther with the physical strength and audacity of Jael.[29] In her prayer in chapter 9, Judith speaks positively of Simeon because she plans to emulate him, rather than Dinah. She presumably is more concerned with killing Holofernes than with being raped, in one scholar's view, and thus she identifies with the avenger and not the victim.[30] This is yet another unusual aspect of Judith: a woman who does not see herself as a victim—a very relevant notion today.

Some feminist writers, such as Pamela Milne, continue to view Judith negatively, believing the text is filled with "androcentric assumptions and patriarchal ideology … Judith is a character who gives expression to men's deepest fears, namely, a woman out of male control who kills a man when he is completely helpless."[31] I feel this judgment fails to take into consideration the context of Judith's behavior and the goal she achieved with this murder. It was not a random killing of a helpless man, after all. As one scholar has pointed out, some readers "have made certain a-historical and a-cultural errors by interpreting the text purely from their own contextual confines," citing negative interpretations of Judith as a good example. Using deception and manipulation is considered acceptable in the Hebrew Bible, and many biblical women achieve their goals in this way. In the cultural context in which Judith was written, these methods were certainly accepted and even praised.[32] It might be seen as an example of the ends justifying the means.

Judith is the only character in the book portrayed with initiative and courage. All the men in the story are weak, stupid, or impaired. This includes Manasseh (although he is dead), Holofernes (who initially displays strength but who is made weak by wine and lust), Bagoas, Achior, and Uzziah. Craven states that "no portrayal of another biblical woman equals Judith in its positive depiction of and praise for a woman as an autonomous agent through whom God's purposes are accomplished."[33] Judith may also represent an Israelite manifestation of the Canaanite Anat tradition, which assigns

[28] Kevin Brine, "The Judith Project," chap. 1 in *The Sword of Judith*, p. 15.
[29] Moore, p. 193.
[30] David Noel Freedman as quoted in Moore, p. 191.
[31] Pamela Milne, "What Would I Do with Judith Now?" chap. 7a in *Feminist Companion to Tobit*, pp. 138–9.
[32] Helen Efthimiadis-Keith, "Judith, Feminist Ethics and Feminist…Interpretation," chap. 8 in *Feminist Companion to Tobit*, p. 153.
[33] Toni Craven, "Judith 2," in *Women in Scripture*, ed. Carl Meyers (Grand Rapids, MI: William Eerdmans, 2001), p. 106.

females a role of military heroism in times of war.[34] But Judith is not represented as a military hero, considering that she leaves Bethulia presumably intending to kill Holofernes but brings no weapon (according to the text). Her trust in God was apparently so great that she was confident that a weapon would appear at the right moment.

The Servant/Slave/"Abra"

Judith's servant is often called "Abra" meaning "favorite slave" in Greek (a variant of this name is often used by librettists); but in the Greek text, she is also called *paidiskē* ("maid" according to Craven, "slave girl" according to Andrea Sheaffer) and *doule* ("servant" according to Craven, "female slave" according to Sheaffer).[35] Sheaffer points out that the distinction between one who has agency and free will, and one who does not, is very important to the modern reader. This distinction has been largely glossed over in librettos and other modern retellings. Sheaffer provided several references from the New Testament where the term *paidiskē* is clearly presented in opposition to a free woman.[36] In librettos, the woman is variously called maid, servant, nurse, and sometimes slave. Judith addresses her directly as "slave" (*schiava*) in only one work discussed in this book, the 1856 Italian play by Paolo Giacometti (see Chapter 3). In the book, she never speaks but seems to have an intimate relation with Judith, since Judith's first and last described actions in the story involve her. Amy-Jill Levine suggests that the patriarchal culture could not deal with more than one woman who speaks and acts. Two such women would compromise the status quo. This could explain the complete silence and also loyalty of her servant.[37] The presence of a servant who is also a confidante recalls Greek dramas, where the servant is often the only trusted companion of the heroine. On the other hand, the servant who acts but does not speak also depicts a power relationship, highlighting the socioeconomic differences between the two women.

Judith's servant is never named, even though her actions when she accompanies Judith to the enemy camp are equally as courageous as Judith's. She was taking as much of a risk as her mistress was. Yet she was still a servant or a slave who probably had no choice but to follow orders. Jennifer Glancy focuses on this character and suggests the slave might have been a Jew, which would explain her commitment to saving the community of Bethulia (as suggested in several musical works). However, Glancy points out that if the slave was a Jew, Judith was legally obligated to release her in the

---

[34] Susan Ackerman, *Warrior Dancer Seductress Queen* (New York: Doubleday 1998), p. 63.

[35] Craven, p. 363; Andrea Sheaffer, "Images of the Indentured," in *Biblical Reception 2*, ed. Cheryl Exum and David Clines (Sheffield: Sheffield Phoenix Press, 2013), p. 82.

[36] Sheaffer, personal communication, June 27, 2019. These are three examples: Gal 4:23: "But he of the bondwoman [παιδίσκης - paidiskēs] was born after the flesh; but he of the freewoman by promise." Gal 4:30: "Nevertheless what saith the scripture? Cast out the bondwoman [παιδίσκην - paidiskēn] and her son: for the son of the bondwoman [παιδίσκης - paidiskēs] shall not be heir with the son of the freewoman." Gal 4:31: "So then, brethren, we are not children of the bondwoman, [παιδίσκης - paidiskēs] but of the free."

[37] Amy-Jill Levine, "Sacrifice and Salvation," in *A Feminist Companion to Esther, Judith, and Susanna*, ed. Athalya Brenner (Sheffield: Sheffield Academic Press, 1995), p. 219.

seventh year (Deut 15:12), so her lifelong use of the slave was a serious violation. Did observance of food laws, then, matter more to Judith than just treatment of a fellow Jew? The reader knows nothing at all of this slave: not a name, not her feelings (did she truly remain loyal to Judith her entire life, or did she have no choice?) Did she herself have a family? These are all unanswered questions, some of which are explored in oratorio and opera librettos. Glancy may be one of the first scholars to explore this mute but essential character. In her words, "The slave is as silent a handmaiden to the narrative as she is to Judith."[38] Of course, the reader assumes the two do speak; the speech is simply not recorded, significant in itself in a book so replete with dialogue. It is a mystery why readers, including feminist ones, have continued to ignore this slave and what she tells us about Judith and the ethics of slaveholding. Many musical settings give this servant a voice—sometimes even a prominent one, in both solos and duets with Judith, amplifying her role and giving her many more dimensions. She is also humanized in many works, called "Nurse," "Mother," or "Sister."

Other scholars believe the "servant" is a slave, but not a Jewish one. Sheaffer argues that servitude was common in wealthy Jewish households in the Greco-Roman period. She believes that Judith's act of freeing her slave only upon her own death proves that she was a non-Jewish slave, because Judith was observant of Jewish law and would have not been permitted to hold a Jewish slave for more than seven years (as pointed out by Glancy, above). In addition, Jewish law expressly forbids holding Jewish slaves (Lev 25:35–46). Since Judith's strict religious observance is a theme running through the book, it is very unlikely that she would have blatantly disobeyed Jewish law. Irony runs through the book (see below), and Schaeffer considers the notion of a slave helping to save the people enslaving her as yet another ironic plot device. She further stresses that no feelings between the two women can be gleaned from the text, and ascribing emotions to either woman is reading into rather than from the text. Composers and librettists, of course, are not scholars and felt free to fill this large gap in numerous creative ways, in every era.

Holofernes

The character of Holofernes, for this reader, is far less nuanced and interesting than the female characters. He is depicted in two dimensions: blustering, or seducing. His prowess as a ruthless warrior is described vividly in Jdt 2:14–28. This sets the stage for a man who inspires fear and terror in everyone—except Judith. Later settings of the story tend to focus less on his ruthlessness and instead suggest he is capable of being infatuated if not intoxicated by Judith. Had she not been so breathtakingly beautiful, however, there would have been no story. Yet the word "love" is uttered by Holofernes's reincarnation in several operas, though it is never clearly established if this is simply part of his seduction technique. In any case, many nuances and new characteristics are added to his character in librettos and operas. The bluster and terror are amplified by music as are his romantic overtures to Judith. In some instances, his music is so

[38] Jennifer A. Glancy, "Judith the Slaveholder," in *Feminist Companion to Tobit*, p. 208.

romantic and appealing that it is sometimes understandable that Judith has trouble resisting his advances, in more modern retellings.

The iconic image of Holofernes in art is, of course, of his head being separated from his body by Judith. It is rare to find a portrait of a living Holofernes. For that reason, I commissioned an artist to create a cover that went against this expected image, and that includes a portrait of the whole man, as he is approached by Judith. The operas and even some oratorios also create a full portrait of Holofernes, and I wanted the cover of this book to reflect that.

Themes and Elements

Three important elements in the book of Judith will be discussed here: humor and irony; the importance of faith; and sexuality.

Humor and Irony

The use of irony is found throughout the book, often through repetition of text used earlier in the book but with a different meaning. For example, in Jdt 2:12 Nebuchadnezzar vows: "I will do this by my own hand," a phrase repeated often by Judith later in the story (8:33, 9:9, 12:4). Ironic also is the suggestion that the mighty Assyrian army should be defeated because its general lost his head to a woman. As Levine puts it, the Assyrian camp is populated by "the beguiled, the besotted and the beheaded."[39]

In the first eleven verses of chapter 10, Judith makes herself as beautiful as she can, prepares her kosher food supplies, bids farewell to the elders, and leaves Bethulia and walks into the enemy's camp. Once there, irony again appears as "Captive Judith captured her captors," in Moore's words.[40] Part of her adornment is bathing—but what about the water shortage? The writer may have failed to explain this because at the time, it was likely understood that Judith would have had a cistern, given that she was the richest widow in Bethulia. Also, in that era people sponged, so the reference is not necessarily to a full bath. Yet another possibility, suggested by Jack Sasson, is that she had her own *mikvah* (ritual bath) on the lowest level of her large house, which she might have forgotten about since the death of her husband. She may have wanted to purify herself ("as would any good Jewish matron"), before venturing into unknown enemy territory.[41]

There are elements of satire and comedy throughout the book. Putting sackcloth on all the animals (echoes of Jonah) and the whole seduction/murder scene could both be read as a parody of what the reader might expect. The meeting between Judith and town officials in chapter 8 is one of the "most memorable and important exchanges in the book" in Craven's words: "The theology may rival that of Job."[42] The scene is both

---

[39] Levine, p. 217.
[40] Moore, p. 204.
[41] Jack Sasson, personal communication, July 26, 2018.
[42] Craven, p. 86.

profound and comic. The passivity and lack of faith of the people, particularly their leaders, is in sharp contrast with the determination and courage of Judith (and her maid) in her plan to enter the Assyrian camp. Though the men assure her that God would be with her (v. 35), clearly none of the men of Bethulia would.

The universal response to Judith's beauty is also filled with both humor and irony, in its sheer exaggeration. From the sentries to the highest officers and general, all are struck by her beauty, rendering them virtually helpless before the supposedly "helpless widow." And the reader should remember that they are seeing her in the dead of night. Beauty in the Hebrew Bible is not treated as a power or strategy of women. If anything, a woman described as beautiful (e.g., Sarah, Bathsheba, etc.) is often a victim and does not use her beauty for any gain. The book of Judith may be the first place that beauty is represented as a weapon.[43] The importance of Judith's arrival in the camp is highlighted by the Greek word *parousia* for arrival, a term usually reserved for the arrival of an especially distinguished person such as a king.[44] Judith's beauty and its effect on men is often amplified and elaborated on in musical works.

In the lengthy conversation between Judith and Holofernes in chapter 11, Craven notes that "truth and hypocrisy are subtly intertwined. Both tell outright lies in their attempt to impress the other,"[45] yet another humorous element, underlined in some musical settings. They are both deceivers: he deceives her in hopes of having sex; she deceives him and his army. Many have commented on Judith's strange ethical priorities: she will not eat non-kosher food, but she lies without equivocation. Moore suggests there is a method behind her stringent food restrictions: by adhering so rigidly to her dietary laws, she is confirming to Holofernes that she would clearly not abide her own people not following these laws. She wants him to think her people's disobedience would lead her to betray them.[46] More irreverently, in Sasson's words, "Holofernes was a fool to expect hanky-panky from a woman who brings kosher food to an orgy."[47] Musical works do not generally deal with Judith's eating habits, possibly finding that aspect of the story too esoteric or difficult to understand.

Faith

It is only Judith's faith that assures her that God will provide what is needed. Her faith sounds like that of Job in the Prologue (Job 1:21 and 2:9). She has no theophany, but in Craven's words, "who knows what happened to her on that housetop?"[48] Notably absent from the story are angels or any display at all of a supernatural power. It is faith that wins the day. Though both Judith and the Israelites prayed to God and gave God

[43] Tikva Frymer-Kensky, *In the Wake of the Goddesses* (New York: Fawcett Columbine, 1992), p. 206.
[44] Moore, p. 207.
[45] Craven, p. 51.
[46] Moore, p. 218.
[47] Jack Sasson, "Did I Lose It at the Movies?" *SBL Panel*, Chicago 1994. Available online: https://cdn.vanderbilt.edu/vu-my/wp-content/uploads/sites/240/2019/04/14092610/lost-it-at-the-movies-SBL94.pdf (accessed October 30, 2020).
[48] Craven, pp. 88–9.

credit for the victory (in the concluding song of praise), they all also recognized that it was Judith's initiative and courage that conquered, and not God. In fact, there is only one verse in the entire book in which God is the active subject: in 4:13, "The Lord heard their prayers and looked kindly on their distress," which echoes Exod 2:23–24. The writer clearly wanted to drive home the point that God was acting through Judith.

Sexuality

Early feminist studies of Judith focused on Judith's androgynous nature. What makes her androgyny so fascinating is that her masculine and feminine traits appear sequentially rather than simultaneously. She is asexual as a widow, masculine when confronting the elders, and feminine in the Assyrian camp; then she resumes her masculine role when she decapitates Holofernes and remains in that role until the Assyrian army is defeated, at which point she reverts permanently to the asexuality of her widowhood. Ultimately, Judith "rises above the sexism of her author's culture."[49] The reader never knows which is the "real" Judith, since her femininity is a ruse, while other elements of her sexuality are not. Ora Brison, too, points to the changeability of Judith's sexual character and notes that the text vacillates between "the need to glorify a woman who communicates with God and to attribute her deeds to stereotypic feminine traits: beauty and cunning."[50] Brison further notes that as the writer presents her, Judith almost seems to internalize the Hebrew Bible's androcentric attitudes, attributing her victory to her own seductive wiles. Clearly the text affirms that a woman may have a reversed-gender role, especially if it brings victory and salvation to her community. But such a reversal threatens the social order, and thus she must retreat from the public sphere and return to complete privacy—including isolation and remaining a widow to her death.[51] Modern readers might be tempted to interpret this as a desire for independence from men, but the writer never suggests this as a motive. Another aspect that goes against the biblical norm is the fact that Judith has both beauty and brains.

A crucial element of the narrative is the (so-called) seduction. The scene in the tent is treated differently in different versions of Judith. In the Septuagint version, Holofernes says that Judith would mock them if he did not "caress" her. In addition, Judith asks God to allow her words to seduce the Assyrians, a line absent from the Vulgate. In general, there is much more suggestive language in the Septuagint. The Vulgate explicitly mentions that Judith "put on new clothes to seduce him" (16:10). But there is no actual seduction: though Holofernes feels lust, he simply passes out drunk. The original text leaves the question ambiguous and murky, of whether or not Judith succumbed to Holofernes's advances, which is probably a deliberate choice. Later retellings generally accepted that Judith resisted Holofernes's advances, with only

---

[49] Patricia Montley in Moore, p. 65.
[50] Ora Brison, "Judith: A Pious Widow Turned Femme Fatale, or More?" in *Feminist Companion to Tobit*, p. 198.
[51] Brison, p. 198.

rare exceptions (Hebbel's play of 1840 was the first to suggest Judith was raped and impregnated; see above).

In conclusion: after reading these librettos and in some cases hearing the music, the reader and listener will never see Judith or her story in the same way again—and will have a better understanding of how Judith was understood, seen, and heard over several centuries.

Part One

Oratorios

1

The Seventeenth and Eighteenth Centuries: Alessandro Scarlatti (Two Works), Antonio Vivaldi, Thomas Arne, Wolfgang Amadeus Mozart

The five oratorios discussed in this chapter were all written by renowned composers. These works have been chosen not only for the high quality and interest of their music but also for how they chose to set the librettos (the text of an oratorio or opera), which is as important as the text of that libretto by itself. Music provides a subtext to the words, adding nuances and suggesting new meanings. The discussion throughout will focus on the many ways in which librettists and composers altered or embellished the original biblical story.

The earliest musical settings of Judith's story were usually in oratorio form, which differs from opera (operas will be discussed in Part Two) primarily in that the work is not staged but sung in a concert setting. Oratorio in the seventeenth and eighteenth centuries also differed from opera in its smaller orchestra, more limited cast of singers, simpler plot, and often a strongly religious content (usually Catholic) or pedagogic aim. At the same time, the two genres of oratorio and opera in that period resembled each other more and more, until the style of oratorios came much closer to being a "spiritual melodrama" (*melodramma spirituale*).[1] In Italy, following the years of popularity of Claudio Monteverdi's (1567–1643) operas, oratorio became the dramatic expression and form that held sway over opera and cantata (short oratorio). Its development is believed to have helped expand the resources of the libretto writers, even when they may have been weak or even below the standard of that time. This will certainly be seen in some of the works discussed here. The oratorio genre originated in Rome and may have flourished in part because of papal opposition to opera in that city.

There is a possible clue to the origins of oratorio, David Marsh points out, in Jerome's Vulgate (early Latin) translation of the story, in which he calls Judith's special place on her roof for prayer (perhaps a tent or tabernacle) an *oratorium*. There is an interesting contrast with this private place and that of Holofernes's tent, also a kind of inner sanctum. There Judith defends her own chastity while saving her people. The

---

[1] Maria Rosa De Luca, "Giuditta versus Oloferne. Un percorso didattico sull'oratorio musicale," *Musica Docta, Rivista Digitale di Pedagogia e Didattica della Musica* 2 (2012): p. 120.

contrast between Judith's public and private spaces is reflected in Baroque oratorio, where both spaces become public. And their performances are likewise public. In this way, Judith's private world becomes immediate for the public audience, and when the final chorus rejoices at their deliverance, "the faithful spectators of a Judith oratorio presumably rejoice with them."[2] Marsh seems to be making this comparison based on the great popularity of Judith as a subject for oratorios in the seventeenth century.

Seventeenth Century

Alessandro Scarlatti (1660–1725)

Alessandro Scarlatti was born in Sicily (then the Kingdom of Sicily). In 1684 he became *maestro di cappella* to the viceroy of Naples, where he wrote numerous operas. In 1702 Scarlatti left Naples for Florence, where he enjoyed the patronage of Ferdinando de' Medici, for whose private theater near Florence he composed operas. Another patron was Cardinal Ottoboni, who made him his *maestro di cappella* and procured him a similar post at the Basilica di Santa Maria Maggiore in Rome in 1703. Scarlatti's music is a link between the early Baroque Italian vocal styles of the seventeenth century and the classical school of the eighteenth century. Scarlatti wrote three other biblical oratorios: *Agar et Ismaele* ("Hagar and Ishmael"), *Il David* ("David"), and *Il Primo Omicidio* ("The First Murder").[3] Scarlatti was an important influence on composers of his own and the next generation.

Scarlatti's two oratorios (1694 and 1697), both called *La Giuditta*, are considered by some critics to anticipate some musical elements of the eighteenth century. This is due to their focus on the more dramatic elements of the biblical story, not previously a focus in oratorios. The librettos for the two versions were written by members of the Ottoboni family, relatives of the Pope. The five-part "Naples" version of 1694 had a libretto by Cardinal Pietro Ottoboni (1667–1740). The libretto for the three-part "Cambridge" version of 1697 (first discovered only in 1960) was written by the cardinal's father, Prince Antonio Ottoboni (1646–1720).

The Naples La Giuditta *(1694)*

In Scarlatti's era, every performance and interpretation was determined by practical circumstances. No two productions would have been the same, nor would they have used the score in the same way. Though this work was called an oratorio, it is obviously more a work for the theatre than a concert. This is due to the lack of a chorus, and the

---

[2] David Marsh, "Judith in Baroque Oratorio," chap. 21 in *The Sword of Judith: Judith Studies Across the Disciplines*, ed. Kevin R. Brine (Cambridge: Open Book, 2010), p. 386. Available online: http://books.openedition.org/obp/972 (ISBN: 978190692417).

[3] Robert Pagano and Malcolm Boyd in *New Grove Dictionary of Music and Musicans*, ed. Stanley Sadie (New York: Grove, 2001), vol. 22, pp. 374–80.

small number of characters (five), as well as its dramatic values. One reason is that in Italy during Lent, when opera could not be performed for six weeks (by Papal order), composers saw an opportunity to utilize similar styles and structures of opera in their oratorios. The five characters, in one commentator's words, are

> enmeshed in a tense, sexy, and rapidly developing story that's told mostly in arias … [which] lie between the freely structured music of the classic Italian oratorio and the formally fixed, ornate da capo form that flourished through much of the eighteenth century; they are beautifully balanced between technique and the emotions of the characters, inspiring English music writer Edward Dent to call Scarlatti Mozart's spiritual ancestor.[4]

Another critic writes: "Scarlatti considered it his finest oratorio, and its dramatic structure, rapidly interweaving brief scenes in Holofernes' camp with events in the troubled city, is remarkable."[5] In another critic's opinion, this work should properly place Scarlatti as "the keystone of Italian Baroque vocal music."[6] The music offers vivid contrasts between scenes depicting a martial spirit, and those of seduction.[7]

Judith: soprano
Ozia, one of the leaders of Bethulia (Uzziah in Greek): alto
Priest: bass
Holofernes: countertenor (sometimes bass, with the notes transposed down)
Achior (called Captain): tenor.

Judith's servant, in this oratorio, is silent, as she is in the original text.
All translations are my own.

Part I

Scene 1

The work opens with a *Sinfonia* or overture. Judith is the first to appear, picking up the biblical narrative at the start of chapter 8. The text is altered considerably from the original, in colorful ways. For example, Judith describes Holofernes as "this captain, girded in gold, who seems already to trample our ruins—who knows, whether it wasn't decreed by Heaven that his glory should end here." Following this recitative, she sings the aria *Trombe Guerriere* ("Trumpets of War"), accompanied by repeated trumpet calls. She asks why the trumpets are silent, since their silence "increases fear in the

---

4 James Manheim, review of 2005 CD, Ambronay edition, https://www.allmusic.com/album/scarlatti-la-giuditta-mw0001395277 (accessed August 8, 2018).
5 Tim Ashley in *The Guardian*, April 13, 2006.
6 Xavier Carrère, CD liner notes.
7 A recording on YouTube is here: https://www.youtube.com/watch?v=RJXVVapmuCw. The Italian libretto can be read here: https://issuu.com/klassiek.nl/docs/digital_booklet_scarlatti_la_giudit (all accessed February 14, 2020).

soul." Then she asks Ozia what he thinks. He sings a sweet aria in response, telling her that he is moved by her calm and the love in her heart, but he says that rage, not love, rules.

The Priest (his bass voice lending authority) pleads with Ozia to let the people submit to the "yoke of suffering" rather than die from hunger. Judith begs him not to despair too quickly. Ozia is unable to make a decision but the Priest urges him to decide quickly so that he can calm the people. Judith pleads with them to wait five more days. After all, she points out, God has fought for Israel several times, citing the stories of the crossing of the Red Sea and David slaying Goliath. She says if in five days there is no change, they can condemn her to death (this detail is invented). Ozia agrees and sings an upbeat aria about hope, which allows him to enjoy the dusk (*sereno*) of their glory. The Priest also agrees but addresses God rather than Judith, praying to God to strengthen them and revive their dying hope. Judith points out in a recitative that the enemy is already approaching and then sings an aria filled with rapid runs. This style is a typical Baroque trope that represents strong feeling or excitement.

Scene 2

A *Sinfonia Bellica* (warlike overture) opens the scene, setting up a powerful "aria of rage" sung by Holofernes. This aria, *Lampi e tuoni ho nel sembiante* ("I have lightning and thunder on my countenance") is filled with long trills and extended 16th-note runs, typical Baroque "warrior" music. It is particularly effective in the bass voice, as it is more often associated with high voices (though Handel later featured bass *coloratura* in many of his operas). In this aria, Holofernes proclaims that thunder and lightning represent him, that he is "the spirit of war and battle," his sword an "anvil of death," and similar sentiments. The music is studded with constant trumpet calls, very effectively suggesting battle in a way that text alone cannot. In the recitative that follows, he admits to being amazed that at the first sound of the feared trumpets, though the foundation was shaken, the walls have not come down. This seems to be a clear reference to Joshua at the battle of Jericho (Josh 6) where the walls *did* come down.

The Captain (henceforth Achior) now addresses Holofernes, as "Invincible hero," and admits that he is afraid. Holofernes asks how he can doubt victory. Achior says that Holofernes will win only if the heavens decree it, and Holofernes, angered, accusingly tells him that his soul and spirit are still loyal to his people. In the biblical story, Achior, an Ammonite mercenary, advised Holofernes not to attack the Hebrews. This is an elaboration of that plot line. Achior now asks Holofernes to kill him, but Holofernes hesitates, thinking of a crueler punishment. He tells his warriors to accompany Achior to the ramparts of Bethulia, the "enemy city" (Jdt 6:10–11), so he will pay for his offense in the general slaughter, and thus "this vile monster shall be a true testimony of our greatness" (*sia valor nostro testimonio fedel così vil mostro*). He tells Achior that he cannot say that Holofernes's victory depends on the heavens. Achior sings a very touching aria, *Della Patria io torno in seno* ("I return to the bosom of my country"), singing that though he fears a terrible slaughter, he will not give in to despair.

Part II

Scene 3

Judith's music is a great contrast with the style of Holofernes's, containing fewer fast runs. Her first aria in the enemy camp, *Se di gigli, e se di rose* ("Though the lilies and the roses") focuses on her beauty and how she would adorn it. She sings gently of wanting to become even more charming and beautiful on this great day. This aria represents her preparations before leaving Bethulia, even though they are not actually described here and seem out of sequence. Holofernes enters and in a recitative with seductive overtones—slow and sinuous music—tells her not to regret her destiny that made her so lovely. She responds that she only wants to please him and appear more beautiful. It is interesting that in this oratorio, Judith's entrance into the enemy camp is not represented. The composer and librettist probably assumed familiarity with the story from their audience. The recitative duet is a wonderful example of the use of the human singing voice to sound seductive, which adds a new subtext to the scene.

Holofernes asks Judith if there is anything she needs, and she tells him she is staying far from his tent and is thus unsure "of the happiness you promise me." Holofernes apologizes and confesses that his soul is transfixed by her beautiful face and tells her to go to the royal tent, where she will be received "amongst my treasures" (*fra tesori miei*). In an aside, Judith sings, "I will be victorious if you are by my side, O Heaven" (*Vincerò, se mia scorta, o Ciel, tu sei*). Holofernes sings an aria, *Vanne, vanne* ("Go, go"), where he imagines Judith should be proud to have a lover who has imprisoned the world (*chi già l'Orbe incatenò*). Though this line might sound comical (or disturbing) to modern ears, it is an indication of Holofernes's megalomania.

Scene 4

This scene takes us back to Bethulia, as the Priest tells Ozia that a foreigner arrested by their troops has asked to see him. Achior enters and falls at their feet, proclaiming himself their loyal servant, though he has been fighting on Holofernes's side. Ozia asks his name and he says it is Achior, an Ammonite mercenary who has been fighting with Holofernes. The Priest suspects treachery but Ozia believes him, and after some discussion they decide to let him explain his situation.

Achior tells them that he silently followed Holofernes in his campaigns, but that he objected to the siege of Bethulia. He reminded Holofernes of the miracles God had performed for Judea. Holofernes was enraged and told Achior that since he was still so devoted to Israel, he could die with them in the slaughter to come. His men seized Achior and left him at the foot of the hill of Bethulia (Jdt 6:10–13). In the oratorio, the Priest asks Achior what he knows about Judith, since only one day remains before their surrender. Achior tells the Bethulians that he saw Judith enter the Assyrian camp dressed festively and feigning love. He expects she will return victorious, with the help of Heaven, with Holofernes's head as a prize. In the original story, Achior was not privy to this information, since he was no longer in Holofernes's camp when Judith arrived. But as a literary device, it creates further suspense. Ozia is thrilled, and Achior sings an aria in which he imagines seeing the "bloody skull of the tyrant trodden down …

and [he] will write the victory of Bethulia with his blood." This passion convinces Ozia, who embraces him and sings a joyful aria.

Scene 5

This is the often-called seduction scene in Holofernes's tent. In an opening recitative, Holofernes praises Judith's wisdom in seeking refuge in his arms. He also refers to her wish to go with him to the heart of Bethulia, an addition to the biblical story. He is so enchanted with her favors and her beauty that, he says, "Your conqueror has become your prisoner" (… *preso di Vincitor: tuo Prigionier son reso*). The duet that follows, *Mio conforto, mia Speranza* ("My consolation, my hope"), is a prime example of the power of the inflections of the human voice to add a subtext between the lines of dialogue. Their duet begins as Holofernes calls Judith "My consolation," to which she responds, "My hope." The music is lilting and lyrical. Holofernes's part was written for a countertenor, which in that era often represented powerful men. Irony is achieved in this duet when they sing similar but not identical words at the same time. She sings "over you I will be victorious" while he is singing "for you alone I will be victorious." They are singing these words, and much of the duet, in parallel thirds and upbeat rapid 16th-note runs—ironically suggesting they are in complete harmony. Though there is some ambiguity in their conversation in the original story (Jdt 11–12), it is less subtle here and greatly amplified by the music, particularly because they can "speak" at the same time.

In a second, faster section, while Judith sings of burning, Holofernes sings of loving. He sings that he will abandon himself to her faith, while she sings that she will soon give proof of her faith to the world and the gods. She also says, "Triumph will be born from my right hand" (*Nato dalla mia destra il trionfo sarà*). In these phrases, Judith uses a notably stronger tone. When he asks how she feels, she responds that his desires will have an end (*Havran termine i tuoi desir*). Then she asks him, since it is night, to take a brief rest while she watches over him. He tells her she should also rest, since he cannot close his eyes while she is awake. She sings in an aside, with sparse, suspenseful accompaniment: "O great God, whose right hand can wound tyrants" (*La tua destra, o Sommo Dio, che ferir suole i Tiranni*). Holofernes comments that "the tone of your song, O beautiful one, is too deadly." She repeats her plea to God, in highly descriptive music, marked *grave e staccato* (serious and with short, broken notes). The effect is one of suspense and breathlessness. The second time Judith repeats her plea to God, the underlying music suggests that she is almost holding her breath. Holofernes is feeling anxious, wondering why his heart feels weary. Judith asks what he fears, and he responds that he doesn't recognize his sadness. Then he says he is giving in to sleep and hopes she will "sweetly join him." The music and his voice fade, suggesting that sleep has overcome him. There is no indication either that they have had sex before this, or that he was too drunk and they did not. This ambivalence is also present in the original text and most librettists echoed that. A notable omission in this opera, however, is a banquet scene or any mention of Holofernes's drunken state.

In the same halting music, Judith sings an aria that opens with a third repeat of her plea to God. She begs God in a hesitant voice to give strength to her hand, so that she can truncate the evil head and bring an end to so many troubles (… *acciò tronco il capo rio giunga fine a tanti affanni*). Returning to recitative, the accompaniment is, as earlier, halting and hesitant. She wonders why she should wait any longer to kill him, since the "impious enemy" is in a deep sleep. Judith prays again for strength for her hand to be able to remove the proud head. Flutes play earlier trumpet motifs, almost mocking the military prowess of the now headless Holofernes. Then in a recitative, she realizes he is dead. The only musical indication of what has just taken place is a pair of rapid orchestral passages. This depiction almost suggests a kind of out-of-body experience. Judith now sings very assertively in a simple recitative, *Ecco diviso il capo dall'esecrando busto* ("Behold the head separated from its execrable bust"). In gentler music, Judith calls on her (silent) servant to cover him with her veil and bring the head back to Bethulia, assuring her that she will accompany her.

Scene 6
Back in Bethulia, the priest sings in a recitative as he waits for Judith to return, that he has lost faith; and he tells Ozia they should surrender. In a dramatic aria, he condemns Achior as a traitor. Ozia admits, with sadness, that he too sees deceit, and sings a sublime and deeply felt aria bidding farewell to liberty (*Addio, cara libertà*). A dialogue follows between Ozia and Achior, in which the latter condemns Ozia for his lack of faith. He continues to insist that he told the truth. Just as the argument is heating up, the Priest enters out of breath, proclaiming the exciting news that Judith has returned and Holofernes is dead. All rejoice, and prepare to kill and "bleed dry" (*svenare*) the infidels. This is a graphic expansion of the original text where the Israelites "cut them in pieces" (Jdt 15:5).

Scene 7
Judith enters and sings a recitative, "Take, and trample, Ozia, this tyrant whom you chose as sovereign of our country. In spite of you, the God of Israel is pouring blessings upon us" (*Prendi, calpesta, Ozia, quell tiran che sciegliesti per sovrano alla Patria. A tuo dispetto piove il Dio d'Israele sovra di noi le grazie*). Presumably she is singing those words as she presents the head to Ozia. She then tells the people to render thanks to God with their voices and hearts, and he will give them freedom and life. The chorus sings that Heaven is inviting them all to joy. Then Judith sings the very upbeat and chipper aria *Combattuta navicella* ("The fragile ship"): "The ship is blown by the treacherous wind, but if a friendly star guides it, it will reach the shore." The ensemble responds in praise of God who can change storms into calm.

Then Ozia sings an aria to the same melody but different text: *Superata la costanza dallo sdegno delle sfere pria che torni la Speranza, scopre il porto del piacere* ("Overcoming the constant disdain of the skies before Hope returns and reveals the haven of pleasure"). The oratorio concludes as all proclaim: It is only the work of God that "changes a sea of tears into a heaven of happiness." The finale is typical of the "madrigal" of seventeenth-century tradition, where all the characters (even the deceased) appear and sing.

This oratorio breathes new life into the characters of the book of Judith, utilizing musical techniques in a witty manner to suggest new layers of meaning and interpretation.

The Cambridge La Giuditta *(1697)*

The libretto is by Prince Antonio Ottoboni, the father of Cardinal Ottoboni, who wrote the libretto for the earlier "Naples" version discussed above. This second version varies in many ways from the first. There are only three characters—Judith (soprano), the *nutrice* or Nurse (contralto, or male alto), and Holofernes (tenor); here too, there is no chorus. The scaled-down orchestra consists only of strings and *continuo*. A reviewer of the *Giuditta* recording on the Dynamic label (2009) points out:

> The Nurse has a musical role wholly equal to those of the other two characters, and indeed some of the most important parts of the score are written for her—a welcome and creative addition. The writing is always very flexible, with rather short recitatives and extremely concise, functional arias, often virtuosic. The conception and idiom of the oratorio are strongly influenced by the simplification of style typical of the closing decades of the seventeenth century.[8]

The oratorio is known today as the "Cambridge" *Giuditta* because its manuscript is conserved in the Rowe Music Library of King's College, Cambridge. The work is a collection of dazzling lengthy arias for each of the three characters, along with duets of many styles and moods, depending on the text. This oratorio, similarly to Scarlatti's earlier *Giuditta* setting, seems closer in style to opera than oratorio, which is true for most of the oratorios he wrote in Rome. Traditionally an oratorio would have been performed in the palace of one of Scarlatti's Roman patrons. The two parts would have been separated not by a sermon, in this setting, but rather by an interval that would have included eating and drinking.[9]

The goal of composers in Scarlatti's time was to succeed through music in moving the hearts of the listener, eliciting emotions (*affetti*, in Maria Rosa De Luca's words).[10] This is known as the "theory of the affects," in German *Affektenlehre*, a theory in the aesthetics of painting, music, and theater widely ascribed to in the Baroque era (1600–1750). In some ways one could say that moving the listener is any composer's goal, but De Luca notes the distinction:[11]

> In the late seventeenth century, the term *affetto* had a particular significance, referring to the so-called theory of affects (Affektenlehre), an aesthetic theory that focuses on the relationship between music and feelings. This theory goes back to the ancient Greeks (Aristotle in particular), was revived in the Renaissance and further developed in the Baroque era. Then, precise relationships were recognized, in vocal and instrumental music, between the "affect" and musical figures. This meant that musical figures were set up to elicit a pre-determined "affect," and Scarlatti in this oratorio arranges such figures in a precise way to move the listener towards a particular "affect."

---

[8] https://www.ccd.pl/la-giuditta-p192791/ (accessed April 23, 2020).
[9] Pagano and Boyd in *New Grove* v. 22, p. 380.
[10] Maria Rosa De Luca, personal communication, September 12, 2018; translation my own.
[11] De Luca, p. 118.

A discussion of the Cambridge *Giuditta* from this perspective can illuminate many aspects of the three characters and their interactions. Both the music and text shed interesting light on the two women and on their relationship. It is notable that the Nurse, Judith's faithful servant, is often addressed here as "Mother," and she in turn addresses Judith as "Daughter" (this is also found in some later works). Her attitude toward Judith is always protective. Her firmness to Judith is tender and considerate but at the same time insistent. This attitude highlights the quality of Judith's temperament, marked by an "ostentatious assurance—ending in her act of heroic effrontery"—that she is acting by divine will.[12]

The choice of voice type in any vocal work immediately suggests character, age, even personality. Scarlatti chose to make Judith a high soprano, a very bright voice with a ringing sound and a clarion (*squillante*) tone. In addition, much of her music is florid, to emphasize particular words or phrases. These musical features, De Luca proposes, suggest in Judith a certain haughtiness or arrogance (*alterigia*) in sharp contrast to the thoughtful and subdued attitude of the Nurse. The Nurse is cast as a lower voice, suggesting age and lower social status. The cautious character of the Nurse is in polar opposition to Judith's unquestioning faith in God, and both are in sharp contrast to the particular qualities of Holofernes's character. He reveals his brutal and bellicose nature from the first moment he appears. His only vulnerability, the sensual attraction to Judith, will bring him down.[13] Yet in his music, this Holofernes is appealing and not entirely unsympathetic. Neither in the biblical narrative nor in this oratorio is Holofernes depicted as a monster. His music in this oratorio is "elegant and sensitive," in the words of one commentator[14]—with which I agree. The tenor voice is always an appealing one, suggesting a romantic and heroic character. This forces listeners to rethink their previous ideas and attitudes. History is written by the victors, after all. From the perspective of the Assyrians, Judith was the villain of the story. And in this oratorio, she seems a particularly calculating and cold-blooded one.

The oratorio is in two parts and the plot adheres closely to the biblical narrative. It opens with a short *Sinfonia* in three sections, which is followed by a sequence of recitatives and arias and a couple of duets. Most arias are rather short, and the singers are mostly supported by the *basso continuo* alone, with the strings playing the *ritornellos* (repeats). In some arias, the strings have a more prominent part.[15] There is a fine recording on the Albany Record label, featuring The Queen's Chamber Band (2007).

Judith: soprano
Nurse: alto
Holofernes: tenor

---

[12] De Luca, p. 118.
[13] De Luca, p. 120.
[14] John Ostendorf, CD liner notes, p. 4.
[15] The whole work can be heard on YouTube: https://www.youtube.com/watch?v=5cB35U5BYXg (accessed February 14, 2020).

Part I

After the opening *Sinfonia* (overture), Judith sings to her Nurse: *Al fato Assiro cedo Bettulia* ("I cede Bethulia to its Assyrian fate"), in which Judith bemoans the loss of both "Israel's heart" and "Heaven's exalted protection," which included "the rod and stone which struck, giving healing waters" (a reference to Num 20:11). She says that though no one in Bethulia is grateful to God, God is not absent (*Manca l'uom grato a Dio, ma Dio non manca*). She still trusts that they are the chosen people, protected by God. A dramatic aria follows, *Turbe timide, che fate?* ("Timid hordes, what are you doing?"). She implores the people to feel anger rather than resignation, to let their thirst be a thirst for glory (*Sia la sete ch'è in voi sete di Gloria*). The strings play a prominent part in this aria, with continual rapid and excited runs matching the voice, all of which depict Judith's anger. The Nurse sings a recitative, *Signora, ah, che le strida del nostro sesso imbelle*: "The cries of our weaker sex are derided or ignored by men" (Who would believe such a phrase came from a seventeenth-century libretto?). This is followed by her aria, *A che giova d'un solo l'ardire*: "What benefit will the ardor of one person bring?," in which she says if it is to be only one person who will struggle and die, that person must be Judith. The melancholy sound is amplified by the prominent use of the viol, creating a virtual duet.

Judith responds with a recitative and aria, *S'il più forte vacilla lo sostenga il men forte* ("If the stronger one falters, let the weaker one help him"). Judith says that "modest behavior is futile in battle" and then confesses that she has a strange idea. She tells the Nurse that they are going to the Assyrian camp. Then she sings *Sciolgo il crin, snudo il sen* ("I will loosen my hair, bare my breast, and dry my eyes"), to very lively and almost coquettish music. She sings that Holofernes will face even graver danger than they themselves are facing now. This Judith is full of confidence if not even swagger. Then she sings the aria *Scordato consigliere de le sembianze mie* ("Neglected attendant of my appearance"), in which she tells the Nurse to make her attractive to the enemy, and that with "charm, tears, and laughter" she will win over her foe. The Nurse, addressing Judith as *Figlia* (daughter), tries to dissuade her from her plan. She tells her how dangerous it is to "test fierce Mars," that she will not save her homeland and will end up in prison. Most powerfully, she predicts that her actions "will make the cold ashes of your dead husband glow with shame" (*il cener freddo de l'estinto tuo sposo arda di sdegno*). The Nurse's music, in her dark voice, is sad and serious, contrasted with Judith's mostly upbeat and bright sound.

Judith, needless to say, does not heed the Nurse's words. Setting out for the enemy camp, the two women sing a duet, in which their lines alternate. The Nurse opens with *Deh, rifletti al gran cimento* ("Please, reflect on the great danger"). Judith responds that what she is planning comes from Heaven. The Nurse responds that Heaven condemns profane acts, to which Judith responds that Heaven is not subject to human laws. In the music for the Nurse's words, the intensity of her urging is reflected in the *fioritura* (florid embellishment of melodic lines), used here for emphasis and to underline the importance of her words. Judith's response is immediate, sung on rapid runs. She responds to the Nurse's repeated requests to reflect by contradicting with her own urging. The ample *fioritura* on the word "Heaven" and reiteration of "laws" exalt Judith's appeal to "the only law she recognizes, that of God."[16]

Their dialogue highlights the differences in feeling and attitudes between the two women. Having a foil in the Nurse allows Judith to express her feelings more than she does in many other works. In contrast to the Nurse's apprehension is Judith's confidence, and her belief that she is acting according to divine will. The difference in their attitudes is underlined by the music, alternating between sad and bright for the two women. The contrast between the Nurse's menacing words and Judith's energy and faith could be seen to symbolize the contrast between human and divine law. Repetitions of certain words in the music underline the primary focus of the two women: for the Nurse, "Think" (*Rifletti*), and for Judith, "Heaven" (*Ciel*). The music for Judith's responses to the Nurse's pleas is shrill and vibrant, intended to denote Judith's determination and confidence. Judith's music on the word "Heaven" at one point involves a bold leap to a high note, underlined further by a long hold on the note. Successive repetitions of the word are sung on descending leaps, possibly suggesting a significance that goes beyond the written text: in De Luca's view, it suggests that Judith's inspiration comes directly from God.[17]

Their cut-and-thrust dialogue (*a botta e risposta*) becomes increasingly lively. Judith, addressing the Nurse again as "Mother," sings an aria, *Segui, madre, il mio passo* ("Oh Mother, follow my lead, for more glorious steps have never been taken by a Hebrew woman"). The Nurse responds that she will follow Judith and then sings the emotional aria *Sommo Dio, ch'in cor di donna* ("Mighty God, who in a woman's heart can rouse the fiercest feelings ... support her heart, and her words").

The scene changes as they approach the camp, and they sing *Ecco le tende Assire* ("Here are the Assyrian tents"). Judith tells the Nurse that they must pretend to be frightened and attempting to escape. These additions to Judith's words create a more interesting character, one who can plan strategically. Judith then sings *Chi m'addita* ("Who can show me"), musically notable as she is accompanied by strings (without *basso continuo*) that play descending figures on the text: "Who can show me, for pity's sake, where to find peace in the midst of all these weapons?" The sparse accompaniment— only violins and violas in unison—effectively conveys Judith's feeling of isolation. The aria is interrupted by a recitative by the Nurse. She points out to Judith that Holofernes's voice is menacing and fierce with his troops, but when he notices Judith, his gaze is gentle and an unexpected smile flashes on his lips. Judith repeats and expands her aria, after which Holofernes enters. He says to Judith: *Donna, de petti Assiri son men forti gl'usberghi* ("Woman, your armor is weaker than Assyrian breasts"). The tenor voice is an appealing one, making him both sympathetic and heroic, challenging listeners' assumptions about Holofernes.

When Holofernes first sees Judith, he tells her that she arms herself in vain "with those two murderous eyes," a very interesting and prescient remark suggesting that he

---

[16] De Luca, p. 115.
[17] De Luca, pp. 112–14.

is aware of her possible subterfuge. The Nurse remarks in an aside: "Ah, how he laughs at our arts [of seduction]." Holofernes grants Judith pardon because of her "weaker sex, beauty, and tender years," and tells her to return to whence she came. He assures her that "it will take more than your wiles to conquer an Assyrian general." This Holofernes is much more aware and cleverer than his biblical counterpart. Though dazzled by her beauty, he exhorts her to return to Bethulia. Deeply disturbed by the feelings she arouses in him, he sings the aria *Togliti da quest'occhi* ("Remove yourself from these eyes"). This aria reveals more dimensions to Holofernes's character than are imagined in the biblical text:

> *Togliti da quest'occhi,*
> *per non ferirmi il cor,*
> *Bellezza infida.*
> *Dei dardi che tu scocchi, si ride il mio valor,*
> *Ma non si fida.*

> Remove yourself from these eyes,
> in order not to wound my heart,
> Treacherous beauty.
> My valor laughs at the darts you shoot,
> but it doesn't trust [them].

The music is upbeat and excited. Holofernes's words suggest conflicted feelings, which unnerve him. His words create a contrast and opposition between love (the "darts") and the concept of a valorous warrior. His bellicose nature is in conflict with the vulnerability of his heart to sensual seduction. Scarlatti suggests Holofernes's conflicted attitudes musically through a strongly rhythmical and bold melody. The aria opens on *f'* which is relatively high in the register, descending a fifth on a strong beat. Musically these elements suggest battles and warriors. The next verses are sung to the same music, confirming Holofernes's agitation before Judith. The second part of the aria utilizes the same rhythm, with a slight change in melody. Several rests create moments of suspension, suggesting hesitation on Holofernes's part. The closing measures of the second part feature a descending motif, a strong musical suggestion of Holofernes yielding to Judith.[18]

Judith kneels and tells Holofernes, *Duce, Bettulia è serva del tuo valor* ("Lord, Bethulia is a slave to your valor"). She tells him there is no safe place for her if she leaves, since she would be "despicable to both friend and foe." She tells him to "cut off this unworthy head, let this beauty, a useless gift, even an accursed one from nature, be extinguished." This is new and original text, and a Judith who asks to be killed is a more manipulative and risk-taking Judith. An aria follows, *Se ritorno, entro le mura*: "If I return, I enter those walls as a traitor and will have to die." She asks him where she really belongs. She says if she dies where she is, she will die innocent, and asks him again to kill her. The aria has a wistful quality, which may be her genuine feeling or

---

[18] De Luca, pp. 116, 118.

may suggest Judith's strategy of softening Holofernes and assuring him that she poses no threat. In music, emotional manipulation is hard to represent, often being in the ear of the listener and difficult to differentiate from the musical expression of true emotions. Holofernes responds in a recitative, *Donna, a torto m'accusi di superbo e crudel* ("Woman, you mistakenly accuse me of pride and cruelty") in which he insists he is offering her liberty and honor. He claims he does not have a heart of stone and truly feels pity for her. He asks her to leave, because in his camp he "neither welcomes nor kills women."

He sings an aria as an aside: *Mi combatte, mi stringe, m'atterra* ("Her suppliant beauty fights with me, grips me, knocks me down"). He tells his strong heart to resist and deny her weeping eyes and seductive lips but confesses that if the wild struggle continues much longer, he knows he will weaken. The music is upbeat and fast, reflecting his confusion and passion. This glimpse into Holofernes's feelings opens up not only his character but also the plot. He is no longer the one-dimensional villain of the biblical story. He repeats his earlier plea to her that she leave the camp. They continue in a duet, *Tu m' uccidi e non m' accogli* ("You kill me and do not welcome me"), in which they sing separately about what they are feeling. Judith says she will leave, but half-heartedly, then says she regrets it. "What shall I do?" is followed by "Will I/you depart?" Finally she states simply that she is leaving, and he tells her if she leaves he is lost (*estinto*), and he begs her remain. He confesses that he is vanquished (*son vinto*), and when she agrees to stay, she says, "I have vanquished/won" (*ho vinto*) in an aside. There are several moments when the voices harmonize, suggesting a kind of accord between them, even if it is being manipulated by both of them. The double entendres and wordplay of this duet recall that of Scarlatti's earlier Naples *Giuditta* (discussed above). This concludes Part I.

Part II

Judith opens with a recitative: *Del pianto vostro, o lumi, labra, de le querele e dei sospiri vi ringrazio* ("I thank you for your tears, O eyes; and lips, for complaints and sighs"). She continues to address her tears and sighs, which were "born from a heavy heart and which she used as sorrow's weapons." Now she asks how to use these weapons of affection against the enemy whose face inspires her with disdain (*odioso dispetto*), in spite of her great sadness. She continues with *Posso e voglio* ("I can and want to"), an ornate aria filled with *fioritura* to depict Judith's determination. There are also dramatic leaps and runs into the stratospheric range of the soprano voice. She proclaims that she will do what she wants, for she rules over herself (*Di me stessa arbitra io sono*)—a wonderful assertion of female power. She sings of how she will let her lips laugh and her eyes glow, while her heart weeps; but her suffering will remain hidden in her heart. This glimpse into Judith's feelings and how she plans to execute her daring act is a wonderful midrash that creates new dimensions in Judith's character.

The Nurse responds in a recitative, *Dell' inimico Assiro sin tra le mura di Bettulia avezzo ero a temer* ("I have long feared the enemy Assyrian since we were still behind the walls of Bethulia"). Addressing Judith again as "daughter" and singing with great feeling, she admits that she is frightened by Holofernes's advances and fears danger;

but since she knows that fear is futile, she says they must be bold. "If you can't escape, you have to go forth and try" (*S'inoltri a tenti chi fuggir più non può*). She seats Judith and grooms her. Judith seemed to have already done this, in Part I (*Sciolgo il crin, snudo il sen*: "I will loosen my hair, bare my breast, and dry my eyes"). It might be that she only did a modest toilette, to make herself alluring, but now the Nurse is adding new elements. The Nurse removes Judith's scarf, puts crimson on her lips, loosens her veil to reveal her white neck, uncovers her breast, and tells her to let the edges of her cloak fall open to reveal a small glimpse of her foot. This last suggestion is too much for Judith, who explains, "Mother, you are frightening me!" They now sing a duet, *Vincerò/vincerai s'il ciel destina*: "I/you will win if Heaven grants such a victory to a hopeful heart … to so lovely a face, to punish the haughty throngs." They sing homophonically, in perfect thirds, the musical harmony representing the emotional harmony between them.

Judith continues with a recitative, *Madre, apprendo il cimento, ne so temer* ("Mother, I understand the risk, I do not fear it"). She says that if she frees her country, she will live triumphant; if not, she will die with it, celebrated. But she asserts that she shall not fail or die, because the God of Israel is with her. She sees Holofernes approaching and tells the Nurse they should change their demeanor and the Nurse is to follow her cue. Then she prays to God to give her strength. While the Nurse is preparing Judith's hair and clothes, Judith sings *Non ti curo, o libertà* ("I do not care for you, liberty"), where she expresses that in the "comfortable prison" they are not truly free, but they will soon know true freedom. The Nurse repeats the aria and then they sing a duet. The music is gentler than the text would indicate. The reviewer of the CD on the Dynamic label suggests that the use of a minuet dance rhythm in this aria/duet "reflects the composer's openness towards new musical experiences and offers a foretaste of the expressive mood of the new century."[19] It also expresses Judith's confident optimism. At five minutes, it is one of the longest arias or duets in the oratorio. Holofernes enters near the end and sings a refrain, after which they sing together, suggesting complete agreement.

Holofernes now sings a recitative, *Bella, non ruotan gl'astri con si soave armonioso* ("Beautiful one, the stars do not turn in such sweet harmony"), in which he tells her she will be freed as she requested. His singing is sweet and expressive. He adds that at dawn, a defeated Israel will celebrate his triumphs, which he attributes to her beauty. He apparently still thinks she has given him valuable information about the enemy. He takes her hand and pulls her up, then sings the fast, energetic aria *Quella terra onde fuggisti*: "That land that you fled, will obey your commands … its priests will make more offerings and prayers to your beauty than to all the gods in their temples." This text suggests that Holofernes was unaware that the Hebrews don't worship multiple gods, either implying ignorance on his part or that non-Israelites were not aware of Israelite practices. Numerous references to the "one Israelite God" suggest the former. Then Holofernes softens his voice and his tone in a recitative, *Ma impallidita al suolo chini le luci*: "But pale, you lower your eyes to the ground and are quiet. Did I offend

---

[19] https://www.ccd.pl/la-giuditta-p192791/; no writer credited (accessed April 23, 2020).

your tender heart through which you expressed your feelings for your homeland, your true love?" Judith responds "seductively" (libretto note) that she will soon surrender as her homeland already has:

> That pity you believe I feel, please reserve some for my country. The love with which you honor me makes me ecstatic and proud. I admire, more than all my own rulers, the Assyrian general.

Holofernes is "moved but unsure of her sincerity" (libretto note) and sings the aria *Bella, mi vuoi deridere* ("Beautiful one, you want to mock me"), which features the same descending fifth that was heard in his earlier aria, a musical expression of self-confidence. The mood of the aria is light, as he tells Judith that she knows how to shatter his strong heart and that only she can laugh at his tears. The music here as elsewhere feels too light for the text, but Scarlatti may have been trying to project a playful or flirtatious side of Holofernes. Holofernes sits down, pours wine for himself, and invites Judith to dinner: *Vieni, e le nostre cene col tuo sembiante onora* ("Come, and honor our meals with your presence"). He also invites Judith to sit beside him. She rejects the offer with dripping sarcasm, saying that she would be honored but that a "prisoner, a slave, a lowly reject" (*una spoglia, una schiava, un vil rifiuto*) is not permitted to sit next to a conqueror. That would be too much, she says, for this "despised and outcast female who is neither welcomed nor killed" (*questa discacciata e derisa femina non accolta e non uccisa*), throwing his earlier words back at him. Judith may have been portrayed here as trying to find a way to refuse Holofernes's invitation to eat his non-kosher food. This issue, prominent in the original text, is rarely raised in musical works.

Holofernes, "stung by her mocking the words he spoke to her" (note in libretto) sings, *Già sapesti ferir, lascia di pungere*: "You already knew how to wound, stop the stinging, you will kill me if you add more wounds on top of these wounds." The music is once again lighthearted and fast. They sing a recitative, *Siedo, ma non già siede l'instancabil pensier* ("I am sitting, but my tireless thought does not rest"), his music sounding seductive and sweet, or reflecting his increasingly drunken state. This leads into a duet, *Piega, o Duce il capo altero* ("Bend, O Lord, your haughty head"), to very gentle music with an undercurrent of irony. (The Italian word *Duce*, though literally "Duke," more generally means "leader"; but in direct address it would be more accurately translated as "Captain" or "Lord.")

Then Judith says to the Nurse: *Madre, perchè i riposi del tuo, del mio signor sian più soavi* ("Mother, so that the rest of our master be sweeter, sing of Achilles and Hercules"). The Nurse does not agree with this choice and chooses instead to sing of Samson, "Israel's own Hercules," in the aria *Ardea di fiamma impura*: "Samson burned with an impure fire for an enemy beauty." The Nurse continues to relate the story of Samson and Delilah from Judg 16. Holofernes stirs and mumbles in his sleep *Che racconto funesto* ("What a baleful tale"). The Nurse reassures him that "it all ends happily" and then continues with a subdued lullaby, *Dormi, o fulmine di guerra* ("Sleep, O thunderbolt of war," the longest aria in the oratorio, at six minutes). She tells Holofernes that he already knows that "bows and arrows launched from beautiful eyes can bring down the mighty." In the very soft and muted accompaniment, the *basso continuo* as well as the repetitions of steady and slow single notes, almost an *ostinato*, create a breathless mood for this suspenseful moment in the story. Both the accompaniment and vocal part grow slower and quieter during the aria, fading away completely into a mood of quiet suspense.

At this point Judith has Holofernes's head in her lap. The Nurse then concludes the story of Samson in a recitative. Judith, thinking that Holofernes is asleep, tries to prepare herself. She comments on the large sword she is unsheathing, then asks Heaven to help her bring down the tyrant. On the last phrase, *l'empio cada* ("let the tyrant fall"), she sings a sudden strong and determined *fioritura* phrase. But Holofernes mumbles in his sleep again and she can't do it. This happens a few times, creating a suspenseful drama not found in the original biblical text. Holofernes mutters such things as "Cruel one, why?" and "Why do you leave me?" The turbulent music paints her indecisiveness. Judith becomes very agitated and almost shouts some of her words. Just before striking him, she sings, *Folle, che bado ai sogni? Il ferro io libro onde il collo non erri, e il colpo io vibro* ("Mad one, what do I care about dreams? I am freeing the sword, that it should not miss the neck, and I shudder with the blow"), after which she strikes. Though this work was not staged, the audience still would assume that his head was no longer in Judith's lap. The music would be expected to be dramatic and intense at this moment, but the vocal part is simply a dry recitative. The *continuo*, by contrast, plays dramatic and vigorous repeated notes to paint the violent act. In this suspenseful and harrowing, bloody version of the story, the Nurse comments graphically on the killing:

Gurgling, choking on wine and blood, the haughty soul dies, and that horrible face threatens violence and revenge even as it dies.

Judith tells the Nurse that "the vile head is not yet separated from the body. I am striking again, I will grasp his hair and lift up the head; nothing else remains to be done." These words are more shouted than sung. She then separates the head from the body. (In the original story, she strikes twice; Jdt 13:8). This text seems to be describing some of the popular paintings of Judith in that era. Dragging out the killing with imagined details—bloody and graphic—humanizes Judith and makes the story very real and vivid.

The Nurse is "horrified" (note in libretto) and tells Judith that she is totally covered in blood—her arms, face, and clothes. This detail is not usually found in paintings nor in other librettos, and definitely not in the biblical text. A librettist writing for an unstaged work would have more liberty to write a graphic description, as this one did. Judith replies exultantly, "A more vibrant purple has never hung from the backs of Hebrew Kings" (*Porpora così viva non pendè mai dal dorso ai regi ebrei*). Then she coolly tells the Nurse to wrap "the bloody booty" (*la sanguinosa preda*) in a linen cloth (*lino*), possibly a pillowcase, before they head back to Bethulia. This libretto alters the placement of the head inside their food bag (which has not been previously mentioned). The Nurse praises Judith for her victory, and Judith reminds her that it was God's work, not hers alone.

Judith sings the aria *Tu che desti' o eterno Nume* ("You who awaken, eternal God"), which contains a very effective virtuosic *obbligato* part for the violin, adding pathos. She asks God, who gave strength to her arm and courage to her spirit, to help them escape in the darkness. When they see the walls of Bethulia, they sing *Ecco le mura amiche*: "Here are the friendly walls, and the watchful guard is already questioning us." Judith orders the gates be opened, and the Nurse comments on the sad faces of Ozias and the people, expectant yet fearful. She tells Judith to show them the head. They now sing a duet, accompanied only by *basso continuo*: *Spunta l'alba più bella, più chiara* ("The most beautiful and clear dawn is breaking … the lights of victory and glory also brighten their faces"). As in earlier duets, they sing in complete harmony.

Judith shows her people the severed bloody head of Holofernes, and in a very calm voice, says: *Amici, eccovi il teschio dell'Assiro Oloferne* ("Friends, here is the skull of the Assyrian Holofernes"). She continues: 'Bethulia can now rest from worry, tyranny is over, the tyrant overthrown" (*cessa la tirannnia, tolto il tiranno*). Judith further tells the people to put the head on a spike and watch the Assyrian legions fleeing (based on Jdt 14:1–4). She tells them that Heaven will fight for them and will conquer with this head, "struck down by a weak woman." Then she turns to the Nurse and says they must dispose of the "bloody remains." Presumably that is the headless corpse, which in the original narrative Judith left in Holofernes's tent. This is a weak plot change, since it is the sight of Holofernes's headless corpse that terrifies his army. In addition, how could two women have carried the corpse back to Bethulia? Judith also tells the Nurse to dress her again in widow's garb and concludes with: "Let the woman who served as Heaven's lightning and sword be seen again." In her final aria, Judith sings: "O mortals, you will have Bethulia's fate if you trust in God. If you yield to treacherous senses, you will have Holofernes' death" (*se cedi ai sensi infidi, d'Oloferne avrai la morte*). "Whether innocent or guilty, always trust in Heaven but also fear it." The oratorio concludes on an upbeat, bright C major chord. Judith's closing words turn the work into a morality play.

Conclusion

The most striking of many wonderful features in this work is the vividness of the characters' emotions, which are conflicted and feel very real. In addition, there is an unexpected "feminist" slant to some of the dialogue, such as when the Nurse talks about their "weaker sex" and their cries of being ignored or derided by men. Judith is depicted as a woman full of confidence, even swagger, which the Nurse tries to tamp down to protect her. This is not in contradiction with her biblical image but rather fills in empty spaces between the lines. Why should Judith not be confident and strong? How else could she have done what she did? Her wisdom, which is praised in the original story, is here clearly manifested by her planning and maneuvers. Holofernes, too, is given more dimensions. He tries to remain strong and to resist Judith's charms, which he suspects are wiles; yet he succumbs to passion in the end. These additions in the libretto make all the characters (Judith's maid is completely silent in the original text) more interesting and three-dimensional, and musical elements underline and amplify these changes.

Eighteenth Century

Antonio Vivaldi (1678–1741)

Antonio Vivaldi was born in Venice, which was at the time a rich, though by then declining, republic. His father wanted him to have a musical career and felt that the Church was the best place to develop that. Vivaldi began training for the priesthood in 1693, when he was 15, and was ordained in 1703. He was often called *Il Prete Rosso* (The Red Priest) because of his red hair. The year he was ordained, Vivaldi became a violin teacher at the *Ospedale della Pietà* orphanage for girls. The *Ospedale*, one of four such institutions in Venice, was famous for the high level of its singers and instrumentalists, and its concerts attracted not only tourists from Italy and beyond, but—even more critically for the institution—also both civic and private financial support. Vivaldi was connected to the *Pietà* for most of his career, from 1703 to 1740: first as violin master, then director of instrumental music, and composer in residence for many years. He composed his first opera in 1713, and it was a moderate success. He wrote several more over the next few years. But his sacred vocal music was particularly successful, and in time Vivaldi obtained commissions for this music from other institutions.[20]

Juditha Triumphans was commissioned by the *Pietà* in 1716 to celebrate Venice's victory over the Turks. This was Venice's last major military enterprise, and composer, painters, and poets all celebrated this victory. The libretto is a rhymed Latin text by Giacomo Cassetti (1682–1757), a minor local poet. The work is labeled a *sacrum militare oratorium* (sacred military oratorio). As Kelley Harness points out, Cassetti wanted his text to be considered "an allegorical response to Venice's ongoing war with the Ottoman Empire." In fact, "he appended an allegorical poem" (to the end of the oratorio) in which he predicted that Judith's victory would foreshadow Venice's victory against its enemy.[21] In the poem, Cassetti spelled out the symbolism that he saw in the story: Judith represents Venice; Abra is Christianity; the besieged Jewish city of Bethulia is the church; its ruler Ozias is the Pope; and Holofernes is the Ottoman sultan.[22] In this scenario, by saving Venice, Judith is saving all of Christianity from the Ottoman threat. There is some irony in this symbolism, considering that Judith is renowned for saving the Israelites in her day.

Vivaldi left about 750 musical works, most of which have only come to light since the 1930s, and others are still being found. *Juditha Triumphans* is the composer's only surviving oratorio of four that he is believed to have written (attested by many music scholars). The oratorio was first performed in the *Ospedale della Pietà*, and because Vivaldi drew his cast from there, all the parts are for female voices. The parts of Judith, Holofernes and the priest Ozias were composed for contraltos (the lowest female

---

[20] Michael Talbot, "Antonio Vivaldi: Italian Composer," *Britannica*. Available online: https://www.britannica.com/biography/Antonio-Vivaldi; (accessed January 4, 2019).
[21] Kelley Harness, "Judith, Music, and Female Patrons in Early Modern Italy," chap. 20 in *The Sword of Judith*, p. 372.
[22] Martin Pearlman, program notes.

voice), while the part of Judith's servant Abra is set for a soprano, suggesting that she is younger and unmarried. Vagaus, Holofernes's steward, is a eunuch in the oratorio as he is in the biblical story: "Bagoas the eunuch" (Jdt 12:11). His part is written for a soprano. This character is not included in most oratorios of that era. In modern performances and recordings, this casting is usually altered.

Visitors to the *Pietà*, where Vivaldi's works were all performed, sometimes commented disparagingly that church services there were too much like concerts. It is possible that librettos were required to be in Latin rather than Italian in order to legitimize the "sacred" nature of the oratorios performed at the four *Ospedali* in Venice at that time.[23]

Vivaldi used every instrument available to him, including particularly exotic ones. Lynne Murray and Alan Maddox comment further on Vivaldi's orchestration:

> The variety of instrumentation throughout the score serves as a means of characterization, which was important at the *Pietà* where the performers would have been barely visible behind grilles draped with gauze. Instruments also conveyed drama and meaning in a religious work where emotions were implied rather than explicit. The score requires recorders, oboes, clarinets, four theorbos, organ, trumpets, timpani, soprano chalumeau, a viola d'amore, and a consort of viole all'inglese (viols) as well as the customary strings and continuo. The military pomp of the trumpets and drums in the opening chorus would have immediately reminded the 1716 audience of Venice's recent victory over the Turks and the allegorical nature of what they were about to hear.[24]

A striking aspect of this libretto is its interpretation of the relationship between Judith and Holofernes, in spite of their supposed symbolic nature. In the oratorio, their relationship is filled with ambiguity. In one critic's words,

> Humanising Holofernes and Judith, Vivaldi and Cassetti pay tribute to what has been termed *oratorio erotico*. Their Judith and Holofernes are variously repellent and seductive, and their scenes together contain … .a charged air of sexuality and intoxication.[25]

This is particularly interesting considering this was an oratorio performed by girls in a church setting.[26]

There are numerous recordings, with widely varied casting choices.

---

[23] Lynne Murray and Alan Maddox, program notes, 2007: https://www.pinchgutopera.com.au/juditha-triumphans (accessed September 5, 2018).

[24] Murray and Maddox, program notes, 2007.

[25] Mark Gaal, program notes, 2007: https://www.pinchgutopera.com.au/juditha-triumphans (accessed September 5, 2018).

[26] Vivaldi's oratorio can be found here on YouTube: https://www.youtube.com/watch?v=6mTEpicRFwM (accessed February 14, 2020).
The full libretto with translation is here: https://cdn.moble.com/w/2056/317281/file/Juditha+Triumphans+program+Pinchgut+Opera.pdf (accessed February 14, 2020).

The oratorio opens with a chorus of Assyrian soldiers and ends with a chorus of Bethulians. It contains ambiguous elements, particularly in its portrayal of Holofernes as a skilled seducer, even a womanizer. In the seduction scene with Judith, the oboe and organ create an erotic and sensual atmosphere. Through his music, Holofernes becomes sentimental if not even appealing and the scene has the feeling of a pastoral idyll. Though Judith resists, it is suggested that she almost succumbs. The plot of this oratorio, as in many musical settings of Judith, differs from the original text in numerous ways. This is true of any modern setting of a biblical narrative, of course, but possibly even more so with Judith, since there is no definitive original text. Attitudes to the book also shifted constantly in different eras (see the introduction of this book).

Juditha Triumphans *(1716)*

> Judith: contralto
> Holofernes: contralto
> Ozias: contralto
> Abra: soprano
> Vagaus: soprano (parts usually altered in modern performances)

Part I

The oratorio opens in Holofernes's camp (Jdt 9) with a warlike chorus, followed by a recitative, "Behold a joyous and blessed day," and an aria, "Arms, battle, burning rage" (*Nil flamma furoris*), where Holofernes sings of the importance of hope in the warrior's heart. The music is appropriately assertive and florid, suggesting a very strong and bellicose Holofernes. Vagaus enters and tells Holofernes the exciting news of the arrival of a beautiful woman in their camp: "A noble lady of the enemy has come to our troops asking after you, mighty Lord, And soon, believe me, she will be yours—you have only to set eyes upon her" (*Matrona inimica Te quaerit ad arma Dux magne Et cito deh, credas Tibi erit amica Si lumina cernes*). The unusual aspect of this retelling is that it begins in Holofernes's camp, with no introduction to Bethulia, the siege, or, most crucially, Judith. From the start, then, the listener is hearing the story from Holofernes's point of view.

Holofernes responds with *Huc accedat Matrona* ("Let the lady approach"), in which it becomes clear that he knows of the suffering in Bethulia, where "there is nothing but fear, nothing but grief, despondency, despair, pain, poverty and floods of tears." Vagaus invites Judith to enter, and she sings the aria *Quocum Patriae me ducit amore* ("Wherever I am led by love of the Fatherland"), in which she expresses the hope that she will be safe among these soldiers. Her servant Abra reassures her in the aria "Before the dazzling splendour of your face, anger fades away, and love smiles" (*Cedit ira ridet amor*). She points out to Judith how these people are "overwhelmed by the glory of your face."

Judith asks the soldiers to bring her to Holofernes's tent. Vagaus and the chorus sing "O how lovely, how fair, O how comely you are, our one and true hope of victory. Honour the tent of our leader with your presence, put all your faith in Holofernes, and have hope." Sinuous oboes are used to suggest Judith's beauty in this ensemble. Vagaus encourages Judith to put her trust in Holofernes. When he sees Judith, he is overwhelmed by her beauty:

> What do I see before me! My dazzled eyes, what is this you are seeing? Surely this is the sun, the splendour of the heavens! Ah, most exalted of beings, whose eyes are more potent than the sun's rays! Stay your path, travellers! Prepare tributes, spread flowers beneath her feet, and let the Cupids come forth to meet their Goddess.

This hyperbole exceeds the biblical text, possibly to create more tension between Judith and Holofernes. Judith greets him as "Greatest of Kings, valiant warrior, heart of King Nebuchadnezzar," also hyperbolic flattery. He flatters her in return, then asks what he can do for her. She says she is asking for help for Bethulia, not for herself. She pleads for his clemency in the aria *Quanto magis generosa* ("How much nobler"): "How glorious would be your power if illumined by your clemency! Spare us, Lord, and sweeten our bitter lot." Judith asks Holofernes for peace, possibly intending that he fall in love with her. An erotic subtext is suggested through a sinuous vocal line and the use of a solo *viola d'amore*. This lengthy aria (10 minutes) could believably soften Holofernes's heart, along with the listener's. The crucial point of the story, however—that Judith was offering Holofernes help in defeating her own people—is omitted here. Judith, in this libretto, has only come to plead for compassion.

Holofernes responds with *Magna, o foemina petis* ("You ask much, woman"). Then he announces that all the engines of war should be stilled, and begs her to sit down, addressing her as "my sweet friend." They continue to praise and flatter each other, one outdoing the other. When she says it is not her place to sit beside him, Holofernes tells Judith it is an order, and then sings the very upbeat aria *Sede, o cara* ("Sit, my dear one, my beloved, my beauty, my living rose, my shining flame"). Her response is to praise him further: "You are Judge and Lord, you are commander of so mighty an army, and the stars are aligned to bless your victorious right arm forever." Holofernes tells her that he has found happiness thanks to her and invites her to dine with him that night, to celebrate their cherished peace. This invitation only occurs after three days in the original book. Her response is a dramatic elaboration of her simple refusal in the biblical version:

> At feasts and banquets, my lips turn numb, accustomed as they are to fasting; sorrowing, taking no delight in food, my suffering soul knows nothing of such pleasures.

She now sings the aria *Agitata infido flatu* ("Tossed about by the fitful wind during its long flight"), a metaphor about a vagrant swallow who weeps as it is tossed about but rejoices when it reaches its nest. In this aria, she describes herself as a bird—first a storm-tossed swallow, then as a turtledove. She is accompanied by a *chalumeau*, a single-reed woodwind instrument of the late baroque and early classical eras (a precursor of the clarinet). The futile fluttering of wings is represented by repeated rapid

16th notes, and a falling chromatic line in the voice and violins represents the fierce storm. The aria is extremely fast and filled with impressive *fioritura*. (This listener was hard pressed to hear a chalumeau through the dense and rapid string passages; see the YouTube link in note 26 above.)

Holofernes, obviously paying no heed to Judith's refusal of his dinner invitation, elaborates further, telling her he will provide a meal "fit for the gods. Whatever swims in the river, whatever flies in the heavens, whatever is nourished by the earth" will be served. He orders Vagaus to take care of this. The sound of four theorbos (large lutes with an extended neck) suggests the bustle of servants preparing the banquet in Vagaus's aria *O servi volate* ("Servants, be swift"). The unique fabric of sound depicts an especially joyous celebration. After Vagaus and the chorus sing about the preparations and celebrating love and honor, he addresses Abra, telling her she will also take part and share in their joy. Abra comments to Judith on Vagaus's boldness, "like his master's," and reassures her that she will remain her faithful companion. Judith now expresses her feelings for Abra in a touching aria, *Veni, veni, me sequere fida*:

> Come, come, follow me, my faithful and beloved Abra, deprived of your husband. Like you, I too lament like the turtle-dove. In this terrible fate, you are my trusted companion; when our thankless destiny is fulfilled, you shall have me as your companion in joy.

This is almost a duet with the chalumeau (a predecessor of the clarinet), which imitates the sounds of the turtledove to which Judith likens herself. In a further layer of meaning, eighteenth-century audiences would have known that a turtledove was believed to remain faithful even after its partner's death, and they would have understood this "as an allusion to Judith's steadfast character." At the same time, the repeated notes in the strings convey Judith's nervousness about the task she has set for herself.[27] The amplified role of Judith's servant in this work is a wonderful and satisfying example of gap-filling, particularly appealing to feminist readers and listeners. Abra is a silent bystander in the biblical version, while here she has a close relationship with Judith, who mentions that Abra has also lost her husband. Such small details breathe life into characters.

Abra tells Judith that she has heard confused voices from Bethulia, where there is hope that Judith will save them: "With one voice the maidens of Judah groan and pray, not knowing what will befall them." A touching female chorus prays for deliverance from God through victory by Judith, concluding Part One.

Part II

In the second half of the oratorio, the focus is a contrast between night and day. This part opens with a recitative and aria for Ozias, one of the leaders in Bethulia. He sings

---

[27] Murray and Maddox, program notes, 2007.

about possessing foreknowledge of victory, but just to be safe, he also offers up prayers in the aria *O Sydera, o stellae*:

> Ye stars and constellations, now at the waning of the moon, be funeral torches to our enemy. In this blessed night, let the godless enemy be destroyed, and may they be discovered lying dead by the light of the rising sun.

Following the aria, Ozias expresses in a recitative that he is convinced that Judith will be victorious and will return soon in triumph.

The fall of darkness for Holofernes suggests seduction, while it suggests something else for Judith. He sings *Nox Obscura* ("Dark Night"). Then a recitative between them continues the hyperbolic language heard earlier. Holofernes apologizes for his "soldierly ways" and for the dishes served that were not worthy "of one who is companion to the gods." Judith responds: "They well show forth your greatness." This might suggest that Judith ate the food he served, though in the original text, her observance of strict dietary laws was a prominent motif. Musical works and their librettos do not deal with that issue in most cases. Holofernes tells Judith she makes his heart swell (a somewhat suggestive phrase), and that her face has made him love her. Judith corrects him by saying: "No image save that of its Creator may be worshipped by any creature on earth."

A delicate mandolin accompanies Judith's musings on the transitory nature of life in *Transit aetas*, her next aria: "Life passes, the years fly by; we are the cause of our own destruction. The immortal soul lives on where the flames of love and passion are but smoke." The solo mandolin accompaniment creates an intimate and slightly wistful mood. This is clearly not an aria sung to Holofernes with seductive intent but rather reveals Judith's thoughtful and philosophic nature. Holofernes's abrupt, impatient, and almost comical response is "Keep all that for tomorrow"—a humorous moment, whether intentional or not. "Lighten up, Judith!" he seems to be saying. The music shifts suddenly from the gentleness of Judith's aria to his brusque recitative. Holofernes tells her that he now knows love is a fire, because he feels his heart burning inside him. Judith advises him to cool his passion and "flee from the flames."

When he continues to rant that he is on fire, she suggests she should leave, and he pleads with her in the aria *Noli ò cara* ("Do not disdain, my beloved"). The aria is scored for two oboes and organ only, and it has sometimes been suggested that oboes signify sexual desire. This sweet lilting music, in the bright key of C major, seems as far from the biblical portrayal of Holofernes as is possible. Here he is an appealing lover— who could kill a man who can sing a love song like this? The text is: "O my beloved, do not disdain the entreaties of a ruler who adores you; at least learn not to shudder at the sighs of a loving soul." The music paints a very appealing picture of the enemy, and the voice adds a pleading and sincere note to the text. Was this intentional? Was it meant to cast doubt on the necessity of Judith's act? This same question will arise throughout this book, relating to musical settings of every era. It remains a rhetorical question only, since the composers discussed in this book are no longer alive to explain their intentions. The recitative that follows has a hint of irony. Judith sings: "I pray that the Lord of Heaven may grant you salvation." Holofernes answers: "Let it be so: as I drink, I hope to be saved by you, and if you will love me, I shall be your salvation." This could be read as a proposition, or a threat, or both. The chorus interrupts with a song to Cupid, asking him to "feed the passion of these divine beings with your sweet flame."

Judith sings him a lullaby, *Vivat in Pace* ("Live in peace"), accompanied only by strings playing in a high register (more soothing than the Samson lullaby in Scarlatti's oratorio). A few moments later, she expresses surprise when she notices that Holofernes is "drunk on wine, asleep at the table!" She calls on his servants to attend to him, and calls Abra to wait with her in the tent, to pray and keep vigil while their enemy sleeps. Vagaus sings a gentle aria wishing his master a "soothing slumber" and in supremely ironic words tells Judith: "How fortune has smiled on you, fair Lady! You have triumphed over so mighty a Commander and conquered the conqueror" (while the listener thinks, "if only you knew"). Judith says to herself that God has heard her "sighs and entreaties," and that this is the work of the King of Heaven. Vagaus, completely unsuspecting, tells Judith to let Holofernes rest while he clears the tables, and then continues: "Lovely Judith, you may savor this time alone with your Commander, and comfort the sorrows of your heart. But here comes your servant: I will leave quickly so that you may have this place for your loving" (*Et sic amori tuo locum concede*). Vagaus, a servant himself, seems to assume that servants are invisible and would not interfere with lovemaking.

Judith welcomes Abra, saying: "Faithful servant, you are most welcome! This is the hour of our glory, and the long-awaited moment of victory." Abra responds: "May all your endeavors be crowned with success, and may you, O my Judith, and your nation be blessed with prosperity and life." These words indicate that the librettist did not consider Abra to be a Hebrew. The biblical text gives no indication of her origins, and several works discussed in this book assume that she is a Hebrew. Judith then instructs Abra to seal the entrance to the tent and let no one enter, and assures her she will be victorious. She instructs Abra to wait for her in silence. Abra's response is a fast and very assertive aria, filled with *fioritura* to express her excitement and passion:

> The child returning home through the savage icy storm is not awaited by his mother more eagerly than I shall wait for you. But the pain of a brief yet cruel delay torments the soul who loves too much with fear, and hope.

Then she closes up the tent and tells Judith she will wait for her, and praises her as a "heroine." It is clear, without either woman articulating it, that Abra is fully aware of Judith's plan.

A consort of five viols provides an otherworldly accompaniment to Judith's recitative and aria *In somno profundo* ("In a deep sleep"), where she stands over the sleeping Holofernes, steeling herself to do the fateful deed. The music is somber and stately, suggesting Judith's nerves are calm and she is determined. Preceding the aria she sings a prayer, with original text and additional biblical references:

> Mighty God on earth, who gave strength to the victorious Jael and to warring Deborah, help us as we pray, and take away our guilt, and with the power of your right hand, raise up my frail arm to be a tower of strength.

The reference to Jael and Deborah is not in the original text but can be found in other Judith musical works. The atoning for sin in advance of her deed is an added element and not out of place. Judith sings: "While he lies deep in slumber, he whom you have cast into sleep cannot be watchful." Some of the lyrics of the aria are far more bloodthirsty than those of the biblical Judith. To more excited music as she decides what to do, she sings:

> Let the sleeper be drained of blood, that I may glory in that blood as it pours forth. Ah, see: the sword of the godless, dishonorable tyrant is hanging here below the canopy of his bed: from the body of Holofernes, O God, in your name, I strike off the wretched head.

The only musical signal of the act is a group of sudden and dramatic rapidly descending leaps of 16th-note clusters in the strings, which stop as abruptly as they started. At the end of the aria, she hands Abra the head and tells her to put it in the bag, sharing her hope that the merciful God will help them leave the camp safely. Abra is puzzled, asking Judith: "What are you giving me? O miracle! You have cut off the head of the horrible dragon, and in the same stroke have singlehandedly defeated them all." It is interesting that she expresses no shock or disgust but after the recitative sings a very upbeat aria praising Judith for her act while nonetheless attributing their honor and glory to God, their "blessed Leader."

At dawn, Vagaus sings a gentle recitative about the approaching dawn. There is an abrupt shift in the music when he looks inside the tent and sees the headless, bloody body of his master. He tells the soldiers that they are lost and should seek revenge. This is followed by a raging aria, *Armatae face* ("Armed with torches"). This is one of the more famous arias in the oratorio, and its extremely fast tempo and impressive *fioritura* effectively express his fury and frenzy:

> Armed with torches and serpents, come forth from your blind, foul kingdom, you savage partners of raging frenzy: Furies, come to us! In death, scourging and slaughter, teach our raging hearts to avenge this murderous deed.

In an extreme contrast, Ozias welcomes the dawn and rejoices when he sees Judith approaching in the distance. He is confident that she was victorious and here the title of the work appears for the first time, in his recitative *Juditha Triumphans*. This is followed by the very upbeat aria *Gaude felix* ("O happy city of Bethulia, rejoice and be glad"). The second part of the oratorio, like the first, ends with a chorus: *Salve invicta Juditha Formosa* ("Hail, Judith, beautiful and undefeated, the glory of our nation and our hope of salvation. You shall forever be the ultimate model of true virtue"). The music includes drums and trumpets, which have not been heard in much of the oratorio. The musical expression of unbridled joy has the effect of a ray of sun bursting forth from a previously dark sky.

Conclusion

Though it has been established that all the characters are symbols in this oratorio, they nonetheless come across as living and breathing people through the music and the text. There are moments of humor in this work—rarely found in a musical setting of Judith's story—especially in the "seduction" scene. Judith, possibly because she is a symbol of Venice, is very righteous and honorable, as well as combative. Vivaldi's music makes the listener wish his other oratorios had survived, as it is powerful and inventive, full of surprising and vivid moments.

Thomas Arne (1710–1778)

Thomas Arne is best known for his patriotic song "Rule Britannia" (traditionally offered at the Last Night of the Proms in London and considered a symbol of the British Empire), which is originally from his *Alfred, a Masque*. This version of "God Save the King/Queen" became the British national anthem. Arne was a leading British theater composer of the eighteenth century, working at Drury Lane and Covent Garden. Between 1733 and 1776, Arne wrote music for about ninety stage works, including plays, masques, pantomimes, and opera. He is generally regarded as the most important English composer of the eighteenth century. Many of his dramatic scores were lost, probably in the disastrous fire at Covent Garden in 1808.

In 1759 Arne was awarded the degree of doctor of music at Oxford, and two years later his oratorio *Judith* was produced. In this period, the musical life of England was dominated by foreign music and musicians. Arne was the most successful and popular native composer, "keeping alive and advancing the traditions of the English baroque school … His second oratorio, *Judith* (his first was *The Death of Abel* in 1743) is considered by some to be one of his finest works."[28]

Harold Watkins Shaw, reference librarian at the Royal College and a well-respected Handel scholar, wrote in 1978, the year of Arne's bicentennial: "The vigour of Arne's ideas, the resource of his instrumentation, and the strong sweep of his writing for solo voice" signify that he "was decisively post- and therefore un-Handelian, and was far from being a matter of mere period attractiveness." Shaw further notes that Arne's oratorio "firmly left the baroque style behind, and moved English music well forward in style." He comments on the many effective instrumental touches in *Judith*, such as a harp *obbligato* in one aria. He concludes that the music for the numerous airs, in their "sweep, vigour, range and inventiveness … displayed Arne as a composer of some power and no small stature."[29]

Arne's *Judith* was first performed in London at Lock Hospital, in 1761. In the eighteenth century, there were hospitals built specifically to treat venereal diseases, most of whose patients were prostitutes. Entertainments were mounted to benefit these

---

[28] "Arne, Thomas Augustine," *Encyclopedia*. https://www.encyclopedia.com/people/literature-and-arts/music-history-composers-and-performers-biographies/thomas-augustine-arne (accessed April 23,2020).

[29] H. W. Shaw, "T. A. Arne & 'Judith,'" *RCM (Royal College of Music)* magazine 74, no. 2 (March 15, 1978): pp. 61–2. My thanks to the reference librarian at the Royal College for providing these documents.

hospitals, one of which was the London Lock Hospital. Published copies of the oratorio were later sold to benefit the hospital, and the oratorio was subsequently performed again at another benefit event. The performance at the Lock Hospital is of particular interest, since the audience included the patients. The oratorio celebrated Judith as an "exemplar of resolute chastity" in a setting where there was clear manifestation of the consequences of unchastity.[30]

Judith's first performance at Drury Lane was at Lent in 1761 and 1762, then at the Chapel of the Lock Hospital in Grosvenor Place for the benefit of a public charity in 1764 (in a revised form), and subsequently at Kings Theatre in the Haymarket in 1765, Three Choirs Festival in Gloucester in 1766, and at Covent Garden multiple times for charity. During a 1767 benefit concert at Covent Garden, a song from *Judith* was accompanied with the first ever public appearance of the pianoforte in England. In a 1773 performance at Covent Garden, Arne introduced women's voices into the choruses for the first time. Arne's *Judith* was commended by Charles Dibdin as an oratorio "that does honour to the English genius," and "was long recognized as an important adjunct of the Handelian form, perhaps the finest such work by a native composer before Elgar. This is opinion is seconded by other scholars, who comment on the 'lyric airs' and forward-looking choruses," calling the work "arguably the finest oratorio by an Englishman before [Elgar's] *The Dream of* Gerontius."[31] The difficulty of establishing an authoritative performing version of the composer's only surviving work in the genre has undoubtedly contributed to its neglect.[32]

The full libretto, by Isaac Bickerstaffe, can be found online.[33]

A full score is available online, but it includes only solos, no recitatives or choruses; and solos are identified by the name of the singer who sang them, not by the character being portrayed.[34]

The work was revived for the bicentenary of Arne's death in 1978 at the Royal College of Music, a performance that was recorded by the BBC and aired the same year. This archived recording can be accessed at the British Library upon request, which is where I was able to listen to it. It is a pity that the BBC has been unable to make this sole recording of such an important work more available to the public.

The casting seems to be fluid, since some singers took on more than one role, even in a different range. For example, Mr. Champness (all singers are identified this way in the score) sings a baritone aria as Charmis, but also the tenor arias of Holofernes. This is either an inaccuracy in the score, or these singers were even more virtuosic than the music suggests. The performance history from 1761 to 1785 as outlined in a supplement to *Musica Brittanica* vol. 100 clearly shows that this score was constantly in flux, with no single definitive version.[35]

[30] Margarita Stocker, *Judith: Sexual Warrior* (New Haven, CT: Yale University Press, 1998), p. 141.
[31] Peter Holman and Todd Gilman in *New Grove Dictionary* (2001), vol. 2, p. 41.
[32] http://research.gold.ac.uk/20739/ (accessed September 20, 2018).
[33] https://c.lib.umich.edu/e/ecco/004799605.0001.000/1:11?rgn=div1;view=fulltext (accessed October 20, 2020).
[34] https://imslp.org/wiki/Judith_(Arne%2C_Thomas_Augustine) (accessed October 20, 2020).
[35] "Thomas Arne: *Judith: An Oratorio* (1761)," http://www.musicabritannica.org.uk/volumes/mb100_performance_history.pdf (accessed September 26, 2018).

Judith *(1761)*

Judith: soprano
Abra, Judith's handmaiden: soprano
Ozias, chief of Bethulia: tenor (countertenor on recording)
Charmis, an Elder: baritone
Holofernes: tenor (in the score; sung by a bass on the recording, which meant
transposing his music down)

Act I

The plot remains very close to the biblical narrative. After a lengthy overture, which
prominently features horns, Scene 1 opens in a public part of the city of Bethulia with
the chorus, "Father of mercies lend thine ear, Thy wretched suppliant People hear, Help,
help, O Lord! or else we dye [*sic*]." The voices of the chorus enter gradually, building
in volume and power. The mood of this chorus is very poignant, amplified by oboe
solos. The citizens are parched and suffering because the invading Assyrian army has
cut off the water sources to the city. Charmis and the chorus continue to bemoan their
fate, and "a man" berates the rulers for not making peace with the Assyrians (libretto
only, p. 2). The scene closes with the air (the term "aria" was not used in English works
in this period) sung by "a woman": "O torment great, too great to bear" (p. 11 in
the score, "Sung by Miss Brent").[36] The woman sings of being thirsty to the point of
despair: "Distraction! Horror! And despair," and begs for a drop of water, "to cool the
fever in my soul." The music is fairly standard Baroque style for an aria describing rage
and despair: continual rapid 16th-note passages in the strings, much *fioritura* for the
high soprano, and many leaps up to a high range (*b-flat"*).

Scene 2 opens with "a man" pleading to let the Assyrians take hold of the city to
end the city's suffering. He says it would be better to serve Holofernes than to "watch
their wives and children die before their faces." Ozias tries to persuade the people to
wait five more days and then sings his air "Be humble, suff'ring, trust in God" (p. 3
in the libretto, p. 17 in the score) in which he tells them God is good as well as great,
and those that complain impatiently are rebels. In the score this is marked as "Sung
by Mr. Tenducci."[37] Both times "God" is sung, the note is held for five measures while
the orchestra continues above the voice, creating the impression of steadiness and
confidence. The mood is steady and calm, until the last page when the strings play
repeated measures of very rapid 32nd-note ascending and descending passages, each
repeat starting on a lower note than the last (p. 19 in the score). This expressive device
suggests more chaos than is heard in the vocal part, in a kind of subtext.

[36] Charlotte Brent was one of Arne's pupils with whom he had an affair when his marriage was breaking
up: "Solo Singers Who Performed at Vauxhall Gardens 1745–1859," http://www.vauxhallgardens.
com/vauxhall_gardens_singers_page.html (accessed October 20, 2020).
[37] Giusto Fernando Tenducci (1736–1790) was a well-known countertenor, also known as *Il Senesino*
but not to be confused with Francesco Bernardi, also known as *Senesino* but far more renowned.
https://www.europeana.eu/portal/en/explore/people/37501-giusto-fernando-tenducci.html
(accessed January 7, 2019).

Scene 3 takes place in Judith's house. Abra, lamenting the fate of the city, is convinced that God will not save Bethulia within the allotted five days. Judith tells Abra that she feels her "spirit stirred with strange emotion" and before she goes to seek God through meditation, she asks Abra to "raise some potent strain." In response, Abra sings the air "Wake my harp to melting measures" (p. 4 in the libretto, p. 20 in the score: marked "Sung by Mrs. Cornelys").[38] The long orchestral introduction to this air aims for the sublime, opening with harp and harpsichord solos accompanied by *pizzicato* (plucked) strings marking every fourth beat. It is notable that the harp only appears in this one air in the oratorio, making the sound more striking and unexpected. The texture of the accompaniment is simple, underneath a beautiful lyrical melody, typical of the "galant" style of the classical era. In music, "galant" refers to the style that was fashionable from the 1720s to the 1770s, featuring a return to simplicity and immediacy of appeal after the complexity of the late Baroque era. Abra sings a virtual paean to music, whose harmony, a listener once said, can send the soul heavenward. The spirit of this lengthy air (pp. 20–7) is sweet and appealing, as one would expect music depicting the beauty of music to be. There is also a subtext about music's power to heal and thus save the day.

Judith returns and tells Abra to take her to the leaders of the city at once. "With some vast design my soul is big," she says, also in wonder that God has seemingly entrusted her with such an enormous feat, that God would use "an instrument so feeble … to blazon [his] glorious name among the Nations." She sings the air "Advent'rous, lo! I spread the sail" (p. 28 in the score, "Sung by Miss Brent"). In this air, Judith uses the metaphor of piloting a ship to explain the adventure she is about to embark on. The audience of that time, in their seafaring nation, would have related to such a metaphor. Notable lines include:

With steadfast heart I quit the shore, nor man's assistance deign to court;
the star of mercy goes before, in promise of a joyful port.

This bravura air depicts a strong and assertive Judith as only music can. The vocal part is filled with large leaps: a full octave descent in the second measure, followed by a leap of an octave and a half in the next. Such vocal leaps could be heard as their own form of daring and bravura. The orchestral background is filled with rapid ascending and descending 16th-note passages as well as many large leaps imitating those of the voice. The overall impression is one of great excitement and adventure. It is also notable how Judith emphasizes her independence, stressing that she does not need the help of any man.

Scene 4 (mistakenly written as Scene 5 in printed librettos, for any reader following there) takes place in a public area of the city again, and Ozias introduces Judith with the words "Brethren, behold! the Widow of Menasses, Judith, for Wisdom, and for Beauty fam'd," and asks her what she needs. Judith scolds the people and the rulers of Bethulia for doubting God, to which the chorus of Israelites responds: "When

---

[38] Teresa Cornelys (1723–1797) was an operatic soprano and impresario who lived a colorful life, which included an affair and a child with Casanova: https://www.british-history.ac.uk/ (accessed January 7, 2019).

Israel wept, no comfort nigh, Thou heardst, O Lord, Thy people's cry." This text is a paraphrase of several different verses from various Psalms. They go on to relate God's salvation in the desert, through water and manna. Judith then tells the people and rulers of Bethulia: "Hear me! I mean to do an Act shall go throughout all Generations" (Jdt 8:32). She further explains that she means to go forth to the Assyrian camp with her "virgin" (identified as a "widow," "maid," or "servant" in other oratorios) and within the time prescribed, "the Lord shall save ye by my hand." She asks them not to question how she means to do it.

She then sings the air, "Remember what Jehova swore" (p. 34 in the score, "Sung by Mrs. Cornelys," who previously sang Abra's air). She recalls God's promises to Abram and his seed, that no power will uproot this race: "Suns may melt and stars decay, both heaven and earth shall pass away, but not his sacred word." The stately opening is marked *Largo* (very slow) in a dotted 3/4 rhythm. Judith's opening word "remember" is repeated twice on descending fifths. But after a few slow and deliberate measures, she begins to sing elaborate *fioritura* passages extending into a very high range, even touching a high C (*c"*). On the final phrase, "shall pass away," the last word is sustained on a high B flat (*b-flat"*) for almost three full measures. This virtuosic singing would not only have shown off the extraordinary abilities of the singer but also effectively highlights Judith's determination and strength.

Scene 5 (marked scene 6 in the libretto) opens with Charmis speaking of how Judith will surely save the city of Bethulia, as she "breathes prophetic strains. ... Wonder not, my Brethren, that upon this Woman's Strength we rest our Hopes of Safety! Through the tribes the fame of her religion is gone forth." In his air, "Conquest is not to bestow" (p. 37 in the score, "Sung by Mr. Champness," probably Samuel Champness, but there were three singers with this name in the eighteenth century),[39] he claims that she will succeed not because of strength but because she trusts in the Lord:

> Victory does not belong to the valiant or the strong,
> but the pious and the just who in Jehovah trust ...
> they shall triumph, they shall live.

Oboes (*hautbois*, a relatively new instrument in England at the time) and horns predominate in this air, adding a new sound. This is the first air heard so far in a bass/baritone voice. It is very upbeat, in the key of C major and a very *marcato* 4/4 time. Elaborate *fioritura* is less commonly heard in a low male voice (though often found in Handel oratorios) and would have been very impressive. There is great musical emphasis on the last phrase, as "they shall triumph" is sung on lengthy runs and then on large, dramatic leaps: up to *f'* (high for a baritone) and down ten notes to *d*; this pattern is repeated, followed by five full measures of continual 8th-note runs doubled

---

[39] Winton Dean, "Champness [Champnes, Champneys], Samuel Thomas," *Oxford Music Online*, January 20, 2001. Available online: https://www.oxfordmusiconline.com/grovemusic/view/10.1093/gmo/9781561592630.001.0001/omo-9781561592630-e-0000005393?rskey=WWDmTj&result=59 (accessed October 20, 2020).

in the orchestra, before a resounding and triumphant conclusion on a bright C major, as the orchestra continues playing lengthy runs to the end (p. 40 in the score).

In Scene 6 (marked as 7 in the libretto), Ozias hails Judith as she departs: "How beautiful she looks …' Tis God inspires her to some great purpose, laud His holy name." The chorus of Israelites closes Act I praising God with "Hear, angels hear!"

Act II

Scene 1 opens in the Assyrian camp. A dialogue between Judith and Holofernes stays close to the biblical account. She explains that she has come because her people have sinned and thus "drawn on themselves the wrath of Heaven." Judith tells him that God will give her the signal when she is to conduct Holofernes to the walls, and then not only Bethulia, but also all of Judea, will "fall prey." Holofernes is amazed by her beauty and intelligence, saying she is a "wonder of [her] sex." Judith pretends to have not heard him, as in an extravagant show of modesty she says: "Spoke my lord to his poor handmaid? Let me not suppose it. Far be such vain thoughts from [this] wretch." This is followed immediately by the air "O strive not" (p. 41 in the score, "Sung by Miss Brent"). She asks Holofernes not to swell her head with praise, since "God be my pride, his holy ways my ornaments alone." The music is sweet, almost a minuet, in 3/4 time. There is no *fioritura* in this air, though there are ample trills and several *seufzer* phrases in the orchestra (slurs that suggest weeping or lamenting). All these elements depict a sweet and humble Judith, clearly the image she herself was trying to suggest to Holofernes. The audience is hearing what he hears, but the listener can also read her manipulation between the lines of music. Arne may be suggesting a hint of sly humor and sarcasm behind her words. She later sings "Another's blemishes I see, whilst I lament my own," with "lament" repeated several times on slurs, then finally sustained on a high B flat (*b-flat"*) for almost three measures (p. 44 in the score). The orchestra concludes with a repetition of her previous melodies.

In Scene 2, Holofernes issues a command that throughout the camp, the Hebrew women are not to be approached (presumably there were Hebrew slaves in the camp) but respected as friends of the "Assyrian king." He orders that they be left free to observe their "laws, customs, and religion." This is a remarkably positive portrayal of Holofernes. A chorus of Assyrians sings his praises, in strongly accented music with loud trumpets. Holofernes shows Judith the "superb pavilion" she has been assigned and sings the air "Adorned with every matchless grace" (p. 45 in the score, "Sung by Mr. Tenducci"). This love song to Judith is set to very lyrical music:

Adorned with every matchless grace
By Heaven from whence she sprung,
We view the goddess in her face,
We hear it in her tongue.
Against such charms there's no defense,
O take, possess me whole!

Holofernes's part is written for a tenor (transposed to a bass in the recorded 1978 performance), a lyrical and appealing voice that is particularly convincing and effective in this declaration of love. Above the sometimes florid vocal line, strings play repeated high slurs over trumpet calls in the background. A chorus of Assyrians rejoices, in upbeat and confident music, that they are about to conquer Bethulia: "Rejoice, rejoice, Judea falls! Yon stubborn city bows her walls."

Scene 3 opens with a dialogue between Judith and Abra. Judith tells Abra that they have been brought by God to the midst of "these idolators," but "like sparks of fire in a heap of stubble we shall soon blaze and consume them." She warns Abra, addressing her as "my Sister" (in contrast to the appellations of "Mother" and "Daughter" in Scarlatti's work) to be wary of their deceptions and not be taken in by flattery. Abra assures Judith that she has been well taught by her example "to scorn the glittering gewgaws [updated to "trifles" on the recording] they esteem." She then sings an air (not in the score), "Vain is beauty's gaudy flower," to very sweet music filled with *fioritura*.

In Scene 4, an unnamed Assyrian man and woman approach Judith. The woman in the army camp is never identified but would most likely have been a prostitute. Camp followers in the context of an army had many roles: cooks, nurses, and others, including prostitutes. The man extends an invitation from Holofernes to Judith to attend a banquet that night. Holofernes says to tell her "charms have the Hebrews, and the Assyrians hearts." The woman is even more persuasive, telling Judith that "our general, amidst the noise of war, has a soul tuned to all the loftier ["softer" on the recording] passions." Apparently Judith smiles, and the woman (sung by countertenor on the recording) happily accepts that as her acceptance of the invitation. An air in praise of "the gardens of delight" follows (p. 53 in the score). The singer is identified as "Mr. Tenducci," who has sung Holofernes's airs up to now but in this case is singing the part of the unnamed woman (a countertenor has the same range as a female alto voice). It is a quick and very upbeat air in 6/8 time, a lilting rhythm, featuring flutes and well as horns and strings. "Haste to the garden of delight, where plenteous pleasures grow … to thank the givers, pluck and eat, and satisfy thy soul with joy."

Scene 5 opens with a duet between Judith and Abra (p. 58 in the score, "Sung by Mrs. Cornelys and Miss Brent"). Judith tells her that they "have the lion … and never shall he stalk abroad again." She tells her that though they are going to this banquet, she will not render up her "chaste body … to fulsome purposes." It is generally assumed that Judith remained chaste in the encounter with Holofernes, as Judith herself asserts in the biblical story (Jdt 13:16). But the issue is rarely raised openly in librettos as it is here, either before or after the "seduction" scene. Judith expresses certainty that God will save them, and invites Abra to join her, prostrate on the floor in fervent prayer. At no time do they ever discuss a plan, which is true to the biblical story. They ask God for inspiration and for both courage and power for Judith. In the music, Abra echoes many of Judith's phrases, and they also sing extended passages in harmony, usually perfect thirds or sixths. In some places, the two voices sing melismatic sections (ornamental passages sung on a single syllable) completely in parallel thirds. The blending of the voices in this way suggests perfect harmony and agreement between them, and a close bond. In the second stanza, Abra sings the opening lines as a solo, then they both sing the lines but not together or in harmony. The final phrase is sung in unison, quite unusual for these measures of elaborate *fioritura* and proof of the level of virtuoso singing in that day. It musically represents complete unity of thought and feeling.

Scene 6 opens in Holofernes's tent as he is preparing for the banquet. He stands with a golden goblet in his hand and tells his attendants to crown him with laurels, because today they are conquerors. He encourages them all to praise and honor "father Bacchus" in an air, "Hail, hail, immortal Bacchus!" (p. 62 in the score, "Sung by Mr. Champness." Champness previously sang an air of Charmis, as a baritone; Holofernes has been sung by a tenor until now). The final verses are: "Hither come in jolly pride, and o'er thy festive rites preside." This focus on Bacchus foretells the eventual demise of Holofernes from drinking to excess, an interesting touch. The music has a jolly drinking-song sound to it, with a rollicking 6/8 rhythm. A chorus of Assyrians repeats the entire air (same text, to the same music), reinforcing the festive atmosphere.

Scene 7 opens with a lengthy dialogue sung in a breathless recitative. Holofernes speaks with great anticipation of Judith's upcoming arrival, equating her with Venus. Judith appears and speaks with exaggerated obeisance: "Behold at thy command, O Holofernes! Thy handmaid stands before thee." She asks if there is anything she can do to make herself yet more appealing. He responds that he is overcome by the lustre of her charms, "lost in a blaze of beauty," and asks to lean his head on her bosom. Since Judith has apparently only now arrived, it would seem that Holofernes has been drinking in anticipation—probably when he was hailing Bacchus in the previous scene. She tells him to recline his head on her breast and let her lull him with song and soothe his spirits.

In this interpretation, Holofernes is more gullible than in other librettos, allowing Judith to be sarcastic and almost mocking without his noticing. Then she sings the air "Sleep, gentle cherub" (p. 65 in the score, "Sung by Miss Brent"), musically a simple lullaby and void of the extensive *fioritura* in most of the vocal music in this oratorio.[40] Lullabies appear at this moment in the story in other works (e.g., Scarlatti's). The accompaniment is limited to *continuo* (harpsichord) and only a few strings, creating a sense of intimacy. This air taken out of context would never be associated with the Judith narrative. Abra, seeing Holofernes and noting that "his senses are dissolved … in wine," orders Holofernes's men to remove him "to the inmost chamber of the tent, beneath the purple canopy, beside his couch," where "the fair shall watch and guard him from Disturbance while he sleeps." The reference to the canopy is interesting, since this is what Judith will pull down off the bed after beheading Holofernes (Jdt 13:9). It is briefly mentioned before the killing in the biblical version (10:21, where its ornateness is briefly described). The chorus concludes the act, ending with "let love and silence reign." The soft ending contains no suggestion of what is to come (in case anyone doesn't know the story). Arne chose not to depict the actual beheading in either text or music. A few other composers also made this choice (Mozart is one example; see below). It must have seemed too violent and ungodly an act to portray in a biblical oratorio, even if it is eventually referred back to and even described after the fact.

---

[40] This air can be heard on YouTube at: https://www.youtube.com/watch?v=_iq8JJtm5YA (accessed October 20, 2020).

Act III

Scene 1 takes place in Bethulia, where Ozias greets the returning Judith and asks her what happened, and specifically how she escaped "undefiled," which he is assuming is the case. Judith calmly relates the story, though she never mentions praying to God for strength before striking Holofernes. Instead, after Holofernes was drunk, she "raised [her] eyes to Heaven" and then: "Then came the Spirit of the Lord upon me, and drawing from his Sheath his shining Faulchion ["dagger" on the recording, not an accurate rendering; it is more of a sword] I smote him twice, and took away his Head." Ozias praises and blesses Judith in virtually the same text as the biblical. He then sings an air, "With heroes and sages" (p. 67 in the score, "Sung by Mr. Tenducci"). The text is one of praise for Judith, promising her fame through the ages. The full orchestra accompanies this air, which has a lilting 6/8 rhythm and gentle sound.

In Scene 2, Judith points out how the weak hand of a woman struck down their enemy. She gives instructions to take the head and hang it on the city walls. In addition, she instructs the Bethulians to gird their swords on their thighs and feign preparing for battle. This will frighten the Assyrians, who will go looking for their general, find the headless corpse of Holofernes ("but no cries wake the dead"), and flee. The Bethulians will then follow in hot pursuit "and overthrow them with a mighty slaughter." All of this stays close to the original story. Excited string passages build suspense between the measures of the recitative. An air for Judith follows, "O Lord our God" (p. 73 in the score, "Sung by Mrs. Cornelys" who had previously sung Abra), in which she sings of going to battle as commanded by God, in very strong and confident music. The orchestra has a major part in this air, playing *marcato* in a strong 2/4 beat. The violins play continuous rapid 16th-note passages while the voice sings longer notes, mostly quarter or half notes. It is like the calm at the center of a storm and a highly effective subtext. The final stanzas are powerful, and are spoken, not sung (note in libretto):

In thine anger hot and fierce, melt their hearts, their hopes disperse.
Sweep their bands like chaff away, and cast them to the dogs a prey.

The scene ends as the Israelites praise God. The first part is sung in a strong dotted rhythm, followed by a lengthy and powerful chorus, "Daughters of Zion."

In Scene 3, a woman tells her companions about Judith's great deed and tells them to raise branches and garlands and march with them through the city in triumph. A man tells the people to prepare a feast in celebration, then sings the air "No more, no more the Heathen shall blaspheme" (p. 83 in the score, "Sung by Mr. Fawcett"). This is another paean to God, accompanied only by strings and including effective solo passages (*obbligato* for two cellos) in striking contrast to the previous two more dramatic airs. The text refers to the Heathen that "shall no more blaspheme, or vex thy chosen race, no more elate with impious pride, thy sacred Sabbath shall deride."

Scene 4, entitled "The Triumph," opens with a chorus of Israelites singing "Breathe the Pipe, the Timbrel sound," and a man singing of the joys of victory in "The Victor on his lofty seat." This is followed by the woman exhorting the people to be grateful and to hail their "Friend and Champion." The chorus repeats both airs.

In Scene 5, Judith shames the people of Israel for acting like heathens by giving the glory of God's works to man. She sings the air "Not unto us, but to his Name the Praise the thanks bestow" (p. 87 in the score, "Sung by Miss Brent"). The air, accompanied by strings only, is filled with elaborate *fioritura* and many high notes such as a high B flat (*b-flat*"). Trills abound, both in the voice and instruments, a chirpy and cheery paean to the God of creation. Perhaps these airs are meant to dispel any notion that Judith herself was responsible for her great victory: it had to be attributed to God.

In Scene 6, Ozias claims Israel should rejoice, for the Assyrians have thrown down their weapons and abandoned their camps. A semi-chorus sings "O bless'd Event!" ending with "And now the Sun of Peace shall rise upon us." Abra and Ozias sing the duet "On thy borders, O Jordan," envisioning an idyllic future:

On thy Borders, O Jordan, again shall be seen,
Rich Industry leading gay Plenty along;
The Pipe of the Shepherds shall wake on each Green,
Every Grove shall resound with the Nightingales Song.

This duet, the last number in the score (p. 92 in the score, "Duet for Miss Brent and Mr. Tenducci"), represents the rejoicing Israelites. The music, marked *Pastorale*, is in the conventional pastoral rhythm of 6/8, evoking pastoral idylls. As in other duets in this oratorio, the virtuosic skills required to sing such elaborate and florid music in perfect sync are astounding. Only in the final few measures does the time signature change, to a slower *Andante* and 4/4 time, as it calms to a quiet ending. This duet evokes a pastoral, peaceful scene in the future, made possible (it is suggested) by Judith's and God's great victory.

In the final scene Judith gives the speech, "Here, O ye sons of Jacob, let us rest!" (a recitative follows the air on the recording) and the chorus of Israelites sings, "Hear, Angels hear! Celestial Choirs." In the revised final scene (1764 edition) Judith's speech is set to music, including an oboe solo, replacing the final chorus. According to one scholar, Arne and Bickerstaff were not pleased with "Hear, Angels hear! Celestial Choirs," so they dropped it completely.[41] However, a final chorus *does* conclude the recorded performance of 1978, a triumphant fugue featuring prominent trumpets. Apparently the scholars who prepared that performance were not in agreement with Tasch's assertion. (It is unfortunate that most of the scholars and musicians involved in the 1978 performance are no longer alive to answer questions.)

Conclusion

There are many striking features to this oratorio, mostly in the very elaborate vocal parts. The characters are quite fully developed, possibly even a little more exaggerated than in some other works explored here. They come across as three-dimensional,

---

[41] Peter Tasch, *The Dramatic Cobbler: The Life and Works of Isaac Bickerstaff* (Lewisburg: Bucknell University Press, 1972), pp. 40–2.

real people. There is a wonderful sense of playfulness in the Judith-Holofernes scenes. But the message is clearly a theological one of God's deliverance, with Judith only the instrument of salvation. This could be why the act of beheading itself is so minimized: Judith was only an instrument, acting through God. Yet at the same time, she is portrayed as a powerful and independent woman.

Wolfgang Amadeus Mozart (1756–1791)

Another important work of this period is Mozart's *Betulia liberata* with the Italian libretto of well-known Habsburg court poet Pietro Metastasio (1698–1782). This poet did not substantially alter the treatment of Judith, which remained roughly the same in works through the eighteenth century. This oratorio, the only one Wolfgang Amadeus Mozart ever wrote (at the age of 15), was not performed in his lifetime. Mozart, Austrian composer, is widely recognized as one of the greatest composers in the history of Western music. Unlike any other composer in musical history, he excelled in all the musical genres of his day. In music historian Stanley Sadie's words, "His taste, his command of form, and his range of expression have made him seem the most universal of all composers; yet, it may also be said that his music was written to accommodate the specific tastes of particular audiences."[42] If Judith stood for Venice in Vivaldi's work, she probably is the embodiment of Vienna in Mozart's work. Or perhaps she is seen as the incarnation of any nation fighting for its freedom against a tyrant. In any case, Mozart's music is very focused on Judith. Metastasio's text was used by several other composers. One of the more well-known composers to utilize this libretto was the Bohemian (now Czech Republic) Josef Myslivecek (1737–1781), a very successful composer in his day and an acquaintance of the Mozart family. Metastasio's libretto emphasizes the doctrinal and devotional nature of the community of Bethulia. In fact, the convert Achior (not featured in all oratorios) has a more important role than Holofernes. The "seduction" scene between Judith and Holofernes is completely absent—a strange choice, but one noted elsewhere (e.g., in Arne's work). Judith's deed is not depicted but rather is related in a messenger's account after the fact, a device also found in other oratorios.

In Mozart's case, the choice is due to the nature of the work as a sacred drama, or *azione sacra*. Metastasio adheres strictly to the Aristotelean rules regarding the unity of action, place, and time.[43] This explains why all events that occur outside the city walls (including the decapitation of Holofernes) are related as narrative, in recitatives. Mozart's challenge was to convey drama when the actual dramatic events take a

---

[42] Stanley Sadie, "Wolfgang Amadeus Mozart: Austrian Composer," *Brittanica*. Available online: https://www.britannica.com/biography/Wolfgang-Amadeus-Mozart (accessed October 20, 2020).

[43] The classical unities, Aristotelian unities, or three unities represent a prescriptive theory of dramatic tragedy that was introduced in Italy in the sixteenth century and was influential for three centuries. The three unities are:

1. *Unity of action*: A tragedy should have one principal action.
2. *Unity of time*: The action in a tragedy should occur over a period of no more than 24 hours.
3. *Unity of place*: A tragedy should exist in a single physical location.

back seat to the epic quality. According to one critic, Mozart's musical language "is headstrong, risky and refreshingly youthful … [enhancing] the vocal parts."[44]

The full libretto with program notes and YouTube performances are available online.[45]

La Betulia liberata *(1771)*

Judith: alto
Ozia: tenor
Achior: baritone
Cabri and Carmi, chiefs of the people: sopranos
Amital, noblewoman of Israel: soprano

There is no singing part for Judith's servant or for Holofernes. This work is unique in that respect. The full work is two and a half hours long, roughly one hour of which is recitative.

Part I

The minor-key overture sets a somber mood, with horns playing martial interjections. The first scene opens with a lengthy recitative by Ozia, who berates the people for their lack of courage, their "shameful faint-heartedness" (*vergognosa viltà*). He warns them that "every storm, however slight, is a fatal tempest to a pilot who despairs." He continues this theme in an elaborate aria, singing: "He who despairs does not love, does not believe." The ornate music spins his words into a passionate declaration. Following this aria is a recitative conversation between Cabri and Amital, talking about their despair and hopelessness, and that of their neighbors. Those who still express hope are derided. Cabri sings an aria expressing similar ideas: How can even the strongest hearts not be discouraged by the sights of anguish all around them? The aria's music is sad and pleading rather than angry as Ozia's was. Ozia's response is to remind them of all God has done for them in the past, during the Exodus—could such a God abandon them now? He reminds them that Holofernes has been threatening them for a long time but has not yet dared to attack. He sees that as a sign of "Heaven's favor," but Cabri points out that the savage general is laying a cruel siege on them. Amital wonders how they can resist such an enemy. In touching words, she describes her despair:

Our swollen tongues, our parched throats by now are incapable even of lamenting.
Our eyes lack moisture for tears, yet there is increasing reason to weep.

---

[44] Christian Mortiz-Bauer, CD liner notes, pp. 11–12.
[45] The full libretto can be found here, along with program notes: https://dsd-files.s3.amazonaws.com/challenge/CC72590/CC72590/CC72590.pdf. There are two recordings on YouTube; the shorter one without recitatives is here: https://www.youtube.com/watch?v=sBHvp8wN8R0. I recommend listening to the full work, as there is masterful, subtle music even in the recitatives: https://www.youtube.com/watch?v=vPHdeM2STPQ (all accessed February 14, 2020).

She continues to lament that the greatest tribulation for her is to helplessly watch her children declining. This libretto, like many others, personalizes the biblical account. Phrases from the book of Judith such as "Their little children were disheartened" (7:22) or "Great lamentation arose from all of them (7:29) are made more vivid and specific with words uttered by specific individuals, such as those above. The music then underlines and amplifies the thoughts expressed. Amital accuses Ozia as the prime cause of their misery and wonders how he can sit inactive and watch his people perish. This is followed by an aria, *Non hai core* ("You have no heart"), in which Amital accuses Ozia as heartless and void of compassion. The music for this text does not equal the intensity of the words, for this listener. To much more poignant music, Amital tells Ozia that if the enemy knew how miserable they were, even their eyes would fill with tears. Ozia responds that they could never hope for peace "from that lawless and faithless people, hostile to our God." Amital says it would still be better to die quickly at the enemy's hands than by thirst. Then she begs him in the name of the God of their fathers to surrender to the Assyrian army. Much of the dialogue hews closely to the biblical text (though there is no biblical character named Amital). Amital tells him that the people are all behind her, and the chorus affirms this. Ozia then bargains with them to wait five days for God to relent, as in the biblical story. He then leads the chorus in pleading with God for mercy. The prayer is accompanied initially only by plucked strings, filling out when the chorus joins in a heartrending plea.

As the chorus concludes, Cabri comments on the approach of a woman, whom Amital identifies "from her neglected tresses, coarse mantle and modest eyes" as "Merari's daughter." This identification is never spoken out loud in the biblical text but appears only in Judith's genealogy (8:1). Amital's description of Judith differs a great deal from the descriptions that usually occur after Judith has prepared herself to meet Holofernes. She is always described as overwhelmingly beautiful, except in this rare instance.

Judith's entrance is dramatic mainly for the striking sound of the alto voice, the first one heard so far in the oratorio. This voice type suggests age and authority (and seduction, but more in later eras) and is rarely chosen for the role of Judith. She is irate with both Ozia and the people and shocked at their agreement. She says both have gone to extremes in different ways: "One despairs of divine mercy, the other dares to limit its extent" (*Quello dispera della pietà divina; ardisce questo limitarle i confini*). She follows this diatribe with an aria, *Del pari infeconda* ("Equally barren"), in which she sounds gentler than in her recitative. She speaks more words of wisdom, such as "Presumption comes from too much hope, faith is lost through too much fear." Ozia praises her words, "O wise and holy one" (*O saggia, O santa*), which he says come from God. He asks Judith to implore pardon from God for them all. She points out that God only tests faith but does not oppress his people, pointing out Abraham and Isaac, Jacob and Moses. They must only have faith. Then she tells them that a great plan "is boiling up in my mind" but insists they not ask her what it is. She informs them she will depart at sunset. Ozia leads another moving chorus, this one also foretelling Mozart's great choral music of later years. In this prayer, they beg God to punish them if they are guilty but not to let the punishment come from others.

Cabri approaches Ozia to inform him that a prisoner was left by the enemy forces "bound to a tree near the city" (a slight twist to the original story); his name is Achior and he is "the prince of the Ammonites." Achior tells his story, basically the same as in the biblical book. This is followed by an aria, *Terribile d'aspetto*, in which he says Holofernes is "terrible-looking … [and has] barbaric manners," and considers himself among the gods or has no god at all. This aria foreshadows arias in Mozart's later opera *Le Nozze di Figaro* (1786). Ozia reassures Achior that God will turn against Holofernes and reassures him of their friendship. Achior is surprised to be treated with such compassion and is escorted to Ozia's house.

Judith enters, and Ozia expresses amazement at her transformation. He raves on about her beautiful appearance, to which her abrupt response is "Ozia, the sun is setting: command the gates to be opened; I must go out." He expresses concern for her going out alone in the darkness, unarmed, but she tells him she wants no one with her except her serving-maid. This is the first mention of her servant, who has a silent role here as in the Bible. Ozia says to himself that Judith's words hold something, "resolution and grandeur … which fills and oppresses me." Yet he is surprised that he dare not ask for her plan, and simply lets her go. She now sings an aria, *Parto inerme*: "I go forth unarmed and unafraid … He who fired me to this great trial accompanies and protects me … I hear him reply that I shall be victorious." She holds the first note of the aria, on "Parto," for several measures, an expression of confidence and determination. The second half of the aria slows and the accompaniment is less excited. Here she sings of her great faith in God who "fired her up" (*m'accese*) for this great trial and who accompanies and protects her. She hears God in her spirit, telling her she will be victorious. A chorus concludes the act, marveling at Judith. It is notable that they comment on the certainty of Judith retaining her virtue, long before anyone even suspects her plan:

> O marvel! O amazement! That a private woman should take on cares of the public, that a weak woman [*donna imbelle*, also found in Scarlatti's oratorio] should not share her counsel with the rulers … she adorns herself with such care, yet arouses not a single doubt of her virtue! She promises nothing but lets everyone hope. Could the Author of such wonders disregard such a being?

Part II

The second part opens with a lengthy recitative: a theological debate between Ozia and Achior. Achior questions the assertion that God is one, and Ozia responds by quoting the biblical God saying "I am that I am" at the burning bush (Exod 3:14). Achior does not accept this as truth, and Ozia tells him that reason will convince him, and that he should seek truth, not victory. This debate continues for some time and adds an interesting element to the story of Judith. The writer Metastasio seems to be trying to convince the audience (or himself) of the existence of the God that Judith so fervently believes is aiding her. At the end of the debate, Ozia sings a gentle aria underlining his assertions about God: "you can see him in everything; if you cannot conceive where he dwells … tell me where he does not dwell." Some of these phrases are embellished and reach high in the range, adding to the persuasiveness of his arguments. Achior remains confused and cannot rid himself of doubts.

Amital enters and asks Ozia why extreme silence has replaced uproar in Bethulia. She sings a virtuosic aria, *Quel nocchier*, in which she compares this state with a "pilot in a great storm [who] is not anxious and does not speak, is close to shipwreck." It is a very lively aria in a major key, representing the storm but without any sense of foreboding in the music. Ozia tells her that "excessive grief does not last long" but that there is still hope. She tells him he is wrong to rely so much on Judith, and at that very moment cries of "To arms! To arms!" are heard from the warriors by the gates. Amital fears the enemy has arrived. Instead, it is Judith, telling the people to praise God, whose "promises are fulfilled": "He triumphs by my hand, he has rewarded our faith." Ozia does not understand the sudden tumult but Judith tells him to await her explanation. Then she tells them Holofernes is dead, and that it was she who slew him. In these recitatives and some of the following ones, the accompaniment is very sparse and Judith sings mostly *a cappella*, musically suggesting her strength and independence. As in the Arne oratorio previously discussed, the beheading scene is not represented.

Judith recounts in a lengthy recitative how she killed Holofernes, which is amazingly effective even though it is not an aria. As she begins to describe what happened after all the servants had left Holofernes's tent, the brief musical outbursts between her words create suspense and drama. On the words "I rose, and silently drew near to where he lay," the music becomes darker and more sinister. She repeats the prayer she sent to God, looking to him for help. Then the music abruptly changes again as she describes her actions, taking the sword down, baring it, holding his hair with her left hand and raising the other "to the full length of my arm," a vivid addition. Between each action, the orchestra plays quick and dramatic passages, suggesting the pauses between each action described. In the end, she says she "smote the blow upon his wicked neck." Ozia praises her courage, while Amital comments on the great danger. The rest of description becomes increasingly harrowing, with textual additions bringing her act intensely to life:

> The barbarian opened his eyes and, still uncertain between sleep and death, felt the sword plunged into his throat. He attempted to rise and defend himself, but his fettered hair prevented him. He resorted to cries, but his voice found the way to his lips barred and was lost.

After several dramatic chords, Judith relates that she repeated the blow until the "fearful head was cleft from his shoulders":

> The severed trunk quivered on the blood-stained ground. I felt the half-dead skull start beneath the hand that held it. I saw that face suddenly lose color, those lips frame mute words, those eyes seeking all round the light of the sun: I saw him die, threatening, and I trembled.

An aria is really unnecessary with such a vivid and dramatic text, surely one of the more vivid and bloody descriptions I have found. Judith pauses in her narrative to relate that when at last she could breathe again, she thanked God for her triumph. She then goes on to relate that she wrapped the "lifeless head" in the canopy that she pulled down from the bed and gave it to her "faithful maid, who had been waiting nearby." The maid, mentioned once before, is silent here as in the biblical account. There is a striking departure from the biblical account here, in that Judith pulls down the canopy from the bed (13:9) and then presents it *along with* his head (13:15). In the original story, she actually puts the head in her food bag, but that is replaced by "pillow," "linen cloth," or similar terms, in other librettos. The notion of a food bag was unfamiliar to many librettists, who in most cases did not deal with the issue of sanctioned (kosher) food and therefore never even mentioned such a bag in their retellings. The idea of the head wrapped in a large canopy, which would be very cumbersome, is an odd alteration.

This is one of the most dramatic accounts of the killing in an oratorio, even though it is related in a recitative with occasional orchestral accents rather than in an aria. The listeners all express amazement and wonder that Judith achieved this feat. Achior wonders how he can believe that Judith could plan and perform this "unarmed and alone," and Judith tells him he can believe as she shows him the severed head. Achior, frightened, recognizes him, as Ozia and Amital note that he is frozen in place. Judith suggests that perhaps "that veil which obscured his mind now is torn away all at once," intimating that he will now accept their God. She also says that Achior may be "unaccustomed to sustain the rush of so much light." She elaborates on this point in an aria, *Prigionier, che fa ritorno* ("The prisoner who returns"), which describes the prisoner "unused to peaceful day closes his eyes to the sunlight … but soon is able to bear the radiant light." Achior's response to all this is to admit he is vanquished. He does not know what has transformed him, but he is now "filled, entirely filled" with the Israelites' God:

> I hate and abhor the false gods and the shameful adulation that I credulously offered them, I love no other, I recognize no other god than the God of Abraham.

He then sings an aria expressing his adoration of God, "infinite Mind, Source of life and of truth." Ozia points out to Judith what a glorious result has come from her victory—as if the conversion of Achior were more important than the conquest of their enemy. This perspective can probably be explained by the author's familiarity with his audience and their expectations. Amital follows Ozia's confession with her own, admitting that her fear and lack of trust were "an affront to divine mercy": "O God, I forgot what thou canst, what thou art." This is followed by an aria in which Amital confesses her sins and begs for mercy. These additions to the original Judith text shift the emphasis from her feat itself to its power to increase doubters' faith.

Carmi relates that Judith's forecasts were true, and "universal slaughter has overwhelmed the Assyrians." He goes on to relate scenes of utter chaos in the Assyrian camp, beyond the biblical description. One summary sentence says: "The event opens up a hundred unusual ways to death." This is followed by a very dramatic aria describing the terror of the enemy camp, where "fear completes the work of the sword." Everyone heaps praises on Judith, whose response is simply *Basta*—enough. "God was the spirit who guided the great blow; I was his hand; let the festive hymns be offered to him." A powerful and upbeat chorus of praise follows, interspersed with solo sections for Judith in which she relates the story, beginning with the siege of Bethulia. After each solo section, the chorus repeats the same text of praise. Only the final repetition speeds up and changes rhythm, and the chorus sings a new text, expressing joy that Bethulia is free and the enemy conquered. They proclaim that the greatest vice is pride:

> Quell it, and with it all its band of followers will be quelled, and you will gather a thousand palms at a single blow.

Conclusion

This oratorio is less about character than about teaching a moral lesson. It is one of only two works discussed in this book that has no singing role for Holofernes (the other is Parry's 1888 oratorio). Because most of the story is told through recitative and after the fact, it has less dramatic impact and the characters are less developed than in other works discussed here. The exception is Judith, who emerges as a strong and confident figure. The genius of Mozart shines through several times, particularly in Judith's long recitative about her feat, in which only orchestral passages provide musical background and manage nonetheless to create a harrowing effect.

Chapter Conclusion

These oratorios inject new life into the characters of the book of Judith, utilizing musical techniques in creative ways—sometimes to harrowing and sometimes to humorous effect—to suggest new layers of meaning and interpretation. Through musical devices utilized in the orchestra and in the voices, characters' emotions come across as conflicted and very real. In addition, there is an unexpected and welcome woman-centered and empowering slant to some of the dialogue, particularly in Scarlatti's Cambridge *Judith*, when the Nurse talks about their "weaker sex" and their cries being ignored or derided by men. To a greater or lesser degree, Judith is depicted as a woman full of confidence, even swagger, in these works. This does not contradict her biblical portrayal but rather fills in empty spaces between the lines. If Judith had not been confident and strong, how could she have done what she did? Her wisdom, which is praised in the original story, is defined in various ways by the librettists and is clearly manifested by her planning and maneuvering, in several works. Holofernes, too, is given more dimensions. In some works, he is doltish and simple, while in others he is represented as struggling to remain strong and to resist Judith's charms, which he suspects are wiles; yet he succumbs to passion in the end. Holofernes is sometimes portrayed sympathetically, adding nuance and ambiguity to the story. These additions in librettos increase the characters' complexity.

In two of these works (Vivaldi's and Mozart's), all the characters are understood to be symbols, yet they nonetheless come across as living and breathing people through the music and the text. In Vivaldi's oratorio, Judith, possibly because she is a symbol of Venice, is very righteous and honorable, as well as combative. At the same time, through her voice and the music, she is very real.

Notable trends found in these works, such as an increased role for the servant, new dimensions to both Judith's and Holofernes' characters, and elaborations of the murder scene, will be noted and highlighted in discussions of the next three centuries of musical retellings.

2

Nineteenth- and Twentieth-Century Oratorios: Henry David Leslie, C. H. Hubert Parry, Paul Hillemacher, Arthur Honegger

The Oratorio in Nineteenth-Century England

The eighteenth-century oratorios of Georg Friedrich Handel dominated the oratorio form in England well into the next century, serving as models for the works of numerous composers. In contrast to oratorio performances in other countries, those in England were performed almost exclusively without staging, costumes, or acting—making the story of Judith a particularly strange choice for this form because the story is so plot-driven and dramatic. However, once British oratorio composers became familiar with Felix Mendelssohn's biblical oratorios (*St. Paul*, 1837, and *Elijah*, 1846), that composer's style of German romanticism began to have a strong influence. Some British composers either shifted from the Handel style to Mendelssohn or created a mix of the two.[1] The two British oratorios discussed here are both good examples of this amalgam.

Henry David Leslie (1822–1896)

Henry David Leslie was an English choral conductor and composer. In 1855 he founded the Henry Leslie Choir, a celebrated *a cappella* ensemble that was awarded first prize in the International Choral Competition held at the Paris Exhibition in 1878. His London concert programs were notable for the large amount of English choral music included. Leslie was a supporter of amateur choral societies and of musical higher education.[2]

Leslie wrote a preface to the published libretto of his oratorio *Judith*, in which he shared his anxieties about using the Judith text. He claimed that Judith is not to be

---

[1] Howard E. Smither, *A History of the Oratorio* vol. 4, *The Oratorio in the Nineteenth and Twentieth Centuries* (Chapel Hill: University of North Carolina Press, 2000), pp. 250, 257.
[2] H. C. Colles and E. D. Mackerness in *New Grove Dictionary* (2001), vol. 14, p. 586.

taken as an example: "It is no lesson for Christians." On the one hand, Leslie wants to ignore the sensationalist aspects of the story that other librettos had not; on the other, he admits that these aspects must necessarily appear. Stocker notes that "this strange apologia, grammatically and logically distorted by its own ambivalence, is equally confused by the story's sacred/non-canonical status."[3] On the one hand, Leslie insists that the Apocrypha is not authoritative; while on the other, he assures readers that he has used no words not found in the original text, so as not to alter "the lofty and lyrical language of Scripture." The music shows very strong influences of Mendelssohn (1809–1847), whose oratorio *Elijah* had premiered in England just over ten years earlier. Mendelssohn himself was influenced by Bach, and this can also be heard in Leslie's work. *Elijah* was very popular with amateur choral groups, with which Leslie was heavily involved, so he would have certainly known the work well.

Judith, Henry Leslie's oratorio or "biblical cantata in three scenes," was created for the Birmingham Musical Festival in 1858, as a hospital benefit (similarly to Arne; see Chapter 1). Such hospital benefits date back to Handel, whose music was intimately connected to the Foundling Hospital in London, the UK's first children's charity, which Handel supported throughout his life. His oratorio *The Messiah* was performed each year in the Foundling Hospital chapel for the benefit of the charity. This tradition continued until the 1770s and Handel conducted or attended every performance until his death in 1759.[4]

Henry Fothergill Chorley (1808–1872), the librettist, began to write for the *Athenaeum* in 1830 and remained its music and literature critic until 1868. While there, he reviewed approximately 2,500 books and wrote reviews and musical gossip columns discussing composers and performers in Britain and on the European continent. Chorley was influenced by Pietro Metastasio's *Bethulia liberata* (even borrowing the unusual name "Amital" from his play or from Mozart's opera). Chorley was much more known, if not always positively, for his translations and reviews than his librettos.[5]

Judith (1858)

Judith: mezzo-soprano
Holofernes: baritone
Amital (Judith's servant): soprano

The work has never been recorded. The score can be found in very few libraries (not on IMSLP). All page numbers cited in this chapter are taken from the scores.

Scene 1 opens in the beleaguered city of Bethulia. After an orchestral introduction, a narrator (tenor, a tradition in Bach oratorios) opens with a recitative quoting the

3   Margarita Stocker, *Judith: Sexual Warrior* (New Haven, CT: Yale University Press, 1998). From the Introduction to the libretto, p. 155.
4   Caro Howell, "How Handel's Messiah helped London's Orphans—and Vice Versa," *The Guardian*, March 13, 2014.
5   Robert Bledsoe, "Chorley, Henry Fothergill," *Oxford Dictionary of National Biography*. Available online: jHttp://www.oxforddnb.com/view/10.1093/ref:odnb/9780198614128.001.0001/odnb-9780198614128-e-5350 (accessed October 17, 2018).

opening verse of Judith. A chorus sings "A day of darkness," in a tempo marked *maestoso*, changing to *allegro* as they rally and sing "Assemble yourselves together, a great people and strong, there hath not ever been the like." A duet between Amital and Ozias, with the chorus, follows: "Spare thy people." Both soloists sing in a very high range, the soprano reaching a high C (*c*"; p. 26) and much of the tenor part lying well above the staff. The subsequent chorus, "God be Judge" (p. 28), is a far more dramatic one. That is followed by yet another chorus, all before Judith enters.

Judith, sung by a mezzo to suggest age and authority, enters to a dramatic dotted rhythm leading to her opening words, "Hear me now" (Jdt 8:11; p. 39). The orchestra switches to repeated *tremolos* when she berates the Bethulians: "Who are ye that have tempted God this day?" On the phrase "and comprehend his purpose," Judith sings a short phrase starting on *f#*" and descending rapidly almost two octaves to *g#*, a very low note. This is followed by the aria "Let us wait for salvation" (8:17) to a conventional, hymnlike melody. The chorus responds: "Pray for us," sung *pianissimo* to an accompaniment in 6/8 time that fluctuates between measures from 16th notes to 8th notes, in a very Mendelssohnian sound. Judith responds with her prayer "O Lord God of my father Simeon" (9:2, 9, 12; p. 43), a beautiful pleading melody, with a more agitated middle section, eventually returning to the calm opening melody. For this listener, these are among the most inspired pages of this oratorio (see Figure 1).

At the conclusion, the tempo picks up and the rhythm is much more excited, as Judith orders her people to stand at the gate as she goes forth, in higher and more dramatic phrases. The final phrase, "The Lord will visit Israel by my hand," includes several of her highest notes, finally reaching *a*" (p. 46), sustained over several measures. Ozias responds in an *arioso*, "Go in peace, the Lord be before thee" (Jdt 8:35, where this phrase is followed by "to take vengeance upon our enemies"). The final part of his solo is "God be merciful unto thee," in a hymnlike tune that the chorus then repeats.

Scene 2 opens in the Assyrian camp, to a martial introduction. Holofernes (baritone, suggesting authority) asks his attendants where the power lies of "these people who dwell in the mountains." He proceeds to sing a very Handelian aria filled with *fioritura*. This is followed by a quartet singing Psalms verses, typical of biblical oratorios. The music is in a square 4/4 time with strumming groups of triplet 8th notes, again showing a strong Mendelssohn influence. Judith sings with a chorus of Assyrian soldiers. A *tremolo*, suggesting trepidation, introduces the chorus asking Judith where she is from. She tells them she is a woman of the Hebrews and fled from them. They ask where she is going and she tells them: "before Holofernes to declare words of truth" (Jdt 10:12–13). The soldiers reassure her that Holofernes will not hurt her. She sings a dramatic aria ending with a rapid run up to *a-flat*" on "O come let us cut them off" (presumably referring to the Hebrews). The Assyrians are excited by her words, and sing "Come, come, come, let us cut them off" repeatedly and *fortissimo*.

There is another interlude as Amital sings Psalms excerpts to very Mendelssohnian music. Then the tempo abruptly changes to *allegro moderato*, as a dramatic introduction filled with 16th-note passages leads into a trio with Amital, Judith, and Holofernes. The rhythm and sound of this trio recalls Verdi, whose music was very popular at the time this work was composed. Holofernes opens, singing words of comfort to Judith (based on Jdt 11:1–3). He closes with the phrase "Be of good comfort, thou shalt live this night

Figure 1 Henry David Leslie, "Judith's Prayer"

and hereafter." This last word is sung on an *f#* octave descending down to a low *f#*; very low in the baritone register. This could be a musical suggestion of both authority and comfort.

In response, Amital and Judith sing a duet, in a slower tempo. They sing the same text but echo one another; some of their music is homophonic (in harmony), while some features interweaving musical lines. They sing fawning compliments to Holofernes, based on Jdt 11:6–9. Several times they sing Handelian runs, once again showing the pastiche of styles used by Leslie in this somewhat derivative work. Holofernes responds in a recitative introduced by the same agitated 16th notes as earlier. He repeats that he still wants to know what Judith is doing there. In a short *andante* section, in a new tempo and key, Judith tells him her plan (an abbreviated version of Jdt 11:5–19). In an aria in 6/8 time featuring a halting rhythm broken by rests, suggesting hesitation, she sings: "I will lead thee through the midst of Judea and will set thy throne in the midst thereof. For these things were told me according to my foreknowledge, and they were declared unto me and I am sent to tell thee" (11:19). Holofernes sings: "There is not such a woman from one end of the earth to the other, both for beauty of face, and wisdom of words" (11:21). Amital and Judith also join in, Judith at one point singing a trill that extends over four measures, over Holofernes's singing. (At times like this, the oratorio seems almost a parody of itself.) The trio is joined by the chorus singing a drinking song in D minor, an odd choice of key that adds an ominous or foreboding element. They sing text that is not found in the biblical story: "Drink now, tomorrow shall be as this day but more abundant" (Isa 56:12). Amital and Judith, presumably aside, also sing new (and ironic) text: "Boast not thy self of tomorrow for thou knowest not what the day may bring forth" (Ps 27:1). Near the end, the drinking chorus switches to a bright D major.

Scene 3 takes place at night and daybreak. After an orchestral introduction, a chorus of revelers is singing in the Assyrian camp. They start with the text from the preceding chorus, about the next day being more abundant than the last. Then they fade as they sing "A little sleep, a little slumber …."

Amital and Judith now sing verses from Judges relating to Jael's killing of Sisera, a reference found in a few Judith oratorios (e.g., Vivaldi's *Juditha Triumphans*; see Chapter 1). "The mother of Sisera cried thro' the lattice 'why is his chariot so long in coming? Let thine enemies perish, O Lord, but let them that fear thee be as the sun when he goeth forth in his might" (Judg 5:31). The chorus of revelers interrupts again, countered with Amital and Judith's "I have seen the wicked in great power, spreading himself like a green bay tree. Yet I passed by and he was not; Yea, I sought him, and he could not be found" (Ps 37:35–36). This episode seems meant to illustrate the pious motives of Judith and Amital, who is never identified (she was named as a noblewoman in Metastasio's and Mozart's *Betulia liberata* but here seems to function more as Judith's servant).

The next scene finds Judith in the tent of Holofernes. Judith sings another prayer, based on verses from Jdt 13:4, 5, 7 and also Jdt 9:10, "Break down," which she had also sung in her earlier prayer. This prayer is far more dramatic than the earlier one, though the opening measures echo the previous prayer. On the words "For the exaltation of Jerusalem" she starts on *a-flat*", one of her highest notes in the oratorio, which she reaches again on "Lord." The final phrase, "Strengthen me this day," takes the voice on a descending scale ending on a *pianissimo a-flat*, a very low note and two octaves below what she had just sung. This is a musical portrayal of both exaltation and relief. But there is no text or music describing the beheading, which is also absent in a few other oratorios. For some composers, it was not seemly to represent such a violent scene in a biblical oratorio (even though it was not staged).

Instead, a narrator relates the rest of the story in a recitative, accompanied by excited chords alternating with *tremolo* measures. Judith reenters, singing in a few *maestoso* measures in D major: "So let thine enemies perish, O Lord" (Judg 5:31, the final line of the Song of Deborah, celebrating a different victory). The word "enemies" is sustained on *g"* for a measure and a half, and "O" sung on a full-measure trill. All of these are musical markers of power, particularly in this musical period.

The final scene is at the walls of Bethulia, with a march and chorus of the Hebrew guards. Soft martial music in the brightest key of C major is heard. Another chorus is singing psalms: "Except the Lord build the house, they labour in vain that build it; except the Lord keep the city, the watchman waketh but in vain, for the lord is a great god and a great King" (Ps 127:1). More martial music follows. Then Judith sings a short solo, marked *allegro agitato* followed by a recitative: "Open now the gate, God is with us." A trio with more Mendelssohn echoes follows, featuring Judith, Amital, and Ozias praising God. The chorus joins and a C- major "Amen" concludes the oratorio.

Conclusion

There is far less character development or depiction here than in the eighteenth-century works discussed in the previous chapter, partially because the librettist used exclusively biblical text, finding appropriate verses to fit the moment—mostly Psalms, and others. This gives the oratorio the character of a religious work more than a dramatic one, but since it is typical of its genre and period, I felt it important to include it. It gives a sense of what the audience of that time expected to hear.

Charles Hastings Hubert Parry (1848–1918)

Charles Hastings Hubert Parry was an English composer, scholar, and teacher. in the words of Parry biographer Jeremy Dibble, Parry combined these three activities with a "forceful personality and social position, [thus exercising] a revitalizing influence on English musical life at a time in the nineteenth century when standards of composition, performance, criticism and education were low."[6] He took lessons with William Sterndale Bennett, a prominent composer of the time, but felt he wasn't critical enough. He applied to study with Johannes Brahms in Vienna but was refused, and then studied with a renowned champion of Richard Wagner, pianist Edward Dannreuther. Parry studied more and more contemporary music, especially Franz Liszt, Pyotr Tchaikovsky, and Brahms, all of which had a profound effect on the

---

[6] Jeremy Dibble in *New Grove Dictionary* (2001), vol. 19, pp. 152–4.

development of his musical language. He also became a passionate Wagnerite, going to Bayreuth several times. He was appointed Professor of Musical History at the newly founded Royal College of Music. Most of his music in the 1880s was symphonic, but commissions from provincial festivals signaled a shift from symphonic to choral music (a shift much lamented by George Bernard Shaw).[7] In 1888, Parry's national renown was consolidated with *Judith, or the Regeneration of Manasseh*, the first of his three biblical oratorios (followed by *Job* in 1892 and *King Saul* in 1894). He was knighted in 1898 for services to British music. He wrote a number of "ethical oratorios" to express his own personal heterodoxy (1898–1908), drawing on biblical texts and his own words through which he tried to elucidate his humanitarian convictions.[8]

In his music, by the age of 18 Parry had fully imbibed the aesthetics of Anglican church music and the oratorio-centered repertory of the provincial music festivals. His early works show a Mendelssohn influence, which was true of many composers of that period (like Leslie, above). While deeply religious, Parry developed a pathological loathing for organized religion. He was a strong influence on the composers Ralph Vaughan Williams and Gustav Holst (who both studied with him), Herbert Howells, and Gerald Finzi. He is probably best known today for the choral song "Jerusalem" written in 1916, and his 1902 setting for the coronation anthem "I was glad."[9]

Parry's *Judith* was an overwhelming success in Victorian England, performed by some of that era's greatest musicians. Hans Richter conducted the premiere; Charles Villiers Stanford conducted the London debut, and Edward Elgar played violin in the orchestra under Parry's own baton in Gloucester.[10] The oratorio was first heard in North America in Toronto, in 2015. The first full London performance since the nineteenth century was in April 2019, at the Southbank Centre, London. In his program notes for that performance, Jeremy Dibble comments on the beauty of the choruses:

> The choruses concerned with the Jewish captivity (notably the last chorus of Part I and the opening chorus of Part II) have an impressive sonority and pathos.[11]

In his Preface to the published score, Parry explains that in his search for oratorio material, he consulted the "learned work" of Reverend Dean Humphrey Prideaux (1648–1724), *The Old and New Testament Connected in the History of the Jews and Neighbouring Nations* (1715–17) for "details of one of the Jewish captivities." Prideaux's theory was that Judith's exploit occurred in the reign of Manasseh. He probably based that on the name of Judith's named (and dead) husband in Jdt 8:2: "Her husband Manasseh belonged to her tribe and family." Prideaux claimed to have worked out the connection to Judith with "some show of historical probability."[12]

---

[7]   Dibble, p. 154.

[8]   Smither 2001, p. 354.

[9]   Dibble, pp. 152–3.

[10] http://www.paxchristichorale.org/news/2016/9/17/the-judith-project (accessed October 18, 2018).

[11] Jeremy Dibble, program notes for London English Song Festival presentation at the Royal Festival Hall, London, April 3, 2019, pp. 8–9. My thanks to the Song Festival for providing me with the full program.

[12] Alexander Gordon, "Prideaux, Humphrey," *Wikisource*. Available at: https://en.wikisource.org/wiki/Prideaux,_Humphrey_(DNB00) (accessed July 12, 2019).

The story of Manasseh is found in 2 Kgs 21:1–17 and 2 Chr 33:1–20. He rebuilt the heathen altars of Baal that his father Hezekiah had destroyed. He also built pagan altars in both courts of the Temple of the Lord, for worshiping the sun, moon, and stars. Manasseh even sacrificed his own children as burnt offerings in the valley of Hinnom. He consulted spirit mediums, fortune tellers, and sorcerers. He angered the Lord by encouraging every sort of evil (2 Chr 33:4–6) and murdered large numbers of innocent people (2 Kgs 21:16). Warnings by the Lord were ignored by both Manasseh and his people, so God sent the Assyrian armies (another perceived link to the Judith story), who captured him and took him into exile. While in captivity he came to his senses and cried out to God for help. As recorded in 2 Chr 33:13, the Lord answered his prayers by returning him to Jerusalem. At that point Manasseh realized that the Lord was really God. He removed the foreign idols from the hills and the Temple and tore down the pagan altars. He then rebuilt the altar of the Lord and offered sacrifices upon it. When Manasseh died, he was buried beneath his own palace.

Parry wrote in his Preface: "I had already been attracted to the story of Manasseh, and its salient features, though merely suggested in the Bible." He explains his intention in his Preface to the score:[13]

> The story of Judith has a breadth of significance and force of character likely to lend themselves to treatment in an oratorio form. It was not my original intention to call the work *Judith*, though her heroism is admirable, but the sanguinary catastrophe of the story is neither artistically attractive nor suitable for the oratorio form. But while working out the subject I was partly carried away by the superior interest of her personality, and her share in the action because it was at least equal to Manasseh's. But I wished to centralize the interest on popular movements and passions, more than only on individuals.

The reader of these words is left wondering which version of the Bible Parry was consulting. If the Manasseh mentioned in the book of Judith is the king, he would still be alive. And his wife is named in Kings as Meshullemet, as she is in the oratorio. Judith is not identified as anyone's wife—in fact, she is not identified at all. Of the numerous reviews that appeared after the 2019 performance, only this reviewer comments on the plot confusion:

> By using Prideaux Parry created two conflicts in Judith, the first the Israeli [*sic*] worship of Moloch during the reign of Manasseh and the demands for child sacrifice, and the second the near-seduction and murder of Holofernes and Judith's escape … Unfortunately, in Parry's version, the tale of Judith and her tantalising of Holofernes becomes bowdlerised; the drama moved to Jerusalem rather than the city of Bethulia which, because of Judith's exploits, protected the larger city and the whole of Judaea … the drama [is] sapped by Parry's refusal to engage directly

---

[13] Full score: London, Novello, Ewer, n.d.

with what was going on. The murder of Holofernes is only mentioned when Judith instructs his head to be hung from the city walls![14]

The story presented in the oratorio is outlined in the Preface to the score:

At a great assemblage of the Israelites for the worship of Moloch, the priests demand the children of Manasseh for sacrifice. The king is overcome by the frenzy of the crowd and acquiesces. The priests take the children from their mother at the king's palace, taking them down to the valley of Hinnom to sacrifice them. Judith, trying to save the children, is almost sacrificed herself by furious worshippers, but the coming of the Assyrian armies saves her. They leave Jerusalem in ruins and take Manasseh prisoner to Babylon.

Manasseh repents while captive and is allowed to return to Jerusalem. He is followed by Holofernes, who demands from the ruined city submission to Nabuchodonosor, his king, and also tribute payments. Judith exhorts the Jews to trust in God and takes it upon herself to save the city in God's name. The Jews and Manasseh wait anxiously as she enters the Assyrian camp and Holofernes' tent. There he is overcome by wine and Judith's beauty and is slain by her that night. She escapes back to Jerusalem and urges the Jews to attack the vulnerable Assyrians. Manasseh and his people are fired up by her heroism and scatter the enemies.

There are clearly numerous changes made to the story of Judith. Manasseh becomes the main character, while in the book of Judith, Manasseh is named only as Judith's dead husband and not a king. In this version, Bethulia is not even mentioned, since the city in question is Jerusalem, and it is not under siege. The entire first part is an invented prelude (or prequel) to the actual story of Judith. Holofernes does not have a singing part in this oratorio, nor is his name ever mentioned (only his messenger). The music adds pathos, longing, fear, and excitement to the text, which however is cobbled together from biblical fragments and thus does not truly depict or develop individual characters. This is typical of biblical oratorio in Victorian England.

A recorded performance is available online.[15]

The London performance of April 2019 was recorded and is now available on the Chandos label.

The full libretto and piano-vocal score can be found online.[16]

Judith, or The Regeneration of Manasseh (1888)

Manasseh: tenor
Meshullemeth, his wife: alto

[14] Andrew Neill, review of Parry's Judith at Southbank Centre, at https://www.classicalsource.com/concert/hubert-parrys-judith-at-royal-festival-hall-william-vann-conducts-the-first-london-performance-since-1889/ (accessed October 21, 2020).
[15] https://www.youtube.com/watch?v=qNH8NpEMvAQ (accessed October 22, 2018).
[16] http://conquest.imslp.info/files/imglnks/usimg/f/f4/IMSLP108864-SIBLEY1802.15027.48cc-39087011304260score.pdf.

Judith: soprano
High Priest of Moloch: baritone

Holofernes has no singing role, as is the case only in this oratorio and in Mozart's (see Chapter 1).

Act I

Scene I: Moloch

After an overture, the scene opens with very dramatic processional music for Moloch worshippers, singing "Hail, Moloch! Hail, awful god!"; some dramatic leaps of descending octaves portray the horrible god. Manasseh enters (a heroic tenor voice; p. 11) telling them to come close and worship. He describes the horrible power of Moloch and they beg Moloch for mercy in more excited, dotted rhythms, sung *pianissimo*, with a *tremolo* in the basses. The High Priest (baritone) in very somber music tells the people they need not sacrifice their children but only those "within whose veins flows the blood of your King." Manasseh is astounded and believes the persons enthroned over Judah should be spared. But the worshippers demand the children of the king, even hailing their god's choice with joy. In pleading music, Manasseh bewails his fate: to condemn his own children; but the chorus of priests tells him the god will not forgo them. Manasseh sings "O horror! Despair! How shall I turn to meet them?" (p. 20) and the worshippers, in steadily building music, tell the king he must not delay in bringing his children. The music is animated and contrapuntal (two or more independent melodic lines are played simultaneously). The key changes now from A-flat major to E major as the worshippers sing, in stronger and more insistent music, "Bring now the children," their voices echoing one another. The worshippers sing of what these sacrifices to Moloch will accomplish: end pestilence and famine and make Jerusalem secure. The scene ends with a resounding chorus praising Moloch and promising the solemn rites will be performed.

Scene II: The Children (p. 34)

The scene takes place in the King's palace, with Meshullemeth and their children. The scene opens with a very lyrical orchestral introduction. Then the children, in a touching tune, ask their mother to tell them again the story of their people, how God brought them forth from Egyptian bondage. Meshullemeth (alto, representing maturity) tells them he is no longer Israel's God, that his courts are desolate and his altars profaned. They ask if there is no one that still seeks him, and if they can't entreat him. These innocent questions heard in children's voices are very poignant. Their mother tells them God has cause to be angry, and recounts all the reasons. Her last phrase, "requited his love with scorn," ends on a *forte a*, low and dramatic. She tells her children that she will recount the old familiar story of the Exodus, so that they can tell their own children of the lovingkindness of their God when she is gone. The anthem, "Long since in Egypt's plenteous land" (p. 39), is almost a folk-like tune and a wonderful example of Parry's melodic ideas. It has since become a favorite English hymn, to the text "Dear Lord and Father of Mankind."[17] The vocal passages are intertwined with yearning passages in the orchestra. Her two boys join in a trio of praise, unaccompanied and madrigal-like. The trio ends on an E-flat major chord, followed immediately by an intrusive B natural to mark a shift to C minor and another chorus of the priests of Moloch, in very ominous music. They tell the mother that the children must come, as their god demands sacrifice. She protests, clearly indicating she is not a worshipper of Moloch, calling them "priests of that monstrous deity whose roaring throat devours our people's offspring." The children say they trust their father (who priests say has called them) and their God, because both love them. Their mother fears for them and prays their God will keep them safe.

The priests praise Moloch and announce that they are bringing a "worthy sacrifice to him" (p. 48). The beginning of this chorus is in E-flat major, but most of the final passage is in C major, which seems to be almost trying to establish itself, in a possible touch of musical irony. The priests exit and a few low passages in the double basses introduce the entrance of Judith (p. 50). She is not identified or acknowledged by anyone. Judith opens, on a soft C major chord, addressing Meshullemeth very sweetly as "Lady, thou Queen of Israel." She then sings text based on Ps 121 with some variations, introduced by a few horn passages. The tempo is *andante molto sostenuto* in 3/4 time, like an anthem. The second part is more animated, with some syncopation in the orchestra. The text is all "biblicized" English, imitating the style of the King James Bible and intermingled with snippets of actual biblical texts. The music becomes increasingly romantic, particularly in some soaring string passages, when Judith is singing about God's power. The final section is more agitated before concluding on sustained passages, with several repeats of *a-flat*" (p. 54). The choice of a light lyric soprano for this role suggests youth and sweetness, qualities not usually associated with Judith and somewhat downplaying her strength.

Scene III: The Sacrifice

This scene opens in the Valley of Hinnom, where the image of Moloch is flaming. Manasseh and the worshippers are assembled and the priests approach, leading the king's children. The opening is foreboding, with horns and low phrases in the double basses. Both Manasseh and the worshippers, in soft music, praise Moloch and greet the sacrifice of the children. The priests interject three times singing "Moloch, Moloch! Give ear!" in darker and more foreboding passages (pp. 61–3). The music grows louder and more dramatic as the chorus ends with everyone singing *fortissimo* "Moloch! Give ear!" underlined in the closing measures by a *tremolo* in the orchestra. At this point, the children are being held aloft and brought closer to the flames (libretto note).

Judith enters (again unannounced and unidentified; p. 67), singing on a *fortissimo g-flat*" "Stay your hideous mockeries!" In declamatory tones, she rails against Moloch and the "weak and faithless king … abused and fallen low, [whose] high and kingly

---

[17] HRH Prince Charles in program notes for London performance, April 3, 2019, p. 3. The Prince further comments on Parry's "genius for melody."

office [is] degraded and shamed." Then she turns to the people in a second section, where the accompaniment changes from ominous *tremolos* and 8th-note passages to more sustained whole notes, as she sings: "Now shall the Lord Jehovah visit you, the Lord ye have forsaken." Then, in more dramatic music, she warns them that "the sound of arms is in the air," accompanied by *tremolo* in the basses. This is followed by an ascending series of chords in the orchestra, sounding increasingly excited as Judith's pitch also rises.

The final section is *presto* (very fast; p. 72) as she sings "The God whom your fathers worshipped" on a leap from *f#"* down to *d#'*; this section is marked by other unusual or wide intervals, expressing strong emotion and musically adding power to her words. She tells them that the God their fathers worshipped, Jehovah, will fight against them and none will help them, only "this black, hideous mass of stone" that they carved themselves. In increasingly stronger passages, she sings: "Call to your Moloch! Hurl in your children!," both phrases opening on a *fortissimo g#"* and then descending. There are strong echoes, both textually and musically, of Felix Mendelssohn's *Elijah*, which was very popular and influential in the decades before Parry wrote this work (see above). In that work, Elijah is depicted in his famous conflict with the prophets of Baal on Mount Carmel (I Kgs 18), when he challenged the false prophets to bring down fire from heaven. It is possible that Parry was inspired by the conflict depicted there to re-create such a scene in his own work. Judith sings "Cut yourselves and howl, he shall not hear' and many similar passages. Musically these phrases feature rapid descending and ascending octave leaps. The section ends with a *ritardando* (slowing down) and sustained "ad lib" *a"* (to be held at the singer's discretion). The references to Elijah in this scene suggest an elevation of Judith's status to that of a prophet.

The people sing, musically almost shouting: "Who is this that raileth against Moloch? Jehovah is gone, his temples are empty, his courts deserted, them that serve him shall Moloch devour" (p. 74). In the book of Judith, the Hebrews are shown to be doubting and even denying God's power, but certainly not to this extent. Nor, of course, does Moloch have any connection to the Judith story. In any case, Judith is a known figure in her own book, but not in this oratorio's scenario. The crowd grows more and more agitated and finally screams "Cast her in the furnace! She hath defied great Moloch! Let her be sacrificed!" to rapidly ascending orchestral passages, with prominent horns, leading to a final *fugato*, where the voices "chase each other."

Judith is saved by the arrival of a messenger, announcing a host of warriors heading their way: "They fill the valleys far and near, like waters of a sweeping flood. Behind them all the land is waste … All Israel is scattered on the hills as a flock whose shepherd slumbers." This text is replete with biblical references. Manasseh reassures his people that their God shall now show his power. But it seems the god he is referring to is Moloch, based on "The fierceness of his flame shall consume them."

Finale: *The Coming of the Assyrians* (p. 81)

The chorus sings highly dramatic music, filled with fast *tremolo* and dotted rhythms, expressing both their fear and confidence. In a partly *a cappella* section, the worshippers sing of their confidence in Moloch to defeat the enemy. Judith sings an unaccompanied passage about Jerusalem being loved by the Lord as a spouse by her husband whom she betrayed (this idea is found in several of the Prophets, e.g., Micah and Ezekiel). At the word "betrayed," a long and loud *tremolo* is heard, as she concludes that now God shall show vengeance. Martial marching music is heard, representing the approach of the Assyrians. The chorus of Moloch priests pray to their god for help, in a prayerful tune but against the background of the marching music, an effective contrast. Women worshippers join in the plea, in homophonic, chromatically descending phrases. Then they all rise and the priests and worshippers together sing this last melody but in a new key and more *marcato*: "Rise in might and scatter our foes."

Now the Assyrians enter, a male chorus of only tenors, a particularly heroic sound (p. 88). The tempo changes to *Allegro spiritoso*, the key from E minor to its relative G major, and the rhythm from 3/4 to 4/4 time. The music is confident and sturdy, buttressed by the tenor chorus. There is a sudden shift to G minor as the Hebrews cry out "Fly!" in a *fortissimo* chorus as they realize "he host of Assur" is upon them. They wonder what happened to their Moloch in a *fugato* sung over groups of triplets, an ominous sound. At the end of this section, the Assyrians enter singing "Slay them!" The triplets stop abruptly and become rapid *fortissimo tremolos*. Now the two choruses sing simultaneously, the army proclaiming what they will do to the Hebrews, the victims relating the terrible sounds of destruction they are hearing. Then the victim chorus continues alone, with the earlier pleading tune to Moloch this time altered to 4/4 time and accompanied by the groups of triplets. This brilliant transformation of a theme highlights the change from fear to recognition of defeat. Near the end, the sopranos hold long sustained notes above a more rapid melody in the tenor and bass sections. At the climax, the sopranos sing a high C (*c''*), very demanding and unusual for an oratorio chorus. The pitches then get lower and more sustained, and quiet down to *pianissimo* as the people realize they are lost.

This sense of resignation leads to the closing chorus, which starts as an *a cappella* six-part anthem: "Jerusalem, that was Queen of the nations, whose glory is gone, her children captive" (p. 102). Gradually the orchestra enters, at first only as a low rumble from drums and basses. The chorus develops into a *fugato* over an ominous bass *tremolo*. This moving and sad note ends the first act. Including a hymn to Jerusalem is an interesting choice, since Parry is best known for another such hymn to Jerusalem that he wrote years later, to the poem by William Blake. It is possible that he was remembering this hymn to Jerusalem from his 1888 oratorio when he wrote the later one.

Intermezzo: Manasseh's Repentance in Captivity in Babylon (p. 104)

The beautiful and poignant orchestral introduction is marked *Lento espressivo* and opens with a plangent cor anglais solo, which sets the mood of lamenting. This introduction is followed by an aria for Manasseh: "I will bear the indignation of God because I have sinned." He has turned to the Hebrew God, it would seem, whose forgiveness and righteousness he is now awaiting. (The final phrases include an optional *forte a'*, not on the YouTube performance).

Act II

Scene I: The Return of Manasseh

The opening chorus ("The Jews in desolate Jerusalem," libretto note) sings: "Wail, wail, ye solitary people." The music is dramatically mournful, in 6/8 time and dominated by descending passages. At the conclusion, the cor anglais briefly repeats the theme of the earlier Intermezzo, a musical reminder of Manasseh's capture.

Meshullemeth now sings a solo, in a square 4/4 time and very slow, almost an anthem (p. 115). Her text suggests that she stands for the believing Israelite, trying to encourage and uplift her people. There is a transition in the middle of the solo, at "He bringeth home your king," into a major key and faster tempo. The music becomes increasingly more triumphant, and the text, all biblically based or inspired, includes such phrases as "The Lord Himself will fight for you … and Jerusalem from her stain shall be cleansed." Meshullemeth is rousing the people as the listener might have expected Judith to be doing. After her solo, the chorus enters, filled with hope as reflected in the more upbeat music. "Our King is come again" is a fugue in which the voices imitate one another. The tempo steadily increases as they thank their God who has answered them. They give the impression of a very fickle people!

Manasseh's next solo opens in the very bright key of C major, in 3/4 time for the anthem that follows his recitative (p. 125). Dibble calls "Behold how great is the mercy of our God" a "quasi-Handelian aria."[18] Meshullemth enters, singing more of God's praises to a new tune with a more dramatic orchestra. Then Judith (again unannounced) joins them in praise, "O that men would therefore praise the Lord," sung to the melody of Manasseh's anthem. The three sing a beautiful and heartfelt trio, with more praise of God. The trio concludes on a unison C, suggesting complete unity of thought. The orchestral conclusion reprises the theme of the trio, ending hopefully on a soft C major chord.

Scene II: The Message of Holofernes (p. 133)

The orchestra opens in *Allegro maestoso* (fast and majestic), and dotted rhythms alternate with triplets, a strong musical picture. The messenger tells the people not to get too cozy, since now they have to bow to Assur's lord (never named), to bring him tribute and ask for mercy. They may find mercy from him, but if they offend him—death. Syncopated chords and trumpet calls underline his words, when he announces that they must yield their city in three days or suffer the consequences—their city will be razed to the ground, "the mountains shall be drunken with your blood," and more such threats (largely rephrasings of prophetic texts such as Ezekiel, Isaiah, and Jeremiah). He spells out those consequences over a *ff tremolo* and the same repeated chord patterns heard in the opening of this section.

The "chorus of Jews" respond: "Woe, woe, our city's walls are broken," repeatedly sung on whole or half notes over an agitated accompaniment (p. 137). After it has died

---

[18] Dibble, program notes, p. 9.

down to *pianissimo* and a low range on "There is none to help us," the orchestra again builds up to a louder chorus on "Doth the god of Israel sleep? Or has he cast us out?" (This text again echoes the famous scene in Mendelssohn's *Elijah*.) This second phrase is repeated several times, one section echoing the other, descending in range on each repeat. Constant shifts from despair to anger are heard in the music, going from loud to soft, high to low range. Near the end, the orchestra plays very effective descending chromatic notes broken by rests, sounding like gasps. The section ends on a hopeful C major chord, signaling Judith's entrance.

Judith, again unannounced, sings praises to God in a recitative (p. 142). Then she announces, over only an ominous *tremolo* in the orchestra, creating suspense, that she will do something to the glory of God (Jdt 8:32–34). From here on, the text is from Judith (KJV). The sound is that of a very strong martial anthem, *fortissimo* in the orchestra, dying down to lead into her lengthy prayer that opens at Jdt 9:11–12, 14, excluding any reference to deceit. Though Judith has seemed to be a minor character in the oratorio up to this point, this solo marks her as a major player. For this listener, this solo is one of the musical highlights of the oratorio. It opens with several unison chords in the orchestra, and then she sings on rising vocal lines "I pray thee, O God," supported only by sustained whole-note chords in each measure (p. 144). When she sings to God that he is the God of the afflicted, the music becomes more animated. After "them that are without hope," a poignant descending phrase is heard in the orchestra, repeated a second time an octave lower, a potent musical representation of hopelessness. The mood changes once again after this passage. The vocal range grows steadily higher, reaching *g*" on "God" in the phrase "Thou art the God of all power and might." The next phrase, "And that there is none that protecteth Thy people but Thou," takes the voice up to a sustained *a-flat*" and then the solo ends an octave below that. The lyrical orchestral postlude ends on a clear A-flat major chord. Then a C is repeated three times before turning into an unexpected C major chord, introducing Judith's ordering the gates of the city to be opened (Jdt 10:9). On the last phrase, "those things whereof we have spoken," she sings the last word on a *g*" and *e'*, a large and dramatic descending interval, followed immediately by a long orchestra *fermata* (held note) C. Judith's announcement is followed by a chorus, marked *Allegro con spirito*. Through much of this upbeat chorus (the text is Jdt 10:8), *staccato* (broken) 8th notes are played in the orchestra under the chorus's sustained line.

Scene III: The Exploit of Judith (p. 157)

Though an oratorio, the libretto nonetheless indicates where each scene occurs, presumably to aid the audience's imagination. This scene takes place at the walls of Jerusalem at night. Manasseh and the watchmen are looking out toward the Assyrian camp. An orchestral interlude opens the scene, starting with high soft chords. The mood is one of calm, filled with lyrical passages in the clarinets and other winds. This is followed by a chorus of watchmen, sung to a very regular 4/4 beat to suggest they are pacing around the wall.

Manasseh sings a lovely *arioso* to Jerusalem, "a city held in the hand of God" (p. 160). The watchmen interrupt his soliloquy, singing of their attentiveness and worry but concluding that God watches over all his people. Manasseh sings another short solo, recalling Israel's transgressions and God's punishment, concluding that now God will hear their cries. The watchmen sing a final chorus, in which Manasseh joins them at the end, as do women in the chorus for a resounding conclusion sung by all—"God succoureth his people!"—ending on an F7 chord that Judith resolves as she enters on a *fortissimo* "Ho!" on a high B flat (*b-flat*). She sings several very assertive and high *a cappella* phrases, starting with "Ho! Ye open the walls! Open to me!" (p. 166, bottom). She announces that the Lord has worked wonders by her hand and their enemies have been brought down. This is one of the most anti-climactic moments in the oratorio. Not only does Holofernes never appear, but Judith's act is only briefly described later.

She presents the head, telling the people to hang it "on the highest place before your walls." Much of this is sung *a cappella*, punctuated with dramatic orchestral passages between her phrases. These passages are either *marcato* chords or rapid dotted ascending passages. When she sings about the enemy finding their leader Holofernes's body, the orchestra enters under her, with a lot of dotted rhythm to denote excitement (the text based on Jdt 14:1–4, eliminating Achior altogether). A triumphant chorus follows, in 3/4 time with trills punctuating the second or third beats. The opening words are adapted from Josh 10:19, "Arise, O Israel! Smite ye your enemies," while other descriptions of God's wrath are original with Parry, though borrowing from prophetic texts.

Manasseh summarizes the events in a solo, "God breaketh the battle" (p. 180), which has a very Handelian sound, not atypical for British oratorio composers of that period. In the second part he announces that the Lord overthrew Assur by a woman's hand, then relates Judith's deed: "Her beauty took his mind prisoner, the falchion passed through his neck." Presumably the audience of that era knew the story of Judith, but for any that did not, they would not have a very clear idea of it from this oratorio. Holofernes's name does not even warrant a passing mention. This final solo disappoints, as the mood remains the same throughout; no dramatic change is perceived even at the mention of Judith's deed.

In the Finale (p. 186), Judith sings an amalgam of many Psalms, starting with "I will sing unto the Lord a new song." It is a lengthy anthem of not great textual or musical interest. On her final word, "Israel," the tempo increases to *allegro molto* and to 4/4 time, all sounds of a triumphal chorus. When the chorus enters, the tempo quickens and is marked *alla breve* (also known as cut time and standing for a very quick tempo). The music becomes a Handelian fugue, switching in the middle to A-flat major but ultimately and predictably ending in a bombastic C major.

Conclusion

Though musically and dramatically superior to Henry Leslie's oratorio, Parry's work also has the same shortcomings. The text is virtually all biblical or biblicized English, sounding more like a religious work than a dramatic one. But the greater flaw in Parry's work is that its focus is on an entirely different narrative—from Kings—and Judith is treated almost parenthetically. For an audience that thought they knew the story of Judith, this work would have been very puzzling. Yet the choral music, which predominates, and some of the solos (particularly Judith's prayer) can still be enjoyed for their power and beauty.

The Oratorio in Nineteenth–Twentieth-Century France

The story of Judith was so known and popular in late-nineteenth-century France that in 1876 the Académie des Beaux-Arts chose a play based on the story for the annual Prix de Rome cantata competition, to be set to music by aspiring young composers. In that same year, Charles Lefebvre's opera *Judith* was performed at the Paris Opera (see Chapter 4). The winner of the competition was Paul Hillemacher.[19]

Paul Hillemacher (1852–1933)

Paul Hillemacher studied at the Paris Conservatory where he won several prizes before winning the Grand Prix de Rome. He was known in his time for stage works, symphonies, and songs. He wrote much of his music in collaboration with his brother, Lucien.[20] The librettist for *Judith*, Paul Delair (1842–1894), was a well-known playwright in his time. It was his play that was chosen for the musical competition.

Judith, Scène Lyrique (1876)

The score can be found online.[21] The work has never been recorded. Translations are my own.

> Judith: soprano
> "Zillah": mezzo-soprano
> King of Assyria (Holofernes, promoted to king): bass

It is noteworthy that there are only three characters in this setting, the same three as in Scarlatti's Cambridge *Giuditta* (see Chapter 1).

No. 1A: Introduction and Prayer

The cantata—really only one long scene but divided into *tableaux* or "images" that the audience of the unstaged work could visualize—opens at chapter 9 of the book of

---

[19] Jann Pasler, "Politics, Biblical debates, and French Dramatic Music on Judith after 1870," chap. 24 in *The Sword of Judith, Judith Studies across the Disciplines*, ed. Kevin R. Brine (Cambridge: Open Book, 2010), pp. 434–5. Available online: http://books.openedition.org/obp/972 (ISBN: 9781906924171). Pasler discusses Hillemacher's work from a slightly different perspective in chap. 24, pp. 231–9, and includes musical figures.

[20] John Trevitt in *New Grove Dictionary* (2001), vol. 11, p. 509.

[21] https://babel.hathitrust.org/cgi/pt?id=uc1.c2821777;view=2up;seq=74;size=175 (accessed November 15, 2018).

Judith. The brief and ominous orchestral introduction opens with passionate waves of chromatic 16th notes and leads into a prayer, based loosely on Jdt 9. But the first voice heard is that of "Zillah," presumably Judith's servant.[22] On a single note, Zillah sings "Judith, the evening has come," accompanied by some unusual and unexpected harmonies. She continues, accompanied by the same murmuring groups of 16th notes just heard, to point out the "triumphal tents" of the King of Assyria. Zillah tells Judith to raise her voice in prayer "above the cymbals" and God's power "will descend into your breast," sung on descending pitches and a large interval.

No. 1B: Prayer (Prière)

Judith's prayer follows (p. 3). It starts softly, marked *Andante religioso* and in C major. But the music quickly grows more dramatic as Judith entreats God to pour from her eyes a "sleep without return" (*sommeil sans retour*, probably implying from her eyes into Holofernes's). As the music shifts into quick 16th-note groups of triplets, she prays for the King to fall under his own sword into the trap of love. This text leaves no suspense about what Judith has planned. While the biblical story remains ambiguous about how much planning went into Judith's act, this libretto leaves no doubts. The key and mood change on the word "love" (*amour*), switching to A major and a broad 12/8 time, with four groups of triplets under Judith's triumphant-sounding music. This particular musical pattern, including frequent suspensions, is found several times in the cantata and is very typical of the music of Charles Gounod (1818–1893). Judith sings: "God (*Jehovah*), may a curse fall on anyone who threatens your holy temple or your race," and sings of the "worm … who voraciously gnaws for eternity" as the music softens near the end. This is not so much a prayer as a declaration of faith in an expected triumph. It could not be further in mood or sentiment from British oratorios of the same period (discussed above).

No. 2A: Recitative and Duet

Holofernes now appears (p. 6), though he is called "the King" in this work (which is based on Delair's play, not the Bible; see above). His music is resolute, filled with strong dotted rhythms that become his *leitmotif*. He notices someone in front of his chariot (a striking addition), and when he sees Judith, he tells his sword to "extinguish its anger." When Judith sees him, she excitedly tells Zillah to look at this "sublime warrior" who "gleams like a tower." A continuous *tremolo* creates suspense under their recitative. Zillah addresses Judith as "my daughter," which was also seen in a much earlier work, Scarlatti's Cambridge *Giuditta* (see Chapter 1). She tells her in highly dramatic phrases that build on the King's *leitmotif* that this is the King of Assyria, their oppressor and Judith's victim. That remark suggests that they have a full plan in place. Surely Judith would have recognized the King, so it is possible she was feigning excitement for his benefit. Yet this is not suggested by the music and is contradicted by a later scene.

---

[22] Zillah is named as Lamech's second of two wives in Gen 4:19; but this is unconnected to Judith's story. Judith's servant is named creatively by librettists in every era, for reasons unknown.

The King suggests that Judith is a "spy for the Jews" (*espionne des Juifs*), an ahistorical term used instead of Israelites or Hebrews. Many works, in several languages, use the contemporary word for "Jew" because it was the most understood at the time the works were written. He commands her to appear before him, addressing her with the intimate *tu*; he says she looks like an imposter and asks what she is doing there. She sings "*Toi!*," which is "you" but significantly also in the familiar form, not generally used to address a stranger and certainly not a king but using the same form he used to address her. He is surprised she seems to know him, and she says she knows he is the King. He denies it, in an interesting plot twist. Holofernes is drunk on his power, figuratively (and later literally), but right now this king wants to be in disguise. Judith tells him that if he wants to deny who he is, he needs to change his traits and his stature, and hide his royalty better. This exchange is sung to very strong and assertive music. He asks for her name and she tells him, and when asked what she wants, she declares that she is there to speak for her God who will speak through her voice.

The music suddenly slows to *Adagio* but with a strong and insistent rhythm, as Judith tells the King: "Prepare for the killing," referring to her own people. She continues, singing only on one note in unison with the orchestra's repeated dotted Cs, as her voice and the orchestra gradually ascend chromatically. Above all this, occasional high piccolo shrieks are heard. She sings: "Walk with the sword towards the fire; for the body must fall, since the soul is corrupt, and these insolent people have disavowed their God." The dotted rhythm continues, a propulsive sound, with the bass descending chromatically through several measures. This music paints a very ominous mood. Judith continues, no longer on a single note: "I deliver them into your supreme hand, like a herd without a leader, O King. And I don't want to leave even a dog there to howl at you," the word "dog" (*chien*) sung *fortissimo* on *g*" (p. 11; this is a paraphrase of Jdt 11:19).

The King is startled at Judith's ferocity, saying: "What? You would lead me against your own people, woman?" In a very resolute phrase that suddenly shifts to F minor, he sings: "Is one who betrays, not cursed?" Judith responds in much slower music, marked *Solennel* (solemn; p. 11): "When God commands, one has no more soul; and without understanding, one obeys." A duet follows, opening with an expansive solo by the King, a melody that will reappear often as a second *leitmotif*. He says that Judith has revealed a God who wants us to love and asks if anything flowers on her rosy lips besides anathema. He concludes singing very lyrically: "I am the King, O beautiful Jewess, and I love you" (p. 15). In faster and more excited music, Judith responds that he should raise his sword "which makes your servant tremble," and in a passionate phrase reaching *a flat*" on *soleil* (sun), that the sun seen from so close causes only dread. The King, smiling (score note), replies that sometimes love can arise from fear and that "women love the sword," to which Judith replies: "I agree." The reader might be tempted to find a Freudian meaning in the king's words.

In increasingly expansive phrases, the King reprises his earlier soaring melody as he sings romantic verses to Judith such as: "I hope the hour that has brought you will bring joy … if my splendor frightens you I will divest myself of it this very evening at my feast and I will place my diadem upon your head. O come to the feast, beautiful Jewess, I love you" (consistently using the contemporary term "Jew"). Judith responds: "To be seen in your company in front of the confused servants? I would rather be lowered into a grave." The King is shocked by her words, asking why she is resisting since if there is no rescue for them, it is better to give in. Judith says it is good to die (*c'est grand de mourir*; p. 16), sustaining *grand* on a *fortissimo g*". In a sudden shift to C minor, the King responds, to a melodic variant of his *leitmotif*, that he sees her wildness and needs to capture her God in order to chain Judith. The music changes mood, slowing down into a very insistent and foreboding rhythm. In an aside, Judith prays to her God to help her break her chains. The duet continues with each of them expressing their own wishes and hopes, unheard by the other (pp. 16–19). Only in music can two characters express their feelings simultaneously, as will be seen repeatedly throughout this book. He is singing about putting her in chains, while she sings of breaking the chains.

A recitative follows, over which the orchestra plays a high *tremolo* and the King's "love" *leitmotif*. After assuring Judith that her "modesty is reassured," the King tells Judith they will be alone at his dinner that night, and his eyes alone will be dazzled by her beauty. He also tells her that her "nurse" can be their cupbearer. Judith, "lowering her eyes" (score note) asks, singing on one repeated note in a hesitant sound, if "your servant" can say no to "the master." The music suddenly becomes faster and louder, marked *Allegro appassionato* (p. 21) as he responds: "She is mine, God has given her to me, Love has submitted her to my laws. And who resists a king?" Judith enters after a few measures singing the same phrases and music but referring to the King. Their voices "step on" each other's, while neither is hearing what the other is saying, and the orchestra plays short sighing phrases. At one point they both sing that "love has submitted her/him" and that "he/she is subject to my laws" (pp. 22–3). Shortly before the final phrase, the two sing a few *a cappella* measures, in which Judith's voice descends chromatically—a subtle musical suggestion that either she is losing the battle of wills or that she wants the King to think so. On the final repeat of "she/he is mine," Judith sustains an *a*" while the King sustains a *c*, both notes high in their ranges and a very dramatic conclusion. They end on a unison E flat, as if they were of one mind. The orchestral conclusion is filled with *tremolos* (p. 25). This is the end of the first *tableau*.

No. 3: Symphonic Introduction

The very martial introduction features trumpet calls coming from both the orchestra and from within the theater (score note, p. 26), a very effective and rarely used device. It was notably employed by Hector Berlioz in his Requiem of 1837, certainly known to Hillemacher. These measures of fanfare are followed by more martial music, marked *tempo di marcia* in the score.

No. 4: Recitative and Aria

In his recitative (p. 28), marked *Allegro risoluto*, the King calls for someone to remove his bloody armor, because the day is for combat, but the night is for love. This leads into an aria that opens to militaristic music and text, where the King sings about the battlefield. But the music suddenly grows quiet as he says the night is for another kind of intoxication. In the aria that follows, the King returns to his militaristic mood, singing of the thirty battles they have won and the thirty kings they have killed. But he sings angrily that Judah, in the mountains, has resisted but will crumble with its God. This is a softened version of the original text in which Holofernes says "we will consume them, and their mountains will be drunk with their blood" (Jdt 6:4). After this phrase is repeated twice in very strong music, the music suddenly shifts to a slow and sad mood (p. 31). The King sings with melancholy (score note), in a lilting, pastoral 6/8 tune, of his beautiful serene gardens, where he has gathered "sensuous figures, women and plants." In slower music, he sings of searching for the most beautiful women, whom his eyes have not yet found. This section creates sympathy for the King, or at least makes him seem more human and multidimensional than the biblical Holofernes. The mood then changes abruptly, almost as though the King is stopping himself from this reverie, into a rollicking 3/4 time drinking song. The King sings that the joy of drums, and of love, is vain and should be drowned in wine. In the next stanza, the King sings of wine—or death—that delivers us from remorse and the sadness of life (p. 34). This passing mention of death certainly lends a touch of irony to the King's drinking song.

No. 5: Scene and Trio

The ensuing trio is between the three characters: the King, Judith, and Zillah. The King opens with a recitative (marked *Poco appassionato*) singing: *Ce vin magique et ton regard de feu, De roi me feront passer Dieu* ("This magical wine and your fiery gaze, from King will turn me into God"). Then he sings a lilting drinking song, in a broad and *marcato* 9/8 time signature: "Pour, pour, O nurse, the dark wine, the wine purple like blood" (pp. 36–7). The reference to blood, though not subtle, is still an interesting touch of irony. He repeats the verses twice, building the second time to *fortissimo*. Judith enters to the same rollicking drinking-song tune, but it is softer and there is a more menacing bass line. This is a wonderful example of music creating a subtext: the same music with a slight change of key or the addition of a contrasting voice can establish an entirely different mood. She tells the King that she dreams of his victories. He asks if not even one of those is worth a kiss. At this, the music shifts to steady foreboding *tremolos* as Zillah tells him ominously that "in a kiss, all your glories will be crushed." Then the rollicking theme returns, but each time it is repeated in different keys to suggest a change in mood. The King asks Judith why she isn't drinking, and she responds that she is dreaming of his wives. He says: "If you like, they will all die." And she answers back: "And from the grave the jealous ones will watch you." The King sings "Ah" to a rapid and loud chromatic unison descent in the orchestra, leading back to the drinking song.

All three now join in to sing it, and it builds continually in speed and volume up to the climactic ending. The tempo suddenly slows as Judith expresses how she feels she is drowning in wine (p. 44). This is an addition to the biblical story that suggests a cleverer and more manipulative Judith. By feigning drunkenness, she will throw the King off guard. Under a soaring new theme, he asks her to cool his face "with your wing, O my dove," and "gather in your arms your King as he succumbs" (p. 45). As the lyrical theme abruptly stops, Judith sings very slowly in an aside, "the arms of the grave." The King, clearly drunk, sings "Alas" several times on long sustained notes and then repeats snatches of his earlier arias under unstable shifting harmonies. Gradually his voice fades and Judith notes that he is asleep.

In a complete change from the biblical plot, it is Zillah who points out where the King's sword is hanging, ready for Judith to seize it and chop off the King's head. This increases the servant's role and decreases Judith's initiative (also excluding her prayers to God for strength). In fact, Judith hesitates and Zillah urges her on. Judith comments on how handsome the King is, and asks: "Who made me executioner?" Zillah very assertively and angrily says: "Doubt and blasphemy!", while Judith murmurs sadly (*con dolore* in the score): "He says he loves me," to which Zillah responds: "It is an insult to God!" But Judith still wavers: "Let God strike him, then; he made me a woman, not an executioner." Needless to say, this is a corruption of the biblical narrative but reflects the thinking of that time. Judith is portrayed as weak and vulnerable while the servant seems to be older and wiser. There was discomfort with the strength and independence of Judith, who was not seen as a role model. So, reading between the lines, the librettist created a story that, while very plausible, runs counter to the original.

Then the King begins mumbling in his sleep (this was found in earlier works, such as Scarlatti's and Arne's; see Chapter 1). Librettists seemed unconvinced that a drunken stupor could not be interrupted. He mumbles about how many kings he has killed and how he will destroy Judah and its God. Zillah points out to Judith how he is singing about his exploits and Judith says: "He has just condemned himself!" It is not clear why Judith did not know of the King's evil deeds earlier or why she needed this kind of proof; perhaps she just needed a reminder to egg her on. To highly dramatic music, Judith sings: "The sword is ready, let's go! Die, die!" (p. 49). Then, unaccompanied, she sings: "His head is at my feet," rising to *a flat"* on *tête* (head), "and my foot on his head," dropping on the last word to *d flat'*, a leap of more than an octave and a half. These measures show a powerful and fearless Judith. In addition, the dramatic musical descent vividly conveys the dropping of the sword and the head. The final measure is a *fortissimo* (actually marked *fff*, which is louder than the loudest) D-flat major chord and *tremolo*.

Judith now sings: "Let us flee, the camp is asleep and God will guide us," over excited 16th-note passages and *tremolos* of chromatically ascending and descending chords (p. 50), connoting fear and suspense. On the final repeat of "guide us," the accompaniment calms to sets of triplets under a duet between Judith and Zillah. The music once again has strong echoes of Gounod and his opera *Faust* of 1859, which was already very popular when this work was written. (Gounod's later opera *Roméo et Juliette* premiered in 1867 and would have also been known to Hillemacher). The time signature is 12/8, with four steady groups of triplets under the voices that follow each other or sing homophonically. They sing: "Jehovah, a curse on those who would threaten your holy temple," and continue praising God's power. The duet ends softly as the two women sing *Seigneur* (Lord) and high chords die out to conclude the cantata, somewhat unexpectedly and very softly. In fact, the marking is *pppp* for the final "Lord," which is meant to be as soft as possible and almost unheard. This would be highly effective when done well.

Conclusion

This work, though called a "scène" or "cantata," has the drama of an opera. New dimensions of both Judith and Holofernes are explored and the dialogue is a refreshing break from the biblically stiff text of the British oratorios explored previously. Music and the original text combine to create a true modern midrash, stimulating the reader to go back and look for nuances in the biblical text never before considered. Judith's portrayal is ambivalent: she seems cleverer than her biblical counterpart, yet she also wavers and seems vulnerable to the King's advances. This mixed picture is more realistic and multidimensional than the biblical portrait.

Arthur Honegger (1892–1955)

Arthur Honegger was a Swiss-French composer, a member of *Les Six*, a group of young composers that also included Francis Poulenc and Darius Milhaud. His musical style, however, was more serious than that of others in the group. Honegger developed unusual musical and dramatic forms in large scale works for voices and orchestra. He was one of the most skilled composers in counterpoint in the twentieth century (counterpoint is basically writing melodies in conjunction with one another), clearly inspired by Johann Sebastian Bach. Though his musical language is essentially tonal, it is characterized by a highly individual use of dissonance. Though Honegger expressed admiration for Claude Debussy and Maurice Ravel, his music is often more uncompromising than theirs. At the conservatory, his discovery of Wagner and Richard Strauss had a profound effect on his emerging musical language.[23] Honegger's musical influences were primarily drawn from three musical cultures: German, French, and Swiss.[24]

Honegger remained in Paris after seven years of study at the Paris Conservatoire. He soon asserted his own strong personality in the incidental music he wrote for Swiss poet Rene Morax's "dramatic psalm" *Le Roi David* (1921, rev. 1923), which catapulted him to international prominence (see Leneman 2010).[25] *Judith* was also originally written as incidental music for a Morax biblical drama. Honegger then revised that version for the stage as an *opéra sérieux* (1926). The work was subsequently transformed into an oratorio, or *action musicale*, for the concert hall (1927). Later, Honegger also produced an *opera-seria* version, which in fact after many transformations, became his first opera. Moreover, two different versions of the *drame biblique* (biblical drama) were also discovered, the second one containing movements that later found their way

---

[23] Geoffrey K. Spratt in *New Grove Dictionary* (2001), vol. 11, pp. 679–84.
[24] Kate Espasandin, "Musical Modernism at the People's Theatre" (McGill University, Montreal, 2013), at https://escholarship.mcgill.ca/concern/theses/6108vf73w?locale=en, p. 28 (accessed November 2, 2018). There is a wealth of information in this online thesis, including the complicated performance history of Honegger's Judith.
[25] Helen Leneman, *Love, Lust, and Lunacy: The Stories of Saul and David in Music* (Sheffield: Sheffield Academic Press, 2010).

into the opera and *action musicale*.[26] This tangled history creates some difficulty in identifying which version is being discussed.

In *Judith*, the chorus is represented as a unified gathering of valued individuals rather than a single entity. Honegger does this by selecting different members of the chorus as soloists. In the work's opening movement, *Lamentations*, for example, a woman steps out from the crowd to address Judith directly in the name of the people of Bethulia. Crowd scenes are given important dramatic value in *Judith* (as they are in many oratorios) conveying a sense of united community, a crucial value to Honegger and Morax's social and humanist concerns.[27] Like most *Judith* oratorios, the work both opens and closes with a crowd scene.

The plot of *Judith* centers on the two women, Judith and her servant. In all the versions, the musical language is fundamentally tonal and strongly characterized by unity and coherence. Stylistic eclecticism is evident, with allusions from Gregorian chant and Protestant hymns to jazz, alongside frequent use of complex polyphony and occasionally polytonality. Honegger also experiments with complex harmonies and dense rhythmic counterpoints. Morax's dramatic treatment of the story, its strong orientalist and erotic flavors, owes more to Oscar Wilde's *Salome* than to the original story. Kate Espasandin suggests:

> The troubled psychological profile of Honegger's and Morax's heroine is not dissimilar to other contemporary (or slightly earlier) operatic efforts whose composers shared a similar interest in psychosis or psychotic characters. These include Strauss with *Salome* (1905) and *Elektra* (1909)[28]

These are interesting parallels, but most readers of the book of Judith would not agree with this assessment of her "psychotic" tendencies. Such modernist readings do not consider historical context or the meaning of the biblical text. This is an example of more "reading into" than "reading of."

Honegger had wanted to write only operas, and even wrote some operas as a child; but later he felt the lyric theater was in decline. In *Judith*, the lack of psychological conflict, development, and resolution in the characterization of its operatic reworking mitigated against its establishment in the repertoire.[29] Espasandin writes of Honegger and Morax's *Judith*:

> Judith's tortuous chromatic lines and exotic dissonant harmonies succeed in depicting her complex and ambiguous psychological journey characterized by both the beauty of her sacrifice and the barbarity of her actions, by innocence and guilt.[30]

---

[26] Espasandin, p. 34.
[27] Espasandin, p. 46.
[28] Espasandin, p. 44.
[29] Spratt, p. 682.
[30] Espasandin, p. 78.

These comments leave the biblical scholar wondering what book of Judith this writer was reading. What exactly is Judith's "sacrifice," also mentioned elsewhere, when it is suggested that Judith "sacrificed her virginity." This, too, is imaginary. And Judith was not considered guilty of any crime at the time the book was written, and in its reception.

Commenting on a newly released and first recording of this work in 1995, on the Vanguard label, commentator Lynn René Bayley writes:

> Judith is a great work; it's just not a great opera. With only two characters, a narrator and a chorus that takes roughly a third of the score, it was a mistake for Honegger to classify it as an opera … The music, though a bit more understated than its more famous sister, is gripping.[31]

Critics agree that the music is relatively static and that most of the interest lies in the libretto. It was performed only a few times in the decades after its premiere, and only once in the United States when *Judith*'s original choral director, Paul Boepple, successfully revived the *action musicale* in 1961 in New York.

In liner notes, music scholar S. W. Bennett writes:

> Honegger's idiom in *Judith* is basically tonal, while exploring the area of dissonant harmonies with searing emotional effect and sometimes approaching the polytonal, in superimposed chords of different keys. His vocal writing, like his orchestral, is particularly beautiful. The prevailing use of freely rhapsodic melodic lines gives extra impact to the contrasting passages of violently propulsive rhythm when they occur, as in the Incantation (No. 7). And one of the most touching uses of the "wordless cry" occurs near the close of No. 8, where it is heard from a distant tenor in interplay with a soft, orchestral fanfare.[32]

Judith, Drame Biblique, Words by Rene Morax (1925)

Judith: mezzo-soprano
Servant: soprano
Holofernes: baritone
Ozias: bass

A recording (2013) of Honegger's first version that I used for this analysis, of the *action musicale* or oratorio, is available on YouTube.[33] The printed score I obtained is Editions Maurice Senart (Paris, 1925), entitled *Opéra sérieux en trois actes et cinque tableaux,*

[31] Lynn René Bayley, "Honegger's "Judith" a Great Find!," *Art Music Lounge*, 2017. Available online: https://artmusiclounge.wordpress.com/2017/07/28/honeggers-judith-a-great-find/ (accessed November 2, 2018). The "sister" referred to here is Honegger's more popular *Le Roi David* (see Leneman 2010).

[32] http://graphicwitness.org/music/linernotes/honegger.htm (accessed November 6, 2018).

[33] https://www.youtube.com/watch?v=bTSF-CIQXqI (accessed May 1, 2020).

which would have been staged; whereas the recording, and the version discussed in Espasandin's thesis, is the unstaged, numbered oratorio version. In order to avoid discussing the two works separately—since the music is largely the same, and only the scene division and the presence or absence of a narrator differentiate them—I am combining the two (indicating which version I am discussing where) in hopes of reducing (hopefully not increasing) confusion.

Part 1 (or Act 1)

No. 1: Lamentations

Summary: The women of Bethulia lament in front of Judith's window where she can be heard praying behind the curtains. The town is under siege with no access to water. A woman in the crowd asks Judith to open the gates of the town to halt the siege.

The opening measures feature eerie high trills on the piano and flute, on a striking dissonant chord of a major seventh: G flat below F (see Figure 2). This is followed by strident, harsh string sounds. This music recalls Bernard Hermann's score for Alfred Hitchcock's 1960 film *Psycho*. Since Hermann studied composers of Honegger's circle early in his life, it is plausible that this shrill opening of the oratorio remained etched in his mind. The opening choral section is "rich in inconclusive dissonant harmonies and obsessive chromaticism which are mirrored in the orchestral part."[34] After a few measures of a women's chorus, Judith sings a solo of lamentation, begging God for pity and acknowledging that God's punishment is for their wrongs. The chorus interjects every few measures. Judith also moans wordlessly for several measures, echoed by the women's chorus. Throughout the oratorio, Honegger makes an especially haunting use of long-drawn sighing wordless phrases. They are heard in this choral scene and again in the second scene. In this passage, the orchestral part's "torturous harmonies … depict Judith's own indecision and troubled emotional state." Honegger explores "grinding harmonies and serpentine chromatic lines for Judith."[35]

No. 2: La Trompe d'alarme *(The Warning Trumpet)*

Summary: Ozias, the Governor, followed by the elders and the guards, enters and tells the women that if reinforcements have not arrived in five days, he will give the town to Holofernes. Ozias then asks the guards to sound the horn of alarm to disperse the crowd. He leaves the stage followed by the elders.

A narrator relates all of this (on the recording; in the score, Ozias sings this text, pp. 7–8). His announcement is followed by mournful sighing phrases led by trumpet. The women's voices sing wordless chromatic and dissonant phrases. In the opera, Judith appears on the terrace with her servant (p. 10) and sings pensively that the people have doubted God. She asks Bethulia if they have lost their faith. Then, accompanied by a repeated group of 16th-note ascending and descending phrases, almost a hypnotic

---

[34] Espasandin, p. 59.
[35] Espasandin, p. 59.

Figure 2　Arthur Honegger, opening music

effect, she sings of seeing the blazing army in the distance from her balcony. But, she says: "Strength is not in great numbers, but in the heart and in faith." As she sings these lines, a soprano sings a wordless lament from the wings, a very effective device.

Judith tells her servant to prepare her festive and most beautiful clothes. The servant asks her where she wants to go (p. 13), while the women's chorus wails in the background. She says she is going to make a sacrifice pleasing to God as voices continue to moan in the background. She tells the servant "that which no man in Israel will dare to do, I will undertake." Then she tells her to leave her alone for her prayers. There might be a subtle suggestion here of the anti-Semitic trope of the weak Israelite man. But more likely, this phrase is intended to show Judith's power and self-confidence. Only the reader or listener can decide.

No. 3: Prière *(Prayer)*

Summary: Judith appears on her balcony dressed in black. She stands up abruptly when she hears the horns. Questioned by her servant, she explains she will be leaving Bethulia that night in her best dress and jewels. She then prays to God asking him to help her seduce Holofernes, concluding: *Je suis l'offrande et je suis la victime* ("I am the offering and I am the victim"). The servant then draws the curtains.

Judith's Prayer is one of the work's most extended and spacious scenes for solo voice in this work. It demonstrates Honegger's expressive, speech-inflected declamatory line, interweaving with the orchestra in a way that Debussy broke ground for in *Pélleas et Mélisande* (1898), although Honegger made this technique his own. Judith's prayer opens with a motif played on flutes, following which she sings *a cappella* phrases pleading with God to listen to her and help her. Judith's first line resembles "a lament with a distinct 'oriental' flavor" in Espasandin's words. Although there are no stereotypical oriental characteristics such as sophisticated melodic ornaments *(melismas)*, the lyrical, expressive melody spans a wider range than previously sung by the chorus and is rhythmically intricate. Espasandin further notes that "the repetitiveness of both melody and accompaniment produces a sense of quasi-hypnotic stasis ... the chromatic *ostinato* in the orchestral part and the open fifth heard in the bass ... also contribute to this sense of otherness produced by Judith's lament."[36]

The music grows more animated and the accompaniment is filled with jagged rhythms as she asks God to "raise your arm as in past centuries ... crush their power ... let the pride of this man feel your anger." In a faster but softer, more intense section, featuring effective muted trumpets, she sings:

> Give my eyes the splendor of desire, let his heart be troubled by my smile and let him be taken in by my sweet words, for I am a woman and weakness is my weapon ... Save my people with your sanctuary. I am the offering and I am the victim.

The text suggests a more self-aware Judith than her biblical counterpart or seen in other librettos. Judith concludes by proclaiming the God of Heaven and Earth, the only, Eternal God, as high ethereal chords rise above her voice. The final measures reprise the opening theme and continue to rise, ending on an unexpected tonic E major chord that has the effect of a ray of hope.

---

[36] Espasandin, p. 57.

No. 4: Cantique Funèbre *(Song of Mourning)*

Summary: The women of Bethulia appear on stage again, lamenting. Night has fallen and Ozias approaches the gate guarded by his soldiers and the elders, and tells them to push the crowd aside. Judith appears, followed by her servant. Ozias attempts to stop Judith but finally agrees to let her go.

This section makes a climactic use of the wordless, sustained cry, here heard from the female chorus under a soaring, high solo soprano line. The mournful sound is atonal but with an occasional unexpected resolution into a tonal moment. A soprano soloist sings: "Oh Bethulia abandoned, we cry but no one consoles us." The women's chorus sings repeated "Ahs" on descending half steps, known as a *seufzer* or sigh; the contraltos echo these phrases an octave lower, after which the soprano chorus repeats the solo line. Then a new section starts, and to a relentless marching rhythm in the background, the chorus sings *De la maison que batirent nos pères Il ne restera plus rien* ("Nothing will remain of the house our fathers built") as the sopranos sing *Pierre sur pierre, et sur le lieu qu'occupait Bethulie ne fleuriront que l'absinthe et l'ortie* ("Stone upon stone, and on the place where Bethulia was, only wormwood and nettle will grow"). The line is first sung in a low register, after which the sopranos echo the phrase an octave higher. There is notable dissonance here as the sopranos sing *d'* over the altos' *c'*. Sopranos continue their wordless lament over the more rhythmic section (p. 21), and throughout. At one point the sopranos and altos sing together in thirds while the soprano soloist sings an octave above them. All the women briefly sing "Ah" on a descending half-step motif. Like the prayer just heard, this chorus also ends on a tonic chord, after a final solo "Ah" sung softly on a slur, echoed by a flute.

On the recording, a narrator describes the departure of Judith, how beautiful she looked, so that no one questioned her but they blessed her. In the score (opera), Judith sings: "Let us prevent this madness at all costs, soldiers, clear this crowd and do not approach the gate; there is no danger tonight" (p. 25). The people murmur excitedly: "There she is, there she is." Ozias approaches and asks Judith if it is from her that this light is coming and this joy is flowing. She tells him to open the gate for her, but he refuses to expose her to "outrage" or even death. She reminds him that he gave her his word as a soldier. He says she at least needs an escort, and she tells him God is with her—what more does she need? Ozias has no answer and orders the gate to be opened.

No. 5: Invocation

Summary: Ozias blesses Judith and the chorus prays for her safety. Judith and her servant walk away.

This chorus (p. 28), marked *lent* (very slow), almost has the sound of a Gregorian chant, but instead of singing in homophonic thirds, the women and men alternately sing repeated notes in a free chant style. The men's and women's voices continue to follow each other as a sort of echo, until they finally overlap. The music continually rises in pitch with eerie string passages above the voices. The tempo gradually increases and then slows down near the end. The conclusion is a unison hum sung by all the voices. They pray to the "God of war ... to protect her [Judith]," who is their last hope, and they beg God to extend his hand to her. In the final measure (p. 30), only altos and basses sing "Ah" but as a hum (with mouth closed; note in score) on an A—low in the range, finally ending on A major but in the first inversion (the tonic is not the bottom note), which feels slightly unresolved.

Part 2 (or Act 2)

No. 6: Fanfare

An orchestral interlude filled with trumpet sounds sets the stage for a military scene.

In the opera version, this is Scene 1 of Act 2. The servant opens the scene, singing that the night is turning into dawn, as the trumpet fanfares just heard play very softly as though in an echo above her voice (p. 32). Judith joins her and says they should remain at the spring, where the water "cooled my burning forehead but not my soul." A tenor soloist sings wordless chants from the wings during Judith's recitative. She asks God to give her a sign, and sings: "I hold up to you this freezing, clear water in my two hands, and my troubled, weak heart that hesitates and trembles. Ah, what have I done that you do not answer?" (p. 33). She is accompanied only by a low sustained chord and the tenor's lamenting chant. He stops when the servant begins speaking. She asks Judith why she is weeping, and Judith responds that she presumed too much of her strength; but the servant reassures her that God will not abandon them. Judith replies that her only hope is in death. Despondently, as the tenor once again chants a lament, she says she does not know what she is supposed to do—*je ne sais pas*, "I don't know," she repeats softly in a low register. The tempo suddenly doubles in speed, repeating the trumpet fanfares, as they exit (p. 34). The section grows much softer as the tenor sings a few more measures of his chant, "sounding far away" (score note) and finally dying out completely.

No. 7 (Scene 2 in the Opera): Incantation

Summary: In front of Holofernes's tent, the priests and warriors of Assur gather around the sacrificial fire. They implore their god, Marduk, to give them Bethulia. Holofernes walks out of his tent to talk to his advisor Bagoas, who tells him that the oracle has predicted a change but not a victory.

This highly dramatic section opens with rhythmic, pulsating music, as the male chorus repeatedly asks their goddess and god of war Ishtar and Marduk how long they still have to wait. The music depicting Holofernes's camp differs in many ways from that attached to Bethulia. It is more decisive and direct, marked by a more precise rhythmic and structural drive. Thus, Espasandin points out, "it contrasts with Judith's and Bethulia's tortuous chromatic lines, intricate rhythms and richer, denser harmonies."[37] Very dissonant and pounding chords in the strings are heard above the chorus's unison

---

[37] Espasandin, p. 60.

prayer. The movement's orchestral part is primarily made up of an animated two-bar *ostinato* with strong, forcefully accented beats. The dissonant harmonies are almost overwhelmed by the *ostinato*'s forceful rhythmic drive, propelling the movement forward dramatically. "When will we take the city?" the chorus sings in *fortissimo* and strongly accented phrases. Sharply dissonant chords play under the unison voices, which are treated rhythmically rather than melodically.

In the second part, the tenors briefly sing a more melodic prayer to Ishtar while the lower male voices continue to repeat *Réponds* (Answer) on an accented descending third (p. 38). The tenors pick up this motif while the basses sing a prayer to Marduk. Then the tenors sing more aggressive texts as the insistent rhythmical and *marcato* accompaniment is played in a much higher range. Addressing their gods, they sing such bloodthirsty words as "Crush them like a hornet's nest, disperse their ashes to the winds, the odor of blood will fill your nostrils" (p. 41). The phrases "When will we take the city?" and "Answer, answer" are reprised in a higher key, sung almost frantically, *fff* (louder than loud), with a sharply dissonant chord repeated with their voices. The chorus continues to accelerate before dying down to lower pitches sung *pianissimo*. The music for this chorus is in sharp contrast to the Israelites' choruses, making a distinction through music of their differing goals and moods.

In the opera, not the oratorio, Holofernes now comes out of his tent to join the soldiers in prayers to Marduk and Ishtar (p. 43), in strongly marked 4/4 time—more militaristic than prayerful. He sings to the "gods of Assur," who will accompany them the next day: "I raise to your mouth, thirsty for vengeance, this cup of wine in which blood is fermented: bring luck to our army tomorrow" (p. 44). Bagoas tells Holofernes he is overheated and offers him wine cooled in the snow (a particularly odd but vivid detail). Holofernes tells him that what he needs to refresh his senses is "that Israelite woman who came to the camp this morning" and orders Bagoas to find her. Holofernes sings to his men about the great victory they will have the next day. He interrupts himself and announces that "it is Ishtar herself who appears to us in the light of our torches," as Judith approaches.

The scene between Judith and Holofernes in the opera (pp. 48–52) is more prolonged and interesting than in the earlier oratorio version (it will be discussed below, with No. 9 bis, the Death of Holofernes).

No. 8: Scène de la Source *(Scene at the Spring)*

Summary: Judith and her servant stop by a spring near Holofernes's camp. The servant expresses doubts and asks Judith to go back, but she refuses.

The narrator describes Judith's approach to Holofernes's "golden tent." She greets Holofernes by bowing to the ground, and he tells her to rise and have no fear. As in the original story, Holofernes is seduced by her beauty. He gives Judith and her servant permission to go down to the spring every night for their purification. Slow and tranquil music now begins. Behind the scene (*dans la coulisse*), the servant sings of staying close to the spring. As she continues to sing, a tenor soloist sings extended melismatic phrases on "Ah," mostly *a cappella* and modal. The servant also sings mostly *a cappella*. This section shows a strong influence of Debussy's *Pélleas et Mélisande* (1902). The singing is interrupted by sudden dissonant chromatic phrases in the orchestra. The tempo doubles as a few bars of trumpets sounding far away are heard, a sort of fanfare. Then the tenor concludes the scene, sounding "very far away" (score note) and dying away on the last phrase. The narrator states that Judith remains in Holofernes's tent.

No. 9: Musique de Fête *(Festive music) (Oratorio Version Only)*

Summary: After a drunken feast, Holofernes retires to his tent and asks Judith to follow him. He falls asleep and Judith beheads him.

This section is for orchestra only. Accompanied by repeated short *staccato* phrases in the strings and trumpets, winds play sinuous phrases suggestive of exotic dancing. These modal passages hint at an "oriental" sound. But the background trumpets insert a contrasting, foreboding element. The narrator announces that Holofernes is "heated up" (*chauffé*) by the wine. In a slight change from the original story, he only now calls for Judith to keep him company—meaning he did his drinking without persuasion. Judith now flatters him, saying she has never met a greater man. Then she offers him sweets, and his heart is "filled with desire." This libretto goes further than others: Holofernes pulls Judith toward him to kiss her lips; she shivers and pulls away. Only then does he feel overcome by wine and lie down, after telling his servant to turn down the sheets. Once he is in bed, Judith prays. In this version, it seems pretty clear that Holofernes passes out before getting beyond a kiss. The tent is closed, and Judith's servant keeps watch.

No. 9 bis: La Mort d'Holopherne *(The Death of Holofernes)*

This is the first of three "bis" (encore) movements, added later and incorporated into both the oratorio and opera versions.

The Opéra Sérieux *Version*

The scene opens with suspenseful music: short repeated piano notes and plucked double bass suggest stealth, while ascending passages in very low bass clarinets add a mysterious sound. Holofernes invites Judith to sit by his side and she says with exaggerated modesty, in sinuous music, "that is too great an honor for your servant." He asks her for her name, then invites her to join him in drinking to their expected victory the next day. She tells him that her law forbids her from drinking unconsecrated wine. This is one of the only librettos I have found that includes a reference to Judith's dietary laws. Holofernes says "all right" gruffly, but she tells him to take the cup on which she wet her lips as a pledge of an alliance. He continues to urge her to come closer, and she asks why he is treating her like a *femme vile* ("vile woman"). He says that her eyes and her mouth are false, and he reads hatred in her heart—but he wants her as she is, beautiful and irritating, like a horse under the spurs. Judith says: "It is not right to deride me this way" (*me railler*), and he responds in faster and more rhythmic phrases: "You think I'm deriding [or mocking] you? Then drink, it's your turn and I want you to." This time Judith gives in, saying she will drink because he wishes it. In the original text, Judith goes to great lengths to avoid drinking or eating non-kosher food and wine, so this addition is not true to the biblical story. Judith's stringent adherence to her laws is an important element of her character. In this version, she apparently decides that giving in is the only way to conquer Holofernes. The music slows and becomes almost sinister as Holofernes sings: "The trace of your lips has been erased, and now it is on your lips that I want to celebrate my victory" (p. 51). The music slows even further as soldiers are heard in the background singing: "Victory to our leader, victory!" In much broader and slower music, Holofernes asks Judith why she is trembling in his arms and turning her eyes away. She replies that the wine and the noise have dazed her. He tells her to go and lie down, as night has fallen and they can meet again tomorrow.

In very slow and languid music, Holofernes muses about Judith: "You are here, near me, and I have always been waiting for you, resplendent and formidable, woman with the mysterious eyes, like death." This last phrase is an interestingly prescient remark. Judith tells him that she came as a supplicant, to implore clemency from him. Angered, Holofernes tells her, over dissonant chords, that he is a hard, pitiless man. Then he asks why she is smiling at that remark. She tells him that being a hard man does not mean he is not just. She is sure he would have pity if he saw the women and children dying of thirst at the dry wells. Holofernes tells her the end is near. A high violin *obbligato* is heard above the orchestra and Judith's voice, adding poignancy to her plea: "These are my people, and this is my city: have pity on them." His answer: "Oh how beautiful your eyes are, filled with tears; come, messenger of pleasure" (*messager de volupté*). Judith answers: "I am yours—but save my people." He reminds her that they dared to resist, while she continues to plead for mercy. This retelling eliminates a crucial element of the original story, in which Judith offers Holofernes her services as a spy. She did not go to him only to plead for her people, because she would have known that was useless.

The tempo suddenly doubles, and under repetitive groups of dissonant and chromatic chords, Holofernes sings on strongly accented notes: "No! I want to annihilate your race! To set your town on fire, massacre your people down to the last one. And I want you in my arms, crying with joy and horror." Several measures of weeping phrases (*seufzer*) follow, as Holofernes asks Judith where she is and tells her to move closer. It has obviously grown dark by now. As Judith responds, horns play groups of triplets (p. 59, bottom). She sings: "I am here, near you." Holofernes sings: "No weakness, no pity; I am strong, and great as a god." This phrase might suggest that he is about to rape Judith, but the next few measures of rhythmically lopsided groups of 8th notes, slowing down and hesitating, suggest Holofernes is already stumbling. Just after these measures, a *tremolo* is heard and Judith sings *mezza voce* ("half voice," very softly) "He is asleep." There is a suggestion that a rape was attempted, but it is ambiguous.

Judith now prays to her God asking for strength and courage. In soft music suggesting stealth and suspension, the servant tells Judith that the camp is sleeping "like a drunkard moaning in his bed." The stealthy music continues and begins to build as the servant tells Judith that she saw clearly that Holofernes was drunk. Eerie strings and flutes play above her voice. Powerful suspense is created through these musical devices. Then the servant asks God if he will really permit this crime. Based on this remark, it would seem that the two women had already made a plan, but it was not included in the libretto. The servant continues: "Time flows slowly, like blood from an open wound." She says she is afraid, then suddenly asks: "Who is walking in the shadows?" Making the moment still more suspenseful, a *glissando* (instruments gliding up and down between notes, an eerie sound) is heard in the orchestra as the servant asks: "Who sighed?" Then she comments on the sounds she is hearing:

> A blow—who struck it? Another blow,
> and something heavy fell to the ground.
> What happened? Who is coming? O, my mistress!

Glissando passages are played between the servant's breathless phrases. It is a harrowing and effective presentation of Judith's act, occurring offstage. This is one of the most effective musical descriptions of the beheading in all the works discussed here.

Judith now appears, carrying something wrapped in a red cloth, a sword in her right hand. (Here as in most works, the food bag in the biblical text is never mentioned.) The tempo is marked "agitated," and in quick, short phrases Judith tells the servant what she did. The only accompaniment to these few measures is a repeated dissonant augmented major seventh chord: *e"-d#"* played off the beat in each measure by *pizzicato* (plucked) strings (pp. 64–5). Then Judith tells the servant they will leave the camp, but they will not run. Suddenly the music stops as a guard asks who is there; Judith tells him it is the two Israelite women, on their way to the spring. He lets them go (as they have gone there every evening). The act ends on an open fifth chord, A-E, an unresolved sound.

Part 3   *(Act 3 in the opera)*

No. 10: Notturno *(Nocturne)*

This is an orchestral interval. The music is surprisingly lyrical and quite Impressionistic. The narrator enters at the end, describing "abandoned Bethulia" where the women light their lamps. It is not clear what "abandoned" means in this context, unless it implies abandoned by God. Judith approaches the gate, awaiting a sign.

No. 10 bis: Retour di Judith *(Judith's Return)*

This is another "bis" scene, added later to the oratorio and opera.

The narrator continues, with more agitated music under his words. The people hear and see Judith and all shout at once, a sense of pandemonium created by the chaotic music. Judith announces her victory and shows the head of Holofernes. The crowd murmurs. As she describes what she has done, the music becomes very excited and polytonal (several keys playing simultaneously). Judith sings in a high range describing what God has done through her hand.

In the opera, the scene opens with Judith calling out to the guards to open the gates. Ozias and a soldier "on the rampart" call out an alert. In a very excited and complex chorus, the people are calling out Judith's name, Ozias is announcing that Judith has returned with "great news," and Judith continues calling out to open the gate (pp. 68–9). As she enters, Judith sings:

Praise the Eternal, he was my right hand.
Look what he has done by my hand.
Everyone, look at this man, it is our enemy Holofernes.

She is obviously holding up the head when she sings these lines. These phrases are sung to rhythmically jagged, excited, and broken phrases, with a steady high *tremolo* above the voice. The chorus responds by singing several unison chromatically descending wordless phrases on "Ah." Then Judith tells them the enemy was going to attack that morning but are now like a flock without their shepherd (from Jdt 11:19). She urges them to attack now, seconded by Ozias who calls on God to disperse the enemy while the people all sing "To battle, to battle." The music adds frenzy to this scene.

No. 11: Cantique de la bataille *(Battle Song)*

In this very dissonant and challenging choral number (for the chorus and the listener), the Assyrian soldiers sing "Ho ho ho" in aggressive and cacophonous music. The trumpets and orchestral shrieks suggest the sounds of a battlefield very effectively. The chorus is divided into two distinct forces: one, the Israelites, speak the text asking Jehovah to disperse the enemy. Their first spoken line is: "Watch out, the rats have come out of their holes." The other chorus, the Assyrians, sings a wordless *ostinato* characterized by a sharp rhythmic profile. This music depicts the action of the battle and the warriors' cries. Espasandin points out that "the two groups are assigned either a purely musical (passive) or a purely dramatic (active) role. The unusual juxtaposition of spoken and sung choral parts in this passage helps create a barbaric and fierce atmosphere for the battle scene."[38] This scene is not enacted on stage (even in the staged version) but only described vividly through music. The spoken text is essential but dramatically enhanced by the music. The final measure ends in an open fifth, as previous scenes have. This is not only an unresolved sound but also suggestively modal and therefore subtly "orientalist."

No. 11 bis, the third later addition, is another orchestral interlude, depicting the calm after the battle. It is slow and soft, and a wistful flute solo plays above a meandering orchestra. In the oratorio, the narrator proclaims that Israel is the victor. All hail Judith, and the "virgins" (or young girls) sing her praises.

No. 12: Cantique des vierges *(Hymn of the Virgins)*

Summary: Judith awaits the return of her soldiers. The chorus of virgins, on their way to meet with the soldiers, stop in front of Judith's house and sing. Ozias, head of the army, approaches and gives thanks to Judith, calling her their "liberator."

Honegger and Morax constantly explore the dramatic possibilities of the chorus by alternating between purely musical and purely spoken dramatic roles. For example, in this number, the chorus has a purely musical role at the beginning, singing a

---

[38] Espasandin, p. 48.

wordless vocalise that pervades the entire movement, before the chorus comments on the enemy's flight. In these passages, the chorus does not take part in the action but establishes a particular atmosphere. The female voices sing a melodic line in thirds that continually repeats, hymnlike, on "Ah." Then a soprano soloist (the servant, in the opera) sings words to this tune over the other female voices: "As a summer day puts the night to flight, the Eternal has arisen and the enemy has fled." They sing more similes comparing nature to God's actions. One commentator calls this section one of "comparatively sweet tunefulness … [where] the use of melodies suggesting old folk songs creates a feeling of happy innocence."[39]

The music grows increasingly more complex. The lowest female voices sing "La la" to a sort of staccato "ditty" while the orchestra plays rapid continual 16th-note chromatic phrases. All of this is going on under the continual "Ah" phrases in the soprano chorus, as the soprano soloist continues to repeat her earlier phrases praising God.

No. 13: Cantique de Victoire *(Hymn of Victory)*

Summary: The chorus praises Judith and God for their victory, then leaves the stage. Judith, remorseful, is left alone with her servant. After a short dialogue, both enter the house.

In the opera, there is a short opening dialogue between the servant and Judith. The servant asks Judith why she is sad when all of Israel is blessing her name. Judith responds, cryptically: *Le coeur qui a donné la joie n'en garde pas pour lui* ("The heart that gave joy, kept none for him"). Is this a subtle expression of remorse on Judith's part, for the killing of another human being? If so, it adds an element of empathy to her portrayal not found in the original or in other retellings.

In the oratorio, the narrator describes the Israelite victory. The music starts in a bright C major with a quick repeated chromatic pattern. It grows more and more complex and remains chromatic. One commentator calls this "compellingly declamatory, searing music."[40] In the opera, Ozias tells the Israelites that they owe their victory to Judith, their liberator, and that they should raise their voices to God in a clamor of joy. The full chorus enters, singing Hosannah in complex rhythms, up to Judith's entrance. She sings *fortissimo* "His name is Jehovah" (this phrase rises from *a'* to *a"* in a few measures): "He is a valiant warrior; he raised his tent among his people; he delivered us from all our enemies." These lines are very broad and declamatory, with jagged rhythms. The orchestra reprises the rapid chromatic phrases after her first few measures, this time on 32nd notes and often in dissonance against Judith's notes. She sings that God struck the enemy by the hand of a woman. At this point the chorus enters, repeating variants of her opening phrase and singing "His name is Jehovah" in a *fugato* (where the voices follow one another). Judith continues singing her own solo line above the chorus.

In the next section, marked *Vivace* (lively), the chorus relates the story as it is in the Bible. Then they sing "Let us sing to the Eternal a new psalm" in a syncopated,

---

[39] S. W. Bennett, liner notes.
[40] Bennett, liner notes.

almost jazzy rhythm. This leads to a new, broader section, with square rhythms, as the full chorus proclaims "Holy holy holy is the name of the Eternal one" and various Psalms texts. Then they sing "Hosannah" as the orchestra plays rapid ascending and descending passages, leading in turn to a *Presto* section (very fast), with a dry *staccato* accompaniment. This section has a very different, accented sound. The chorus continues to build; at one climactic point there are seven voice parts. On the final repetition of the *fugato*, the orchestra plays almost an *ostinato*, on the same ascending and descending 16th notes heard earlier. On the final repetition, all the voices in unison sing the same pattern together, ending on "Jehovah" sung on *a*" and *fff*. Rapid chord patterns in the orchestra are interrupted by three measures of three half-note pealing bells on E flat, followed by a surprising finish on a tonic D major chord.

The opera, however, does not end this way. Instead, Judith sings in a brief, pensive solo: "I see his eyes watching me, his eyes full of sadness and reproach." A few measures repeat the theme of her Prayer from the beginning of the opera. Over this theme, she sings: "I am giving my life to God to forget." A few measures reprise the Prayer theme before dying out softly on a completely unresolved chord. This is an entirely different conclusion from not only Honegger's original oratorio version but also from every other version discussed in this book. Honegger and Morax dared to imagine that Judith had regrets about her action. This elevates her from a symbol into a complex and multifaceted human being. In his opera, Honegger retained the overwhelmingly upbeat and ecstatic closing chorus, yet returned to the intimacy of Judith's innermost thoughts. This retelling will encourage readers to return to the biblical story with a new perspective.

Conclusion

Honegger's work, like Hillemacher's, defies easy categorization. In addition, the composer created several versions of his *Judith*, staged and unstaged. Yet the music is essentially the same in all of them, and it is one of the most original and striking scores explored in this book. It varies from modal, almost primitive sounds of wailing, to expressively tonal passages, to eerie dissonant ones. The choruses are differentiated by the action being depicted as well as by the singers: the Assyrians' music differs sharply from the Israelites'. All of these aspects stand out for their originality.

Critic Bennett writes interesting remarks from the perspective of parallel histories between the time of Judith and Honegger's own time:

> The Assyrians have been defeated, a menace has been beaten off. Israel is still free, but menaces will rise again, and Judiths or their counterparts will again be needed. Indeed, this was as the actual historical situation of ancient Israel, a small people fiercely prizing their independence, situated at the crossroads of great warring Empires which continually threatened to trample over them with their armies. And it is perhaps this situation evoked by the story that appealed to Honegger in the 1920's when a war had been won, a menace had been removed, but there was no lasting promise of peace.[41]

---

[41] Bennett, liner notes.

Chapter Conclusion

These four works differ vastly from one another, in their musical styles, their librettos, and character portrayals. The first two are English oratorios of the Victorian era, while the third, Hillemacher's, is a late Romantic French work with a very creative libretto. It only depicts one scene from the book of Judith, differentiating it from most works discussed here. Like the fourth work, of Arthur Honegger, its genre cannot be clearly defined, lying at the border between oratorio/cantata and opera. Leslie's oratorio contains some fine musical moments but does not add anything textually innovative to the interpretation of the story because it utilizes strictly biblical quotes. Parry's oratorio also sticks to this convention except in his case, the primary biblical source is not even the book of Judith but rather the book of Kings. Nonetheless, Judith's story is woven in creatively, even if she remains somewhat peripheral to the plot. The music, however, is often inspired, making this work worth hearing and exploring.

The prize-winning cantata by Paul Hillemacher is in a class by itself, since it is an expansion of the Judith-Holofernes encounter from chapter 9 of the book of Judith. Interestingly, the presence of only three characters—Judith, her servant, and Holofernes—mirrors exactly that of the Cambridge Scarlatti work of almost one hundred years earlier. It could be speculated that the librettist of this work was familiar with that earlier one, especially as it shares other similarities with the Scarlatti work. Like the Cambridge Scarlatti work of the seventeenth century (discussed in Chapter 1), this work stands out for its originality and provocative alterations among nineteenth-century works. The same could be said for Arthur Honegger's work, which in its various iterations was an oratorio, unstaged opera, and staged opera. The music and text of all versions are highly original and add a great deal to the story. The ending of the opera, in which Judith expresses remorse and regret for her act, is one of the most illuminating ideas found in any work about Judith. It challenges readers or listeners to think about how Judith actually might have felt about what she did. If she was tormented by remorse, that would explain why she cloistered herself for the many remaining decades of her life. No other retelling offers an explanation for Judith's choice. The writer of the original story never speculated about this, but we as readers are free to, and obviously the librettist for Honegger's work came to his own conclusions.

Part Two

Operas

3

Influential Nineteenth-Century Plays

Some of the operas to be discussed in the next two chapters were inspired by two nineteenth-century Italian dramatic retellings of the Judith story and by a German play of the same era. They inspired librettos for several operas, the scores of which unfortunately have not all survived. Some of these librettos in their turn were influenced by the popular play *Judith* by the German playwright Friedrich Hebbel. I am discussing two plays, by Hebbel and Paolo Giacometti, as important examples of creative gap-filling and as inspiration for several composers. Not only were they a strong influence on librettos later used in operas, but they themselves also shine a light on attitudes to the book of Judith in that era.

The two most popular Italian plays about Judith in the mid-nineteenth century were Giacometti's (1857) and Marco Marcelliano Marcello's (1860) plays, both *Giuditta*. Marcello acknowledges his debt to both Hebbel (whose play dates to 1840) and particularly Giacometti, in the foreword to his play. (Marcello's play/libretto is discussed in tandem with Achille Peri's opera, in Chapter 4). These writers seem to be advocating women's greater participation in the move to liberation. But Marcello is less revolutionary in his thinking, and many parts of the libretto desexualize Judith. They confirm the thinking that the murder of a tyrant could not be done by a woman, only a man. This view is present more subtly in the biblical story, where Judith refuses to remarry, never has children, and remains a widow till very old age. These are indicators of an almost sexless woman, not defined in any way in relation to a man—not even in her genealogy.

Christian Friedrich Hebbel (1813–1863)

Christian Friedrich Hebbel was a German poet and dramatist who added a new psychological dimension to German drama, focusing not so much on the individual aspects of characters or events as on historical changes that led to new moral values. In 1863, on his fiftieth birthday, Hebbel won the Schiller Prize and died later that year of pneumonia.[1] His play *Judith* was a big success in 1840 when it was performed in

---

[1] "Friedrich Hebbel: German Dramatist," *Britannica*. Available online: https://www.britannica.com/biography/Friedrich-Hebbel (accessed Apirl 24, 2020).

Hamburg and Berlin. Hebbel's name was known throughout Germany after these performances, celebrated all over Europe as the "greatest living German dramatist."[2]

In one writer's opinion, Hebbel's version of Judith's story subverts the tradition of the original story, namely, that Judith is the savior of her people and a hero, by making her a woman "concerned about her desirability as a female body."[3] I do not entirely agree with this assessment.

The artist Horace Vernet (1789–1863) painted a portrait entitled *Judith et Holopherne* in 1831 (located in the Musée des Beaux-Arts de Pau, France), which apparently was the inspiration for Hebbel's drama. Hebbel first saw the scene as a lithograph and four years after his play was written, he saw Vernet's full-length portrait. In a letter, Hebbel wrote: "I stood in front of the painting for a long time … it expresses the same sentiments in the painting as I portrayed in action in my tragedy." Curry wonders what it was about the painting that was so provocative that it inspired Hebbel to write his very influential play. Both the painting and the drawing by Vernet reflect his feeling that Judith and Holofernes were lovers as well as enemies, something which is very much a part of Hebbel's tragedy.[4] Most readers, including myself, do not see any indication of their being lovers in the play.

Peggy Curry, in her study, believes that what is behind Hebbel's and others' contemporary remakes of Judith is each playwright's belief that "violation of the body is a male prerogative and women who trespass will pay with their lives."[5] In Hebbel's creative retelling, Judith suffers from the experience of having her desire and her body shunned by her husband on their wedding night and every night thereafter. She is deliberately deprived (seemingly by God and also by the playwright) of knowing why. In Curry's words:

> This Judith fits in with her time in that she has a vivid idea about masculine courage and finds her would-be suitor, Ephraim, lacking it. Thus, when she arrives at Holofernes' camp, she is swept away momentarily by his strength … Judith decides to counter his tremendous confidence by telling him directly that she plans to kill him.[6]

Holofernes taunts her, saying: "I need only make you a child!" Is he insinuating that by impregnating her, he will demean her? When Judith says: "I have to—I want to— curses on me now and forever if I can't," is she referring to being raped, or to killing him? Is Hebbel suggesting she wants and needs both? Killing and raping are mixed together in Hebbel's ambiguous phrasing. When Judith later describes the rape, it is clear that it was her motive for the killing. Holofernes's death effectively ends Judith's

[2] "Christian Friedrich Hebbel," *Theatre History*. Available online: http://www.theatrehistory.com/german/hebbel001.html (accessed April 24, 2020).
[3] Peggy L. Curry, "Representing the Biblical Judith in Literature and Art: An Intertextual Cultural Critique" (University of Massachusetts Amherst, 1994), at https://scholarworks.umass.edu/cgi/viewcontent.cgi?article=1730&context=open_access_dissertations, p. 101 (accessed April 27, 2020).
[4] Curry, pp. 97, 99.
[5] Curry, pp. 101–2.
[6] Curry, pp. 102–3.

life, in this misogynist retelling, because, in Curry's words, "she has been constructed as over-reaching her place by defending her body." She also showed ego and in Hebbel's view, "that is a crime against femininity."[7]

In his diary, Hebbel admitted that his transformation of Judith was essentially to teach her her place. The diary entry is dated November 24, 1839:

> I can't use the Judith of the Bible. That Judith is a widow who lures Holofernes into the net with her trickery and cunning; she is happy to have his head in her sack and sings and expresses her jubilation with all of Israel for three months. That is mean. Such a character is not worthy of success … My Judith is paralyzed by her deed; she is petrified at the possibility that she might bear the son of Holofernes; it becomes clear to her that she has exceeded beyond her limits, that, at the very least, she has done what is right for the wrong reasons. (p. 35)[8]

Hebbel basically uses the original biblical story as merely a frame, seeing it as in need of fixing. With great hubris, he completely ignores the plot and historical context of the book of Judith—both of when the original book was written and when the events depicted supposedly occurred. Nonetheless, his play appealed to opera composers through the years, obviously because of its dramatic (even melodramatic) elements. Most notably, one nineteenth-century composer (Russian Alexander Serov; see Chapter 4) and two twentieth-century composers were inspired by his play: Emil von Reznicek (*Holofernes*, 1922) and Siegfried Matthus (*Judith*, 1984)—both discussed in Chapter 5. In addition, the play was translated and known in Italy, and influenced the Italian playwright Paolo Giacometti (see below). Marcello, in the foreword to his libretto, called it *la strana tragedia tedesca* ("the strange German tragedy"), indicating mixed feelings about it (Marcello's play is discussed in Chapter 4). This interest may demonstrate an attraction to Hebbel's distortion of the original narrative, "producing a tragedy in which a woman trespasses into male territory and is punished."[9] But Hebbel's most egregious distortions of the original story (particularly the rape) did not find their way into librettos until the twentieth century.

The full Hebbel play in an English translation is available online.[10]

Judith, A Tragedy in Five Acts (1840)

Act I opens in Holofernes's camp, a choice found in several retellings. This establishes from the opening that Holofernes is the central character. In a completely invented plot line, Holofernes invites any soldiers to approach who have a complaint. One does, recounting that he captured a beautiful slave in the assault of the day before. She was so beautiful he was afraid to even touch her. A captain entered his tent later when he was

[7] Curry, pp. 102, 105.
[8] As recorded in translator Marion Sonnefeld's introduction to the play; in Curry, p. 105.
[9] Curry, p. 107.
[10] https://quod.lib.umich.edu/g/genpub/AJD8469.0025.001?rgn=main;view=fulltext (accessed April 27, 2020).

not there, and finding this slave, he killed her when she resisted him. Holofernes orders that captain killed, along with the warrior who made the report. The warrior doesn't understand why, and Holofernes explains that it was just a test. If he were to allow everyone to complain, who could guarantee there would not be complaints against *him*? The warrior reminds Holofernes that he spared the woman. Holofernes says he will reward him for his good intentions: the warrior can get drunk on his best wine before he is killed. This anecdote immediately portrays Holofernes as not only evil but also a complete megalomaniac. He delivers a long philosophical monologue that confirms this impression. Contrary to his portrayal in the original version, Holofernes here expresses disdain rather than adulation for Nebuchadnezzar:

> Nebuchadnezzar, alas, is nothing but an arrogant figure that beguiles the time by multiplying itself forever by itself. If I should withdraw with the Assyrians, nothing would be left of him but a human skin stuffed with fat. I will conquer the world for him, and when he has it, take it from him again!

Elsewhere in the play, Holofernes is portrayed as sarcastic and biting, which makes him more interesting—and almost likeably evil—than his biblical counterpart. After Achior answers Holofernes's question about the Hebrews and their god, Holofernes's response is essentially the same as in the original story: he angrily orders Achior to be taken to Bethulia. But he also says: "Whoever at the capture of the city shall slay him and bring me his head, to him will I give its weight in gold." The reference to decapitation is an ironic one, but this also suggests a crueler Holofernes than his biblical counterpart.

Act II opens with Judith recounting a dream to her servant, here named Mirza (name of Persian origin). In the dream, she was running, pulled by an unseen force. She reached the top of a mountain, where she saw a deep chasm, filled with smoke and vapor. Frightened, she called out to God, and heard a gentle voice say: "Here I am" (echoing the Hebrew *Hineni* uttered by Abraham and others who were called by God, to indicate their submission. Having God say this is counterintuitive for Jewish readers). Judith felt herself resting happily in the arms of someone she could not see, but then he let go because she was too heavy and she sank, feeling hot tears fall on her cheek (echoes of the Genesis *Aqedah* story here). Judith speaks in the same kind of philosophical language as Holofernes, wondering what the dream meant. Mirza tries to change the subject and asks Judith why she will never talk about Ephraim (a man in love with her), and Judith responds that she "shudders at men."

When Mirza reminds her she had been married, Judith reveals what happened to her on her wedding night with Manasseh. This extensive gap-filling is intended to explain why Judith was married but never had children. In her account, she was 14 when given to Manasseh, which is probably more accurate historically than most retellings and artistic renderings of her as a mature woman. She vividly describes their wedding night, including such details as the moon shining in her face as she lay on the bed. But when Manasseh approached her, it was as if an unseen hand had clutched him, and he pulled away. He repeated over and over: "I cannot, I cannot." Judith felt defiled, and their relations were cool after that night. Six months later, in this account, when

Manasseh was dying of sunstroke (over three days, in this version), she pleaded with her dying husband to tell her what had happened that night. But as he was beginning to answer, he died. She tells Mirza she is sure Manasseh was mad. Mirza tells her to look in the mirror, to realize how beautiful she still is. Judith's response—Hebbel putting his own, misogynist words in Judith's mouth—goes against everything she is described to be in the original story:

> A woman is nothing; through a man only can she become something; through him can she become a mother. The child that she bears is the only thanks she can offer nature for her existence. Unblessed are the unfruitful; doubly unblessed am I, not a maid, nor yet a wife!

Other plays, and librettos, have filled in the gaps around Judith's relations with men and attitudes to childbearing, but none have strayed so far from the essence of her original character. When Mirza asks why Judith cannot still be married and bear children, she answers: "My beauty is that of the deadly nightshade; enjoyment of it brings madness and death." She obviously came to believe this because of her ominous wedding night experience. This play portrays Judith as mentally unbalanced. Hebbel clearly could not accept a "normal" woman behaving the way Judith did.

Ephraim now enters and describes the frightening sight of Holofernes's army approaching in force. He says that he knows much about Holofernes's brutality: for example, that he likes his meat broiled by the flames of the cities he has burned. When he saw Bethulia, he was said to have asked his cook if he could roast an ostrich egg by that fire. Judith muses: "If only I could see him," and Ephraim tells her Holofernes kills women with his embraces and kisses, and that if he knew Judith were here, he would come just for her. She playfully suggests that if that is the case, she need only go to him, to save the city. Ephraim is upset that what he thought would frighten Judith and draw her into his arms instead has stimulated her. She suggests, in a metaphor laden with irony: "If the giant's head towers so high into the clouds that you cannot reach it, why, then throw a jewel at his feet. He will stoop to pick it up, and then you can overcome him with ease." Ephraim pleads with Judith that she needs a male protector, but she continues to reject his advances. They have a dialogue about unrequited love, at the end of which Judith tells Ephraim simply to do something for her: to kill Holofernes. Then he can ask for a reward. He asks her how that is possible and she says she does not know either, only that it must be done and so maybe she should be the one to do it. Neither of them has ever seen Holofernes, but they have fearful images of him. Yet, Judith comments wisely: "There was a time when he was not; therefore, one can come when he will be no more."

Ephraim claims that Judith is only suggesting he do this deed out of hatred for him. She responds passionately that if he had been exulted at the thought of such an act, or had even impulsively grabbed a sword, she would have loved him for that. He challenges her to show him the one who can make possible the impossible. She responds that such a one will come, must come. Then she adds: "If your cowardice is that of your whole sex, if all men see nothing in danger but a warning to escape it— then has a woman won the right to do a great deed ... I must prove that it is possible!"

Judith's words here on the surface sound less misogynist than those expressed by the playwright earlier. Yet the idea expressed here is still that a woman can only be strong if all the men around her are weak, and not in her own right.

Act III takes place in Judith's room. Mirza complains that Judith has been sitting in the same position for three days, not eating, drinking, speaking, or even sighing. She reminds her that the courage she showed at the imminent danger had put the men to shame, but then she seemed to close up. Judith motions her to leave. A lengthy monologue, a kind of prayer, ensues. She tells God she has reached out to him, but cannot ascend to him—he must descend to her. She is lying here, out of time, waiting for a sign from God to rise and act. When danger drew near to her people, she rejoiced, confident that God would glorify himself among his chosen people. She saw that what uplifted her debased the others. She felt God's finger had pointed at her, as if triumph would lead from her. She noticed, with rapture, that those to whom she might have relinquished the "great work" all "groveled, cowardly and trembling." She was so sure it was she who would do this work that she lay down and swore a solemn oath to never get up until God "showed her the way that leads to the heart of Holofernes." One thought has continued to return to her, which she could not believe came from God. But with a sudden flash of recognition, she now believes it really was from God, and says: "The way to my deed leads through sin! I thank you, Lord! You make my eyes clear. In your sight, the impure becomes pure." Realizing what she will have to do to defeat Holofernes, she now understands why God made her beautiful and gave her no children to love. Looking at her image in the mirror, she declares:

> Holofernes, all this is yours; I have no longer a share in it. I have withdrawn to the inmost depths of my soul. Take it, but tremble when you have it. I shall emerge at an hour when you do not expect it, like a sword from the scabbard, and pay myself with your life. If I must kiss you, I will imagine that it is with poisoned lips; if I embrace you, I will think that I am strangling you. God, let him commit atrocities before my eyes, bloody atrocities, but save me from seeing any good in him!

In the original story, Judith prayed to God to make her deceitful. Here she is praying to not be attracted to Holofernes, an interesting alteration. But she clearly knows what she is setting out to do, which is ambivalent in other retellings.

Mirza enters and tries to persuade Judith to eat, but instead, Judith insists she adorn her. Mirza suggests they drink, since it may be the last time, explaining that all the water supplies have been cut off. Judith rages about this cruelty, depriving people of necessity instead of simply killing them. Mirza tells her that Ephraim obtained a small amount of water and brought it to Judith instead of to his own brother. Mirza sees this as an act of love, while Judith sees him as a man who sins even when trying to do good. She comments:

> Every woman has a right to demand of every man that he be a hero ... A man may forgive cowardice in another; a woman, never. Can you pardon the prop for breaking? You can hardly pardon your need of a prop.

Women's reliance on men for physical protection was a reality throughout much of history, and these comments reflect that. Yet the portrait of Judith that emerges here is ambivalent: on the one hand, she is powerful and determined; on the other, she sees herself as weaker than men. This slightly contradicts Judith's earlier comments about the men of Bethulia who were "cowardly" and who "trembled." Those descriptions could contain subtle undertones of anti-Semitism.

The scene changes to an outdoor gathering in Bethulia, where men are bickering about their thirst, how to find water or food, and whether they shouldn't just open the gates and let Holofernes enter. Men variously recount biblical stories, or some pretend to be prophets. The mood is one of the population of any small town gathering in a crisis, trying to reach an accord but continually bickering among themselves. Judith joins them and tries to mediate some of the arguments, but they pay little attention to her. Just as the crowd has decided to open the gates, thinking Holofernes will show more mercy if they surrender, Achior appears. He tells them of Holofernes's plan to annihilate them all. Finally, all agree on a limit of five days. Judith solemnly announces that this means Holofernes must die before then. She suggests they attempt to exit the city in small groups in search of water, but all are too afraid. People start bickering, asking why they listen to Judith. Some say she is an angel, and the most God-fearing woman in the city, who always keeps to herself unless she is making a sacrifice, or if her people need her. She is there now to comfort them.

Judith asks Achior to tell her more about Holofernes, whom he knows well. He tells her stories of his daring and power, and admits that he was in thrall to him, that he can only praise him when he speaks of him. Judith asks if Holofernes loves women, and Achior says he does, the same as he loves food and drink. He tells her of a woman he knew who loved Holofernes but whom he disdained. She stole into his chamber and stood by his bed with a raised dagger. When he awoke, he could not stop laughing, until she stabbed herself. This is an interestingly prescient story to insert here. Judith thanks Achior for telling her all this and says she now will have the courage of a man. She entreats all those who have been killed by Holofernes to rise up and show her their wounds, to let her read in their eyes how guilty he was. She says she wants to avenge the dead and protect the living. Then she turns to Achior and asks if she is beautiful enough for a sacrifice, to which he responds: "None ever saw your equal."

Judith tells the Elders that she "has business with Holofernes" and demands the gate be opened, which it is. They ask what she means to do, and she says only God can know that. They all pray that God will be with her. She asks Mirza if she has the courage to come with her, and Mirza responds that she would not have the courage to remain behind. This is an interesting addition, since neither in the original story nor in other retellings does Judith ever give her slave (or servant) a choice. Judith addresses all the people and tells them to think of her as one who is dying, and to teach the children her name. When she is outside, everyone but Ephraim falls on their knees. He refuses, insisting that she only went out expecting the men to follow her, and that he will do so, also hoping to change her mind. Some critics have suggested that the addition of a "savior" man weakens Judith's character, but I disagree. She never asked Ephraim to come and she ignores him.

Act IV takes place in Holofernes's pavilion. After more philosophic musings from Holofernes, a captain enters and tells Holofernes that they found a veiled Hebrew woman approaching a fountain:

> She came toward us and went to the fountain. One of the guards went to meet her. I thought he would even lay violent hands upon her, for the soldiers are fierce from long idleness, but he bowed, drew water, and handed her the vessel. She took it without thanks and raised it to her lips, but before she had drunk, she put it away and poured it out slowly. This vexed the watchman; he threatened her with his sword. Then she threw back her veil and looked at him. He all but cast himself at her feet. She, however, spoke: "Lead me to Holofernes. I come because I wish to humble myself before him and lay bare the secrets of my people."

This is a very dramatic and imaginative retelling of Judith's entering the Assyrian camp. Her gesture of pouring out the water is meant to show scorn and to demonstrate that she is unbowed by the siege. Looking straight at the guard indicates that she trusts the power of her beauty. These are rich additions to the action, even while her words remain close to the biblical text. Holofernes orders her brought to him. While he waits, he muses on the one woman he wants never to see: his own mother. He claims he was abandoned in a lion's den and suckled by a lioness. This is why he once crushed a lion in his arms, making Holofernes almost a mythical, superhuman hero.

Judith is brought in and falls at his feet; Holofernes is visibly smitten. One captain says to the other that they hope this diversion will "smother his wrath with her kisses." He is so overwhelmed by her beauty that he swears to never again have anyone blinded—another example of almost comic evil. Then he tells her to rise and he questions her about her motives. He tells her no harm will come to her because she pleases him more than any woman ever has, and she says that is her goal. She explains how her people have sinned and roused their God's wrath, in an elaboration of her speech to Holofernes in the original text, which is equally obsequious. In a lengthy dialogue filled with twists and turns, Judith ultimately confirms that Holofernes was sent by God to annihilate her people—and she claims that God is speaking through her:

> I came to you because my God commanded it, commanded me to lead you to Jerusalem, to deliver my people into your hands like a flock that has no shepherd [Jdt 11:19]. … He pronounced sentence of death upon my people; He laid upon my soul the hangman's office.

There are more quotes from Jdt 11, such as Holofernes swearing that Judith's god will be his god if he is victorious, and Judith telling him that the food she has brought will suffice her before "God performs what He intends." When Mirza meets Judith to accompany her to their tent, she curses her for betraying her people. Judith weeps with joy because she has succeeded in deceiving even her servant. As they exit, she says: "I shudder at the power of a lie in my mouth."

Act V takes place still in Holofernes's pavilion, but at night. Holofernes asks his captain for an update on Bethulia, and the captain reports that its people wander the streets dying of thirst, bashing their heads against walls, wailing; Holofernes laughs, saying they have often seen such things. Then he asks for confirmation that tomorrow is the fifth day, adding that if Bethulia surrenders as Judith had predicted, the city and its stiff-necked people will come groveling at his feet. And if they really surrender without a fight, Holofernes swears to adopt their god as one of his—a new twist. In the original story, he tells Judith that her god will be his god, but never that this newfound faith would result from Bethulia's capitulation.

Holofernes asks the captain what the Hebrew woman is doing, and the captain replies that she is beautiful but also coy. Holofernes suspects that the captain has tried to seduce her, and when confronted, the captain is confused and asks how he could dare when he knew she was pleasing to Holofernes. Assuming his guilt, Holofernes kills him on the spot, saying: "Take that, dog!" in yet another example of his ruthlessness and cruelty. (This incident was included in the libretto for both Serov's and von Reznicek's operas; see Chapters 4, 5). In a monologue, Holofernes rhapsodizes about the act of conquering women, particularly when they hate and resist him. He brags that he has conquered many, that his greatest triumph is to bring women who despise him to rapture. This text reads like the confessions of a serial rapist, and it is deeply disturbing to think that this play had such great popular success in the 1840s and even later. Most commentators have said that Hebbel created a superman out of Holofernes. But this text seems to make him hateful, rather than admirable.

He describes his plan for Judith:

> Judith—indeed, her glance is kindly and her cheeks smile like sunshine, but in her heart dwells none but her god, and him will I now dislodge. In the days of my youth when I met an enemy, instead of drawing my own sword, I would wrest his from his hand and kill him with it. So will I undo this woman. She shall fall before me through her own emotion, through the perfidy of her own desire.

Notably absent from his words is the word "love," which is true to the original version. However, in almost all librettos discussed here, Holofernes declares his love for Judith repeatedly. But Hebbel's Holofernes would never use that word, or even recognize that emotion—as will be seen shortly.

When Judith enters, the initial banter is based on Jdt 12:17–18 but quickly deviates when Judith shudders at the sight of fresh blood at her feet. This is the blood of the captain Holofernes just killed, who was dragged out moments earlier. Holofernes orders more carpets brought to cover the blood and tells Judith she should be flattered: blood was spilled because it was "kindled with passion" for her. In an aside, Judith says her hair is rising, but she thanks God for showing her this horror, because it will make it easier for her "to kill such a killer." Holofernes asks her if he terrifies her, and she asks if he would despise her if she could love him. He is so startled that he says he does not know that word and gives her a golden chain for using it. Then he asks if she ever cursed him, when the siege began, and she answers that she hoped her God would do it. He then kisses her, and in an aside she mutters: "Oh, why am I a woman?" Whether this line is said with terror, anger, or resignation would be determined by the actress's tone of voice. Musical works that included parts of Hebbel's text employed musical devices to imply Judith's emotion at that moment (see discussions in Chapters 4 and 5). Holofernes continues to needle her, then becomes more and more inflamed, and says to himself: "Be welcome, lust, distilled at the flames of hate. Kiss me, Judith. (She does it.)" It would seem that the second kiss was reciprocal. He then pours her wine and invites her to drink, and she does, saying: "In wine there is courage." (She raises no objection to unconsecrated wine, unlike in the biblical original.) Holofernes asks why she needs courage to meet with him and kiss him, and she begins to cry. He goads her to admit she hates him, and finally she stands up and shouts: "Yes, I hate you and I curse you! Now you can kill me." He says he may do that tomorrow, but tonight she is going to sleep with him. She says to herself: "Now may I do it."

They are suddenly interrupted by a messenger announcing that a Hebrew has entered the camp and needs to be seen urgently. Holofernes quickly asks Judith for the names of her kindred and friends, whom he will spare if Bethulia is about to surrender. This quick moment reveals a compassionate side of Holofernes seen nowhere else in the play. Ephraim is brought in. He bows to Holofernes and asks if his life is assured. When told yes, he pulls out his sword and tries to strike, but Holofernes strikes back. The guard at the door rushes in, ready to kill Ephraim, but Holofernes orders him to stop and Ephraim unsuccessfully tries to fall on his sword. Shamed before Judith, he is now dragged away to be caged as a curiosity: the only one who ever struck at Holofernes and lived. Holofernes equates an attempt to kill him as to "quench the lightning that threatens to consume the world; to crush the seed of an immortality." Judith forces herself to say to him: "You are great and others are small." But then softly to herself, she says: "God of my fathers, save me from myself, that I may not honor what I abhor! He is a man." This is another line that suggests Judith's conflicted feelings. Holofernes rambles about his world, "wretched and steeped in blood," which he feels he was born to destroy. He knows that many curse him, but it has no effect. Judith, in an aside, says: "Cease, cease! I must slay him, if I am not to kneel before him!" Holofernes rants about having no true opponent, that he respects power and longs for someone to come and try to overthrow him, because now he respects only himself. His words become increasingly horrifying and mad, until finally Judith screams: "Man, monster, you force yourself between me and my God! I must pray at this moment, and I cannot." These brief moments of reflection suggest that Judith is struggling against herself and her desires, but it is an ambivalent portrayal.

Holofernes tells her to fall down and worship him. Judith says she cannot understand him, and he says: "One must not wish to make anything comprehensible to a woman." Judith replies: "Learn to respect women! A woman stands before you to murder you, and she tells you of it!" to which Holofernes replies: "And tells me so as to make the deed impossible!" This dialogue goes completely against the original story. The whole point of the killing was that it was accomplished through deceit. Had Judith shown her hand in this way, she would have known her attempt would be thwarted. In this play, it simply becomes a contest of wills, rather than a woman setting out to destroy the enemy of her people.

Holofernes now accuses Judith of cowardice, saying she is only threatening him because he will not go to bed with her. Shockingly, he says: "To protect myself from you I need only to give you a child." She protests that he has not known a Hebrew woman, only women who feel happy when they are degraded. Holofernes tells her he will know her and tells her to stop resisting. He signals to the guard to leave, but Mirza remains. She struggles to have faith in Judith when she goes to an adjacent room with Holofernes. She hears someone being murdered in that room, but she does not know who. She wants to believe all Judith's looks and gestures were deceitful but cannot be sure. She remarks that a woman "should bear men, not kill them." Judith rushes in, her hair loose, reeling. The curtain to the other room is open, and Holofernes can be seen sleeping. Mirza is relieved to see them both alive and tells Judith they should flee. Judith responds:

> He dragged me off, he pulled me down upon his shameful couch, he stifled my soul. Would you endure all this? And now that I will be repaid for the annihilation which I suffered in his arms; now that I will avenge myself for his brutal attack upon my humanity; now that I will wash off with his heart's blood the degrading kisses which still burn upon my lips—now do you not blush to draw me away?

Mirza asks Judith what she will do, and she replies: "Murder" and says that if she falters, Mirza need only whisper in her ear "Holofernes made you a harlot, and yet he lives" to give her the courage to be a hero. Judith relates what happened:

> I threw myself down upon my knees before the monster and groaned, "Spare me!" Had he listened to the cry of my anguished soul, never, never would I—but his answer was to tear off my neckerchief and praise my breasts. I bit his lips when he kissed me. "Temper your rapture; you go too far," he laughed in scorn … I was nearly unconscious, all a convulsion, when something bright glittered before my eyes! It was his sword. Upon that sword my reeling senses seized. If I have forfeited in my degradation the right to exist, I will win it back with this sword. Pray for me; now will I do it.

She enters Holofernes's room, sees him sleeping, and says:

> This quiet sleep after such an hour, is it not the bitterest offence? Am I a worm that one may tread upon me, and then, as if nothing had happened, go quietly to sleep? I am no worm. (She draws the sword from the scabbard.) He is smiling. I recognize it, that hellish smile. Thus he smiled when he drew me down to him, when he—kill him, Judith, he deflowers you a second time in his dream; his sleep is only a beastly chewing of the cud of your dishonor. He stirs. Will you delay till desire, hungry again, awakes him, till he clutches you anew and … (She strikes off his head.) See, Mirza, there lies his head. Ha, Holofernes, do you respect me now?

Vivid and harrowing as this account is, it demeans and distorts the meaning of the original text. This becomes a fantasy of rape revenge, not only the killing of an enemy. Judith even intimates that had he not raped her, she might not have killed him (above: "Had he listened …"). In fact, Mirza asks what Judith's original intent was, since she came to the camp dressed in her finery. Judith recalls the suffering of her people that inspired her to the deed, but in the end, she has to confess she did it for herself. Mirza asks what she will tell the child she might bear, and Judith, in despair, wants to go out and display the head so that a mob will descend and kill her on the spot, but Mirza begs her not to. Judith rambles, sounding as if she has gone mad. But they know they must leave. Judith insists they take the head with them and orders Mirza to put it in a bag. Mirza shudders and resists as she does so. This detail fills a gap in the original story, where the servant seems strangely nonchalant about doing this. Other retellings discussed in this book have not dealt with that peculiarly flat moment in the original story, including those based on Hebbel's play.

The next scene is back in Bethulia at dawn, where the people are still suffering and feeling doubts about God. A woman unable to breastfeed asks a priest if he can offer her any consolation, and when he says no, she says: "Your God sits nowhere but on your lips." Two men talk of the fear that their wives might be considering cannibalizing their own children when they die. Then someone reminds the group that five days have passed and Judith should be returning, so rescue may be close. Judith and Mirza call out for the gates to be opened. With little ceremony, Mirza throws the head on the ground and asks who recognizes it. Achior falls on his knees in praise of God, identifying Holofernes. He then takes Judith's hand and realizes it was that hand that accomplished the killing. All praise Judith as their savior who has set them free. A priest wants to put the head on a spike, but Judith orders it be buried at once, without explaining her motivation. In the original story, it is Judith who orders the head to be hung on the city walls (14:1), which is done at dawn (14:11); but the Assyrians discover Holofernes's headless corpse before they see the head anyway (14:15). Meanwhile, guards at the ramparts call out that the Assyrians are fleeing in disarray. Ephraim has escaped being tortured and killed, and has returned to muster all the soldiers for an attack. He tells them that with Holofernes headless, so are all his troops.

The Elders praise Judith and ask what reward she wants. At first she rejects the idea but then makes them pledge they will honor whatever she demands, and they do. She tells them they must kill her when she asks them to. Judith tells Mirza that she refuses to bear Holofernes's son and only hopes God will be gracious to her and make her womb unfruitful. That is the end of the play.

Conclusion

Hebbel's play distorts the original book of Judith more than any other retelling. He creates a Holofernes in the image of an evil superman, a bloodthirsty megalomaniac. Some writers have suggested this was an ideal in Hebbel's day, but it is hardly a positive portrayal. Therefore, the reader can sympathize with Judith. But her portrayal, too, has contradictions. She initially seems inspired and determined to save her people by killing Holofernes. Once she spends time with him, she comes to despise him more and more. When he rapes her, she almost loses her mind and kills him. It is never suggested that either of them is drunk, which was a crucial element in the original story. How else could such a powerful man be decapitated in his sleep? This is never explained in the play. Ultimately, Judith's act is twisted into a revenge for rape, which goes completely against the main point of the original story. She is a hero to the Israelites because she single-handedly cut off the enemy's head. Perhaps her motive doesn't matter to the people of Bethulia, but it does matter to the reader. The intimation here is that Judith only had the strength and courage to kill Holofernes because he raped her, not because he was the enemy of her people. To reduce the story to a rape fantasy/rape/ rape revenge is not only reading into the story but also reading completely outside it, using it only as a frame. It has been said that Hebbel's play was so popular in its day that many Germans thought they knew the book of Judith from seeing the play. That is probably the most disturbing aspect of this play and its success.

Paolo Giacometti (1816–1882)

Paolo Giacometti was an Italian dramatist who studied law in Genoa but at the age of 20 found some success with his playwriting and from then on devoted himself to the stage. For financial reasons, he attached himself to various touring Italian companies, and his output was considerable. The leading actors of those companies helped to make many of his plays great successes. A collection of his works was published in Milan in eight volumes (1859 et seq.).[11] *Giuditta*, considered one of his best plays, was performed in Madrid in 1857, having won first prize in a dramatic competition in Torino the year before. The work was commissioned and performed by Madame Ristori (Adelaide Ristori, 1822–1906), an internationally renowned Italian actress, and her dramatic company, with whom Giacometti had a long and fruitful collaboration. In this work, the historic/biblical reality is suppressed (as in Giacometti's most popular play, *Elizabeth Queen of England*) in favor of the theatrical exigencies of the protagonist. In this view, Judith was torn between love of her country and self-sacrifice. This approach was very successful with the "bourgeois public." As war with Austria loomed, this public leaned toward a political reading of Judith's story.[12]

After success in Germany, Poland, and the Netherlands, in 1858 Ristori and her company brought *Giuditta* to Paris where the censors were reluctant to allow a performance. The police in the Veneto region did not permit the play to be performed, but it was well received in Torino, applauded there by King Vittorio Emanuele II. Camillo Cavour requested a copy of the play's text and proposed conferring honors on the author.[13]

[11] "1911 Encylopaedia Britannica/Giacomett, Paolo," *Wikisource*. Available online: https://en.wiki source.org/wiki/1911_Encyclop%C3%A6dia_Britannica/Giacometti,_Paolo (accessed January 23, 2019).
[12] Francesca Brancaleoni, "Giacometti, Paolo," *Dizionario Biografico degli Italiani* 54 (2000). Available online: http://www.treccani.it/enciclopedia/paolo-giacometti_%28Dizionario-Biografico%29/ (accessed December 18, 2018); my own translation.
[13] Brancaleoni. Cavour (1810–1861) was a leading figure in the movement toward Italian unification.

Giuditta (1857)

This play is available online as an e-book,[14] in Italian and English, though the English is not always accurate.

There are several interesting changes and additions to the Judith story in this play. First, there are new characters: Gothoniel, an Elder in love with Judith (Gothoniel is the father of Chabris in the biblical book: Jdt 6:15); Arzaele, queen of Holofernes's harem and in love with him; and Dinah, a second servant of Judith who takes orders from the primary servant, here Abramia (from Abra).

Act I takes place in Bethulia. In Scene I, one of the Hebrews tells the crowd about "a pious woman, the daughter of Merari ... [who] by her prayers and her fasting, by her chastity and virtues ... is acceptable to the Lord. The spirit of Deborah is hers." He suggests they consult her for "wise counsel." This is a dramatization of the original narrative, where some of this information is relayed only by the narrator of the story, not expressed aloud or publicly.

In Scene II, a group from Bethulia is in the hills searching among the rocks for water. This interesting addition suggests a less passive and resigned people than that described in the biblical account. While they are searching, they hear trumpet calls in the distance, heralding the approach of their high priest, here Eliakim (instead of Joachim). He tries to encourage and uplift the people by reminding them of biblical heroes who triumphed against odds. In Scene III, excited shouting is heard, announcing the discovery of a spring and the arrival of Judith, "the prophetess."Judith is here conflated with Miriam, as a prophetess who can find water. To those who wonder who she is, Gothoniel explains that she is "the purest of Bethulia's daughters ... who chastely lives a solitary life, always filled with saintly ecstasies."

In Scene IV, Judith arrives out of breath and kneels at Eliakim's feet, asking for his blessing. She then tells the assembled that Heaven has disclosed a spring to her. A woman who has come with her young child calls Judith "the angel of Hagar," who was also searching for water for her child (in Gen 21). Judith next relates at length how she wandered in the hills at night and saw a vision of Holofernes below, at the Assyrian camp, in dark armor. Right after this vision, she saw a swan shaking water from its wings, and this led her to a stream. Everyone now thinks they are saved, and they rush to get water. (This plot line was copied by Marcello in his libretto; see Peri in Chapter 4). Eliakim blesses Judith, placing his hands on her head and saying: "May the spirit of Deborah and Jael rest upon thee!" These biblical references suggest not only that the audience of that day was biblically literate but also that Giacometti knew such frequent nods to the Bible would appeal to his audience. His choice of women "warriors" here was surely deliberate.

Scene V opens with a conversation between Judith and Gothoniel, an Elder in love with her. She shares with him how "filled with horror" she was at Eliakim's reference to Jael, asserting that she could never, never be a Jael. He agrees and tells her he is sure she is pained even by seeing the blood of a sacrificial ox on the altar (mistranslated by

14   *Giuditta*, with English translation by Isaac C. Pray (New York: John A. Gray & Green, 1860). Available online: https://play.google.com/store/books/details/Giuditta?id=Wkb4aGv6YioC&hl=en_SG.

Isaac Pray in the 1860 publication as "lamb," possibly deliberately, to suggest Jesus). She says that that blood is consecrated to Heaven, but whoever sheds the blood of another person should be cursed. Gothoniel wonders aloud why Judith never remarried and didn't want children. She is shocked by the question, stating that it is God's blessing to make her childless, because she is mother to all the "daughters of Israel," particularly those taken as slaves into harems. The prophet Deborah, too, was childless and yet known as a Mother in Israel ("I arose, a mother in Israel," Judg 5:7). This interesting gap-filling idea explains why the author had Judith remain both unmarried and childless—an uncommon choice in her society.

Act II opens in a sparsely furnished room in Judith's house, with steps in the back leading to her "oratory" and doors shut with dark tapestries. Since Judith's room is never described in the biblical version, this offers some satisfaction to those who would like to visualize it. Judith's bridal gown and all her jewelry are laid out on a table in the middle of the room, and Dinah, the second servant, expresses her astonishment at seeing them again. Abramia silences her, and Dinah suspects she has a secret. Dinah also tells Abramia how she has noticed a change in Judith, who seems preoccupied by some "strange thought." And most alarming, she has watched Judith seize the "sword of her ancestors, suspended on the wall" and wield it over her head. Abramia is surprised to hear this and begins to think Judith may be preparing to confront the enemy. She is thrilled at the chance of joining her. In this creative gap-filling version, Judith planned what she was going to do long before she headed out, a suggestion barely even implied in the original story.

In Scene II, Judith descends into the room from the oratory with a sword in her hand, which she drops to the ground with its point downward. In some ways, these actions create less suspense for the climactic moment of the story, and less shock at later seeing Judith wielding a sword. On the other hand, preparation was not a bad idea. Judith, looking at her bridal gown, asks Abramia if she is still beautiful, since she has aged. In reality only three years have passed (in the biblical version) but that is not mentioned here. Abramia tells her she is, but questions what power beauty has, and Judith answers: "Much!" She then asks Abramia if by chance Judith found herself face to face with Holofernes, if Abramia thinks he would fall in love with her once he saw her. Filling another gap in the story—did Judith's servant come along with her to the Assyrian camp because she had no choice as a slave, or because she wanted to?—in this version, the latter is suggested. She confesses to knowing Holofernes because she was once enslaved in his harem.

Abramia describes him as "a horrible monster, both ferocious and effeminate" (an unusual combination that suggests "effeminate" was a very negative term), who has endless orgies in his camp and his perfumed harems. "His cup is a horrible mixture of blood and wine. He intoxicates himself with this drink, for he is as mad as he is cruel." She asks Judith if knowing all this, she can still have hope. This is one of the darker descriptions of Holofernes found in retellings. Yet Judith responds, half to herself, "He is drunk when he leaves the feast," suggesting she is already making a plan. Abramia tells Judith she should tremble if she is relying only on her beauty, and Judith responds: "I would I could see him here at my feet." Abramia warns her that it would be Judith at *his* feet, left dishonored and helpless, unable to avenge herself. Holofernes brandishes a sword, she says significantly, that "no woman's hands could lift." Judith dismisses Abramia, who says to herself as she leaves: "She is only a woman."

Scene III opens with a long soliloquy for Judith. Instead of a lengthy prayer, as in the original story and so many librettos, here Judith muses about power, weakness, beauty, and her dreams. She is contemplating an act of violence and then catches herself. Yet she says: "I would crush Holofernes and trample on him." Anger is never expressed by the biblical Judith, but it adds an interesting new element. In Scene IV, Gothoniel enters and tells Judith that the people are enraged with her after discovering that the spring she found was poisoned (a plot device copied by Marcello; see Peri in Chapter 4). All who drank from it have died. This alters the original plot, in which the Assyrians simply blocked all the water sources, which would have been sufficient to eventually kill off or weaken the whole city. Poisoning springs is another level of evil, and much more dramatic. Judith is horrified that the people she tried to help, she has killed. But in the next scene (V), Ozias reassures her that he knows the Assyrians poisoned all the nearby springs, and he will direct the people's wrath to them. But the Elders agree that surrender is necessary.

Judith suggests learning from Scripture, and reads from a papyrus the story of Eglon, king of Moab, who was slain by Jehu with a sword hidden under his mantle (Judg 3:12–30). When she finishes relating the story, she raises her sword and asks: "Who here will be Jehu? Rise, and seize the sword." No one volunteers, and Judith says with some scorn: "You are warriors, and you tremble?" They mumble lame excuses, including that treachery even toward an enemy is not acceptable. Judith responds that if it is a crime to save their people, perhaps it must be a woman to undertake this task. They are shocked that she wants to even consider this. Sarcastically, she retorts: "What, perform a terrible task which pales the cheeks of soldiers bronzed by the sun in battle?" She further wonders aloud, with sarcasm, how she could succeed, "fatigued and wasted by fasts and prayers." Answering her own question, she says that for women, "the spindle, the shuttle, and the needle" (*il fuso, la spola, e l'ago*, from a Grimms Fairy Tale of that name) are the permitted weapons. In addition, women have "smiles, glances, and kisses." So, Judith concludes, she has no use for this tremendous sword, which she throws down. One of the Elders reaches to take it, and Judith tells him not to touch it. She then makes them all swear to let her go out through the gates that night without questioning her. Believing that God speaks through her, they accept her request.

In Scene VI, Gothoniel remains alone with Judith and tells her he understands what she is setting out to do. But she tells him to close his mouth when he implies that she will offer herself to Holofernes. Then she dismisses him, harshly saying that since he does not know how to kill with a sword, he should leave her to kill Holofernes with the poison of her eyes. Gothoniel tries to speak but she silences him with a gesture, and he leaves, "overcome by her superhuman dignity." These additions to the original create not only a more powerful and commanding Judith than her biblical counterpart but also one with more personality and wit. In the next scene (VII), Judith calls in Abramia and tells her to prepare all her richest clothing and jewelry.

Abramia is terrified when she realizes they are going to encounter Holofernes, whom she says she cannot tolerate seeing. Judith assures her she will not have to see him, only Judith will. Abramia tells Judith that if she sees him, misery will come to her;

Judith counters that the misery will be his. Then she abruptly tells Abramia to oppose her no more and to prepare herself, ending with: "Slave, I command!" (*Schiava, lo impongo*). This may be the only retelling in which Judith's slave is actually addressed as a slave. The biblical Judith never speaks to her slave this way, but this Judith is much more imperious and commanding. Closing the scene, she says to herself: "And now come back to me, you burning, fatal power of my eyes. Deborah, rouse your harp, and whistle now, stone from David's sling—To work! To work!" (*All'opra!*).

Act III opens inside Holofernes's tent, described in very luxuriant terms: "A rich carpet and other furniture give the idea of luxury and the effeminacy of the Assyrians," repeating the apparently derogatory term "effeminacy" from earlier. In Giacometti's period this would have been a great insult, as it then implied being more like a woman than a man (but not necessarily with the innuendo of homosexuality). Holofernes is surrounded by his slaves, harem, officers, and eunuchs. He talks with pride about all his victorious battles and his frustration with the siege of Bethulia, which he feels should not be necessary. Vagaus reassures him that the poisoning of all the springs should bring some victory. Holofernes states that he will find a shortcut through the mountains, and when asked who will guide him, he says: "The young Jewess who entered the camp four days ago." This is an interesting dramatic device: Judith's initial arrival and subsequent days in the camp were never mentioned or described until now.

Holofernes tells Arzaele, queen of his harem, that Judith is his "star" who will guide them and through whom he will vanquish the God of Israel. He describes their initial encounter thus: "Scarcely had I seen her … in all the brilliance of her beauty, than I felt in my soul a profound secret, a new life, a great fascination, and a feeling sweeter than I had ever experienced." Arzaele, obviously jealous and threatened, suggests that Judith could be a "bad spirit in the form of an enchantress who has come to seduce and betray you." Holofernes realizes she would say this because Judith could be "fatal" to her—as she well could be, he agrees, since he loves Judith. He further reminds Arzaele that she has no right to be jealous, for she may be the queen of the harem but is still his slave. He makes it clear that he has chosen Judith over her and that she is obligated to honor Judith.

In the next scene (II), Arzaele bemoans her fate and hopes to find a weapon to kill Judith. She wants Judith to tremble before Holofernes's slave as she trembles before him. In Scene III, Judith arrives, richly dressed, and tells Arzaele that she has come at the chief's order. Arzaele asks her if she is not queen here, and Judith is startled. When Arzaele compliments Judith, she also tells her she was ordered to do so by Holofernes, "my lord, and your lover." Judith protests, but Arzaele insists that he has been proclaiming this every hour. The scene closes with Arzaele telling Judith that she hates her and that "the great hate of a slave is death."

As Holofernes enters (Scene IV), he overhears these words and threatens Arzaele with death. He tells Judith he will kill Arzaele on the spot if she has offended her, and Judith says she does not want the blood of a woman. Holofernes announces that Arzaele will be her slave forever and forces Arzaele to kiss Judith's sandals. She does so, and as she exits the tent, murmurs "Vengeance!" A long dialogue between Holofernes and Judith ensues (Scene V). Holofernes describes how much he loves Judith and proclaims that though Arzaele had reigned over his heart, now Judith reigns over her.

Judith says somewhat cryptically: "May it be a short reign," but Holofernes responds that it will be forever. He goes on to describe what he sees as their future, as he takes over the entire world and rules as both high priest and god, with her at his side. Judith can hardly conceal the horror she feels, and she moves away. He continues with his hyperbolic vision, telling Judith that after he has destroyed the harems, she will be his wife and they will enjoy the pleasures of love. Aside, Judith says: "Hiss, hiss, serpent. I am not Eve! I will crush you." (Some of this text is what many of us would love to hear coming from Judith's mouth). Librettists who borrowed from Giacometti often incorporated serpent imagery in Judith's lines, but with a different sense.

Now in a complete plot twist, Judith tells Holofernes she is not yet his bride and was sent to him by Heaven in order to guide him toward "Zion" (meaning Bethulia, presumably). In the original version, it was this offer that gained Judith access to Holofernes. But here, he rebuffs her offer, saying he never asked her for help. In fact, he says, it is an insult to even suggest he needs help because he is so all-powerful that his sword can "open every road," and more hyperbole of this kind. In the end, he tells Judith she must choose between two deities: hers, or himself. Judith proclaims her God is the only one, and Holofernes tells her to return to Bethulia, where he will find her. He tells her of the plan to attack Bethulia the next day and assures her that no one will escape the massacre: "Children will be torn from the wombs of their mothers and hurled into the air as stones." This Holofernes is truly a monstrous literary creation. Judith reconsiders when she learns of the plan for the next day, and offers to remain, to "accomplish what I have commenced," which has a double meaning (as in the original story). Holofernes tells her it is not enough, because he still thirsts for her lips. She promises he will have them next day, and he is overjoyed, telling her she will be the mistress of his destiny. She responds: "I will prove it to you," yet another double entendre.

In Scenes VI and VII, Holofernes's men bring him a prisoner: none other than the high priest Eliakim. Judith is shocked to see him and tries to hide in the shadows. Eliakim had been on the mountain to invoke God's thunder against Holofernes, who jokes that his God must have been sleeping when he was just now taken prisoner (a reference to Elijah's words in 1 Kgs 18:27). Spotting Judith, Eliakim asks her why she is there, and Holofernes answers that she is his "spouse and lover." She has to pretend in order not to betray herself. Eliakim is shocked and curses her, which enrages Holofernes, who wants to kill him on the spot. Judith pleads for his life because he has preserved the faith of their ancestors and is justified in his anger. Eliakim faces up to Holofernes, telling him he will be defeated by God. Then he continues with a prophecy: "From the root of Jesse shall spring the robust tree destined to gather ... the scattered tribes. A breath new and pure ... announces God, born of a virgin of Judah, Redeemer of the world" (from Isa 11:1 and 7:14, viewed by many Christians as a foretelling of the birth of Jesus).[15] Giacometti has astoundingly inserted a verse

---

[15] Alice Ogden Bellis, Professor of Hebrew Bible at Howard University School of Divinity, says: "Because Isaiah 11:1 is quoted (from the Greek Septuagint) in several New Testament texts, Christians have traditionally understood the image of the root of Jesse as referring to Jesus." Bellis, personal communication, April 29, 2020.

considered by Christians to be a prophecy of the birth of Jesus in the mouth of an Israelite High Priest! This might subtly suggest that the purpose of Judith's triumph was to allow the Israelite people to produce Jesus. Presumably his audience would have appreciated this.

Holofernes's response is: "But before he is born, you will die. Now!" Eliakim says he is ready to die, but Judith pleads for his life. She throws herself at Holofernes's feet, while Eliakim continues to beg for death. Judith pleads desperately, looking at Holofernes with great passion and reminding him that he had made her queen. Holofernes agrees with her and spares the priest's life, since he does not want "to deign to strike such a weak foe." He tells his men to escort Eliakim to Bethulia. Turning to Judith, he tells her that her reign has now begun. When Holofernes leaves, Eliakim again asks to be killed, but Judith approaches him and in a very low voice, orders him to return, and to tell the people to prepare for battle, when the head of the Assyrian chief will be seen on a long spear. Eliakim wonders if she is trying to deceive him, or if she is mad. She tells him to look at her face and tells him she is offering "sweet promises" to Holofernes today in order to kill him tomorrow. Eliakim now understands and berates himself for cursing her. He then blesses her, saying: "Isaac's angel descends to shield thee with his chaste wings," suggesting she will be saved by the same angel that saved Isaac from sacrifice. Then the guards take him back to Bethulia.

Act IV opens in Holofernes's tent, where loud music, singing, and cries are heard. Abramia is sitting alone thinking of Judith at the feast, when suddenly Judith approaches (Scene II). She tells Abramia that Holofernes got very drunk at the feast and other officers tried to approach her, but she was able to escape. (This sequence is acted out in Marcello's libretto and elsewhere, rather than just being recounted; see Chapters 4 and 5). Judith is now waiting for Holofernes, though Abramia discourages her from doing that, saying that Arzaele has been watching Judith with contempt, awaiting her moment. Judith hears voices approaching and realizes it is Holofernes. She says to herself: "Perhaps his slaves are waking him from a sleep for the last time" and Abramia asks what Judith said. Judith just tells her to raise the curtain in preparation for Holofernes's arrival.

In Scene III, Vagaus enters and tells Judith that Holofernes is enraged. He did not sleep for long and when he saw that Judith had left the banquet, he found out she left because his officers had disturbed her. He is now very drunk but also furious, and Vagaus says only Judith can calm him. She reluctantly agrees, while Abramia hides in the corner. In Scene IV, Holofernes rushes in, followed by his officers. Thrilled to see Judith, he asks which of the officers offended her, offering to cut them to pieces as he brandishes his sword. She tries to calm him and asks him to give her the sword. He smiles and lets her feel the weight of it, saying that no human hand can wield it: "It is lightning and I turn its point against heaven." At that moment, thunder is heard, brought on, in Holofernes's mind, by his voice. The dramatic device of a storm in this scene is also employed by Marcello, and in several operas (see Chapters 4, 5).

Holofernes continues to rant for some time before collapsing, dropping the sword and struggling to breathe as he falls on the couch. Judith asks Vagaus if he is dying, but Vagaus assures her that Holofernes is always like this when drunk, and that he revives after sleeping. Judith encourages Vagaus and the officers to carefully place Holofernes on the couch. Judith says to herself: "Samson's hair at last is cut off, and the sacrifice to God is ready!" After they all leave, she says: "You have now closed the tomb of Holofernes—and mine, perhaps, but to that I am resigned."

Now she addresses Abramia, who has come out of the shadows and is shocked that Judith chose to remain alone with Holofernes. Judith tells Abramia that she cannot hate him as much as Judith does, and Abramia corrects her. For the first time, she confesses that she was taken captive as a girl to Babylon, where she was forced to be in Holofernes's harem. Judith says that she has therefore done well. Abramia does not understand but Judith sends her away. She lifts the curtain to the room where Holofernes is sleeping, and in a long soliloquy she hesitates out of fear that he might awaken. His eyes seem to be open and looking at her, which terrifies her (this dramatic device was used in early oratorio librettos; see Chapter 1). She is contemplating how to perform the act. As she reaches for the sword, Holofernes begins talking in his sleep (a device used in early oratorios and also by Marcello). Finally she tries to lift the sword, but it is too heavy for her to raise off the ground. Now she turns to God, in the first and only lengthy prayer heard (contrasted with the numerous prayers in the original story), praying for strength and asking God to show his power. At that moment, lightning is seen, which she takes as a response. Now able to lift the sword, she still hesitates. In Marcello's libretto, she interprets the thunder as God's response.

In Scene V, the rejected and jealous Arzaele enters stealthily and approaches Judith, intending to kill her. She threatens Judith with a dagger but Judith raises up the sword, threatening to take her head off, as Holofernes had previously offered. Judith is inspired by Arzaele's presence to carry out her act. She runs back to the alcove, from where Holofernes's cries are heard. Judith reappears with a bloody sword and Arzaele asks what she has done. Judith answers that "your couch is smoking with blood; go, behold how the kiss of a Hebrew woman burns." Arzaele screams and is about to denounce Judith but when Judith raises the sword over her, she falls lifeless. Judith expresses relief that God took care of it and she did not have to strike another time. Though covered in blood, she is "unstained." She calls Abramia and tells her to tear down the "silken curtain" and quickly wrap the head in it, which Abramia does joyfully. Judith wraps herself in a mantle and hides the sword (an interesting addition to the original story, where the sword is never mentioned again after the beheading). Abramia wonders how they will get away and Judith reminds her that she is the queen and will not be questioned.

Act V takes place back in Bethulia. The Elders are wondering why Judith has not returned, since the five days have passed. One Elder comments that they deserve the slow and horrible death they have chosen, since they trusted their safety "to the promises of a pretty woman. Women fight now instead of the soldiers of Judah." This is yet another reference to "effeminacy," or women taking over men's roles. Gothoniel, in love with Judith, tells him to be quiet, as he weeps for Judith's (assumed) lost honor and for Israel. All the others take his side. Suddenly, trumpets are heard, and the people think it is the enemy. Instead, it is Judith approaching, accompanied by their own trumpets, and she is bearing a sword.

In Scene II, Judith tells the assembled that the sword is Holofernes's and it was used to "cut from his body his horrible head." She tells them she placed it on a lance and in front of the camp, frightening the enemy. This is a slight change from the original, in which she brings the head back to Bethulia and there displays it on the walls. People are shocked and in wonder, and want to kiss Judith's robes, but she stops them, insisting that she has done nothing, that it was all done by God.

Gothoniel is the only one who doubts Judith, wondering how she could have executed such a blow and remained pure. Judith is irate and convinces him and everyone else of his error. In the third and final scene, Ozias returns from battle, announcing a total victory. All the assembled want to kneel before Judith but she instead kneels before Eliakim as she presents the sword, which they will place on an altar. She then announces that she is throwing off her fancy garments as a soldier throws aside his armor after battle and returning to her quiet home in her veils of mourning. She gives a final sermon, telling all to teach her name to their children, to tell them "war is sacred when the stranger threatens the land which God has given us for our country." This text would have resonated for Italians during their struggle for independence. She further promises that if they are ever threatened by an infidel people again, she will return to lead them to battle. Wrapping herself in her mantle, followed by Abramia, she leaves. All watch her in silence, "filled with admiration and marvel." This ending has a very different tone than the original one, which included a lengthy hymn in praise of Judith and God. It is also, unusually, a quiet ending.

Conclusion

This play, very popular in its time and a strong influence on librettist Marcello (who copied many elements of it), adheres to much of the original story while adding interesting new elements. Judith's slave, here Abramia, is given more dimensions. She relates that she was in Holofernes's harem in Babylon and therefore has personal knowledge of him, along with fear and horror. Judith displays conflicted feelings about strength and weakness, both in the Hebrew men and in herself (this theme is found in many librettos). The most unusual addition is that of the Hebrews' water sources being poisoned by the Assyrians (also found in Marcello's work). This makes Bethulia's suffering even greater and the Assyrians even more evil. Another addition is the character Arzaele, queen of Holofernes's harem and also in love with him. A love triangle, of course, has always appealed to the Italians and is a crucial element in many operas. In a jealous rage against Judith, who has just killed Holofernes, Arzaele approaches her with a sword but is struck down on the spot. Judith thanks God for saving her the trouble of killing another person, which sounds almost comical but was probably not meant to be. An addition that goes counter to the original story is Holofernes refusing Judith's help, insisting he is strong and smart enough to conquer Bethulia on his own. All he wants from Judith is her body. So in this retelling, Holofernes himself was deceitful, agreeing to let Judith into his tent because he pretended to want her assistance in defeating her people. The ending is triumphant but not exuberantly so, as Judith walks off wrapped in her mantle and all watch her in quiet admiration.

4

Nineteenth-Century Operas: Achille Peri, Domenico Silveri, Charles Edouard Lefebvre, Alexander Serov

The term "nineteenth-century opera" immediately evokes Giuseppe Verdi's brilliant operas or the *bel canto* masterpieces of Gaetano Donizetti and Vincenzo Bellini. But unfortunately, the composing giants of that century did not find inspiration in biblical stories, including the book of Judith. A popular Judith play by Paolo Giacometti (1857: discussed in Chapter 3) and an equally popular libretto by Marco Marcello (1860) inspired several Italian composers who were popular in their time to set these texts to operas. Two of these composers were Achille Peri and Domenico Silveri. The former wrote his opera in 1860, the latter in 1885. The most notable French opera of that era based on Judith was by Charles Lefebvre and dates to 1877. Even a Russian composer, Alexander Serov, found inspiration in Giacometti's play, as well as in an earlier play by Hebbel (see Chapter 3) for his Judith opera of 1863. I will be discussing these four operas in this chapter.

The most striking musical development in early nineteenth-century Italy was the decline of oratorio and the rise of opera. Opera was seen as the perfect genre for collective, national actions, which accelerated its development in Italy. In the nineteenth century, a time of increasing national identification (rather than city or regional) and nation-states, heroes had to be strongly connected to the nation. Since Judith acted independently, she could not fulfill "the typical nineteenth-century ideal of a hero."[1] In France, composers in the late nineteenth century were interested in exploring female strength and depicting it through music. At the same time, painters were depicting Judith as a predatory femme fatale associated with evil. But in the 1870s, in the wake of the French defeat by Prussia, Judith was seen as a role model both for her faith and her willingness to risk her life for her country. This became an allegory for a new political identity based on these qualities. By the 1890s, the perspective changed to one that

---

[1] Paolo Bernardini, "Judith in the Italian Unification Process," chap. 22 in *The Sword of Judith: Judith Studies Across the Disciplines*, ed. Kevin R. Brine (Cambridge: Open Book, 2010), p. 398. Available online: http://books.openedition.org/obp/972 (ISBN: 9781906924171).

was fearful as well as misogynist.[2] Judith's story ran counter to the general portrayal of women in the Romantic era, particularly in opera. The majority of Romantic operas end with the lead soprano's death/martyrdom. This was true of that era's literature as well. Women were condemned to suffer—that was their role. Not only is Judith not a woman who suffered, she also did not die until long after her heroic deed. In addition, women in the Risorgimento era (about 1815–70, the period of Italian unification) were expected to remain within the domestic sphere, not the public one.[3]

The story of Judith became so known and popular in France that in 1876 the Académie des Beaux-Arts chose this story for the annual Prix de Rome cantata competition, to be set to music by aspiring young composers. In that same year, Charles Lefebvre's opera *Judith* was performed at the Paris Opera (see below). The winner of the competition was Paul Hillemacher.[4]

In nineteenth-century Italian opera, there is typically far more music for chorus than in oratorios, which is usually the reverse in other countries. The chorus plays a crucial role—that of "the people"—in many operas. One representative work of the period is the opera *Giuditta* by Venetian Jewish composer Samuele Levi (1813–1883), with libretto by Giovanni Peruzzini (1815–1869), a prolific author well versed in Risorgimento ideology. The choral action is central to this opera, overwhelming Judith. There are choruses of women, warriors, and priests.[5] Unfortunately, there is no extant score, only the libretto (therefore I am not discussing it here).

Achille Peri's *Giuditta* (1860) and Domenico Silveri's *Giuditta* (1885)

The libretto for both of these operas was by Marcello, who collaborated with many opera composers. Though the two operas were written twenty-five years apart, the text in both is more or less the same. For that reason, to avoid too much repetition, I am treating them together here, rather than chronologically. The operas will be discussed in blocks of scenes, after the introductions to both composers.

Achille Peri (1812–1880) was born in Reggio Emilia where he began his musical studies, which he later continued in Paris. There he founded a touring opera company but returned to Italy after it failed. He then began working as a conductor, and ultimately wrote ten operas, many of which were successful and which were said to be influenced by Verdi. In fact, his music echoes the *bel canto* style of Donizetti even more than Verdi. *Giuditta* (1860) was one of his most popular operas and possibly one of the most important musical works based on Judith during the Italian Risorgimento. The premiere of this opera at La Scala received enthusiastic reviews, with one calling it "one

---

[2]   Jann Pasler, "Politics, Biblical debates, and French Dramatic Music on Judith after 1870," in *Sword of Judith*, p. 431.

[3]   Alexandre Lhâa, "Marcello and Peri's *Giuditta*," in *Sword of Judith*, pp. 420–1.

[4]   Pasler, p. 435; see Chapter 2 for full discussion. Hillemacher's work was an opera/oratorio.

[5]   Bernardini, p. 405.

of the best melodramas to come out for many years."[6] The opera received its American premiere in 1863, performed by the Maretzek Italian Opera Company in New York. An advertisement and a review for the performance state:

> The opera of "Judith," from the pen of a young but gifted composer, Achille Peri, was written at the breaking out of the Italian war in 1859. The story of Judith and Holofernes was taken as being typical of the expected deliverance of Italy from the bonds of her oppressors, and the text of the opera everywhere expresses the longings of a down-trodden people for freedom.
>
> The great success which attended the production of "Judith" at every prominent theatre between Naples and Milan did not arise wholly from the political bearings of the opera, since the vigor and originality of the music added largely to its popularity. The work is recognized in Europe as a standard composition, and as such is now presented for the first time in this country.[7]

Not all reviews were equally favorable, for example, this one:

> "Giudetta" [*sic*] is the name of a "biblical opera," by Peri, which was performed twice, and, we hope, will soon find that rest, from which it should never have been disturbed. An ordinary opera, by any of the followers of Verdi, is already bad enough, but a "biblical opera" is decidedly worse. The story of "Judith and Holofernes," put to test by the brass of a modern Italian composer, puts it in a considerably more hideous light than it enjoys already by itself. The effect of a prima-donna swinging the head of a man she has just cut off, in the air, may be very fine, but sustained by the music of Signor Peri, it is positively too fine to be enjoyed by us. But, after all, we have to be thankful to be made acquainted with these modern Italian operas, for they make us understand why Verdi could become so popular. We shall, here after, enjoy Verdi's music much better.[8]

In any event, the opera disappeared from the repertoire. At the time of these performances, its success occurred in spite of the prevalent view in that era that the story of Judith was widely considered inappropriate for dramatic or musical formats. This was due to an important change in attitudes toward women in the nineteenth century. It was now considered inappropriate for a single woman to perform any violent act without the assistance of a strong man.

It is quite possible that the enthusiasm for Peri's opera was in part due to how it addressed current attitudes to the Italian war of independence. Alexandre Lhâa suggests that the librettist Marcello infused the Judith narrative "with the nationalist-patriotic ideology of the Risorgimento." He was attempting, in this opera, to make

---

6   *Gazzetta dei teatri*, March 27, 1860; in Lhâa, "Marcello and Peri's *Giuditta*," p. 413. An entry in *New Grove Dictionary* (2001) contradicts this sentiment: there, Giovanni Carli Ballola writes that the 1860 premiere was a disaster, and *Giuditta*'s success came only in 1862 (vol. 19, p. 397).

7   https://www.musicingotham.org/event/26950 (accessed January 24, 2019).

8   Musical Review and World, "Review," *Music in Gotham*, November 21, 1863, p. 28. Available online: https://www.musicingotham.org/event/26950 (accessed February 20, 2019).

Judith a symbol, or "emblem of the national movement of independence."[9] In Paolo Bernardini's opinion, Judith's action is marginal in this opera and is made possible by the victory won by the Jewish army against Holofernes's troops. In this interpretation, not only is Judith's act "almost unnecessary," but her servant also is replaced by a strong Jewish captain in love with her.[10] I do not agree with this assessment. Judith's character is quite well developed in the libretto; she experiences many emotions found only in the margins of the original book and is portrayed as a strong woman.

The closing word of the final chorus is "Liberty," repeated several times. Marcello spelled out his own intention to give a political dimension to Judith's story in a prefatory note, where he writes that he saw Judith as "the Charlotte Corday of Jewish history," evoking the playwright Paolo Giacometti's words (see Chapter 3). Giacometti himself refuted that parallel, insisting that politics was not connected to the "purely religious and theocratic war" described in Judith.[11] Yet both the audience and critics of the opera did perceive allusions to their current situation of the Risorgimento, whether deliberate or not. Lhâa points out some rhetorical cues throughout the opera. For example, the use of the term "barbarian" for the Assyrians would have been familiar to nationalistic writers as a reference to the Austrians. Another cue is the willingness of the entire community of Bethulia to take an oath of loyalty: such a collective oath can point to the "birth of a political community." Yet another cue is Judith's willingness to be sacrificed to obtain honor (as Charlotte Corday had done). Lhâa astutely notes how the Risorgimento's attitude toward sacrifice "merges with the operatic discourse that makes the sacrificial dimension a major characteristic of the Romantic heroine."[12]

Choosing a biblical narrative, particularly that of Judith, could well be the librettist's attempt to legitimize the Italian movement for independence by identifying it with the Hebrews, who clearly had God's support. As Lhâa points out, the words for God—*Iddio* and *Dio*—are used over twenty times by the Hebrews in Peri's opera. This God often appears as a warrior God, thus justifying the war against Assyria (symbolizing Austria). In addition, the conflict is called a holy war (*santa guerra*) and Judith's piety is emphasized throughout. She is described as a "holy woman," even an "angel"; and also as "Jael's sister" and the "new Deborah." The identification of the Italian people with the Hebrews is not unique to this libretto. Risorgimento thinkers (particularly Vincenzo Gioberti) saw the biblical narrative as a paradigm of history and the Italian people as "the Israel of the modern age."[13] An earlier and very influential opera that would have served as inspiration and confirmation of these ideas was Verdi's *Nabucco* (1842) with its extremely well-known "Chorus of the Hebrew Slaves."

In Peri's opera, Judith's character is a paradox: in Lhâa's words, she is "sandwiched between the nationalist usage to which she lends herself and the gender structures of contemporary Italian society." Her femininity is denied on some levels, even while she is praised as a liberator. Ultimately, she is "plagued by the interpretative needs of a

---

[9] Lhâa, p. 413.
[10] Bernardini, p. 405.
[11] Charlotte Corday killed Marat, during the French Revolution, and would have been very well known in that era; Giacometti quote in Lhâa, p. 414.
[12] Lhâa, p. 415, footnote 18, p. 416.
[13] Vincenzo Gioberti, in Lhâa, pp. 418–19.

male-dominated society."[14] Marcello's libretto was subsequently altered and the opera was performed again at La Scala, for the last time, in 1862.

The libretto in Italian can be found online (all translations my own).[15]

A translated libretto can be found online.[16] However, the translation is not completely accurate and some text is not included.

The score (Milano: Francesco Lucca, 1861) is not available online, and the opera has never been recorded. Scores are available in a handful of libraries, for example, the British Library[17] and the library at the University of California in Berkeley. The frontispiece on the score provides the names of the singers at the premiere but not their voice types. That has to be gleaned from the vocal range of their music (on which I based my classifications).

Count Domenico Silveri (1818-1900) was born to a family of nobility, in Tolentino, Italy. His family sent him and his brother to Rome when Silveri was 18, to enter the Pontifical Noble Guards (*Guardia Nobile Pontificia*), an honor bestowed only on noble families. While in Rome, he pursued musical studies, both cello and composition. Around 1843, he met Gioacchino Rossini, who praised and encouraged Silveri's compositions. His first major success was a work he composed for the Mass celebrating the election of a new Pope in 1846. The work, *L'Armonia Religiosa*, was very successful and was played from then on for many special occasions at Saint Peter's. In Rome, Silveri came to know many leaders of the Risorgimento and became their followers. Years later, because of these activities, he was expelled from the *Guardia* because of the anti-pontifical leanings of the Risorgimento movement. He continued to work in local administrative and political positions, while also pursuing music. He married a countess in 1853 and they had ten children, most of whom died in infancy or childhood. Throughout his life, Silveri wrote primarily religious works. The opera *Giuditta* falls loosely in that category and is considered one of his most significant works. Written in 1885, it premiered at the Teatro Comunale of Catania.[18]

Achille Peri's *Giuditta* (1860)

Piano-vocal score: Stabilimento Musicale F. Lucca, Milan, 1885; page numbers refer to this score.

Judith: mezzo
Abramia (servant): alto
Eleazaro (a Hebrew): tenor

[14] Anne Eriksen, in Lhâa, p. 423.
[15] https://ia801808.us.archive.org/13/items/giudittamelodram00peri2/giudittamelodram00peri2.pdf (accessed October 22, 2020).
[16] https://babel.hathitrust.org/cgi/pt?id=hvd.32044044300440;view=1up;seq=17 (accessed October 22, 2020).
[17] I owe a debt of gratitude to my London friend and colleague Rev. Dr. Ann Jeffers, who kindly devoted many hours in the British Library scanning the full score and making it available to me. Without her generous help, I could not have discussed the music in the same depth.
[18] Enzo Calcaterra, *Talento e nobiltà: Domenico Silveri, un uomo una città un'epoca* (Phoenix: Tolentino, 2002), pp. 109–11.

Holofernes: baritone
Gionata (young warrior in love with Judith): tenor
Pontefice/Eliachimo: bass
Arzaele (queen of Holofernes's harem): soprano

Domenico Silveri's *Giuditta* (1885)

Piano-vocal score: Stabilimento Musicale F. Lucca, Milan, 1885; page numbers refer to this score. The score is not available online but can be found in several libraries.[19]

Judith: soprano
Abramia: mezzo
Gionata: tenor
Holofernes: baritone

I will discuss these two operas side by side, broken into scenes or acts. The scene division varies a great deal between the operas and often even diverges from the libretto's division. Where the action is identical, I will only summarize it in the discussion of Silveri's opera. Some onstage action indicated in the libretto is also written in the score, but not consistently so. I will highlight significant alterations to the original libretto, and differences between the two composers' musical interpretations. Silveri (or his publisher) sometimes chose to indicate which instruments in the orchestra are playing specific passages; such indications are absent from Peri's score (with few exceptions). Therefore, I cannot accurately compare orchestration in the two works. In general, Silveri is influenced by Verdi far more than Peri, whose music more often mirrors that of *bel canto* composers Donizetti (1797–1848) and Bellini (1801–1835). The differences between these two settings can be attributed to many factors, among them the style of music popular in their day as well as political and social attitudes.

Act I

Peri: After the overture, the introduction to Act I opens with a brief lamenting passage and then a short solo by Eleazaro, a Hebrew (p. 18). This differs from most operas that start immediately with the chorus. The chorus does join in after a few measures to echo Eleazaro. The great pathos in the music is amplified by the rhythm of three groups of sighing triplets. As the people of Bethulia grow more agitated, singing about suffering thirst from the siege, the music remains plangent but becomes more rhythmical. Eventually the 8th-note triplet groups become 16th-note groups, a more agitated sound, building to the climactic phrase "Lucky is the one who will die by the enemy's sword" (p. 25). After this, the music calms again as they continue over a steady 4/4 beat to sing of those who will be lucky and will not see their homeland prey to a new insult, and won't experience the pain of servitude. Silveri's setting of this text is more

---

[19] To locate one, search https://www.oclc.org/en/worldcat.html.

soaring than Peri's. Eleazaro berates the people, in very dramatic and angry phrases, for abandoning their God. He says that since they have done so, the better choice now would be to surrender Betulia.

In Scene II (p. 29), Gionata (an invented character; in love with Judith) comes running when he hears the people, exclaiming in strong phrases over rapid 16th-note passages in the orchestra: "Who here speaks of surrender?" Two long rests suggest the people's hesitation. They murmur: "We will die of thirst." Gionata continues, over very excited music in the broad time of 9/8, that it is better to die of thirst than become slaves to a barbaric king. He tells them to gather the courage of their ancestors, but he despairs that they have lost hope and faith. While he is singing those lines, the chorus sings very softly that Holofernes is more powerful than they. Gionata's music becomes increasingly passionate.

In Scene III (p. 34), after a long pause, the key changes to B-flat major and the tempo increases, as trumpet sounds are heard approaching. The people fear it is the enemy but then realize it is their High Priest (*Pontefice*) Eliachimo, and this renews their hope. The music for his entrance is marked *Maestoso, sostenuto* (majestic and sustained). The people bow before him as he blesses them (confusing Jewish with Christian practice, but since his audience was largely Catholic, they would have related to this practice). Gionata tells him the people want water, and Eliachimo tells the people that war is all around them but the day is near when their God will avenge them. In soft but fast and rhythmical music, he encourages them to fight back. The chorus sings, in lively and upbeat music: "The old courage has been reawakened, we do not want to suffer servitude to the foreigner." In the metered, rhyming Italian verse:

In noi s'è destatò antico coraggio,
Soffrir non vogliamo straniero servaggio.

After a long pause, Gionata sings forcefully that everyone must swear that, rather than give in to "the barbaric" Holofernes, they will bury themselves in their "native grottoes" (not explained) since it is better to die this way than succumb to vile servitude (p. 38). These lines are sung to rousing music. He also encourages them by saying that the fury of a people often buys them liberty. Such sentiments would have resonated with the Italians during their fight for independence. The chorus repeats Gionata's words in a faster tempo while Eliachimo reassures them that the God of war will fight alongside them. This ensemble goes on for some time, repeating the same lyrics. The women sing a heartrending plea to Eliachimo about their children, who "like wilted flowers, bend their heads, thirsty and exhausted." Eliachimo reassures them that God will restore them. He follows this with a *bel canto*–style aria filled with biblical passages, notably about Moses getting water from a rock (Exod 17).

Silveri: An orchestral prelude introduces themes that will be heard in the opera. Drums, muted cymbals, and timpani are heard first as Scene I opens. The people of Betulia are lamenting the siege of the Assyrians. When the scene opens, at first only timpani are heard, then a mournful tune is heard first in the double basses, then in other instruments. The music amplifies the sense of desperation and exhaustion. The voices follow one another, rather than singing together in harmony. Eleazar, a Hebrew, sings the first line: *Sventura a noi! Per la nemica spada beato chi spirò* ("Unlucky us, and lucky is the one who dies by the enemy's sword"; also heard in Peri's opera). The tempo picks up and the chorus sings most of that phrase in complete unison, representing unity of thought. They continue in a new key, B-flat minor, in a soaring melody over throbbing chords: "That lucky one will not see his homeland prey to a new insult and won't feel the pain of being in servitude" (p. 12). They continue in this vein until finally, in another key change, they agree to submit to the enemy, saying: "It is the people's will." They start walking to the walls to open the gates to the enemy.

In Scene II (p. 19), Gionata comes running when he hears the people (as in Peri's opera). In strong music (to be sung *con forza*, forcefully), he sings in unaccompanied phrases, rising to *g'* in the second measure: "Who speaks here of surrender? Is there anyone here so blind and cowardly, that would dare to repeat these hateful words to my face? Please, approach." They all pull back but then sing a few unaccompanied measures in unison ("'grumbling amongst themselves," *mormorando fra loro*): "So we must die of thirst! O, our misfortune." His tenor voice continues above the full chorus. The rich and changing harmonies musically underline the people's despair. Most of this text was in the Peri opera, but Silveri's music in this section is more passionate, particularly the part of Gionata. When they build to the line "Lucky is the one who died," Gionata stands in the middle of the people and "with emotion" tells them it is better to die of thirst than become slaves to a barbaric king (as in Peri's opera). The passionate music rises to *a'* over a throbbing accompaniment. Gionata tells them to gather the courage of their ancestors, but he despairs that they have lost hope and faith. In faster, more anxious music, the people sing that Holofernes is more powerful than they, and there is no hope of breaking him. Gionata responds in rousing music, singing in a very high range—up to *b-flat'*—that God brings faith to people who have lost hope (p. 23). At this early stage of the opera, Gionata is playing the role Judith is expected to play, rallying the people and giving them hope. His casting as a heroic tenor further underlines this role. But ultimately, he does not replace Judith in any way.

As Scene III opens, the people hear trumpets approaching and fear it is the enemy, reflected in dissonant chord groups in the orchestra. Then they realize it is their High Priest (*Pontefice*) Eliachimo, whose entrance is in C major to express their renewed hope. The people bow before him (as in Peri's opera). Eleazar, speaking for the people, tells the Priest that the people want water or they will surrender. Eliachimo is shocked and tells them they must have hope, for the day will come when their God will have vengeance on their impious enemies. His music starts very solemnly but grows increasingly animated as the tempo quickens. At its climax, the encouraged people sing the passages about their courage reawakened in *fortissimo* and *allegro vivace* passages. Gionata reassures the people that if the old ardor arises in them again, their beloved country will be free. His *Giuramento* (vow; p. 35) is sung with great force (*gran impeto*). In contrast to Peri's setting, these lines are mostly unaccompanied, with sharp, rhythmic groups of chords between them. On the last line, the chorus joins in, repeating the opening phrases of the vow. The rousing chorus concludes with a repetition of Eliachimo's earlier encouraging lines that God will take vengeance on their enemies. The choral repetition is in a major, not minor, tonality and very assertive. Eliachimo reassures them that the God of war will fight alongside them. Fired up by Gionata, the crowd joins him at the walls.

In Scene IV (p. 45), which is still Scene III in Peri's opera, Eliachimo, singing very lyrical passages, tries to give hope to the women, who cannot bear to watch their children dying of thirst. He tells them God will save them and then sings an aria filled with biblical passages, about the powerful rod of Moses that performed miracles and is not broken. "Already, already, the burning thirst is ceasing, the yearned-for hour is not far!" This phrase is accompanied by high strings, a "holy" sound.

Judith's Entrance

Peri: No act or scene is indicated, as suddenly some of the people start shouting "She is coming!" (p. 48), initially singing *a cappella*. Others ask "Who?" and Eliachimo sings "Judith." The people and Eliachimo identify Judith as "the pearl of Betulia, the holy woman, inspired daughter of Merari, the widow of Manasseh" as the orchestra plays soaring music above them. In the original story, Judith is only identified by the narrator, not by the people. Eliachimo tells the people to put their hope in Judith, who will herald an auspicious event.

Judith enters and proclaims that she has just discovered water, singing *Una fonte!* ("A stream!"; this is from Giacometti's play: see Chapter 3). This may be a subtle nod to Miriam, known for her ability to find water in the desert during the desert exile (in the books of Exodus and Numbers). The people all sing that God sent Judith. She responds in a recitative (p. 51) that if God has chosen her, praise should go to him, since she is only his instrument. This is followed by a soaring melody in the orchestra. Then Eliachimo solemnly says that when their homeland has such women, the ark is safe in Zion, to which the chorus responds with a lively *Viva Giuditta!* ("Long live Judith!").

The people now gather around Judith to hear her story. Over a steady accompaniment of 16th-note motifs, creating a sense of suspense, she tells them she heard a mysterious voice. On this word, the rippling 16th-note passages abruptly stop. Over sustained chords, she repeats what she heard: *Esci, Giuditta* (Go out, Judith). She obeyed the command, not knowing where she was going. As she continues her account, the 16th-note phrases return. In a soaring phrase, Judith relates how she heard the laments of her city as she walked away. The music grows very soft (*ppp*), with mysterious *staccato* (detached) notes in the orchestra. A sudden flash of light shone in front of her, convincing her that God had chosen her to find a stream, which "gave wings to my feet." On that excited phrase, she sings a *g*" followed by a rapid descent of an octave and a fifth (to middle C), evoking a sense of flying. As Judith continues her account, the people sing "O blessed one, God has sent you to us!" in shimmering, elated music with many *tremolos*. An ensemble follows in which Judith continues her narrative over the chorus singing her praises. Judith's line is very *legato* and broad, while the chorus sings more broken and hesitant phrases, as if unsure of how to react to Judith's story. The soaring melody doubles Judith's line, and both the melody and rhythm strongly echo Verdi.

When Judith begins singing about her sighting of water, the accompaniment is very rapid groups of 32nd notes (p. 58). On the text "my heart burst out of my chest," she sings elaborate *coloratura* phrases, a *bel canto* style of expressing joy reminiscent of Donizetti (p. 59). The phrases end on a series of trills. The chorus sings a single *a cappella* measure ("Betulia can breathe") but Eliachimo breaks in, in more somber music, and reminds them that the holy war is not over and Holofernes is still a strong enemy, who has "as many warriors as the sea has waves" (p. 60). Under a *tremolo*, Judith "enthusiastically" proclaims, in another *coloratura* passage, that when the Lion of Judah boldly rises up, they will see the enemy completely destroyed, like insects.

Eliachimo, in a lyrical and poignant *bel canto* aria (p. 60), recites a prophecy of Isaiah after telling Judith to kneel—a Christian image. The people proclaim that God speaks through the Priest, who compares Judith to Deborah and Jael, telling her that Heaven has chosen her to accomplish a special mission. The chorus repeats these words. This slightly shifts the crucial roles of both God and of Judith herself to the High Priest. Judith remains kneeling for some time, as though "oppressed by the sublime prophecy." She rises slowly, lost in thoughts she cannot yet comprehend. Looking around, she remains stunned, seeing everyone quietly admiring and watching her. She repeats the Priest's words about the "new Deborah, the sister of Jael," protesting in soft, halting phrases that her ignoble (or worthless: *vile*) name cannot be mixed with theirs. Then she feels her soul filling with a great thought (*L'anima ferve d'un gran pensier*), her excitement again expressed in a *coloratura* passage (p. 63). The people comment that God is inspiring and exciting Judith with her own power. Judith, seeming outside of herself, wonders if it is God or Hell that is awakening such thoughts. In extended *coloratura* passages, often representing madness in the *bel canto* tradition, Judith envisions blood spraying in her face, which does not grow pale from terror. "I will be great, or a criminal, but I will save my country!" The people praise her, and say "there is nothing left" of a woman in her; she has the skirt of a widow, but her heart shows her a heroine:

> *O prodigio! In lei di donna*
> *Or più nulla ormai restò.*
> *Di una vedova ha la gonna.*
> *D'eroina il cor mostrò.*

Judith protests that she is only an instrument of God and it is he that should be praised. As a triumphant theme enters in the orchestra, the scene ends with Judith repeating *La patria salverò* ("I will save my homeland") several times, on the final repeat reaching a high C (*c"*) after a cadenza. She sustains this dramatic high note through the concluding measures (p. 68) (see Figure 3).

Silveri: In Scene V (p. 52), the people suddenly start shouting "She is coming!" and identify Judith as "the pearl of Betulia." Eliachimo emphatically adds: "the holy woman, inspired daughter of Merari, the widow of Manasseh." They sing these lines *a cappella* in a hymnal sound. The people all welcome her, and Eliachimo solemnly tells them to put their hope in her, while high *tremolos* play above him.

Judith appears high on a mountain, radiant with joy. The people proclaim that she will be the harbinger of auspicious events. She descends rapidly, proclaiming that she has just discovered water (as in Peri's opera). Judith's opening line, sung in three very

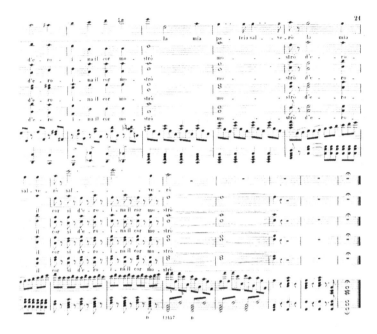

Figure 3 Achille Peri, Judith and Chorus

excited measures, is 'A spring, a spring!' (*Una fonte*; p. 52). The music immediately calms as a beautiful cello solo is heard, followed by a four-part hymnal-sounding chorus. The people praise and bless Judith, singing that God has sent her. Judith throws herself humbly at the Priest's feet, and the very lyrical music, to be sung "with great expression," switches to 6/8 time and D major (p. 53). Judith calmly insists that if God did choose her, then praise should go to him; she is only his instrument. As she sings, soldiers and servants are bringing vessels filled with water, and people are rushing to quench their thirst. Many return to the mountain for more water. Eliachimo tells everyone to praise Judith, which they do in rousing phrases. Then they ask her to relate her story.

A gentle theme in the woodwinds introduces Judith's account and runs through it. In a calm voice, she relates that she was praying, as the dismal night slowly surrounded her. In a sudden declamatory burst, in unison with trumpets she sings: "Go out, Judith" (*Esci, Giuditta*). The music dies down and picks up again, with bass *tremolos* and a throbbing beat. Judith says she heard a mysterious voice giving her that command, which instilled both courage and fear in her. She arose without a goal, walking in the shadows where the mysterious voice went quickly ahead of her. The music is quiet and suspenseful. In more passionate and soaring phrases, she sings: "The plaintive moans from our city wounded my heart." The music quiets down to a steady but nervous beat, as Judith describes a sudden flash of light that shone in front of her, convincing her that God had chosen her to discover a stream. This inspired idea, she sings over a more strumming accompaniment, "gave wings to my feet." In more measured, calm music, she sings of how she struggled in the "trembling, uncertain moonlight," thinking her eyes betrayed her in that dark night. On this final phrase, her voice, with the orchestra, descends to *b*, a low note for a soprano and very descriptive of darkness. Now the tempo picks up as she sings, over steady groups of triplets, that she finally heard the murmur of a stream from the hillside and cried out "It's water!" The music picks up, marked *con abbandono* (with abandon) as she cries out "O joy!" up to an *a"* (p. 61). She blesses God for the water and tells the people that this sight made her heart burst in her chest. She repeats this line twice, the first time high and then, over breathless music, on a lower note. In strong, triumphant music, the people ecstatically call her the saving angel of her people. Though the action and text are almost identical to Peri's opera, there is far more variation and drama in the musical elements.

Introduced by trumpet calls, Eliachimo solemnly recites a prophecy of Isaiah in a kind of chant (p. 65). The rest of this scene is the same as in Peri's. But after Eliachimo's prophecy, Silveri omitted several lines of the libretto. When Eliachimo has finished his prophecy (p. 70), ending on a low note, the orchestra plays a few measures of very high tones and a lyrical *ppp* melody in the violins, all suggesting "heavenly" sounds. During this music, Judith remains kneeling for some time before rising slowly, "lost in thoughts she cannot yet comprehend." In a new section, marked *Allegro vivo* and with a triumphant sound, Judith envisions blood spraying in her face, which does not grow pale from terror. In propulsive, exultant music, she sings: "I will be great, or a criminal, but I will save my country!" (see Figure 4) On the final repetition of this phrase, she sustains a *b-flat"* (*c"* in Peri, where Judith is a mezzo, making that high note even more dramatic). This aria has very strong echoes of Verdi, particularly his *Don Carlo*, which had been revised and performed in the same period. This section in Peri, by contrast, has more echoes of *bel canto*. In equally exultant music, the people repeat her words, saying: "She will save her country." Judith repeats "I will save my country" to the same melody one final time, again reaching the same *b-flat"*. But the chorus sings under her this time, a very effective device (pp. 76–7). Silveri does not use the exact text of Marcello's libretto here. The constant repetition of *la patria*, "the country," had deep resonance for Italians in that era. The act ends on a strong F major chord with the chorus sustaining *a"*, followed by fast trumpet calls.

Peri: Part II, Scene I opens in Judith's house (p. 69). The libretto includes a description of the room, with stairs in the back and several doors, an ebony table in the center and chairs. All the furniture is "severe and draped in mourning," with curtains over both the doors and windows. Hebrew maidservants and girls (*ancelle e fanciulle ebree*) come from the internal rooms, laying out rich and splendid women's garments on the table. Over a light, upbeat melody, a cheerful female chorus sings brightly about the beautiful garments and how they recall happier days. The music grows increasingly more upbeat up to Abramia's entrance.

Abramia (Abra in other librettos) appears here in Scene II for the first time, having overheard the women and girls. Though bright music continues, her singing is sustained and subdued. She tells them that the pious Judith does not break faith with Manasseh's ashes (this is presumably meant figuratively since cremation is taboo for Jews). In a recitative, to very sparse accompaniment, the women ask her for the meaning of all these festive clothes, and Abramia responds, unaccompanied: "Who can

Figure 4 Domenico Silveri, Judith and Chorus

read her thoughts?" They protest that Abramia, even though Judith's slave (*schiava*), is also her "sister" (a notion found in early oratorios; see Chapter 1). This character is rarely called a slave in librettos. Abramia confirms, in a wistful phrase sung *a cappella* to accentuate her loneliness, that Judith has pity for her many troubles (*affanni miei*). The women sing "Always so sad! What is it that troubles you?" in a dotted rhythm imitating a funeral march. In a mostly *a cappella* recitative (p. 74), broken by sparse chords between her words, Abramia shares her story of being captive in Babylon as a child, prey of the Assyrians. Now, she says, she lives "only on tears and sighs." In her aria *Nei Giardini di Samaria* ("In the gardens of Samaria"; p. 75), she describes herself in metaphoric verses clearly suggesting that she was repeatedly raped. The wistful music suggests an idyllic setting but also provides a subtext, since what she describes is far from an idyll. The music in in sharp contrast to her bitter words, suggesting that she kept her feelings buried for many years. At the end of the light aria, the tempo slows and the music becomes more emotional. In melancholy phrases, Abramia says she would have been better off never born, since her fate gave her such grief. The text is an elaboration of the same idea in Giacometti's play (see Chapter 3).

Part II, Scene III opens with Judith's arrival (p. 77). To soft and suspenseful music, including trills, dotted rhythm, and mostly *staccato* notes, the women sing that the "holy woman" (*santa donna*) is coming down from her *oratorio* (an oratory is a small private chapel). Silveri's music for this opening is more somber than Peri's. Judith enters very slowly, wrapped in a large cloak, absorbed in deep meditation and holding a sword close to her chest. She is so lost in thought that she walks into her servants and quickly hides the sword (score notes). She expresses surprise at seeing them there, and they remind her that they have been preparing the bridal kit (*il nuzial corredo*), which is now ready. In a recitative sung over a long sustained chord, Judith murmurs to herself that she does not want to look at these ornaments of her former modesty, since they will soon become the ornaments for the lustful passion (or lewd fire: *lascivo foco*) of an impious mortal. She is almost repenting what she had asked for (libretto note). Then she orders the servants to cover all the garments with a brown veil not to be lifted by anyone and dismisses them.

Scene IV, between Judith and Abramia, opens with an orchestral interlude marked "expressive" but which is light and very soft, with a dotted rhythm. It may be intended to represent anticipation. In a recitative dialogue accompanied only by sparse chords, Abramia confesses she is afraid, because their country is languishing and dying. Judith asks if she no longer has faith in God, and Abramia says she does, and also in Judith. Judith momentarily exults but catches herself and humbly says: "I am a weak woman and need to pray." Abramia ardently says: "There is a time to pray, and to act." Judith cries out: "Oh, if I could!" and lets Abramia see the sword. Abramia is surprised that it is Manasseh's, which Judith had inherited. Judith says she will offer it as a sacrifice at the temple, but Abramia says that vengeance would be dearer to God. Judith, over sudden *tremolos* and "shaking involuntarily" (score note), says: "You speak to me of blood? And if it were a crime?"

In response, Abramia opens the Bible that is on the table and reminds Judith of what is in the book of Judges. In a Verdian melody, very *legato* over a *staccato* and rhythmic accompaniment (p. 80), she sings of earlier victories over oppressors, particularly "a woman with strong language" (*una donna col forte linguaggio*). This woman gave courage to Israel. Interestingly, in this early part of the duet, no names are mentioned. The soaring opening of the duet that follows is sung in unison. They sing of the enemy who knew the escape route (referring to Sisera in Judg 4). Then returning to the earlier melody of Abramia's solo, they recall Deborah and Jael (p. 83), calling them both immortal and retelling the story in a duet, with great enthusiasm. Near the end, they describe Jael's deed in unison, as if in one voice, in soaring passages. They conclude singing a cadenza together in perfect thirds (p. 85).

Judith says, in an *a cappella* recitative, that the horrible legend fills her heart not with fear but with fire and ardor. After two measures of anxious music followed by *tremolos*, Judith wonders if the ferocious Holofernes would like her if he saw her. In a sudden key change, Abramia tells her to be quiet, because she knows Holofernes. Crestfallen, Judith wonders if she is seductive. These expressions of self-doubt are very interesting gap-filling moments that make Judith more human and three-dimensional, if not also weaker. Abramia is alarmed by Judith's question, but when she asks, in very strong music, what terrible plan she has in mind, Judith pulls back and imperiously dismisses her. Abramia, in parting, says she is trembling.

Scene IV opens with Judith alone. She sings in an *a cappella* recitative, in strong phrases, that she hears the voice of the supreme will calling her (p. 88). A few high orchestral passages suggest a heavenly voice. She continues, saying that the idea that was unsure in her mind is now taking shape, and it comes from God. More high orchestral passages are heard. This section is musically more dramatic in Silveri (below).

Act II

Silveri: Scene VI (still Act I in Marcello's libretto and Peri's opera) takes place in Judith's house. The orchestral "Prelude" opens with a few trumpet notes, followed by brass, then a high lyrical melody in the violins. The music sets a somber mood, more than in Peri's opera. The libretto includes a description of the room (the same as in Peri's). The female chorus sings about the beautiful garments and how they recall happier days, in simple and gentle music, ending with a lilting and homophonic (harmonic) section (p. 85). Abramia appears here for the first time. The rest of the scene is identical to Peri's. Only the music differs, for example, when Abramia confirms only in a brief melodic passage, that Judith has pity for her long travails. When Abramia describes being taken captive in Babylon as a child, her music is simple, melodic, and wistful. She sings of her "virgin breast" being "opened up like a solitary rose," clearly implying rape. After she adds that she also "recoiled from soft kisses," there is a sudden change of tempo to *presto*. Abramia angrily and forcefully sings that she believes she would have been better off never born. Building still more, in *fortissimo* and declamatory passages, she adds: "if your fate gave you such grief." On the final repeat of that line, her voice descends, singing *a cappella*, down to *g* below middle C—a very low note, expressing despair. (Silveri did not include the second stanza of Abramia's account from the Marcello libretto.) This is a very sympathetic portrayal of Judith's slave. She displays more grief and anger than in Peri's depiction, where she is wistful.

The next scene, VII, opens with Judith's arrival. The opening music, marked *molto espressivo*, is a mellow and Verdian lyrical melody (p. 92). Judith enters slowly, wrapped in a large cloak and "absorbed in deep meditation," holding a sword close to her chest that she later will hide in her cloak. The subsequent action is identical to Peri's opera. The next scene (IX in the original libretto, VIII in this opera) opens with slightly suspenseful music, leading up to the duet between Judith and Abramia. The dialogue is virtually identical to that in Peri's opera. Themes introduced in the opening of the scene are heard throughout the duet, which has powerful echoes of Verdi. When Abramia opens the Bible that is on the table and reminds Judith of earlier victories over oppressors (p. 97), she begins with "So is it written in Judges," punctuated by trombones. Judith listens to the story, "agitated by a thousand different thoughts, letting herself little by little be won over" (libretto notes). Abramia sings, to a simple melody, the story of Deborah and Jael. Her music is punctuated throughout by trombones. They join together before repeating Abramia's final lines. The last phrase, "she hammered his head to the ground," is sung by both women with exaltation, underlined by the bright C-major ending. To very dramatic music, abruptly shifting to C minor, Judith sings that "the horrible legend fills my heart not with fear, but with fire and daring," the voice rising to *a-flat* (p. 105). This is followed by highly dramatic and fast orchestral passages, filled with 16th-note runs and jagged rhythms, all reflecting the turbulence in Judith's mind. This is a more dramatic presentation of the Judges text than Peri's version.

Suddenly the music grows very soft, and over *tremolos* and sustained chords, Judith studies her image in the mirror. As in the Giacometti play (and Peri opera), she asks Abramia, in hesitant lines, if the years of mourning and widowhood, prayers and fasting, have left their mark. Abramia, in lilting music, assures Judith that she is still as beautiful as a morning star. Judith wonders if the ferocious Holofernes would like her if he saw her. The sweet, almost seductive music for this short duet may contain an element of irony. The rest of the scene is the same as in Peri.

Scene VIII is a short monologue by Judith. The four-measure orchestral introduction is marked "mysterious, with great expression" and features a clarinet solo and *tremolos* that continue over Judith's voice. In very dramatic lines, with winds and horns over her voice, she says she hears the voice of the supreme will calling her. Then continuing in an *a cappella* recitative, she says that the idea that was unsure in her mind is now taking shape, and it comes down directly from God. She repeats this last phrase twice, rising to *a"* and then descending an octave and a fifth, musically suggesting the descent of God (p. 110). This section is also more dramatic than Peri's version.

Peri: Scene VI continues with no scene break. Gionata enters to very fast and ominous music, marked *Allegro agitato* (p. 89). Judith does not seem happy to see him and asks him brusquely why he has come. He tells her: "To save you," ' to which she responds: "What danger threatens me?" In a Verdi-inspired aria, marked *Allegro agitato* and in a very strong 4/4 beat, he tells her in propulsive music that their people are coming to kill her. In more sustained passages, he tells her that while she was once blessed, she is now cursed. In increasingly louder and more excited music, he begs her to flee. Undaunted, she says she will remain and offer herself to the furious mob. He stops her from leaving and she asks him what he is hiding. The duet that follows is in the same agitated strong rhythm as the aria just heard. The orchestral music builds slowly, over *tremolos* and continual octave leaps in the bass section. Gionata finally tells Judith that the water she had found for the people was poisoned by the enemy (based on the Giacometti play; see Chapter 3). The final word of this phrase takes him to a high A flat (*a-flat'*). The music suddenly grows softer and hesitant, with *staccato* 8th notes creating tension. Judith says: "You are lying," but Gionata tells her that he himself saw some drink it and die. Voices calling for her death are heard approaching. To an excited 9/8 time signature with repeated breathless groups of triplets, Judith asks whose voices they are. Gionata begs her to pity his dismay if not her own. In broken phrases, he pleads with her to leave but Judith insists she is safe where she is.

Gionata tries to pull Judith out of the house as the music builds, but she rejects him, singing *Taci* ("Quiet"), *a cappella*. The music suddenly stops as he kneels and confesses his love for her in a long unaccompanied phrase: "If you die, I will die!" (p. 94). In a resigned voice but with passion, he sings in highly lyrical and soft music that he will only confess this to her once, and begs her to take him as her companion on her "strange journey" (*vago cammin*). In faster and more confident music, Judith tells him she swore to be faithful forever to her spouse's ashes, that she has consecrated herself to heaven and her country. She does admit that if she could love, it would be only him. After this phrase, their voices come together as they each sing their own thoughts in a very effective duet. The influence of Donizetti, particularly his 1835 opera *Lucia di Lamermoor*, is clearly heard in this duet. Louder cries are heard, calling for her death.

The music grows increasingly excited, as Judith says she is not afraid and will not hide, because she knows God is watching over her. Gionata pleads with her again to flee with him. The act ends with this final duet, as they both sing their own thoughts in fast and dramatic music.

Silveri: Scene IX (XI in the libretto and VI in Peri's) introduces Gionata. The action and text are the same as in Peri's (above). When Gionata pleads with Judith, the music is agitated, pleading and very Verdian. In short, breathless *staccato* (broken) notes, Judith asks him what he is hiding, the music creating a sense of mystery and confusion. She imperiously orders him to tell her what has happened. Gionata reluctantly tells her that the water she had found for the people was poisoned by the enemy (as in Giacometti's play and Peri's opera). His breathlessness is heard in the hesitant music and many rests. Judith's cry, "You're lying!," is followed by loud trumpet and trombone calls (p. 115). Gionata tells her he himself saw some drink it and die. Voices calling for her death (*Morte a Giuditta!*) are heard, in propulsive, dramatic music. This scene is more dramatic and stirring in Peri's opera.

When Gionata kneels and confesses his love for Judith, he sings soaring lines over a throbbing accompaniment. His confession of love, sung in a poignant and beautiful *bel canto*–style aria, relates that Judith is the angel of his destiny. On his final plea, he sustains an *a"*. Judith tells Gionata "it is in vain," sung on a descending chromatic phrase, down to *ppp* (p. 120) Then in strangely lighter music, she tells him that she has consecrated herself to heaven and her country. On the repeat of "country" (*patria*, a very important word in Italy in the 1880s), her voice soars to *b-flat"*. When she admits that if she could love, it would be only him, the phrase is marked "expressively and passionately." Silveri deviates from Marcello's libretto here. Gionata repeats Judith's words in short phrases, while Judith continues to repeat that she would love only him, if she could love. This soaring love duet ends with Gionata singing another *a"*. Their final measures are sung in harmony and *a cappella*. There are some similarities between this duet and the duet in Peri's opera.

There is no break as the F major just heard turns into F minor. Such an abrupt change is always an ominous musical subtext (p. 125). Louder cries from the riot are heard approaching, calling for Judith's death. Judith says she is not afraid and will not hide, because she knows God is watching over her. The rest of this scene adheres to Marcello's libretto, which Peri's opera does not. Gionata pleads with her again, then unsheathes his sword and prepares to exit and defend her. He says that without her love, it is better to die. In the opera, she tries to hold Gionata back but cannot. Their duet concludes with both singers sustaining *a"* together with the chorus singing the same note (p. 127). Over turbulent music, Judith cries out to God to watch over her. She sings an ascending line that culminates on a high C (*c"'*, although alternate, lower notes are written in the score as an option). Judith falls to her knees, calmly and confidently resigned, bending her head and crossing her arms over her chest. The orchestra plays an exciting, *prestissimo* (very, very fast) ascending scale to conclude the act.

Peri: Act II, Scene I takes place in the enemy camp (p. 100). The short orchestra prelude is ominous and suspenseful. The libretto describes the scene vividly, with Holofernes's imposing "pavilion" (*padiglione*) filled with rich purple cloth, gold, and golden columns. Judith's white tent is seen nearby, with flowers and fountains inside. Captains, Assyrian warriors, satraps, and eunuchs are seen gathering around Holofernes's pavilion, which is still closed. In a *staccato* and rhythmical chorus, they sing of conquering the world "behind Holofernes' fatal footprint" (*orme fatal*). The music continues to grow louder and more menacing. They sing of victories past and future, hoping to see the "empire of Jehova" destroyed and the city of Nebuchadnezzar (*Nabucco*) and the god Bel reign over all cities (Bel was the chief god of Babylon—Bel means "lord" or "master" in Akkadian; he is also referred to as an idol in Dan 14:22). The music for this text changes to a major key and is sung with great feeling (p. 103).

No scene change is noted, but this is presumably Scene II. The opening measures have an ominous sound. The curtains of the large pavilion are opened and all bow. Holofernes is lying on luxurious cushions, lion and tiger skins under his feet (representing the ultimate luxury for the period when this was written) and women all around him, next to Vagaus, his eunuch. He sings a recitative over a sustained and unsettled chord (a diminished triad, or two minor thirds stacked on top of each other, creating an unresolved sound; p. 106). Holofernes sings of being accustomed to the heat of action and now feeling weighed down by the inertia of a day of rest (*Uso alla foga del torrente ..., mi pesa l'inerzia di un sol dì*). Vagaus reminds him, over *tremolos*, that Heaven has sent him this very beautiful Hebrew woman to dissipate his boredom. Holofernes agrees, in a recitative, that she is like a serenading star for him. As *tremolos* resume, Vagaus explains that she has escaped from Betulia to help deliver that "rock" (referring to Betulia, which was on a rocky perch) and lead him to Zion. Holofernes leaps to his feet, shouting: "Jerusalem, it will be the greatest of my victories!" In this plot, Judith's entrance into the camp is never described, and an earlier conversation between Judith and Vagaus, not in the original version, is suggested. It is not clear when Holofernes first saw Judith, but he seems to already be aware of her presence. In an *a cappella* recitative—an indicator of strength—he says: "Only two things do I ardently yearn for: universal servitude, and dominion over the entire world—and her love" (the third is an add-on):

> *Due sole cose ardentemente anelo:*
> *L' universal servaggio, ed io signore*
> *Del mondo intero, e di costei l'amore.*

He names the first two in dry recitative, but the final wish is sung with a romantic flourish. Holofernes exits the pavilion and turns to look at the white tent beside him. To throbbing, Verdian music, he wonders aloud if Judith is the angel that will guide his destiny, or an "opposing demon." Either way, whether demon or angel, phantom or mortal, he sings in increasingly soaring phrases, this love may be fatal to his heart (p. 109). The music accelerates and he sings several *fioritura* phrases (florid embellishments) to express his growing excitement (p. 110), ending with a cadenza. This music has great appeal, and since Holofernes is singing only his own thoughts, the charm of the music is not intended for Judith's ears. Holofernes as depicted here clearly has a heart—but what would unappealing or heartless music sound like? Two possible examples might be the music for Iago in Verdi's *Otello* or that of Scarpia in Puccini's

Tosca. Those two villains do not sing "appealing" music. Whether Peri was just catering to his audience, or really believed Holofernes had a softer side, can only be guessed.

There is no scene change, though this is presumably Scene III. The mood changes and the key is a bright C major as Holofernes sings: "She is coming!" Arzaele (Holofernes's harem favorite, based on the Giacometti play), together with slaves and handmaids, meets Holofernes as he heads toward Judith's tent. Over lighthearted *staccato* and dancelike music (with strong echoes of the opening scene of Verdi's *La Traviata*), he asks Arzaele what "that woman" is doing, and Arzaele feigns ignorance, asking: "Who?" Holofernes answers strongly: "Is there another woman in the world in my eyes, O slave, but Judith?" Trembling inside, she says to herself: "I suspected that." The other women tell him that Judith is lost in thought, resting and praying. The lighthearted music abruptly stops as Holofernes disdainfully says: "My rival will always be this God … I want to be the only divinity (*nume*) in her heart." Arzaele says mysteriously: "You should be afraid!" and when he tries to silence her, she says insistently: *Bada!* ("Be careful!" or "Beware!"). Holofernes announces that "that queen is staying with me in the camp; if Holofernes bows to her, here everyone will adore her." A *bel canto*–style aria follows (p. 113) after a few measures of ominous music. Holofernes sings: "If I thirst after new glory, if I want a throne in the world, it is only to give to her as a gift, in return for her heart." He calls her his angel of love, who has descended to be at his side. In faster and increasingly more upbeat music, the chorus sings that Bel has sent Judith to him as a reward for his great valor (p. 114). Holofernes repeats the earlier refrain, ending in the grand conclusion with the chorus (p. 117).

In Scene IV (p. 118), Arzaele says to her servants that "this impious Hebrew (*Israelita*) has subjugated Holofernes."[20] They all see the tent open and say: "Here she is! I tremble." In the libretto, Judith is described as "brilliantly dressed, a precious crown on her head, the tresses of her hair covered in pearls and gems." Arzaele and the slaves, despite their jealousy, are dazzled by such beauty. The dialogue that follows, between Arzaele and Judith, is taken directly from Giacometti's play. Arzaele calls Judith Holofernes's lover, which puzzles Judith, but over sudden rapid repeated chords, Arzaele says Holofernes has affirmed that. In an aside, Judith says: "God has blessed me!" Over the same propulsive and hammering chords, Arzaele informs Judith that she herself had been queen, that she hates Judith, and that the hate of a slave is death. As in Giacometti, Holofernes overhears this, and in frenzied music, he rushes toward Arzaele and tells her that she is the one who will die. In much slower and very expressive phrases, Judith asks him to forgive Arzaele's jealous anger, and Holofernes orders Arzaele to kiss Judith's feet. A few measures of hesitant music, including long rests, suggest Arzaele's feelings. As she obeys the command, she murmurs that she

---

[20] Arzaele's use of the term *Israelita* is puzzling, since it appears almost nowhere else in Judith retellings. Based on context, she uses the word negatively and with scorn. Generally, however, the more common *ebreo*, which simply means Jewish, has been used negatively far more throughout Italian history, than *Israelito*. An Italian journalist writes: "The word *ebreo* was used negatively in those centuries and even earlier by the Catholic Church first, and then by the Fascists and Nazis. Ultimately, defining a person with the term *ebreo, israelito, giudeo-* depends on the context and the tone of voice (Pupa Garribba, Roman journalist, personal communication, March 10, 2019; my translation).

will have revenge. Judith very softly tells her to be quiet (this last element is not in the Giacometti play; it suggests that Judith is trying to ally herself with Arzaele). In contrast to Giacometti's play, Arzaele does not appear again after this scene.

Act III

Silveri: Act III (in this opera; Act II in Marcello's libretto and in Peri), Scene I takes place in the enemy camp. The opening music prominently features martial trumpets. There is far more martial-sounding music in Silveri's opera than in Peri's, although instruments are not notated in Peri's score. The description of the scene is the same as Peri's opera. In a chorus to the same martial music as the opening, the soldiers sing proudly of conquering the world "behind Holofernes' fatal footprint." Near the end of this chorus, the tempo suddenly slows from *Presto* to *Adagio* (p. 139) and becomes a hymn. Then the tempo picks up again for the bombastic finale (p. 143).

In Scene II, the curtains of the large pavilion are opened and all bow. The music is soft as Holofernes sings in a wistful recitative of being accustomed to the heat of action. It feels to him as though "the wings of the hours have been clipped and the lazy chariot barely drags the sun." These lines transmit Holofernes's impatient nature. Vagaus reminds him about the beautiful Hebrew woman. Holofernes sings forcefully: "Peoples and kings I have trampled, I have them under my feet. Now I want to do battle with the gods." Holofernes's vocal line is characterized by a wide range and many large leaps, all suggesting power. Peri utilizes *a cappella* recitatives to the same end.

In an abrupt musical change, a soaring lyrical melody is heard in the orchestra, setting the tone for Holofernes's next words about the things he most yearns for (the same as in Peri's opera). Then he wonders aloud, to the romantic melody just heard, if Judith is the angel (*angelo* in the libretto, changed to *celeste spirito* in the score) that will guide his destiny, or an "opposing demon." Either way, he knows, whether demon or angel, phantom or mortal, this love may be fatal to his heart. The aria ends as Holofernes repeatedly sings *O amore, O voluttà* ("O love, O voluptuousness"), text not found in the Marcello libretto or in Peri's opera. He ends on a long sustained and soft *e-flat'*. In this very romanticized image of Holofernes, he seems completely overcome by love and lust for Judith. Humanizing him this way makes it hard to hate him: who could despise a man who sings such beautiful music? This issue was also discussed in reference to Peri's portrait of Holofernes.

In Scene III (p. 153), Arzaele, together with slaves and handmaids, meets Holofernes as he heads toward Judith's tent. The key has suddenly changed from E-flat to E major, a shift that suggests a mood change. When Holofernes asks the other women to tell him Judith's whereabouts, they respond over a sweet, almost pastoral and Mozartean melody in the orchestra. They tell him that Judith is lost in thought, resting and praying. The tunefulness of these measures may be meant to represent a modest, prayerful Judith, or a group of submissive women. A very loud and brusque passage is heard in the orchestra as Holofernes says disdainfully: "My rival will always be this God" and more brusquely: "I want to be the only divinity (*nume*) in her heart." The rest of their dialogue is the same as in Peri's opera. Holofernes announces in ominous, threatening music that "that queen is staying with me in the camp; if Holofernes bows to her, here everyone will adore her." He exits his pavilion. (In Marcello's libretto, he tells Arzaele that he will give her to Judith as a gift, but not in either opera). In the very brief Scene IV, Arzaele says to her servants in a breathless recitative that "this impious Hebrew (*Israelita*) has subjugated Holofernes." In the previous scene, Vagaus had referred to Judith as an *ebrea*. There might be a negative connotation to the term Arzaele uses (discussed above, footnote 20). All the women see the tent open and say: "Here she is! I tremble."

At the opening of Scene V (p. 158), Judith is described just as in Peri's opera. The music is soft, very slow, and in the bright key of C major. Arzaele and the slaves sing among themselves about Judith's surpassing beauty. The dialogue that follows, between Arzaele and Judith, is taken directly from Giacometti's play (and is the same as Peri's). When Arzaele furiously calls Judith Holofernes's lover, Judith in an aside says with jubilation: "Heaven supports me" (*mi seconda il ciel*). (In the original libretto and Peri's opera, she says: "God has blessed me!") In a sudden shift from C major to C minor—an ominous subtext—Arzaele informs Judith that she herself had been queen, that she hates Judith, and that the hate of a slave is death. Silveri adds a female chorus to this section, who sing new text softly under Arzaele: "She too was his lover, left and abandoned; the throne of your beauty will also crumble." The music for this section strongly recalls Verdi, with its sweeping groups of 8th notes in the orchestra. As in Giacometti and Peri, Holofernes overhears Arzaele, rushes toward her, and condemns her. His condemnation is accompanied by a rapid descent of loud chords over a *tremolo*, followed by a long pause. In pleading, lyrical music, Judith begs Holofernes to forgive Arzaele's "jealous anger." In forceful phrases, Holofernes agrees but orders Arzaele to kiss Judith's feet. As she bends, frightened, to kiss the hem of Judith's garment, she murmurs that she will have revenge. An ominous bassoon solo is threaded through these measures, along with continual bass *tremolos*. Judith tells Arzaele *sotto voce* to be quiet (this last element is also in Peri's opera though not in the Giacometti play). As in Peri's opera, Arzaele does not appear again after this scene, which ends in very soft, ominous low *tremolos*.

Peri: Though the next scene is Scene VII in the libretto, there is no break or scene change in this opera. Arzaele and the other women exit, leaving Holofernes and Judith alone. He asks her why, in the four days she has been in the camp, she has not directed a single look or word to him, to at least "calm the fire burning in his heart." This is all sung as a mostly unaccompanied recitative. Under sudden *tremolos*, Judith hesitantly responds that the brightness of his glory radiating on his face affects and disturbs her. He tells her he can lay down the mantle of his majesty when she is near him. Holofernes sings in a lyrical, almost wistful Verdian aria (p. 121) that he was born in the midst of war and has passed his life in tents; massacres and extermination were his footprints. To a lighter accompaniment, he sings of loving beautiful slaves who were like the perfume of flowers. After a brief interlude, he continues in a new melody, with a new key and time signature: "Then I met you, now I want to live only for you, pulling a veil of oblivion over the past." He repeats the final words several times, the last time on a short cadenza for emphasis.

The key suddenly shifts from F major to F minor, introducing a change in mood. Holofernes asks Judith what she wants. She tells him, in an expansive melody, that if he loves her, he should not oppress her people, her deserted and afflicted people that are dying (p. 123). Under her sustained line, continuing 16th-note groups are heard. In more soaring music, she sings: "Before I give in to the charm of your flattering words, do not let me despair of obtaining this mercy from you." ' She continues to plead with him. As the music continues to build, she tells him that if he magnanimously will save Betulia, he can possess her. This speech, of course, runs counter to the original narrative, where Judith gains access to Holofernes because she offers to be a spy against her own people. Here she is simply begging him to be kind in exchange for her body, which she surely must have known would be fruitless. And her words also do not sync with the earlier dialogue between Holofernes and Vagaus, who had told him Judith was there to help him defeat Betulia.

After a short cadenza, the key changes and the accompaniment is now a simple light *staccato*. Holofernes says it is useless to ask him for mercy, since his star has sent him to destroy. She tells him to just kill her in that case (p. 125). Holofernes begs her forgiveness, saying she is imbuing his heart with virtue. She accuses him of deceiving her, which he denies, but he asks her to reveal who she is. She sings in a sweet and expressive aria to a steady throbbing 4/4 beat with triplet groups that she is a solitary and unknown person who has withheld affection from any man. She sings in a *coloratura* passage that his glorious name reached her in the shadows and she dragged herself to come before him. In lighter and more upbeat music and a key change, Holofernes tells Judith it was "decreed in the stars," and she should be happy, for she is now his queen. His rest is near after he has conquered the world, and his reward for the labors of war will be her. This becomes a duet (virtually a love duet but a one-sided one) in which they both repeat the words they have just sung to each other (p. 128). They end by singing a cadenza together. Holofernes says her reign has begun and Judith says to herself: "God, help me," both lines sung *a cappella*.

The tempo suddenly quickens as Holofernes asks if she loves him, and shivering, she responds: "Don't you see it in my terror?" which is equivocal but probably implies that for Holofernes, terror is the same as love. He asks again and she forces herself to say yes. The key changes to G-flat major, and in a much faster tempo, Holofernes enthusiastically says that her words have exalted him and his heart is inebriated. To herself, exultantly and not softly, she sings: "In the slippery coils of the wily serpent, the ferocious tiger, strangled, will die." This vivid phrase is an elaboration of a similar one in the Giacometti play (see Chapter 3). She pledges to give herself to him that same night, and he says that she will be queen of the world when she has her throne in his heart. After these pledges, both sing another refrain of their previous words, this time together (p. 132). While he is singing of his passion and exaltation, she sings of strangling him like a tiger in a snake's coils. She repeats this phrase several times, the last time reaching *b-flat"*, while Holofernes sings of being inebriated by Judith's voluptuousness. Only in opera can two characters be expressing such opposing thoughts simultaneously, unheard by each other.

Silveri: In Scene VII (p. 163), Holofernes, in a recitative and in his sweetest voice, addresses Judith with the same questions as in Peri's opera. He sings mostly *a cappella* with soft string passages playing between his measures. The music suggests a softer Holofernes. She offers the same hesitant response, singing in a broken recitative, amplifying her hesitance. Holofernes moves closer, to the sound of heraldic trumpets and trombones, and sings "proudly" and rhythmically about his life in army camps. In Peri's opera, these remarks were sung wistfully. The mood changes as he composes himself, and to a gentler accompaniment, he sings of loving beautiful slaves who were like the perfume of flowers. After a long pause, he continues in more expansive music: "Then I met you, now I want to live only for you, pulling a veil of oblivion over the past." This is one of the most appealing and romantic portraits of Holofernes in the repertoire. Do both the librettist and composer sympathize with him? Or do they want the audience to side with him and against Judith? It is impossible to know their motive, but this work might alter some listeners' ideas about the original story.

When Holofernes asks Judith what she wants (an addition to the libretto, also found in Peri's opera), the music shifts to the unusual key of G-flat major, accompanied by the frequently used Verdian groups of throbbing triplets. Judith starts softly and builds gradually. In poignant, deeply moving music augmented by *seufzer* or sighing phrases in the orchestra, she pleads: "Before I give in to the charm of your flattering words, do not let me despair of obtaining this mercy from you." She asks him to save Betulia, in the same exchange seen (and discussed above) in Peri's opera.

The music changes abruptly from sweet to forceful, and the key moves from G-flat major to F# minor (the F# is enharmonic with G flat, making the change more startling). Holofernes, of course, tells her this request is in vain, because his star sends him out to destroy all those who rebel. On the word "star" his voice reaches *f#'*, quite high for a baritone. The key in this scene changes frequently, increasing the feeling of instability. Judith tells him, in very assertive music, that he should in that case strike her first. Then in weeping music, she adds: "if it is not possible to mitigate your mortal fury." The sad tone with which she infuses those words suggests she is manipulating him with her voice. Holofernes in 'expressive' tones begs her forgiveness and says she is imbuing his heart with virtue. (The dialogue from the original libretto that follows this, in which Judith explains how she found him, does not appear here but was used by Peri). Moving closer to Judith, Holofernes tells her, in soaring phrases, that her reign has begun. Judith pushes him away, saying to herself: "God, help me." Over long descending cadences and throbbing groups of 16th notes, Holofernes asks Judith if she loves him, and shivering, she responds, in a low range dropping to *b* over rising cadences in the orchestra: "Don't tempt my oppressed heart" (in the libretto and Peri's opera: "Don't you see from my terror?"). Though her voice has dropped, the orchestra continues to play rising cadences, building excitement. In the next few phrases, their voices step on each other. He asks again and after a long pause, she forces herself to say yes.

The key changes again and the music is lighter and gentler, as Holofernes abandons himself to unbridled joy in calm but elated music. He tells Judith that her words have exalted him, over high *pianissimo* passages in the orchestra. To herself, she says "ecstatically": "In the slippery coils of the wily serpent, the ferocious tiger, strangled, will die" (also in Peri's opera, above). While she is singing that line, Holofernes continues to express his exaltation and excitement, singing ironically of her "dear words." Judith sometimes repeats Holofernes's notes (p. 174). The same effect was achieved in Peri's opera, where the two characters are expressing opposing thoughts simultaneously.

With "feigned abandon," she pledges to give herself to him that same night, and he says that she will be queen of the world when she has her throne in his heart, that night. In the opera only, Judith adds "he will die" before they sing "tonight" the last time, in perfect harmony. They embrace for an instant, then stop as they hear someone approaching.

Peri: In Scene VIII in the libretto, called Finale II in the opera (p. 134), Vagaus quickly approaches Judith and Holofernes. Judith, relieved to be interrupted, says to herself: "Finally I can breathe." In fast, agitated music, Vagaus tells them that two strangers have been captured nearby. Judith suspects the worst, as reflected in suspenseful music. Eliachimo and Gionata have been captured near the camp and are now brought in. This in some way minimizes Judith's deed of venturing there by herself, with only her maid, although their plan was not known to her. They identify themselves as "Sons of Israel." When Holofernes asks what brought them to his camp, Gionata defiantly says, in strong, assertive music: "We ran here to inflame the anger of our brothers against our oppressors" in somber phrases, with only sustained chords under their voices. Holofernes orders them killed. They defiantly state: "God will avenge our blood." Holofernes calls them fools, informing them that their God is calling him to Zion and that "this, your angel" is showing him the way. This is an interesting assertion, since up to now Judith has never discussed helping Holofernes in his battle plan (although Vagaus previously made a reference to this).

Holofernes pulls a resisting Judith out of the shadows. The two men are stunned to see Judith by Holofernes's side. Very agitated music suggests their emotions as she appears before them (p. 137), and they call her name twice, in amazement and shock. In the libretto, Holofernes notices their amazement and also Judith's pallor, and looks at all of them grimly. Judith, to avoid suspicion, embraces him. (These actions are in the original libretto but are not indicated in the score.) Both men call Judith a traitor, Eliachimo in particularly frenzied music. Holofernes tells them Judith is his lover; Gionata says he is lying, asks Judith to answer, and then says: "O misfortune, if it is true." Judith says to herself: "What terrible sorrow" while Holofernes assures Gionata that he is not lying. Most of this is recitative over continual *tremolos*, which only stop when Eliachimo curses Holofernes (p. 138). Most of this scene was omitted by Silveri.

After Holofernes orders the two Hebrews taken prisoner, a highly dramatic orchestral interlude describes the strong emotion of the moment (p. 139). As it dies down, Gionata sings a heartbreaking plea to Judith. In slow and plaintive music, with a "gasping" accompaniment, he tells Judith she was deaf to his love, which he nurtured with tears. Then in more flowing, aching music, he calls her "impious" (*empia*) and accuses her of betraying honor, country, and God. He says he can still see on her face the kisses that the oppressor gave her. All the words spoken by the different characters from this point on are heard simultaneously as part of a large ensemble. Gionata continues to repeat what he just said, while over his voice, Holofernes sings that anger is boiling in his breast, to oddly bouncy music suggesting he is making a joke of all this. He adds that that no man can be his rival and that "the chill of death can extinguish audacious ardor" (*Perchè il gelo della morte spegner può l'audace ardor*; p. 141).

The chorus of bystanders sing among themselves, remarking on the furor of these "vile, oppressed people," confident that Holofernes will take vengeance on them. Judith prays fervently in an aside, asking God to sustain and support her in this difficult ordeal, to give her strength and protect her so she does not fail in her grand plan: "The holy love of my country renews and reinforces me." Gionata tells Judith that her virtues were lies and her modesty false. Eliachimo also rails against Judith: "You were the lily of Israel, for your virtue and purity; now stained and unfaithful, you are the horror of your people!" Abramia sings of the difficult test Judith is going through and prays that the love of her country will renew and reinforce her. The music becomes steadily more dramatic and insistent. This lengthy ensemble must have been a musical highlight of the opera, as Silveri's version also surely was.

Silveri: Scene VIII (titled *Finale* in the score) is in most respects identical to the Peri scene described above. Eliachimo and Gionata cry out when they see Judith by Holofernes's side. Holofernes notices their amazement and also Judith's pallor, and looks at all of them grimly. Much of the action described here in the libretto was left out by Silveri. After the two prisoners cry out, Holofernes turns to Vagaus and says: "Bring everyone to me," meaning his attendants and soldiers. It is a more abrupt ending than the original libretto's, but leaving so much unspoken is in some ways more effective.

Scene IX opens as all Holofernes's men and slaves approach, along with Arzaele and Abramia. The short orchestral introduction is foreboding. The action here, too, is very close to the Peri scene. Judith is beside herself, while Gionata defies Holofernes's fury and resists Eliachimo's attempts to hold him back. Pale and trembling, Gionata approaches Judith. In short, broken phrases, he accuses her of being deaf to his love. Then in more flowing, aching music, he accuses her of betraying honor, country, and God. The word *patria* (homeland) is stressed far more in this opera than in Peri's. On the final repeat of this word, Gionata reaches and sustains a *b-flat'*. As in Peri's opera, a large ensemble begins here, in which the different characters express their thoughts simultaneously. The text, from Marcello's libretto, is virtually the same as in Peri's work. Silveri pulled out all the stops for the lengthy ensemble. It must have been very impressive to hear, more than can be gleaned from reading the score. Gionata first repeats all the words he has just spoken, in a "suffocated voice." The text is the same as in Peri's ensemble, above. When Gionata sings the heartbreaking line "On your face I see the kisses that our oppressor gave you," the orchestra doubles his voice for emphasis. Unlike Peri's version, the orchestra doubles Judith's soaring lines through most of the ensemble. In the final measures, Judith's voice sustains a high C and then a B flat (*c", b-flat"*) on the words *santo amor* or "holy love" (p. 199).

Peri: When the ensemble ends, Holofernes, in a brusque recitative, orders Eliachimo brought before him (p. 148), and then unsheathes his sword and prepares to kill him. Judith courageously puts herself between them, assertively singing *Duce! Arresta!* ("Captain, stop!"). In the libretto, she then caresses Holofernes, but this action is not indicated in the score. In soaring phrases, she asks him to stop and look at her, because she has a favor to ask. In suspenseful music, she asks him to free the old man, which he agrees to do. In more dramatic, faster music, she then asks him to hand over Gionata, "this impious one," so that she alone can avenge herself, since she was the offended party. Holofernes instantly agrees. Gionata cries out: "Kill me!" but Judith tells him quietly: "You will live." Holofernes orders Eliachimo back to Betulia. A few measures of lighthearted dance music intrude here (p. 149).

Suddenly, at Holofernes's signal and as if by magic, trumpet calls are heard all around them, answering each other (p. 150). Warriors teem everywhere, covering the plain and the hills with flags. Tenors, then basses introduce the full ensemble after the warriors sing a battle chorus. Judith repeats *Vendetta* ("Revenge!") several times, her voice soaring over the others. While the Hebrews bewail their fate, the soldiers, over a teeming orchestra, sing of war and upcoming victory. Holofernes confidently proclaims his upcoming victory over Judah. He sings in a brief solo, his line doubled by the orchestra for emphases, that he will erase the memory of Judah (p. 153). The different groups—Hebrews and soldiers—often sing in unison, each expressing their unity of purpose. Eliachimo and Gionata sing together that a people who defend their native land will remain unconquered. Holy Zion will never succumb and will be defended even by the old and by women. "We all swear to die rather than suffer under the yoke of a foreign oppressor," they sing, a sentiment that would have resonated powerfully with Italian listeners of that time. Judith sings in an aside, on long sustained notes above the ensemble (p. 160), that the terrible hour is approaching quickly and the mystical voice is speaking to her heart. "The old courage is growing and doubling." Arzaele and the female slaves sing of a flash of light on Judith's face and sense danger for Holofernes. "Her perverse genius is spurring him to his death; the alluring Hebrew has seduced that heart":

> *Al duce sovrasta novello periglio.*
> *A morte il suo genio perverso lo sprona.*
> *L'Ebrea lusinghiera sedotto ha quel cor.*

Judith's final word of the lengthy ensemble, soaring over the other voices, is *Vendetta* ("Vengeance") sung on a sustained high B (*b*"). Heraldic trumpets close the act.[21]

Silveri: After the ensemble, Holofernes orders Eliachimo killed. The rest of the action is the same as in Peri's opera. There is a small musical difference when Judith asks Holofernes for a favor. A light minuet-like tune is heard, suggesting Judith is putting on her sweetest airs. She asks him to hand over Gionata in stronger phrases (p. 203). When the trumpet blasts are heard, both a band and orchestra play several minutes of martial music. The rest of the act is the same as in Peri's opera. When Holofernes sings of wiping out the Israelites, so that in the future not even the history of where they lived will survive, the music is appropriately warlike, with more trumpet calls. At this point, the entire ensemble steps to the front of the stage (score note). All sing their lines simultaneously, with a soaring melody in the orchestra. Abramia states her belief that the death sentence for the "impious one" has already sounded, and Judith already knew it in her heart. The rest of the scene is based on the libretto but absent from Peri's opera. The soldiers' final words are *All'armi!* ("To battle!"). The act concludes as Eliachimo is taken out of the camp by guards and Vagaus escorts Gionata to Judith's tent. In an

---

[21] In Marcello's libretto, the soldiers sing another battle song, ending with the boast that their phalanxes are like a thousand torrents, spreading horror over the terrified world. There the act concludes as Eliachimo is taken out of the camp by guards, Vagaus escorts Gionata to Judith's tent, and Holofernes embraces her and pulls her toward his pavilion while Arzaele and the slaves follow them.

addition not found in Peri's opera, Holofernes embraces Judith and she falls into his arms, but with an expression on her face indicating that she is already thinking of the next part of her audacious plan (score note). Holofernes pulls her toward his pavilion while Arzaele and the slaves follow them (p. 219).

Peri: Act III, Scene I takes place in a remote area of the Assyrian camp (p. 163). The scene is vividly described in the libretto: Holofernes's pavilion is "splendidly illuminated inside," and beyond this is an "immense plain under a cloudy sky, in which from time to time the moon appears." Gionata is seen, chained and alone. The opening music is very soft and mysterious. In a recitative over *tremolos*, Gionata says he wishes he were stronger, to overcome these torments. Over a single sustained chord, he sings of his despair, believing that Judith has forgotten her brothers and her virtue amid the splendor surrounding her. Inside the large tent, the sounds of clinking glasses can be heard, as well as occasional shouts and singing. He hears voices singing praises to Judith in a lively drinking song in 6/8 time: "Dreamy Hebrew, your beauty transports us to paradise; you spread, with your laughter, infinite voluptuousness":

Ci trasporta in paradiso,
Vaga Ebrea, la tua beltà.
Tu diffondi col tuo riso
Infinita voluttà.

Gionata is burning with jealousy and in a recitative says it is time for action (p. 166). Judith is in the arms of the barbaric oppressor of their people, smiling at him with her resplendent beauty, embracing him. "This bitter thought chills my heart!" he sings. A lyrical and plangent aria follows, in which Gionata sings that he wishes Judith could hear his anxious voice: "That unfaithful soul would hear ferocious accusations." He repeats these words in increasingly more passionate and expansive music. Finally, he prays for the tremendous anger from heaven to fall on her, this curse first accompanied by *tremolos* and the final time sung *a cappella*.

Scene II opens with Judith quietly leaving the illuminated pavilion, looking for someone. She is dressed beautifully, studded with jewelry, a crown of flowers on her head, breathing seduction (or "giving off" seduction: *spirando seduzione*). The music is marked *Allegro risoluto* and reflects the anxiety of the moment, with a sense of stealth. Gionata rushes to meet Judith, as she calls out for him softly. He tells her not to come closer because she disgusts him (*ribrezzo* sung on *a'*; p. 169). Judith tells him not to worry about her, that she fled undetected to untie and free him. These lines are sung breathlessly with sparse accompaniment. Gionata insists he doesn't want his life saved by her, but after untying him, she simply says in two strong phrases with chords accenting her words: "Hate me and leave." He responds in a propulsive and Verdian aria (p. 171), marked *Allegro risoluto* and shifting to a minor key with dotted rhythms pushing the music forward.

Softly but intensely, he protests that he cannot live far from her knowing she is in another man's embrace. In the same driving rhythm, Judith tries to dissuade him, telling him he should give his life for his country and forget this foolish love, or he is a coward. Gionata, mad with jealousy, continues in slower and more resolute music to say it would be better to die if he cannot have her; but he wants to kill her so Holofernes cannot have her (p. 173). To a new, but still driving rhythm of three 16th-note groups, she sings in soaring phrases: "If I come out of this conflict impaired, would you want to reproach my holy deed?" She knows the task she must do for her country is dangerous. Whether she is the victim or the victor, Gionata must know that it is God's will. Returning to the earlier rhythm, he joins her, singing that if she gave herself to Holofernes, the ground would swallow her up. They continue to each express their own thoughts.

Suddenly, the music quickens and the key changes (p. 177), as Gionata, in breathless, anxious music, tells Judith to leave the terrible burden (or undertaking: *incarico*) to him. Without responding, she tells him it is late and he must return to Betulia and inspire his people, as she pushes him to the exit. Very softly (*sotto voce*), over steady murmuring *ppp* 16th-note groups, she tells him how to escape at dawn, before the moon has waned, getting past the enemy guards. Gionata says he dares not believe her. Over constant rippling 16th-note groups, the music grows louder and faster. In a continually rising line, Judith reveals the signal that they are free: it will be the bloody head of his rival (p. 179).

Finally convinced, Gionata rails against the horrible veil that had covered his eyes until now. The key has changed and the accompaniment is softer and in a square 4/4 time. He calls Judith the one chosen by Heaven and falls at her feet to adore her virtue. To the same music, she tells him: "If I die doing this mighty deed, or am unavenged or pierced through, you must save my name from infamy and offense. You must say: Judith died to free her homeland!"

> S'io morrò nell'alta impresa,
> Od inulta ovver trafitta.
> Dall'infamia, dall'offesa,
> Il mio nome dèi salvar.
> Tu dirai: morì Giuditta
> La sua patria a liberar!

The tempo suddenly speeds up to *Vivace* and the key changes as the *banda* (brass band) is heard and the chorus is singing "Judith, Judith" from the large tent. The key changes again (p. 181) as Judith tells Gionata time is passing and pushes him to run to Betulia. In a fast duet, Gionata sings again that he wants to fall at Judith's feet to adore her virtue, while she sings that he should tell their people Judith died to free her homeland (p. 182). He blesses her and asks for pity on them both. In even quicker music, they say their goodbyes. There are long rests between their final words *addio ... va ... pietà* ("Farewell ... go ... pity"), to reflect their hesitation (p. 183).[22]

---

[22] In Marcello's libretto, Judith tells Gionata where to hide before he escapes. In the revised version, she tells him to hide behind the tent and if he hears her cry out, he should come in and avenge her. When he doesn't understand, she tells him that Heaven has sent her there to kill Holofernes. This later version weakens Judith, so it is possible that the audience of that day could not accept a woman who acted entirely alone, as in the original version. In Peri's opera, there is no mention at all of Gionata hiding.

Act IV (Act III in the original libretto)

Silveri: Scene I opens with a short orchestral prelude featuring a lamenting cello solo, setting a mood of despair, but interrupted abruptly by trumpet calls (p. 221). The description of the scene is the same as in Peri's work (above). The opening measures of music feature the chorus singing joyfully "Long live love!" (*Viva l'amor*), heard from far away before dying out. Gionata sings in a recitative that his strength and his heart are broken by his terrible torments. In a few measures marked "sweetly and with great expression," he sings that he loved Judith like a holy thing, but he is interrupted mid-phrase by voices from the tent. Gionata is burning with jealousy, and in a recitative sung "darkly," he says it is time for action. The music shifts every few measures, depicting his confusion and anguish. At first, he sings only over *tremolos*; then a few measures of a plangent melody are heard. He believes that Judith is in the arms of the barbaric oppressor of their people, smiling at him with her resplendent beauty, embracing him. On those last words, his voice rises to *a-flat'*, which is followed by a long pause. Then in a much lower range he sings: "This atrocious thought chills my heart!" (Silveri changed the original *acerbo*, "bitter," to *atroce* in the score). The key changes to E major as Gionata sings a wistful and melodic aria: "Why can my anxious voice not reach her? That unfaithful soul would hear ferocious accusations." The music builds as the orchestra shifts from a light accompaniment into steady, pounding chord groups. To this music, Gionata prays for Heaven's tremendous anger to fall on Judith, ending on a strong *g#'* over *fortissimo tremolos* (p. 251). Both composers effectively depicted Gionata's shifting moods in this aria.

Scene II opens with hushed, hesitant music as Judith quietly leaves the illuminated pavilion. She calls out softly to Gionata, who is affected by her voice but tells her not to come closer, because she disgusts him. In the recitative duet that follows, their words are interrupted only by sharp chords. Judith tells him "coldly" not to worry about her. The rest of the dialogue is the same as Peri's opera. After Judith says: "Hate me and leave," Gionata protests in a propulsive aria (marked *Agitato*), with steady 8th-note groups driving the music, that he cannot live far from her knowing she is in another man's embrace. In a completely different musical tone, steadier and more lyrical, Judith tries to dissuade him. Peri did not shift the moods in this duet. Judith tells Gionata that he should give his life for his country and forget this foolish love. In more agitated music, Gionata says if he has to lose her, it would be better to die. Then he embraces her as she calls him a fool, and she tries to pull away, saying: "Leave me!" In "an excess of passion," Gionata swears that Holofernes shall only have her dead (p. 256). As the key suddenly shifts to G major, the music is marked both "agitated" and "very expressive." The orchestra plays steady low *tremolos* while soaring melodies are heard above them. Gionata swears to suffocate Judith in the arms of that sacrilegious man (*profano*) with his own hands. This phrase takes him to *a'*. He says if he were guilty of letting Judith be with that man, the ground would swallow her up.

Silveri altered and eliminated some of the original dialogue, found in Peri's opera. In fast and breathless music, Judith asserts that everything Gionata says is in vain, and now is the time to act. On the repeat of this phrase, she reaches *a"*. The music is marked *Allegro vivace* and short *staccato* notes punctuate each beat (p. 258). She tells him it is late and he must flee, as she pushes him to the exit. She tells him how to escape, taking him by the hand and telling him the great secret: the signal that they are free will be the bloody head of his rival. As the tempo steadily increases, on this last phrase, her voice rises to a high C (*c″*).

As soon as they hear people approaching, trumpet calls are heard in the orchestra (p. 246). In very fast, almost frantic music, Judith presses Gionata to leave, to hide and wait. No specific plan is spelled out. This is from the original Marcello libretto, not the revised version in which she tells him to listen for cries for help. While Judith is pushing him to leave, Gionata prays that God's love will protect her. Though they are singing different lines, their voices unite on a high sustained B (*b″*), highly dramatic heard in a tenor and soprano in unison. Then they sing their goodbyes and Gionata ends with: "Ah! Mercy for me ... and for you." Their final measures of *Addio* ("Farewell") grow softer until the music dies down to *ppp*—softer than *pianissimo*, and in C major, signaling hope. Gionata hides behind the pavilion and "Judith is reassured" (score notes).

Peri: The next scene, not marked in the score but presumably Scene III, takes place in the great tent adorned for the feast. The lengthy description in the libretto can be summed up as "everything exudes pomp and voluptuousness." Holofernes and Judith are sitting, waited on by handmaids, cupbearers, and eunuchs. Dancers swirl around them, spreading flowers, while several slaves sing and play lyres and drums. Vagaus stands behind Holofernes and Abramia can be seen coming and going in the back. The chorus sings drinking songs in the standard 6/8 time of an operatic toast. The upbeat, catchy music reflects the romantic text. Holofernes sings erotic words about Judith's lips touching the glass with her divine mouth, from which he will absorb the fragrance of the drink. In a sudden switch to 4/4 time and lilting music, Holofernes sings of seeing Judith's image in the goblet. He concludes with: "Leave me, O woman, to be drunk on wine, and love in your arms!" to be sung "with great transport" (p. 188). Everyone's enthusiasm and inebriation steadily increase as they resume the previous chorus in 6/8 time. Holofernes toasts Judith again with new verses. He sings that she will be a gem adorning his crown when he is victorious over Jerusalem. There is no clear musical indication of Holofernes becoming more drunk, though there is a note in the score. His music reverts back to the 4/4 time with a suggestion of swaying movement. The chorus gradually dies down, ending in unison, unaccompanied, singing: "Dawn is breaking" (p. 192). At a sign from Vagaus, the songs and dances abruptly stop and the women all leave. Vagaus announces that Holofernes is asleep.

Judith, both "anxious and bewildered" (*trepidante e sbigottita*), realizes that the great moment is approaching, and she prays to God to steady her arm and let it conquer. Some of the remaining drunken men spot Judith and surround her when they notice that Holofernes is asleep. In light and graceful music, but hinting at a sense of danger, they tell her their Captain is drunk and they can take their pleasure with her unimpeded. Judith is enraged by this "new obstacle" and she screams at the men: *Stolti, indietro!* ("Idiots, get back!"). They are indignant and just then Abramia sees them and screams loudly. This plot addition is also found in Giacometti's play, but there it was only recounted and not played out. As the light music stops, *tremolos* are heard as Judith, discreetly hiding behind the sleeping Holofernes, screams: "Fear my fury!" These words are sung on ascending pitches, up to *a-flat* and large leaps. All the commotion wakes Holofernes from his stupor (p. 194).

The music is slower and more subdued now. Furiously rubbing his eyes, Holofernes wonders who is screaming and who woke him up. Then he sees Judith through the darkness and in a soaring phrase says she is the only star now, in his eyes. When he notices she is perturbed, the key abruptly changes and the music speeds up, becoming almost frenzied as he asks why she is trembling and then accosts the captains. He asks who the coward is who offended her with a look, reminding them that no one rules except him. Continuing in frenzied music, he tells them to fear him, their king, and commands them: "Prostrate yourselves, O slaves, on the ground." When they resist, he raises his enormous scimitar (a short sword with a curved blade, originating in the East) and menaces them, forcing them to kneel (p. 195). To quieter and measured music, he orders them: "Down, in the mud—at her feet!" Frightened, they obey. He brings Judith over to them, telling her she is queen and should walk on their heads. This incident shows the ruthless side of Holofernes, but on the other hand, he is also portrayed as a hero defending the woman he loves. Such a positive trait is not even hinted at in the biblical version.

Holofernes now begins tottering and mumbles that he cannot feel the ground beneath his feet. With the earlier dance music in the background, he orders everyone out, as Vagaus holds him up. He tries to recall his memories of the party but is confused. Echoes of the earlier party music are heard, suggesting they are in Holofernes's head. These echoes continue under his voice, as he even tries to sing his *brindisi* (toast) but his voice falters (p. 197). Throwing the scimitar aside, he approaches Judith and tells her: "the hour approaches … for which my heart has yearned … O Judith, you are queen, this is the hour … of love." He gradually falters and falls into the arms of two eunuchs, who carry him to the alcove. At that moment, the curtain that had separated the two parts of the pavilion falls. Judith remains alone on one side, trembling. One of the major departures from the original text is this entire scene, which instead of a "seduction" scene between Judith and Holofernes, is a big party. He gets drunk because everyone is drinking at his party. This change has been noted in several other works, of every era.

Silveri: The scene description above is the same for Silveri's opera. The opening chorus, called "Assyrian Hymn," sings "Honor and glory to the unconquered leader." This is followed by the first dance, during which the chorus sings drinking songs and Holofernes toasts Judith in his own *brindisi*, holding his glass and turning to Judith (p. 262). The music and text are the same as in Peri's opera. When the chorus returns, the time shifts from 6/8 to 2/4, a quicker rhythm. They sing *Viva il vin, viva l'amor!* ("Long live wine, long live love!"). Everyone's enthusiasm and inebriation steadily increase. Holofernes tries to reprise his toast but slows down and, holding his glass up, he staggers. He sings, still in the *brindisi* tune, that Judith will adorn his crown when he conquers Jerusalem. Then, "overcome by the wine and the fire of love," he tries to embrace Judith. Shuddering, she pulls away. He totters, finally falling on a cushion in the middle of the tent, surrounded by slaves and concubines who dance around him.

At a sign from Vagaus, the songs and dances abruptly stop and the women all leave. In the silence that follows, a storm is heard in the distance, with lightning and thunder. This is a completely invented detail but a very popular device in Italian opera, also found in the Giacometti play. Vagaus calmly announces that Holofernes is asleep (p. 274). Judith, alone now, realizes that "the great hour is getting close." She prays to God, over the sounds of thunder, to steady her arm and let it be unconquered (*invitto*), sung on *b-flat*". Dramatic storm music ensues.

Silveri eliminated the superfluous scene of a group of men accosting Judith. Its only purpose seems to have been to show a chivalrous side of Holofernes. Peri included it but it originated in Giacometti's play (see Chapter 3). Instead of the commotion waking Holofernes from his stupor, it is the sound of thunder. In dramatic storm music, Holofernes tries to get up. Transported, he sings: "Come, come." Then in soaring romantic music, he tells Judith "the hour approaches … for which my heart has yearned … O Judith, you are queen, this is the hour … of love." He sings these lines exultantly, with most of the notes over the staff—high for a baritone. He reaches one of his highest notes, *g'*, on these words. The accompaniment is "very sweet" (*dolcissimo*). After concluding on *f'* his voice then drops an octave as, faltering, he falls into the arms of two eunuchs who carry him to the alcove. He begins tottering and mumbles that he cannot feel the ground beneath his feet. He orders everyone out, as Vagaus holds him up. Trying to recall his memories of the party, he is confused. As he approaches Judith, he lets the scimitar drop (in the original libretto and Peri's opera, he throws it aside). The music changes abruptly, becoming much faster and more excited. At that moment, the curtain that had separated the two parts of the pavilion falls. Judith remains alone on one side, trembling.

Peri: Scene IV (p. 198) finds Judith alone in the dark tent, with thunder and lightning outside. The tempestuous music of the opening could suggest a storm or terror—or both. In a small addition to the libretto, Abramia enters, out of breath, calling out *Fuggi!* ("Flee!"). In mostly unaccompanied recitative, Judith calmly replies: "It is time," and Abramia asks her if she is not afraid. Judith asks what there is to fear, if God is calling her to this great deed. Abramia tells Judith, to agitated music, that everything around them is silent. Judith calmly tells her to leave and to pray for her, to which Abramia responds: "You make me shudder" (*raccapricciar*). She grudgingly leaves (*a malincuore*). Thunder and lightning are heard now (score note; p. 199) and Judith says *Notte fatal* ("Fatal night"), a line found in countless operas, commonly in response to a storm. Judith's greatest fear is that the thunder will awaken Holofernes, a plot line unique to this opera.

Over continual ominous *tremolos* on diminished seventh chords, Judith walks on tiptoes (score note) and raises the curtain of the alcove, overtaken by shivering. The soft and stealthy-sounding *staccato* passages in the orchestra vividly describe this mood. Holofernes mumbles in his sleep *A Betulia! A Betulia* ("To Betulia"). The notion that Holofernes was partially awake before Judith killed him has been found in several other works, dating back to Scarlatti's oratorios of the early eighteenth century (see Chapter 1). It certainly adds suspense and a sense of horror and foreboding. Shaken by his words, she sings out *O Patria Mia! Ed io vacillo ancor?* ("Oh, my homeland! And I still hesitate?"). Verdi famously used those first words in his opera *Aida*, which was written ten years after this work. The second line is from Giacometti's play.

Judith, to very agitated 16th-note passages, runs around as if outside of herself, and her foot smashes against Holofernes's sword (*scimitarra*), which he had earlier thrown to the ground. She exclaims: "Heaven has handed it to me," as she grabs it and runs to the alcove. Several measures marked *Allegro risoluto* feature loud *staccato* chords, suggesting Judith's determination. She worries aloud if Holofernes might still be awake. The same *staccato* chords are now higher and softer, creating suspense. As she listens at the entrance to the alcove, shaking, she hears him still talking in his sleep, calling out her name. The measures played between her speaking are hesitant and suspenseful *staccato* notes. She walks toward him slowly, saying: "I'm coming." Trying to lift the sword, she finds she cannot, as it twists in her hand. She cries that the sword is too heavy, in a dramatic unaccompanied vocal descent from *a-flat"* down to middle C, almost two octaves. Then more softly, she says her arm is too weak.

She tells God she trusts in him. Suddenly inspired, she throws herself to the ground in fervent prayer, leaning on the sword. Her prayer (p. 202) is sung to a very slow, soft, and light accompaniment of *staccato* triplets, in B-flat minor. In a poignant *bel canto*–inspired melody, she prays to God to let his powerful spirit enter her, to restore her heart and her arm. She tells God that if he loves his people, he can take her honor and even her life. In the more soaring sections of the aria, the orchestra doubles Judith's notes. There are high cadenzas, touching *b-flat"*, before her prayer for redemption (p. 203), begging God to redeem and free his faithful tribe. That text is sung with increasing passion, ending on a long cadenza and a trill. The storm rages, lightning flashes, and the thunder doubles frighteningly. Judith interprets the thunder and lightning as God's response, "as he answered the holy prophets," which gives her renewed strength. (In Giacometti's play, it was the lightning that Judith interpreted as God's response.) Now she sings assertively, over loud *tremolos*, the second line doubled in the orchestra: "It is written in the eternal decrees: by my hand the tyrant will die!"

> *Scritto è già negli eterni decreti:*
> *Per mia mano il tiranno morrà!*

Judith rushes into the alcove, now waving the sword with ease. Several measures of music provide a description of the violent act, building quickly to *fortissimo* before abruptly dying down to *pianissimo*. In addition to many *tremolos*, the music also suggests long sighs. Vagaus cries out: "What a scream!" (*O qual grido!*). Then Arzaele sings that she heard a strange noise coming from that tent, which then stopped. Whether or not a scream was included in performance cannot be known. In suspenseful music—sighs alternating with *staccato*—Vagaus comments: "What a horrible night, I am struck by fear." The dialogue between these two characters is an addition to the libretto. Arzaele suddenly hears sounds of tumult as trumpet calls sound (one of the only places an instrument is indicated in Peri's score), and Vagaus says they are being attacked by the Hebrews. Arzaele tells him to wake up Holofernes.

They realize that they have been betrayed by their enemy, and Vagaus rushes into Holofernes's tent, calling out to him. The music suddenly becomes more frantic, accented by loud *tremolos*, as they sing: "What a grim sight" (*O vista truce*) on a harsh chord. After a pause, they sing together in a poignant melody that the blast of the trumpet can no longer awaken Holofernes. This is a rare expression of compassion in the opera. The underlying message could be that even an enemy is still a human being. The chorus sings of the sound of armies around them resounding. Arzaele and Vagaus decide to flee.

Highly dramatic music in the orchestra vividly represents the action, as the scene changes to one of growing chaos. Fleeing and frightened Assyrian soldiers are pursued by Hebrew warriors with bloody swords led by Gionata. This greatly minimizes Judith's role, focusing more on the results of her killing Holofernes than on the courageous act itself. The music abruptly grows very soft, with high *ppp tremolos* gradually modulating to C major. This, considered the brightest key, always signals a happy turn of events. And indeed, the scene suddenly changes to Betulia, where an ensemble including Abramia, Gionata, Eliazaro, and Eliachimo all sing, in a joyous C-major chorus, of the brightness of the new day in their redeemed land. The chorus opens with the basses, singing *a cappella* together with Eliazaro and Eliachimo, followed by the full chorus still singing *a cappella* until the orchestra joins in. The effect of slowly building excitement and joy is powerful.

Peri altered the ending.[23] In his opera, Judith simply appears, signaled by a shift in the rhythm and mood. The accompaniment changes to four groups of rippling 16th-note groups and Judith sings a *bel canto*–style aria, still in C major (p. 210). She tells them that the powerful scepter of the tyrant was broken "like a weak cane" (*debole canna*). She urges them to join her in shouting "Hosanna!" on this, the day of their freedom. Judith's final word is *Libertà*, followed by the full chorus singing "Hosanna" in bright and triumphant C-major music, as the opera ends.[24] Notably missing is Judith displaying the severed head, to be displayed on the walls.

Silveri: The first part of Scene IV is the same plot as in Peri's opera. The thunder and lightning are represented here too by very loud, dramatic music. When Judith raises the curtain of the alcove and is overtaken by shivering, there is a small addition to the original libretto. Judith hears Abramia from the other chamber singing a verse from a song heard earlier in the opera, "In the gardens of Samaria" (p. 277). Judith recognizes this as the signal that it is time to act. She walks cautiously up to the curtain of Holofernes's alcove, listening for any sound. The music is very suspenseful. Then she cries out: "He is sleeping! Shivering overtakes me." This is followed by *pianissimo*

---

[23] In the final scene of Marcello's libretto, the chorus sings: "Holofernes is dead! The barbarian oppressors flee!" Gionata asks where Judith is, and the chorus points to her, "radiant in splendor" as she approaches, holding up the bloody sword. All kneel to her. This action and text were not included in Peri's opera.

[24] In the libretto's subsequently revised ending, Gionata sees Judith with the bloody sword and proclaims that Judith has freed her country. He kneels at her feet "to adore her virtue" and all sing: "The day of freedom has come" (*E giunto il giorno di libertà*). The opera concludes on the word "freedom," but in the original version, it was Judith who proclaimed it. And the Hosanna chorus was eliminated from the revised libretto.

staccato phrases in the basses, musically imitating her shivering. When Judith sings out *O Patria Mia!* ("Oh, my homeland!"), the soaring melody is cut off almost immediately. Then Judith sings softly, almost speaking: "And I still hesitate?" When Judith stumbles upon the sword, Silveri inserts a rousing short prayer, sung over steady throbbing groups of triplets—a very Verdian sound (p. 279). Looking heavenward and leaning on the sword, Judith prays:

> In this terrible hour, O God, help me; double the strength and boldness in my heart; let oppressed Israel that languishes, that dies, be saved. Let me run to accomplish the deed.

She holds up the sword and runs to the alcove. Worried that Holofernes might still be awake, Judith listens at the entrance to the alcove, shaking. She hears him still talking in his sleep, calling out her name. She walks toward him slowly, saying: "I'm coming." Her subsequent prayer, found in Peri's opera, is not included. Deviating from Marcello's libretto, Silveri cuts to the chase. Judith rushes into the alcove, waving the sword with ease. After a scream is heard (not indicated in the score, nor is the beheading suggested musically as it is in Peri's opera), the scene changes to one of growing chaos, as fleeing and frightened Assyrian soldiers are seen and the sun rises. A chorus is heard singing "Horror!" As in Peri's opera, this minimizes Judith's role, almost erasing it. The orchestra describes the chaos of retreat and victory. In the final scene, the chorus sings: "Holofernes is dead! The barbarian oppressors flee!" This is an abridged version of the scene; more of Marcello's libretto was included in Peri's opera.

Silveri made considerable changes to both of Marcello's conclusions. The final scene opens as Betulia is seen illuminated by the sun, with flags spread out over the rocks and the walls. The Hebrews advance, led by Gionata, and then the High Priest. Judith appears, her hair disheveled and her clothes stained with blood. She announces that the sun of the fifth day is shining. The astonished people greet her, singing in unison, as one unified voice. Continuing in a declamatory style, unaccompanied, she says: "This hand, still drenched in blood, carried out the pact that it faithfully swore." The chorus responds in pulsating music, opening in complete unison: "For a people who languish, suffering the shame of vile slavery, only the blood of the oppressors can wash them clean":

> *Un popolo che langue di vil servaggio l'onta,*
> *Degli oppressor nel sangue, solo lavar potrà.*

This verse would resonate strongly in the period of the Risorgimento. Judith tells the people that they should praise Heaven for the great deed and prostrate before God, let loose a song. All kneel, except Judith and the High Priest. Everyone sings praises to God, who had pity on them. To expansive, triumphant music, they conclude singing: "Let the sun of freedom rise more resplendent," ending the opera on *libertà*. Judith's voice rises above the full chorus, ending on a sustained a''. This altered ending is more satisfying in that the focus remains on Judith and her deed, rather than on the resulting military victory led by Gionata.

Conclusion

In both these operas, the biblical plot, based on Marcello's libretto, is dramatically altered. Choruses of women, old men, warriors, slaves, eunuchs, and priests from both sides dominate the action, somewhat sidelining Judith. These extensive choruses also establish a sense of place and mood. There are quite a few plot additions from the original biblical book in Marcello's libretto, which Silveri and Peri changed in only a few places; both also incorporated elements of Giacometti's play. Judith has a very close relationship with Abramia, who in this retelling was in fact her nursemaid and confesses to having been a slave in Holofernes's harem when she was very young. These extra dimensions create a rounded and very sympathetic character. The invented love interest, the tenor Gionata, gives both composers the opportunity to write wonderful love duets (and tenor arias); but Judith rejects his love, so the plot device does not weaken her. If anything, it adds an element of independence to her character, for it would have been very unusual for a woman to reject a loving suitor, both in nineteenth-century Italy and two thousand years ago.

Other major additions are Judith's discovery of water that turns out to be poisoned (from Giacometti's play), which adds nothing to the original story but creates more drama and attributes still greater powers to Judith; and the presence of both Gionata and Eliachimo the High Priest in Holofernes's camp. But they did not come to find Judith, only to confront Holofernes, and finding Judith there creates yet more dramatic conflicts. But these too do not diminish Judith in any way. Yet another addition is the character Arzaele, queen of Holofernes's harem, a tool for an operatic love triangle. She is introduced and then dropped, unlike in the Giacometti play, where she is present even at the killing of Holofernes. (She appears very briefly near the end in Silveri's opera.) More subtle additions are Judith's expressions of self-doubt, which give her more dimensions while not contradicting the original text. She is more real and vulnerable when she shows doubts. Holofernes, too, has more dimensions in both these operas than in other works discussed here, alternately showing rage and expressing poetic and loving thoughts. It is hard to hate him, and it is not clear if that was the intention of either composer.

Though one might be hard pressed to recognize the apocryphal book in the Marcello's libretto and these two operas, the gap-filling does not always contradict the original text, and the music fills the gaps colorfully and dramatically. Despite the underlying symbolism in the libretto (discussed earlier), it nonetheless adds new dimensions to the main characters—not only Judith and Holofernes, but also Judith's servant Abra or Abramia. They get a "back story" that makes them more rounded as people. Judith's motives as well as her doubts are presented as more complex than in the original book, which in turn makes her more human than symbol. The focus in the conclusions of the operas is more on the results of Judith's brave act, which enabled the Hebrews to defeat the Assyrian forces, than on the act itself. But this plot does at least acknowledge that Judith was responsible for the Israelite victory, if not very overtly.

As for the music, echoes of Verdi in both operas were often mentioned. But to describe an opera as "Verdian" is not necessarily negative. It is imitation, not mockery, and this was what the public of that day wanted. Verdi's orbit in the latter part of the nineteenth century was almost impossible for aspiring composers to avoid. Peri's music often echoes the *bel canto* style of Bellini and particularly Donizetti, whose music in turn influenced Verdi in his early works. Calling both composers' music derivative does not mean it is not appealing or effective. The operas include stunning, frightening, uplifting, and moving music. This music illuminates and adds new colors to the portrayals of all the main characters, by expressing and amplifying a wide range of emotions in both the soloists and the choruses.

Charles Edouard Lefebvre (1843–1917)

Charles Edouard Lefebvre studied law before entering the Paris Conservatoire, where he studied with Ambroise Thomas and Charles Gounod (whose influence can be clearly heard in his opera *Judith*). He won the Prix de Rome in 1870 for his cantata *Le Jugement de Dieu* (The Judgment of God). He was highly regarded as a composer by French critics in the late nineteenth century, even if they recognized that his music was not on the same level as leading composers of the time. The style and texture of his instrumental pieces recall Felix Mendelssohn, while his *Judith* anticipates the twentieth-century French predilection for opera-oratorio typical of *Les Six*, particularly Darius Milhaud and Arthur Honegger (see Chapter 2).[25] Paul Collin (1843–1915), the librettist, was primarily a poet, who later wrote libretti and collaborated with contemporary composers of the second half of the nineteenth century, including Pyotr Tchaikovsky, who set several of Collin's shorter poems as songs. Collin also wrote the libretto for César Franck's 1880 oratorio *Rébecca*.[26]

Judith, drame lyrique en 3 acts 4 scènes, poem by Paul Collin (1877)

This work is an opera-oratorio; it is not known in which form it was ever performed.[27]

Judith: soprano
Holoferernes: baritone
Ozias: bass
Nassar: tenor

There are no recordings but the score is available at IMSLP.[28]
All translations are my own.

In Act I, the opera, like many other musical settings of Judith, opens and closes with a chorus of Hebrews. The opening scene takes place in a public square in besieged Bethulia at sunrise. (The parallel action in the book of Judith is chapter 7). In the

[25] Elaine Brody in *New Grove Dictionary* (2001), vol. 14, p. 472.
[26] See Helen Leneman, *Musical Illuminations of Genesis Narratives* (London: Bloomsbury T&T Clark, 2018), pp. 214–19.
[27] Dedication page to Madame Pauline Viardot (1821–1910), renowned mezzo-soprano of his time: *temoignage de reconnaissance et d'admiration* (a token of recognition and admiration).
[28] https://imslp.org/wiki/Judith%2C_Op.31_(Lefebvre%2C_Charles) (accessed October 22, 2020).

opening lamenting chorus, the people sing about dying of thirst, cruel suffering, and burning lips. The orchestra plays chromatic rising and descending passages. Other musical devices include dissonant intervals intruding in the otherwise tonic harmonies, and plodding chords in the bass, suggestive of slow and difficult walking. The chorus sings in a very low range, hesitantly, almost speaking their lines, to effectively evoke their dry throats. The old men express the hope that their soldiers have broken through the enemy ranks. The tempo speeds up and becomes much more rhythmic as a group of armed men enters, describing their failure to break through (p. 4). Everyone joins together in a chorus, singing: "This is too much sadness and suffering, it must end, we have to surrender." Several passages of chromatically descending phrases very effectively suggest despair. The chorus builds to a *ff* climax over orchestra *tremolos* and chromatic clusters (p. 8) and continues in this loud and excited music when they see Ozias, one of the rulers of Bethulia. They decide to ask him to do their will (p. 16).

A dramatic *fortissimo a cappella* chorus follows (marked *Largo*, very slow), singing in unison to suggest they are all of one mind. Rapid passages or single chords are heard between their phrases. Over *tremolos* and loud *marcato* chords, they sing:

> Ozias, all our troubles are your work, you thought there would be a treaty and the enemy would be disarmed. Your mad pride has repelled peace like an affront (*Ta farouche fierté a repoussé la paix comme un outrage*).

Ozias asks what they want (p. 18). With their voices following one another, they tell him their hopes have been vain, only illusions; they will die of hunger, they must give themselves up. Their final phrase, "We must give ourselves up," is sung on a *fortissimo* ascending passage, in unison, reaching *a-flat*", which is held for several beats over excited tremolos (p. 22). The music underlines and heightens the sense of desperation in their pleas.

In a sudden key shift from C minor to C# minor and in a slower tempo, Ozias responds over continual *tremolos* and ominous descending notes in the bass:

> What, deliver Bethulia to the worshippers of false gods? Let the holy land where our ancestors sleep be vilified by proud foreigners? You would not want to buy your salvation with this ignominy, to bend your heads and humiliate yourselves under their hateful yoke.

In faster but more flowing and plangent phrases, now in G# minor and accompanied by waves of rolling 16th-note passages, the people reply that exile, slavery, and shame do not matter: they will submit to them. Even death, if it is quick, is better than the horrible fate they are suffering now. The orchestra plays soaring poignant phrases above the chorus (p. 28). A Hebrew (named Coryphère) asks Ozias if he knows another way, in this extreme danger, of saving their children, wives, themselves. A tenor chorus repeats these phrases.

Ozias asks for five days, by which time he hopes they will find help. In a faster tempo, the people sing repeatedly: "Help! Help! Who will give us that?" At this moment, Judith appears in the doorway of her house, magnificently dressed (p. 30). (This is a fast-forward through Judith chapter 8.) When the people ask "Who will give us help?" one last time, the tempo slows down abruptly by half as Judith answers: "Jehova our father." Her voice rises to *g"* before descending over an octave, ending on *d'*. Such dramatic intervals musically suggest strength. The chorus sings Judith's praise in a sweet, lilting, and almost hymnlike melody. They sing: "Virtue, grace and beauty, the inconsolable wife in her faithfulness." Then as if suddenly noticing how she is dressed, they ask: "When did she abandon her black widow's garb? What splendor and majesty."

Judith responds in a recitative that develops into an aria (p. 35). She scolds her ungrateful people, who in these days of testing didn't raise their hearts to God or ask him for light or the invincible support of his paternal arm. She firmly orders them to kneel and have hope, reassuring them that God (Jehovah) can still pardon them. (The reference to Christian rather than Jewish practice in this action has been previously discussed; see above). She asks if they have forgotten Moses's hymn of deliverance. In her aria, *Andante maestoso* and sounding like a rallying cry in marked 4/4 time, she sings:

> They were numerous and magnificent, the proud enemies of the Lord. As in an instant the highest weeds fall under the hand of the reaper, and as in winter a dead leaf falls under the wind that blows and carries it—so they fell, these proud enemies of the Lord. Our Lord said: Go, I will deliver you, and so the sea opened its waves to make us a path.

On the final phrase, the key and tempo change, and the accompaniment is sparser. This adds emphasis to Judith's pronouncements. She goes on to relate the whole saga of the parting of the sea. The passages about Pharaoh feature chromatic two-note phrases, a weeping sound (*seufzer*) over a steady *tremolo*, a very dramatic effect (p. 39). One music scholar suggests that the *tremolos* represent the voice of God speaking through Judith.[29] Judith reprises the first part of her song, and the chorus responds that her intrepid voice, intimidated by nothing, awakens virtue in their downcast hearts. They are fired up and their fear is fading. Their strong and confident music reflects this mood.

Now Ozias asks Judith why she's dressed in finery, with necklaces and rings and a golden diadem on her head "as in happy days of old." The music throughout this dialogue becomes increasingly more excited. She says she is carrying out heaven's decrees and he shouldn't try to understand the mystery of these secrets but should only pray to God to watch her back (p. 50). Her voice dies down as suddenly very high loud *tremolos* are heard (a "heavenly" sound) and she sings, "seized by a sudden inspiration" (score note): "People of God, raise your heads, know that the almighty one will not let you be oppressed, you are a people loved by God." Then she bids them adieu, accompanied by highly lyrical arpeggiated passages. As she exits, she tells them to pray for her, as they follow her with their eyes. The scene ends on an unresolved seventh (dominant) chord, which leads directly into the final chorus.

---

[29] Pasler, p. 439.

In this chorus, the sopranos sing an expansive melody (marked *Dolce*, sweetly), accompanied by *staccato* 8th-note chords. They sing: "Go, Judith, go, noble woman, where duty calls you, and God guides your steps, let him inspire your soul." A full six-part chorus, plus soprano *obbligato*, repeats the sopranos' melody, building to a big climax. Then the music suddenly dies down as they kneel and sing a few measures over very spare accompaniment, almost hymnlike (p. 56): "You see us kneeling, God of Abraham and Moses." Rising, in a sudden and sharp change of mood, they sing in a broader melody over *ff* chords and *tremolo*: "We invoke the promised alliance, save us." This final chorus received particularly high praise at the first performances.[30]

Act II takes place in the Assyrian camp. A rapid orchestral introduction has a martial character, suggested by fanfares; this is followed by a martial chorus of Assyrians singing: "Our gods are the only real gods, everywhere; today they will make known the supreme power of their glorious arms; let's sing to them and to our master, the king who is always victorious." The music grows increasingly loud and high. Though the chorus is in D minor, the final sustained chord is in D major, underlining the triumphant mood. This is followed by an aria for Holofernes (p. 64), marked *un poco maestoso* and both martial and pompous in style. The rhythm is *marcato*, with strongly accented beats. There is a rumbling low *tremolo* and from time to time, very high quick passages are played, most probably by flutes or piccolos, to suggest storms. He sings: "More menacing than the hurricane or the flood pushed by the north wind, the Assyrians rushed to subject the world to their laws." He sings about their fierce courage that has sown terror wherever they go and how they have nobly accomplished their task—subduing all their enemies.

The tone becomes sweet and sustained as he sings under lyrical orchestra passages: "And soon returning to Assyria where a calmer destiny awaits us, we will return to our homeland, rich with honor and with booty." The music momentarily reminds the audience that Holofernes is a human being, with the same dreams and even homesickness as every other soldier. But immediately the music resumes its martial character, as Holofernes concludes with a recitative: "Only Bethulia, under a long siege, laughs at our effort and believes itself protected by its god." The chorus interjects: "Death to anyone who resists us!" Holofernes reprises the first part of the aria, ending an octave higher, on *g'* instead of *g*. This is a high and dramatic note for a baritone (p. 70). The soldiers reprise their earlier chorus.

Holofernes now addresses the Hebrew slaves (p. 73): "Why these menacing looks? Resign yourselves to your altered destiny; your god does not see your powerless tears. Be our cupbearers at this joyous party." The presence of Hebrew slaves in Holofernes's camp is suggested in only one other work: Chadwick's 1901 opera (see Chapter 5). Historically, the Israelites were at one time captives in Assyria, as related in 1 Chr 5:26 and 2 Kgs 15:29. A Hebrew woman sings: "The miserable man! He curses and insults you, God of the universe." The other Hebrews repeat this, while the Assyrians try to quiet them down, telling them to stop ruining their merry concerts. They tell the Hebrews that their God will never break their chains. A remarkable double chorus

---

[30]   Pasler, p. 440.

follows, the Assyrians and the Hebrews engaged in a battle of wills. These two choruses go on simultaneously, the Hebrews' music sustained and intense against the more dotted rhythms of the Assyrians'.

Holofernes interrupts the chorus and tells the Hebrews "ironically" (score note):

> If you find your chain too heavy, then pray, invoke your all-powerful god; he will not remain deaf to your cries; he will put your city back together and will crush us under his avenging hand!

Trills and dotted rhythms in the music heighten the irony and sarcasm. The Hebrews respond (p. 79), initially singing in unison, which increases the effect of a chant. The three-part chorus (no altos, creating a more modal and "religious" sound) sings that in this hour, in their distress, in this place, they cannot sing the hymns (*canticles*) of God (based loosely on Ps 137). Continuing in this hymn-like music, they sing:

> Our glory is withered, our dear homeland is bent under your laws; we can only sing the songs that our lyre played then; those sweet songs our fathers, in better times, taught to all of us.

On the word *modulait*, or modulated (played), they begin to sing in three parts, underlining the text (p, 80). Suddenly the tempo picks up dramatically as they sing in much stronger tones and in unison: "No! these sacred hymns will not be delivered, tyrants, to your contempt." The Assyrians respond in double the tempo, over rapid 16th-note phrases:

> Race of slaves, we are your masters, their audacity to threaten their conquerors, let's strike these traitors! Let us take vengeance on this mob without mercy.

This leads to another double chorus, in which the Hebrews sing long sustained lines against the choppy, rhythmic music of the Assyrians (p. 86). There is much dissonance between the two choruses, a musical way of underlining their sharp differences. For example, the Hebrews hold *B* and *C* against the Assyrians' *C* and then *D*. The Hebrews sing in a unified voice, in unison; while in contrast, the Assyrians sing to a lively 3/8 rhythm in short phrases and divided voices (not homophonic), suggesting more chaos and less unity. The Hebrews' homophonic singing suggests unity and pride, while the lively but harsh Assyrians' music features short phrases and divided voices.

As the chorus ends, several measures of rapid *tremolos* are heard (p. 92). Holofernes's servant Nassar announces that his soldiers surprised a Jewish woman (*une Juive*) near his tent.[31] In slower music, he describes her "proud bearing and stunning finery," which attest to her high rank. Holofernes tells Nassar to bring her in. Her entrance

---

[31] The use of a contemporary term for Jew has been discussed in reference to other works. Why her identification differs from the identification of the Israelite slaves as Hebreux is not clear but was probably a convention in that era.

(p. 94) is signaled by a reprise of the music of the first act chorus. Judith opens with a recitative: "From the greatest of heroes I am begging for power (*J'implore la puissance ...*) ... yes, how decent and sweet he is ... he will protect the innocent who comes seeking refuge on her knees." This sounds like a soliloquy, but it is not entirely clear if Judith is already in front of Holofernes. He asks for her name, and to a spare accompaniment of only sustained chords, she tells him she is Judith and her birthright allows her to expect a noble welcome from enemies like him. Instantly smitten, as underlined in the music by rapid *tremolos* with a soaring melody beneath, Holofernes says to himself: "I feel an unknown ecstasy before her" (p. 96). Then he asks Judith why she has come. In slow and deliberate phrases, she responds:

> Lord, I had to leave the beloved walls of Bethulia that the Hebrews in their madness insist on disputing with you. These walls which they should have given up to you while imploring mercy from you, in vain in their pride they still hope to defend.

The music becomes more dramatic as she continues:

> Tomorrow it will be over for us! Everything conspires for our ruin, and those who are spared in the assault, will suffer the horror of famine!

After a long silence, her voice grows much softer as she reprises the opening melody:

> This is why I said to myself, let's leave this funereal city which is pursuing the wrath of Heaven; let's throw ourselves at the feet of the victor!—Ah!

The last phrase is sung on an ascending scale, the final exclamation reaching *a-flat"*, before the music dies down. Holofernes tells Judith (p. 100) that she is wise and has not counted on his goodness in vain, promising "on my honor I will protect your days." The chorus of Assyrians sings about Judith in a bright C major: "Look how beautiful she is, the sun shines less brightly in the eastern sky than in her radiant eyes" and more such superlatives. Holofernes sings over them, as the orchestra soars (with strong echoes of Gounod's *Romeo et Juliette*, written ten years earlier) about the spark of flame (*étincelle*) he sees when she gazes at him. "For a single kiss from her, I would betray my gods, my country and my faith." Then Judith sings in unison with Holofernes, a musical element that usually suggests unity of thought. In this case, it is used with some irony. For several measures, she repeats his words about her, about the effect of *his* gaze. But then while he sings about a kiss from her, she sings: "To be victorious over the infidel, let's enjoy his confusion, let's increase his excitement!" (*Profitons de son trouble, éxcitons son emoi*). While this is going on, the double chorus (Hebrews and Assyrians) praises Judith as a saint, who is betraying and renouncing her unhappy people today. An interesting and unusual element in this opera, as noted above, is the presence of Hebrew slaves in the Assyrian camp, observing Judith. The music is very rhythmical and excited, featuring some striking dissonance, such as minor second chords of *c-d-flat*. Throughout this large and dramatic chorus, Judith and Holofernes continue to sing over them. The ensemble closes with the two protagonists singing two bars in harmony (p. 108) about the effect of the looks the other gives—musically like a love duet, increasing the sense of irony.

Judith tells Holofernes she needs to talk to him without witnesses, to tell him important secrets, which she can reveal only to him. She sings these words in a recitative accompanied only by *tremolos* and occasional *seufzer* phrases in the orchestra; all of this creates suspense. In an aside, in lyrical phrases, Holofernes sings that he can't resist her tempting voice. Softly he tells Judith to come to his tent after dark, where they will be alone and where he will wait. An ominous repeated phrase under *tremolos* creates suspense. Then he pointedly adds in a strong phrase: "A curse on your people if my wait is in vain!" Judith sings in an aside: "He is falling into the prepared trap all by himself." Over steady bass *tremolo*, he asks softly if she will come to his tent that night, and she says she will. In these final measures, a sustained C major chord is held while short fast phrases in dissonance with that key are heard in the bass, steadily ascending in pitch. The scene ends in a strong mood of suspense and apprehension, created by the music (p. 111).

The Hebrew slaves now sing a very slow funereal lament, singing the same chromatically ascending notes, echoed in the orchestra, that were just heard in the conclusion of the Judith-Holofernes scene. Such musical devices tie all these scenes together. They sing: "O guilty woman! Who would have believed your heart capable of such infamy?" In steadily building music, they continue: "Shame on you who deceived us!" over which Judith prays to God for strength while the Hebrews curse her in dramatic and dissonant music. Clearly Judith is not close enough to hear them. Then the Assyrians resume praising their gods. It is not clear how the Hebrews would have known who Judith was, or even that she was a Hebrew.

Act III takes place in Holofernes's tent. Scene 1 opens with a short orchestral interlude, some of it highly reminiscent of Gounod. This is followed by dancing music accompanied by chorus (p. 117). Men ask women to dance and sing to help them forget war; this is followed by a lengthy drinking chorus, then several dance numbers. There are numerous references to drinking, dancing through the night, and enjoying the orgy. There is extensive dance music without chorus, as ballet scenes were traditionally expected in nineteenth-century French opera. Many Judith operas include lengthy "banquet" scenes like this, absent from the original story but creating a context and background for the later private Judith-Holofernes encounter.

Nassar points to Judith approaching Holofernes's tent (p. 140) and tells the others that Holofernes wants to be alone with "this Jewess," and they should leave. The sounds of the drinking and dancing choruses die down to nothing. Judith enters and sings a recitative and prayer. The recitative is sung in highly dramatic tones, while fragments of the dance music are heard in the background:

These foolish people, what blind delirium! They say they will sing tomorrow but they are wrong. One who seems weak and you disdain is strong. Hurry up with your singing and laughing, for I am bringing into this place silence and death. (p. 143)

Judith now addresses God in a passionate aria, filled with sweeping melodies and large intervals with an ominous bass line throughout. In the first part, she prays to God whose voice has so often commanded her as to what to do, even this time, when God planted the seed of this audacious plan to pull his people out of the abyss: "Help me to achieve my virtuous crime." After this line, the music becomes increasingly passionate, changing here from A-flat major to E major with a much more throbbing and excited accompaniment (p. 145). Moving from the abstract to the concrete, Judith reminds God that he helped the child David bring down the giant Goliath, and she wants him to pour the same strength into her soul. On this phrase, she reaches *f#"* and then plunges down to *b*, an interval of a twelfth. She sings the final words unaccompanied, a musical suggestion of vulnerability. Intensity builds as Judith cries: "This is the hour, that my vengeful arm will rise up over the proud tyrant," sung over ascending 32nd-note chromatic octaves, one series after the other. After these passages, the original key of A-flat major returns. In resolute and triumphant music, the prayer reaches its apogee on a leap of a seventh up to *a-flat"* when she pleads with God to strengthen her arm: "When I take hold of the sword, my weak hand will not tremble. My God, make my hand firm!" (p. 148).

The duet that follows (p. 149) contains some dissonant intervals that create a sense of foreboding. The opening recitative measures have a very sparse accompaniment. Holofernes asks Judith what secrets she has and warns that even her beauty would not defend her against him if she dared trick him. Ominous-sounding dissonant minor seconds are heard in the orchestra. She falls to her knees singing, to sinuous music: "All right then, strike me! I lied," over very dramatic intervals and chords. He answers "violently" (in the score): "Curse you, woman, have you not come to deliver Bethulia to me?" She rises and in a much steadier beat, asks: "I call upon your genius, oh Master, do you need such help?" The calm heard in the measured music, with many whole notes, is a subtext suggesting Judith's state of mind. He asks her what her goal is, and she says she is ambitious, that "it is a rare and beautiful triumph my heart desires, an illustrious conquest, that I dream of." He asks her what conquest, and she says: "Yours, proud victor." She is offering to align herself with Holofernes.

The accompaniment now changes to a steady 6/8 beat of repeated chords and moves from E-flat major to G minor. Such an abrupt change is a musical technique indicating a sudden change of mood (p. 152). The lyrical vocal line is doubled in the orchestra as the music grows steadily more powerful. Judith explains that she has tried to find the old virtues in her own people but that her warriors have the hearts of women, and the terror of Holofernes's name has beaten them down. After a full measure's rest, she continues: "You, sent by heaven to punish these infamous ones, you appeared to me like a divine being!" Trumpet calls are heard at this phrase. On the last held note of this text, the key changes back to G major. In this libretto, Judith goes beyond what her biblical counterpart says to persuade Holofernes. She is convincingly portraying herself as a traitor, demonstrating both cleverness and deviousness.

The tempo speeds up as Judith sings to Holofernes in very rhythmic phrases: "Take this intoxicating smoky cup, O Master, in your valiant hand. I drink to your greatness, to yesterday's triumphs and tomorrow's success." Holofernes sings, increasingly louder and higher, of how her look shines "like a shooting star in a summer night." She sings in an aside: "My God, let drunkenness come and break his strength and vigor." While she sings that, he rhapsodizes about the pride in her look, how beautiful she is. She also sings: "Lord, let it be your hand through mine that strikes him" (*Que ce soit ta main par la mienne qui le frappe, Seigneur*). They are singing these very different texts simultaneously, something possible only in music.

Love duets—even ironic ones like this—played an important part in the allegorical meaning of the texts. As Pasler points out, this was particularly true in that era in France for republicans, to whom love was an essential part of their freemason-based ideology. The power of love heightened the significance of choosing duty to country. Judith and Holofernes, representing different countries, could have expressed the complex relationship of France to Germany at that time. Judith's story illustrates what it means to be the weaker of two and how the weak can relate to the strong with the end result of overpowering him. Composers and librettists writing about Judith demonstrated the tactics she used, thus also teaching listeners how they might empower themselves.[32]

In an abrupt modulation to B major, and to pompous marching music, Holofernes now sings: "Yes, I have gone from conquest to conquest, I won all, bent everything to my law. But now it is my turn to bow my head, Judith, conquered by you." He takes off his sword, as the key suddenly shifts from B major to D major. Judith says: "Here it is, this sword that has never shown mercy, and that, terrible in battle, shines like wild lightning in space." Judith takes the sword from him, and Holofernes asks what she is doing: "What temerity, your child's hand can't lift this sword." She responds that the arm is strong when the soul is hardened (*trempée*). Over only *tremolo* in the orchestra and to a faster tempo, he tells her to rather pour him the fiery liquor: "I want to drink, Judith, to your conquering charm. Pour, pour." The tempo increases further in a *brindisi* or toast as she offers him the cup. She salutes him and drinks to his greatness. It is not clear if Judith actually drinks from the cup, since in the original story she never breaks her dietary laws that forbid drinking unconsecrated wine. Librettos in general do not deal with this topic.

Signaled by a change in the music, he interrupts her and sings: "No more delay, I give in to the transports that possess my heart thirsty for burning sensuality. Come, let a kiss from your lips soothe or double the fever by which I feel myself being devoured, near you" (p. 161). The music becomes faster and more excited. Judith protests that the God of Israel and all her race will curse her. To reassure her, in a bitterly ironic line, he responds that he will erase any trace of Bethulia and all will fall under his blows—"so then who can curse you?" She asks: "What about the wrath of your gods on you?" to which he replies: "All erased, gods and kings, at my wish. Let us love one another." The excitement builds in the orchestra during this increasingly passionate exchange. Holofernes grows more and more excited, amplified by the continual 16th-note passages in the orchestra: "Be mine, in my veins a fire has been lit that is consuming me." Judith sings in an aside: "He has to die," then, "For my country I have to do it, the time is here." Holofernes continues with more passionate entreaties. In an aside, Judith murmurs: "It is love he is calling—and death that will come," which she

---

[32] Pasler, p. 50.

repeats several times, while he is singing: "Your beauty belongs to me, come, come." In a violent movement, he tries to pull Judith, who fights back and is able to disengage. Holofernes totters, and wonders about his sudden dizziness. Erratic musical phrases paint his physical state, as he wonders what force holds him back, feeling his eyes cloud over and his knees buckle. Then he falls onto the bed.

Rising chromatic chords are heard, gradually growing louder under a constant *tremolo*. Judith sings (p. 169): "Heaven do for me this marvelous miracle. You who with a breath fight the strength of the powerful, let your immortal glory be known in all places. My God, your work is done!" Some *tremolo* is heard, followed by several rising chord clusters. Finally, Judith strikes Holofernes (marked in the score, but with no mention of raising the sword) to the accompaniment of harshly dissonant chord clusters—three shrill eleventh chords—played *ff* and off the beat. This vivid musical depiction creates far more excitement and tension than words alone ever could. After Judith's act, only a sustained low B flat is heard along with a *tremolo* on that note. Since it is clearly indicated in the score that Judith strikes Holofernes (*Judith frappe*), it would be interesting to know how this was depicted on stage. There is also no mention of what Judith does with the head, since this is one of the few works that includes no part for her slave. Unfortunately, there are no records of performances of this work.

In this lengthy "seduction" scene, the music expresses both unspoken and spoken exchanges that characterize seduction. Unsettling conventional relationships by making the strong weak and the weak strong is accomplished by charm. And music utilizes the voice to both initiate and express charm. In this opera, Judith tempts Holofernes with her voice, which he himself says he cannot resist. The music of this duet suggests attraction in several ways: for example, they sing on the same pitch at certain moments, and also sing passages in parallel thirds. When Judith sings of approaching death, they sing octaves, which musically can suggest the ecstasy of sexual union. But before they reach a musical climax, Holofernes collapses, and the momentum grinds to a halt. The music might suggest to listeners that deceit and seduction are closely related.[33]

An orchestral interval precedes Scene 2 (p. 170). The scene opens as Judith is heard from offstage, accompanied by martial music, singing: "Open the gate, Bethulia! The time for trembling is over. Rejoice, people, the impious one has been struck down." The pattern of repeated 8th notes in 12/8 time continues throughout her recitative. Scattered groups of Hebrews onstage are gradually joined by many others. They wonder what is going on, what this joyous announcement means. In small groups, they sing: "What does this mean?" "Listen! ... Can we believe this?" Then they recognize Judith, whom they hadn't hoped to see again. The music, continuing the same repeated 8th notes, builds in excitement as the people see her coming. First they recognize her voice, and then they finally see her. Only when Judith enters does the rhythmic pattern change, as rapid ascending passages lead up to her entrance. The key changes to a bright F# major and the tempo is marked *Maestoso* (p. 182). The orchestra briefly reprises the first act melody. Then to a sparse accompaniment of only *tremolos* or rapidly ascending passages, Judith proclaims:

---

[33] Pasler, pp. 445, 448.

Look! By the hand of his humble servant, he struck a mortal blow against the one who struck fear into the children of Israel. Here is the head of the barbarian. I promised you help, you have had it. The enemy has no captain, they are fleeing far from our walls.

She now reprises the aria from the first act: "They were many, they were proud" (p. 185), joined by the chorus. The final chorus is introduced by Ozias, who sings: "Honor to you, Judith, God has blessed you, your arm has brought down the enemy of Israel. Glory to you, and to God who has saved Bethulia." He then instructs the Israelites to address their hymn to God. A few bars of military proclamation lead to the fast finale, in the brightest key of C major. The opening lines are from the closing hymn in the original story (Jdt 16:1–3). It is a cut time fugue (very fast), in which the middle section grows more complex, when they sing about the Assyrian terror. The music vacillates constantly between dissonant and consonant chords, building up to the repetition of the opening. Throughout the chorus, they sing "Glory to Judith" and "Glory to God," but they conclude singing praises only to God. The opera ends triumphantly and securely in C major.

Lefebvre wrote two different conclusions to the opera. The second one cut the final chorus of praise for Judith by more than half and completely eliminated the exuberant "Glory to God" chorus. The composer apparently wanted one ending to reinforce God's actions through Judith, and the other to focus on Judith's actions aided by God.[34]

Conclusion

This very appealing opera/oratorio is dominated by extensive and varied choruses, all very expressive and effective. But this does not lessen the impact of the main characters' roles. The Judith-Holofernes duets feature irony in abundance, and the composer brilliantly uses the potential of the singing voice to convincingly suggest power, passion, meekness, and other emotional states. A long banquet scene is included, as in most works discussed here. Musically of great interest is the periodic and unexpected use of dissonance to build suspense and anxiety. The plot is less altered than in other works discussed, though it is one of very few works to include no role for Judith's slave. Another unusual deviation is the inclusion of Hebrew slaves in Holofernes's camp. This adds a new element to the plot, though it is never explained how they would know Judith. They could not have come from Bethulia, so this remains a gap. But the expansive choruses succeed in projecting the importance of the people in the story, be they Hebrews or Assyrians. There may well be underlying political messages in this opera, but the listener can derive great pleasure from the music and empathize with the fully developed main characters, without awareness of those messages. Of course, at the time the work was written and performed, those messages would have been much more obvious and meaningful to the audience.

---

[34] Pasler, p. 437.

Alexander Serov (1820–1871)

Alexander Serov was born in St. Petersburg. His maternal grandfather was of German-Jewish origin. Serov worked as a lawyer for ten years before giving it up to pursue music in 1850. He married his student Valentina Serova (1846–1927) who was also a composer. When he died suddenly of a heart attack in 1871, she completed his final opera. Their son Valentin Serov (1865–1911) became a noted and highly distinguished painter (who designed the sets for his father's opera).[35] Serov's first opera (and first large-scale work) was *Judith* (*Yudif*), which premiered in 1860 at the Mariinsky theater. Because Serov had been fortunate to receive a crown stipend and also patronage, no expense was spared for the production. It won the approval of the Moscow Conservatory and one of its most distinguished students, Pyotr Tschaikovsky, who said of the opera: "It is written with a great deal of fervor and at times reaches summits of tremendous power."[36] So successful was the opera that the Tsar granted Serov a royal pension, and Serov became a major celebrity almost overnight. Aspects of his style that had a strong influence on later composers include the profound musical contrasts between opposing national identities—Assyrian and Israelite—as well as the distinctive "oriental" style heard throughout *Judith*.[37] The libretto was inspired by Giacometti's 1857 play (see Chapter 3), which circulated widely in Russia at that time. In fact, it was a performance of that play by the touring Italian actress Adelaida Ristori (see Chapter 3) at the Mariinsky Theatre in 1861 that inspired Serov to finally write a "musico-dramatic creation" inspired by Wagner. He was not only inspired by Giacometti's play but also confessed he had always been attracted to the stories and characters of the Hebrew Bible. Less than three years later, the 43-year-old Serov finally made his operatic debut with *Yudif*. At this point in his life, Serov had been Russia's foremost music critic for more than ten years, but none of the music he wrote had been performed or even published. As Serov scholar Richard Taruskin notes, "such a retarded development may be unique in the history of music, and it could only have happened in Russia." The opera was performed twenty times to full houses in its first season, an extraordinary success for a Russian opera.[38]

Though initially popular, the opera has almost completely dropped out of the repertoire. The role of Holofernes was one of famous Russian bass Feodor Chaliapin's favorites.[39] In fact, *Judith* was performed only as long as Chaliapin was singing in it.

---

[35] These set designs can be seen at https://www.google.com/search?rlz=1C1CHBD_enUS856US856&q =valentin+serov+Judith+sets&tbm=isch&source=univ&sa=X&ved=2ahUKEwjd84COoZTkAh VFzlkKHfzWDpwQsAR6BAgJEAE&biw=1366&bih=625#imgrc=PO_VXIsH3AC_tM (accessed August 21, 2019).

[36] Quoted by Julian Haylock, CD liner notes, 2011.

[37] Haylock 2011, liner notes.

[38] Edward Gorden and Stuart Campbell in *New Grove Dictionary* (2001), vol. 23, pp. 137–8; and Richard Taruskin, "The Case of Serov's Judith," in *Opera and Drama in Russia* (Ann Arbor: University of Michigan Research Press, 1982), pp. 34–5, 52.

[39] Haylock 2011. Many images of Chaliapin in this role can be seen here: https://www.google.com/ search?rlz=1C1CHBD_enUS856US856&q=chaliapin+as+holofernes&tbm=isch&source=univ &sa=X&ved=2ahUKEwiy05PR1q3jAhVHSN8KHa-BC9gQ7Al6BAgJEA8&biw=1366&bih=625 (accessed August 21, 2019).

The only time any part of Serov's opera was performed outside of Russia was in Paris in 1909, when the fourth act was produced by Sergei Diaghilev.[40]

Though unknown outside of Russia today, Serov was not a "cipher in history," in Taruskin's opinion, but an essential link between Russian music of the first and second halves of the nineteenth century. For his libretto, Serov engaged several different writers without informing any of them that he was doing so. He presented them with his scenario and asked for a libretto, while he composed the music first. He eventually engaged a prominent poet, Apollon Maikov (1821–1897), to help him complete the work. In the end, Serov took credit for the libretto himself. In addition to Giacometti's influence, Hebbel's play also inspired some of Serov's libretto. The composer expressed admiration for that play (see Chapter 3) but did not incorporate many of the major alterations Hebbel made to the original story.[41]

There was a 2016 performance of excerpts at the Mariinsky Theatre in Moscow.[42]

The score can be found online (it should be downloaded one act at a time because of its length, 380 pages).[43]

There is a fine recording, widely available at Brilliant Opera Collection, 2011, Bolshoi Theater Orchestra. The singers are uniformly excellent.

Yudif/Judith (1863)

Judith: soprano
Avra: mezzo-soprano (the Russian version of Abra, from Giacometti's play, and
      originally Metastasio's libretto; see Chapters 1 and 3)
Ozias and Eliakim: both bass
Achior: tenor
Holofernes: bass
Bagoas: tenor

In Act I, the lengthy and dramatic overture features poignant passages that depict the despair predominating the opening scene. Lengthy harp passages introduce several themes from the opera. There is no break between the overture and opening of the opera, in a public square in Bethulia. Ozias, Charmis, and Eliachim sing about their people's suffering and God's abandonment of them. They are introduced by slow and very low passages in the orchestra. Their recitatives have only sparse accompaniment, a solemn sound with mostly sustained or short chords. They refer to Holofernes as "the instrument of God's rage … scourge of God" and complain of the almost total loss of water. Eliakim bursts in over sudden *fortissimo tremolos*, railing at the others to stop their "blaspheming complaints." He rouses them by reminding them of all the miracles God has performed for them in the past. The mood changes suddenly to a few lyrical measures marked *cantabile*, where he assures the leaders that God is with them. Then to steady groups of 8th-note triplets, and with increasing passion, he tells them

[40] Taruskin, p. 67.
[41] Taruskin 1982, pp. 48, 52.
[42] https://www.mariinsky.ru/en/playbill/playbill/2016/3/31/7_1901 (accessed October 22, 2020).
[43] https://imslp.org/wiki/Judith_(Serov%2C_Aleksandr) (accessed October 22, 2020).

a miracle will take place, the enemy will perish and glory will be restored to them; but they must continue to pray.

A chorus of the people now sings of their suffering and anguish, pleading with Ozias to open the gates. He persuades them to wait five more days. This is all based on the original story. The chorus, in increasingly urgent music, opens with male voices and quickly builds to *fortissimo* when the women enter. There are constant changes in mood in both the orchestra and chorus, evoking panic and dismay. At the end, now a *fugato* with the voices following one another, they sing: "Let the bloodstained sword of Holofernes put an end to all our woes," and plead again to surrender to the enemy. Ozias begs them to be patient and hope in God. When he again pleads for five more days, they respond: "Five days of suffering!" and he promises that after the five days, they will surrender the town to Holofernes.

Suddenly, very fast loud passages are heard in the orchestra as the people ask: "What is that? Is it an alert?" and wonder if they are going to battle. The gate is opened and Hebrew warriors carry in Achior, announcing that he was found "bound and half dead" and that he demanded to see the Elders. He recounts what happened to him (based on Jdt 6), opening in simple and sparsely accompanied music, almost a recitative. The music changes several times during his account. It sounds almost hymnlike in spots, then increasingly confident and almost triumphant, as he reaches a high A (*a'*; p. 63). In the final section, he sings sustained notes over continual 8th-note passages in the orchestra, which eventually become *tremolos* to create a very excited atmosphere. The final measures are very sustained, with each sung half note supported by a chord. On his final note, the key abruptly modulates from B minor to B major, like a burst of sunlight through clouds. The new section is marked *molto cantabile ed espressivo* (smooth and expressive). The Elders and the chorus together sing a lengthy prayer to God, which sounds very hymnlike, particularly the *a cappella* sections. This is followed by an aria for Achior singing an aria, before a soft chorus concludes Act I. In general, Serov tried to give a "religious" sound to the Hebrews' music and did so with "saccharinely 'Protestant' and 'Mendelssohnian'" music, in Taruskin's view.[44]

Act II opens with Judith's monologue (p. 78), where she is seen "alone, in deep thought" (score note). The text is based largely on Giacometti's play (see Chapter 3) rather than on her lengthy prayer in the original story. The opening phrases in the orchestra include a lyrical oboe solo, with an almost *bel canto* sound. Then the music becomes more passionate and agitated, building suspense before Judith's entrance. The tempo slows for her opening recitative. As in Giacometti's play, she bemoans the Hebrew men who "do nothing but weep, like women." Wistfully, in lamenting music, she remembers Manasseh as the only "real man" among them and wishes he were still with her. In the original story, Judith does not talk about Manasseh, which makes her more independent than she is in most retellings. Here she says she is sure he would have led his people into battle, and therefore it remains to her to accomplish what would have been his exploit. She next sings passionately, in triumphant music, about taking his place. When she repeats this line a second time, she reaches *g#"* on "I" (*Ya*), exuding strength and confidence. Judith's recalling Manasseh brings to mind a slightly

[44] Taruskin 1982, p. 74 (n. 99).

later opera (1901), by American George Whitefield Chadwick (see Chapter 5). In that opera, Judith has a vision in which Manasseh gives her instructions, suggesting that she could not have accomplished her feat without his support. Serov does not suggest this, only that Judith feels compelled to do what Manasseh would have done.

The mood immediately changes again, along with the key, which is now C minor (p. 83). Judith wistfully sings of her quiet childhood in very lyrical, flowing music that reflects this mood: "I grew up in holy silence, and now I must commit a murder." In this retelling, Judith plans the murder from the outset, which is not as clear in the original story. She fears that shame and captivity may await her but has faith in her beauty, which she believes "will be my sword and the salvation of Israel." Her plan is to "blind Holofernes with my beauty … and beguile him with my words." In the original story, she prays to God for deceitful lips, but here she expresses more confidence in herself. She acknowledges that a "voice from on high" has called her and that she knows that God will bless her, and the wings of angels will keep her "safe and pure."

The constantly shifting tempos and keys in the music convincingly delineate Judith's changing moods. She expresses her doubts in softer music, but after a long rest (pause in the music), the entire tone changes as she proclaims, in very energetic music, that her beauty was not given to her in vain. The tempo broadens from 2/4 to 4/4 and she sings over steady repeated 16th-notes groups. In the next section, when Judith announces her intention to go to the enemy, the key modulates from C minor to D-flat major and the unusual time marking of 9/16—two groups of repeated 16th-note chords followed by a final beat that is sung. This has a distinctly martial and triumphant sound, even when the repeated chords become arpeggios and the key shifts into A major. This tonal instability reflects Judith's excitement and uncertainty, as she wavers between fear and determination. When she sings of the brightness of the sun, she reaches her highest note, high A (*a"*) on "sun." As she continues to plot, her self-confidence grows, and the music again reflects that. The key shifts once more back to D-flat major and this time, the orchestra plays the groups of 16th-note chords along with arpeggios beneath them. Her increased determination is clearly heard as the range becomes higher and higher, up to a high B flat (*b-flat"*) when she refers to her songs lulling Holofernes to sleep.

After this climactic moment, the tempo changes to a steady 4/4 beat with *tremolos* in the orchestra over ascending figures in the bass. As the key changes to C major, Judith sings of saving her people, on steadily rising pitches. After the climactic note, the harp begins playing steady rippling arpeggios as Judith sings softly of the "voice on high." Harps are often a musical trope for Heaven. When she sings of returning victorious, the arpeggios are replaced by *tremolos* over strong bass notes. She sings twice that God will save her, the second time almost an octave higher than the first. She repeats both that phrase and "the wings of angels will cover me" several times, accompanied again by harp, first plucked, then strumming, as her voice reaches higher and higher. The climactic high note is a high C (*c"'*, marked "optional"). The orchestra repeats an earlier soaring melody before dying down to nothing, but clearly in C major. The bright key is a musical signal of hope.

The next scene is between Judith and her servant (Avra here; a mezzo, suggesting age). It opens very softly (p. 94), as in a sparsely accompanied recitative; Avra tells Judith they have only a few drops of water left. Judith responds that all is the will of God. Avra tells Judith how much she is loved, recalling that Judith has provided food for her people thanks to her "flocks and fields." This is an interesting addition, not mentioned in the original story or most retellings. In fact, in the original story, Judith lives off the cattle and land that Manasseh left to her (Jdt 8:7) with no mention of helping others. Avra asks Judith (addressing her as "my child," a suggestion of her young age and their age gap) why she wants to talk to the Elders, and Judith says it is about their people's salvation. Avra doesn't understand; after all, she says, "Who could save us if it is God who is punishing us?" As she sings that line, the key suddenly switches to G major, from A-flat major. Such sudden modulations are always a musical signal of a changed mood. Avra tells Judith that the people have lost their faith, and only Judith still believes. Then she asks how she could save the people, since she is not Deborah or Jael. The mention of these two women is found in other retellings but not in the original story. Judith asks Avra to sing the story of Jael to her, which she does. References to Deborah were also made in Giacometti's play, while both Deborah and Jael are mentioned and even sung about in Marcello's libretto (see above).

The song she sings about Jael's triumph (p. 98) is almost like a folk song with military overtones, strongly rhythmic and upbeat, in a bright E major. This fits with Judith's comment that "the people sing her song," as this sounds like a sing-along. It is strophic, with each verse sung to the same rollicking tune. Judith joins Avra in the conclusion: "God fights for his people," which they repeat twice. Avra will later compare Judith favorably to Jael, in the conclusion of the opera.

In the next scene, the Elders join Judith and Avra. Judith's speech to them is a summary of the much longer one in the original story (Jdt 8:27) but with more stress on God as inspiration and savior. The scene is initially a sparsely accompanied recitative. But when Judith speaks of the suffering their forefathers have endured, her line becomes lyrical, sometimes echoed or doubled in the orchestra. In a more solemn section, she tells them that all life comes from the "King of Kings." These measures are sung slowly on long held notes over sustained chords. The final chord under "Kings" is in a bright C major. This is followed by a very lyrical section, with a flowing accompaniment and plangent clarinet doubling the voice. Here Judith encourages the Elders to feel gratitude to the Eternal. Ozias responds: "Judith, the Creator has given you the wisdom of a man." Nothing resembling this misogynist sentiment, masked as praise, is ever uttered in the original story or in any other libretto. Charmis and Ozias sing a brief duet, most of it in unison to portray their unity of thought. They admit that their vow was a sin before God, but the people can no longer bear the thirst. They beg Judith to pray to God for rain. In a simple recitative, she tells them God will indeed send salvation through a miracle and then asks their permission to go to the enemy camp that night, but tells them to keep her plan secret. The music for that text is marked "mysterious," with continual *tremolos* in unstable harmonies (p. 113).

Avra is shocked to hear Judith's plan. Judith does not reveal her destination in the original story. There, she tells the Elders not to ask about her plan (Jdt 8:34), though when she leaves, she tells them she will carry out the things that they talked about. That line has been interpreted as irony or sarcasm on Judith's part, since they never had such a discussion. In the opera, she reveals where she is going, making her plan pretty obvious. But talk from all the characters about God's protection and praying to God dominates the conversation. Ozias and Charmis bless her, in solemn and hymnlike music. Their casting as low voices evokes the sound of Russian Orthodox church music. The scene ends on a C major chord, musically a flash of optimism.

The next scene (p. 116) opens with fast, agitated phrases in the violas, suggesting Avra's feelings. Alone with Judith now, Avra begs her to explain her plan. She is shocked that they are going into "that godless and debauched camp" where, she warns, Judith's beauty will be her downfall. She sings mostly *a cappella* with agitated phrases punctuating her words between measures. On the final phrases, her voice is doubled in the orchestra, an amplifying effect to underline their significance. "Your beauty will be your downfall" is repeated several times, on lower and lower pitches, down to *b flat* (below middle C), a sound of foreboding. A sudden key change (p. 118) from A-flat major to E major introduces Judith's response. She angrily says "No!" and affirms that it is God's will, that he is guiding her and she hears his voice. She sings these assertions strongly, with sustained chords under her voice. But when she avers that God will send his angels to her, her voice rises over a murmuring accompaniment, up to a long sustained *b-flat"* on "help."

This lengthy duet continues, now marked "agitated," reflected in the repeated murmuring 8th-note groups in the bass. Avra repeats her earlier phrases several times, and Judith responds forcefully, telling her: "Away with these fears!" which initially does not calm Avra down. Their battle of wills is mirrored in the orchestra, where the repeated 8th-note groups grow louder and louder, suddenly changing key, from E major to D-flat major. Though the tempo is still *agitato*, there is now a more pleading tone in both their voices. Avra repeats her previous plea. Judith replies again: "Away with these fears," in a high range, reflecting her passion (p. 120). Under Judith's voice, Avra continues to repeat her alarm. Then the time signature and key change, back into D-flat major. These two keys—E major and D-flat major—fluctuate continually through the duet. The tonal instability adds a sense of anxiety and uncertainty. The unusual new time signature is 9/16, which sounds like a very broad 3/4 time, with the tempo now *Andante* (p. 122). In strong, assertive phrases, over a throbbing accompaniment, Judith explains that she will cover herself in a veil and enter the enemy camp adorned; she will have "the purple brilliance of the twilight and golden beams of the dawn" and she will blind Holofernes with her beauty. These predictions express great self-confidence. Her vocal line soars higher and higher as she sings this text. Avra repeats "What is she saying?" softly, almost as if under her breath.

Avra continues to murmur under Judith's line that Judith seems to have forgotten "all restraint and shame," as Judith's music soars higher and higher. The accompaniment shifts from strumming to loud hammering chords, after which Judith reaches her highest pitch, *b-flat"*. By this point, Avra is still repeating the same text, but an octave higher (p. 125). Then their voices descend and only a single measure of a *pianissimo* murmur is heard. Then the tempo shifts into 4/4 cut time—very fast—and the new key of A-flat major. A few measures marked *Agitato assai* (rather agitated) of repetitive violin phrases on descending pitches lead into the next section, marked *Cantabile, molto espressivo* (songlike and very expressive). In a lyrical and melancholy melody, Avra reminisces about her long relationship with Judith, recalling that she suckled Judith at her breast and Judith "bloomed like a lily of paradise." The idea that Judith's servant/slave was originally her nursemaid (though not necessarily her wet nurse) puts a new twist on the relationship and appears only in this opera. In early Italian librettos, they often address each other as "mother" and "daughter," implying a similar idea. She is also called "nurse" in some settings. Avra reminds Judith that she has shed many tears for her and begs her to take pity.

The accompaniment changes from long arpeggiated phrases to hammering ones in the bass, with high sustained chords above. Judith sings "God is with me!" and then orders Avra to prepare her wedding garments. Avra tries to block her, and in the plangent melody of her earlier plea, begs Judith, on her knees, not to go, because dishonor awaits her there. Over her pleading, Judith repeats "Go!" several times, then "Away with your fears!" She tells Avra she will accomplish her duties because God is guiding her. Her final repetition of this phrase takes her to a sustained *b-flat"* over Avra's *g-flat"* (p. 134). Then the music dies down to *pianissimo* as Avra pleads one final time, on lower pitches that suggest resignation. Her final "Judith!" is sung below Judith's "Go!" as the orchestra continues to murmur and die out.

Act III opens in the Assyrian camp, introduced by an Entr'acte called "The March of Holofernes," an orchestral march. Extensive choruses of "Odalisques" (female slaves or concubines) and dancers are introduced by a sinuous melody heard on cor anglais (English horn) and harp. Occasional bells and tambourines add to the "oriental" quality. To the same melody, the slaves sing of their attachment to Babylon and the languid nights of the Orient. Some of the slaves step forward to sing solo lines. Then they seductively sing: "Come, my beloved, I am lonely. The banquet is prepared for you beneath the golden tent." This chorus is interrupted twice by very fast dances, after which the slaves resume their song. The contrasting moods and tempos of the chorus and dances offer a context for the Judith-Holofernes encounter.

In a sudden shift of mood, Holofernes enters with Bagoas, master of his harem, and Asfaneses, his retainer (an invented character; p. 161). He abruptly dismisses the dancers and singers of the harem. Then he expresses his fury and frustration at waiting thirty days to attack Bethulia, "this pitiful brood." Trumpet calls are heard in the orchestra as Holofernes proclaims, in martial-sounding music, that "the trumpets of victory resound in every corner of the world like the thunder of heaven, celebrating our fame." In less martial music, Holofernes claims that "potentates and gods are prostrate at my feet," yet they are reduced to "contemplating a miserable hovel." In increasingly dramatic music, with loud *tremolo* in the orchestra, he says his patience is at its end and he has decided to attack the next day. He predicts that "the remembrance of the Hebrews will be erased from the face of the earth." Holofernes's music is strong and very *marcato*, projecting strength as well as anger. This impression is reinforced by his wide vocal range. Asfaneses confirms that the troops are restless and it is time to go into battle. He advises Holofernes to address the troops now, and Holofernes orders the trumpets be sounded. They sound, both in the tent (onstage) and then from the orchestra (score note). During the orchestral march that follows, Holofernes orders horses to be brought. The march becomes increasingly dramatic and loud until finally dying down to nothing (this short scene is not on the CD).

Suddenly, a crowd approaches noisily (p. 174). Bagoas sees a group of chieftains rushing toward them and asks what is happening. A chorus of Assyrians responds, in very fast and excited music, that "a Hebrew of a beauty never before seen has arrived among us." They continue, saying she is heading for Holofernes's tent and wants to be presented to him. They proclaim her beauty: "What a bosom! What eyes!" Solo voices from the chorus sing intermittently, which humanizes the group. Their final phrase, "She exudes passion, she has bewitched us all!" is marked *dolcissimo* (very sweet). The lengthy chorus is now in five parts, with voices following each other in a sort of *fugato*, expressing the group's utter amazement. To very agitated music, Bagoas comments that Holofernes is approaching, having heard the commotion. The chorus enters again, singing that no one can take their eyes off Judith, who "shines like a star of the East."

Judith enters and falls to her knees. Holofernes, smitten by her beauty (score note), tells her gently to rise and not to be afraid, and asks why she has come (p.192). This adheres closely to the original story (Jdt 11). The sweet, almost seductive tone of Holofernes's voice in this scene contrasts sharply with all his earlier music, which was brusque. Both voices, Judith's and Holofernes's, change tone in different scenes to highlight what they are trying to project about themselves. This can also be done with fine acting, but music adds a powerful subtext. There is a sudden transition from A major to A minor when Judith answers. Such musical transitions always signal a change—in this case, an ominous one. Judith, "quiet and dutiful, initially timid" (score note), tells Holofernes that if he puts his trust in her words, his way "will be crowned with glory." Her music is simple, in a sustained and calm 4/4 time signature. Her tone is more muted than it has been in previous scenes, highlighting the impression of innocence she is trying to project. Text alone, no matter how well it is recited, can never have the impact that music does in moments like this.

Bagoas and the chorus, in much faster and more excited music, again comment on Judith's surpassing beauty and her wisdom that "is not inferior to her beauty." Judith continues, in measured and calm music, to relate that everything Achior said to Holofernes was true. Since her people have denied God, she says, the road to Jerusalem is open to him, as revealed to her by God. On this final phrase, her music becomes more excited, filled with *tremolos*. She sings some measures completely *a cappella*, a musical signifier of strength and confidence, as she is standing "alone," without the backing of the orchestra (p. 201). Avra murmurs to herself in horror: "What do I hear? Almighty God!" Judith continues in the new key of A major, telling Holofernes to trust her message, and soon he will "raise the standard of Babylon over Zion." (The kingdom of Babylon followed the fall of Assyria; the two are sometimes conflated in librettos, which do not aim for historical accuracy.) The tone of Judith's music has changed: the orchestra is no longer calm and steady; she sings higher pitches and even two long descending runs.

Holofernes responds that he is happy about their meeting (p. 203). He does not know if her God really sent Judith, or if she came on her own. But he confesses that he would never have imagined finding a beauty like hers "among these arid mountains." Shyly, Judith responds in lilting, melodic music in C major and a pastoral 6/8 time, with an oboe, a common "pastoral" sound, playing a solo above her voice. She tells him that their mountains are barren, with only rock and sand, and adds: "the women stay at home at their spinning wheels and only assemble when they go to the well." There is an echo here of a line in the Giacometti play, where Judith tells the Elders that for women, "the spindle, the shuttle, and the needle" (from a Grimms' Fairy Tale of that name) are the permitted weapons (see Chapter 3). Here in the libretto, she is using the phrase in a different way, but there may be a subtext in which she is suggesting that women have no power, in order to reassure Holofernes that she is no threat. If this was her intent, Judith is clever and manipulative; but the line is ambivalent. She adds "ingratiatingly" that she would never have dared approach Holofernes if a heavenly voice had not commanded her to. Her voice rises to much higher pitches on this last phrase, after which it dies down.

The chorus enters to faster and louder music, now in A major. They sing praises of Judith, of her passion and tenderness, and especially her wisdom, which dazzles them. The key suddenly shifts again and Holofernes says to himself, over low-pitched *tremolos*, that he has never seen such beauty and that passion is burning in his blood like a fire. This opens an amazing ensemble (p. 208), with Holofernes joined by Judith, then Avra, Asfaneses, and Bagoas. Each is expressing his or her own thoughts, in individual musical lines. Yet they all come together in such a way that the listener can hear them all at once. This is one of the particularly powerful ways in which music transmits words. Judith sings to herself triumphantly that Holofernes has been captivated by her beauty and has believed all her lies, that he is "bewitched as if by a spell." She repeats these words, woven into the words and music of the others, occasionally in high soaring lines. As in all opera, a suspension of disbelief is necessary to imagine that no one else on stage can hear the soprano's soaring lines, supposedly sung "to herself."

Holofernes, in the ensemble, repeats his earlier lines about Judith but now adds: "she is mine, her love is mine." Asfaneses echoes Holofernes's sentiments about Judith but then renounces his desire, since he thinks Judith's love is directed toward Holofernes. Both Asfaneses and Holofernes are played by basses, and the two low voices are very effective against the higher voices of Judith and Avra. The orchestra doubles Judith's soaring lines, underlining her importance. Avra's is the last voice to enter. Horrified, she sings in broken phrases that "it was no dream, no mad raving; those were Judith's words." While she sings that text, Judith stops singing, making Avra's the highest voice, now doubled in the orchestra (p. 209). When she laments: "Oh my unhappy people! Is it really your blood that flows in her veins?" Judith's voice has returned, again doubled by the orchestra. She sings in soaring phrases of how Holofernes believed in her lies with all his soul. The quartet concludes, after one measure's rest, on an A-major chord, suggesting a kind of resolution—at least musically.

Holofernes now speaks directly to Judith, telling her to remain with them. If she keeps her word, he says, he will raise her above all the queens in the universe. She tells him, in solemn and deliberate musical phrases, that she is pious and asks permission to go out with her servant Avra at sunset to say their prayers. She is waiting for God's commands. This is one of the very few works that includes this part of the original story. Holofernes orders Bagoas to let them come and go freely. He tells Judith she shall be their queen and all shall obey her orders. Then in a puzzling phrase, he says to Asfaneses with a smile: "The Hebrew God must know the strength of our sword!" And he concludes *a cappella*: "Into our power he delivers the fate of his people." Perhaps he is implying that God knew Judith would be safe with him, but the phrases are ambivalent. Asfaneses proudly replies that there is no other power in the world but theirs, so no one could oppose it. A military chorus concludes the act, singing of how they dictate their laws to the whole world: "There is no power on earth equal to ours." Near the end, the female slaves join the soldiers' chorus.

Act IV opens with a prelude, Bacchanalian dances, festive choruses, and the "Orgy of Holofernes." The music in this scene strongly influenced composer Alexander Borodin (1833–1887), whose last opera *Prince Igor* was written almost thirty years later but whose well-known music for the "Polovetsian Dances" powerfully echoes the music in this scene of Serov's *Judith*. The chorus sings: "Fill the cups with wine. Women, sing and dance, you alone adorn life. The rest is only empty words." After several dances and choruses, Holofernes tells Bagoas to sing, since he knows so many songs. Obsequiously (score note), Bagoas offers to sing a Hindu song. There was a fascination with India in this period (1860s) as well as "orientalism" in music, both of which are reflected in this lovely tenor aria that is filled with modal harmonies.[45] Holofernes brusquely comments that such songs about women are suitable for the harems of Babylon, but he would rather hear a battle song. Then he proceeds to sing one. To a heavy martial beat, Holofernes sings about marching forward with his soldiers, their horses and camels perishing, and only the brave advancing. The melody is harsh and repetitive. As Holofernes re-creates this battle scene, the music builds slowly. Holofernes continues: "After the long marching, behold, upon the azure steppes a golden town appears. An army advances … Friends, cut it to pieces, do not weaken." Trumpet calls are heard, after which for the first time, the quarter notes in the steady bass theme are replaced by eighth notes, building to *fortissimo* and finally becoming high *tremolos*.

The key suddenly shifts from F major to D major (p. 266). Steady quarter-note phrases resume but now under very high *tremolos*. In this section, Holofernes sings about all the women they find in the town, whose streets are "paved with gold." He instructs the soldiers to "massacre them all, throw everything under the horses' hooves" and then they can crown themselves king. This aria portrays a very ruthless Holofernes. On the final repeat of his commands, the marching theme in the orchestra finally dissolves into all *tremolos* as both tempo and volume increase. He repeats the last phrase several times, and the chorus repeats it again after him. After the very triumphant conclusion, Holofernes, laughing, declares that "that is our kind of song!" and the chorus sings "Hurrah! Glory to Holofernes!"

Suddenly remembering Judith, Holofernes asks where "the most magnificent pearl of my feast, my fair Jewess" is. Bagoas says obsequiously that Judith herself said there would be no greater honor for her than to join him. Holofernes asks Asfaneses if he appreciates Judith's beauty. As he poses this question, the key suddenly switches to D minor (from A major) and a sinuous theme is heard (p. 270). The slightly foreboding music may suggest that Holofernes is laying a trap for his slave. As the key returns to A major, Holofernes adds that it would bring shame to him if he didn't succeed in "winning" a woman like that. Asfaneses candidly responds, *a cappella*, that she is "as fair as a star of the East, but cold and distant as the rocks of

---

[45] This was the most successful number in the opera and clearly the model for Rimsky-Korsakov's greatest hit, "The Song of India," from his opera *Sadko*. Taruskin, p. 100.

her country." Holofernes answers "darkly": "Ah! Cold? You have put it to the test?" implying that Asfaneses has tried to seduce Judith. Holofernes's words are softly menacing and unaccompanied, with long rests between phrases, all of which builds suspense. Then, calling Asfaneses "miserable dog," he stabs him. As he does so, a loud and dissonant *tremolo* is played, E minor together with C major, musically describing this harrowing and unexpected moment. This plot turn is taken straight from Friedrich Hebbel's play (see Chapter 3), where it was a captain that Holofernes stabbed, because he called Judith "coy" rather than "cold." This incident portrays Holofernes in a darker light than most librettists did. (The scene is also found in Emil von Reznicek's 1923 opera; see Chapter 5).

Judith and Avra enter now, their terror reflected in breathless-sounding music. Bagoas signals all the slaves to leave. Holofernes, speaking gently (score note), tells Judith that the blood was spilled in her honor and adds that she should not be afraid, because it was only the blood of a slave. Judith approaches Holofernes cautiously and explains in a soft, sweet voice, that her fright is involuntary, because she is a woman. Avra, horrified, says to herself in a breathless recitative: "Why are we here, among these dogs? Debauchery, blood, a shameful orgy, a mortal sin!" and she begs God to protect them. Holofernes barks out the order to take the body away and spread out new carpets, as in the Hebbel play. Then his tone changes abruptly to a sweeter one as he asks Judith to rejoice with him and partake of the feast. He assures her she "will be honored more than anyone else, more than a queen." Judith says: "This reign will not last long!" which would be sarcastic if said in an aside. But here she says it aloud, and Holofernes immediately responds that her reign will be eternal. In a simple recitative with sparse accompanying chords, he relates that the "magi" he once consulted had predicted his destiny would be linked with that of a woman, and now he is convinced she is that woman. In a certain sense, of course, he is right—he just hasn't figured out what that destiny is going to be. He tells Judith to prepare for a new life.

A key change (from D to G major) signals a change of mood as Holofernes tells Judith of all his plans. This is still a recitative, and he sings mostly unaccompanied, projecting power as he stands alone without the orchestra supporting him. Holofernes tells Judith that when he returns to Babylon with her, he will possess the crown of king of the world. But rather than lay it before the throne of the King of Assyria, he will have himself crowned and she will be his queen. This last phrase is sung very strongly, in Holofernes's "warrior" voice, but the final line is sung "sweetly" (marked *Dolce*). These changes in his voice reflect subtleties that only music can. There is a sudden, dramatic shift in the music now: it is marked *Agitatissimo* (very agitated; an unusual marking) and suddenly changes from G major to E-flat major, filled with *tremolos*. Judith says to herself, anxiously: "Satan, do not try to blind me or trouble my senses!" In the original story, Judith does not express fear of being "blinded" or infatuated, but it is an interesting and not unrealistic idea that also appears in other librettos. She repeats "predictions of the prophet coming true before me," quoting Isa 14:13: "For you said to yourself, 'I will ascend to heaven and set my throne above God's stars.'" In Isaiah, this verse is preceded by one in which Isaiah describes the fall of a king with those aspirations:

How you are fallen from heaven, O shining star, son of the morning! You have been thrown down to the earth, you who destroyed the nations of the world. (Isa 14:12)

These verses are believed to refer to the death of an Assyrian monarch of Isaiah's time. But they fit remarkably well with Holofernes's previous speech and it is interesting that one of Serov's librettists knew his Bible well enough to insert this quote here, coming from Judith's mouth. Other operas (Silveri, for one; see above) suggest that the Priest quotes Isaiah, but the actual quote does not appear. The accompaniment is *tremolos* throughout this section, and as Judith's voice gets stronger, the orchestra doubles her notes for emphasis.

Holofernes, who obviously heard nothing of Judith's monologue, tries to embrace her. She avoids his touch, but he is not dissuaded. In slow, majestic music (marked *Lento e maestoso*), with the tempo broadening from 3/4 to 4/4, he sings in soaring lines that they will share everything, with the starry sky above them and "beneath our feet, in the dust, all the people!" (p. 278). He sings of "a single throne, a single sovereign on earth … king, priest and god of everyone." Judith suddenly gets up, and at the sound of a crashing *fff* chord over very loud repeated arpeggios and *tremolo*, she sings in a high range: "God of Israel! Do not delay your righteous wrath! Let your thunderbolt strike down this pride!" The key changes from E-flat major to G major for this tirade, which is not marked as sung "to herself." But clearly Holofernes does not hear her, based on his next line, which is sung triumphantly: "Wine! A single throne, a single sovereign on earth!" The key has changed again for this line and the next section, to E major.

Bagoas and the chorus sing softly that when Holofernes speaks like that, "heaven and earth listen in terror." Judith and Avra, on the other hand, listen in anger and comment that Holofernes "is inhabited by the spirit of Satan" and that his words disgust them. Judith prays: "O Heaven, when will you send him his chastisement?" The two women sing these lines softly, first following each other and then together. Bagoas joins the chorus as they sing that as slaves, they await their fate in terror. Holofernes continues to repeat the same line "A single throne …" over and over. A large ensemble develops, with Judith's voice soaring over all the others, as Holofernes's full retinue joins in. All the parts are marked *piano* (soft) throughout, though Judith's repeated *a-flat*" notes would be a challenge to sing softly. Only Holofernes's part is marked *fortissimo*, which if successfully done would certainly be a musical marker of his power.

This ensemble ends on an unresolved seventh chord, leading right into the Finale. The plot follows that of the Giacometti play very closely (see Chapter 3). In very fast, excited music (marked *Allegro con fuoco*), Holofernes sings: "Where are you, Jewess?"[46] In excited and upbeat music, Holofernes tells Judith she should be happy and will always celebrate with him. She responds that she did not come to serve his pleasures but to show him the way to Zion, to punish her people. Her music is a little slower and more measured, showing her control. But it quickly gains in intensity as she sings the final measures on high pitches and over *tremolos*. In slower, more ominous

---

[46] He has addressed her as Jewess several times in the opera, whereas in the original story, she is called a Hebrew but never addressed as one. There is no real equivalent in modern languages for a Hebrew, and librettists generally use the term "Jew" or "Jewess," which was known in their time.

music, and a key change to D major, Holofernes tells Judith that he can find his way himself, and, trying to embrace her (score note), passionately declares: "You are mine, mine!" He also asks: "Where could you go from here?" Several measures of passionate music in the orchestra serve to describe Judith's turmoil, as she cries out: "O God of Israel!" Holofernes tells her to forget God and acknowledge no one but him. As the key suddenly shifts to C major, Judith responds rapturously that Jehovah is great, the king of heaven and earth. On the word "Jehovah," she reaches and sustains a high C (*c"*), a significant marker of exaltation. The phrase ends two octaves lower, on middle C.

Holofernes angrily asks Judith why she is there, though in an earlier scene she had promised to help him. "You do not want to?" he says, implying to have sex. "No? Then go back to your own people where I will find you tomorrow morning!" With horror, Judith repeats the last phrase, singing *pianissimo*: "Tomorrow morning?" realizing he is referring to a planned attack she did not know about. Triumphantly, Holofernes confirms that the trumpets will sound the next day, as trumpet calls are heard in the orchestra. In very martial and strong music, he sings:

> My sword is thirsty for blood! We will not leave one stone upon another in your town. The Jews, women, the old, will be massacred … your children will be shattered against the walls, and on your hideous corpses we will have a feast such as has never been seen before, with blood up to the elbows!

This text is inspired by Hebbel's play, where he wrote: "Children will be torn from the wombs of their mothers and hurled into the air as stones." Serov's additions have made the description even more horrible. Many aspects of this libretto seem designed to paint a portrait of Holofernes as barbaric. The music for this section amplifies the graphic horror of his words.

Judith is so horrified she can only cry out "O God of Israel!" to which Holofernes immediately responds in a snarling voice: "We'll see what he will say!" Judith pulls back and tells Holofernes she will remain with him to fulfill her vow "and then …." It is unclear what vow she is referring to, or when she made one. He pushes her to finish her thought, and shyly (score note), she says she will submit to him entirely. The time signature now changes to 3/4 and the key moves from C major to A-flat major. The music is marked *allegro appassionato* as Holofernes ecstatically sings Judith's praises in his sweetest voice: "O my dove! You are sweeter than myrrh, sweeter than wine" (a nod to Song of Songs). He says he would give all the gold of his conquests and all the glory of his battles for her beauty (p. 292). As he continues to woo her, Judith sings to herself but together with Holofernes: "God will help me!" Continuous rolling groups of 16th-notes in the orchestra create momentum and excitement. They continue singing their own thoughts without hearing each other. Only in music can two soliloquies occur simultaneously. While Holofernes declares that he would give everything for her beauty, Judith sings: "I must perform a terrible deed this very night." Holofernes tries to pull Judith into his arms, but she avoids him, and he collapses on his couch.

The steady accompaniment stops for a few measures, while Holofernes sings, in an unaccompanied recitative: "he is resisting again! Like a serpent, she has escaped from me." Italian librettist Marcello also used snake imagery, but through Judith's words and with a different sense entirely: she is the snake entrapping Holofernes (see above, the Peri and Silveri operas). Holofernes sings "But no!" as the accompaniment returns, and then it stops again (p. 296). After this, the accompaniment changes every few measures, creating a sense of instability and unpredictability. He sings: "Let your God come in person to tear you from my arms! Come here, Judith! Jewess!" The music brilliantly paints the picture of a drunk, deranged man. Modest Mussorgsky's opera *Boris Godunov* (1868–73) sounds strongly influenced by Serov's opera. The music of Godunov's death scene in particular certainly reflects that influence. Holofernes raves that his slaves are hiding Judith from him and threatens to destroy them all, calling them dogs and worms, while swinging his sword around. The slaves all shrink back (score note). The music is almost shrieking during this episode. Then Holofernes spots Judith and calms down. In a delirium (score note), he tells Judith not to trust his slaves, who are all traitors corrupted by the king of Babylon who fears Holofernes. Then he remembers that he himself is the king of Babylon, "and there is no other king in the whole world." Continuing his rant, he says he will show the "sacrilegious usurper" in Babylon who the real king is. He sings "Sound, trumpets, into battle!" as trumpet calls are heard (p. 300). Then he looks around for enemies and sees nothing, so he calls out for light. Then he begs Judith not to leave him, or "they will kill you." Saying he feels heavy, he falls unconscious at Judith's feet.

Still following the Giacometti play, Judith, shuddering, asks Bagoas if Holofernes is dying, and he quietly reassures her that this always happens when he gets drunk, but sleep will restore him and "tomorrow he will wake up happy and strong." As he sings these words, tinged with irony, a very low note is held in the orchestra for several measures, a subtext with a sense of foreboding. Judith agrees that he needs a "deep and restorative sleep" and adds: "Above all, do not awaken him." Bagoas says "slyly" (score note) that he assumes Judith will remain with Holofernes, the slaves will all leave and he will lock the doors (it is unclear what kind of locking doors a tent would have had). But she requests the one door remain open, since she and Avra have permission to use that one. Bagoas agrees, since Judith is the queen. They say their goodbyes—his with a wink. After he has left, Judith she says to herself: "When daybreak comes, you will no longer want to make fun of the Jewess!" (p. 303). Following the Giacometti text very closely, in a quiet and hesitant recitative over low sustained chords, Judith sings that the terrible night has come and her heart is trembling. She wonders if her hand can really raise itself to kill a man, a hero. In a simple, lyrical melody (p. 304), she sings: "I grew up in holy silence and now I shall commit a murder." The line builds quickly from soft to loud. Avra interrupts her thoughts, saying: "My child, come to your senses." She expresses her fear that such a crime will "unleash God's vengeance" on them. Judith responds over Avra's lines, which run together. She says she knows the risks, but her decision is firm and God's vengeance will fall upon the sinner. This dialogue is accompanied only by continuous *tremolo*.

Judith now sings her prayer (p. 306), asking God to give her strength, sustain her hand, and "forgive the involuntary terror" in her heart. Then in much more assertive music, she sings: "No, Avra! I will remain alone with Holofernes." She orders Avra to leave the tent and pray. The key changes from E-flat major to E major and from 4/4 to 3/4 time, all suggesting a change of mood. Judith glances at Holofernes to see if he is sleeping deeply; then, kneeling, she sings on steadily rising pitches: "God of my fathers, God of strength, God of victories! Save your children and cast down the wicked!" On this phrase, she reaches a high B flat (*b-flat*"). Then in a final burst of energy, she sings: "God, give me strength!" The first word is sung on *a*" as rapid descending 16th-note runs begin, accentuating her own descent. Then a very rapid ascending scale is heard in the orchestra, reaching a dissonant chord of F# minor in the bass against a D. This is followed by three sharp chords, the first and last *fortissimo* but the middle chord soft, as if Judith is regaining her strength for a second strike. Each chord is followed by a measure of rest, and the last one by a long pause. Clearly this music represents the actual beheading, though there are no notes in the score indicating what she is doing. Instead, the notes state that Judith leaves the tent, pale and exhausted, leaning on the bloodstained sword. In a weak voice she calls to Avra, who enters, sadly. She goes to Holofernes's bed and there sees his head lying at Judith's feet. She cries out: "You are God's chosen one!" and at a sign from Judith, puts the head in Judith's bag. As in the original story, Avra shows no sign of shock or fear. The tempo suddenly increases to *Presto* as the two women sing in harmony: "Let us hurry to our delivered people!" and the act ends.

Act V opens with a "Chorus of the Starving," with Achior, Ozias, the High Priest (here named Eliakim), and the people. The opening orchestral passages set a mood of utter grief and despair. The people, believing God has abandoned them, are turning away from him. They sing the same sighing, wailing phrases just heard in the orchestra. The volume continually swells and diminishes. In strong, assertive phrases, Achior sings of his certainty that a terrible punishment awaits these blasphemers who want to open the gates. Ozias reminds them they promised to wait five days, and he is sure Judith will yet save them, because God speaks through her. The people complain that they have waited in vain and push to open the gates, in increasingly insistent, impassioned music. The High Priest enters (p. 328) and tells them threateningly that God will smite them, but the people no longer believe in this God. The Priest's music contains many octave leaps, both ascending and descending, a voice of great authority. His words finally have an effect, and the chorus joins him in soaring music, affirming that "the people will rise again thanks to their fervent prayers and their faith." At that very moment, they hear Judith calling from outside the gates, proclaiming victory. Trumpets are heard from the city walls. The very excited chorus is accompanied by constant loud *tremolos*. When the people realize it is Judith, they run toward her carrying lamps and sing: "She returns to us victorious, and God guides her." This six-part chorus (three female, three male) creates a very triumphant sound. It ends inconclusively on a D7 chord, leading directly into Judith's solo, resolving into G major (p. 342).

She announces: "Here is the head of Holofernes," presumably displaying it. Her music has a proclamatory sound, with several descending octave leaps. She continues, with irony: "Here is that mighty warrior, the master of the universe, the terror of Israel!" Achior is the first to express amazement at what he is seeing, and he proclaims the greatness of the God of Israel. The people follow, exclaiming that their God has heard the prayers and tears of his children. Judith tells them to put the head on a spear and place it on the ramparts for the enemy to see. This is followed by a chorus of warriors singing very militaristic music (p. 345). A long victory chorus ensues, ending in "Glory to God, Glory to Judith, Heaven's chosen one!"

As the key shifts to C major, in phrases marked "solemn," the Priest announces that the one who rose up against God has been vanquished by God (p. 351), giving no credit to Judith. Projecting authority, his voice ranges in a few measures from *c* below middle C, up to *f'*, almost an octave and a half. Achior, bowing before Judith, says that she is the most amazing woman and wonders that she was able to "venture fearlessly and alone into the lion's den." On the words "lion's den," trombones are heard, effective word painting. *Tremolos* begin now, as Achior continues "in terror" (score note): "He was the scourge of all the people on earth, yet here you are, unhurt, with his head." In calm and stately music, Judith tells them that God blessed her. As her voice rises, the orchestra doubles her notes two octaves higher, a heavenly sound, as she sings about angels: "The wings of his angels protected me and left me unscathed." On this last word, her voice rises to a high C (*c''*).

Avra, Achior, and the High Priest join the chorus now, each singing their own text. Avra sings: "Judith, you are more glorious than Jael," while the Priest sings the same phrase but comparing Judith to Deborah. The chorus sings that Judith is a shining example for them and that they have been delivered from their enemies by the hand of a woman. They hear the sounds of the fleeing Assyrian armies—stampeding horses, screaming troops. They sing a rousing chorus, excited that they are hearing the shouts of battle and the earth trembling under the enemy's horses. The music imitates the sound of pounding hooves and also includes trumpet calls (p. 355). Ozias enters and proudly proclaims that he has returned from the battlefield where very few of their men have fallen, but the hordes of their enemies "have vanished in a stormy haze." The final chorus follows. The tempo is faster and more animated, and the key shifts from C major to A-flat major. The soldiers and the people sing, in a double chorus: "Victory!" They proclaim that they have conquered the enemy and owe it to Judith alone. They sing: "Glory to Judith, Heaven's chosen one, to her alone." The crowd loudly rushes up to Judith to kiss the hem of her garment. Continuous 8th-note triplets in the orchestra give a sense of turmoil and excitement.

Suddenly the music grows calmer as Judith silences the crowd and reminds them that only God should be glorified (p. 367). The music is marked *Grave* and high *tremolos* play over Judith's steady line, as she sings: "God has dispersed the might of our enemies like dust." Then the key suddenly changes from A-flat major to E major and the music grows louder, while the high *tremolos* continue. Judith sings: "Sing his praises, he alone has vanquished our enemies." The tempo becomes broader and the tone shifts from proclamatory to prayerful, as Judith repeats the same text in a hymnlike melody with prominent harp accompaniment (p. 368), joined by the chorus. She then sings another prayer, in a slightly faster tempo and a time signature of 6/4, a very broad rhythm. She praises "Jehovah" who is "thrice holy ... the rampart of those who pray." She thanks God for having pity on them and hearing their prayers. The chorus joins her. The orchestra plays continual 8th-note groups, mostly arpeggios but near the end, repeated rising scales, giving great momentum to this chorus. Near the end, Judith also sings ascending and descending scales and then rises by steps up to high B (*b''*), which is sustained for two full measures, soaring over the chorus. A few measures later, she exceeds this feat with a high C# (*c#"*), following a few *coloratura* passages, the only such in the opera. This note is rarely heard outside the *coloratura* repertoire and is highly unexpected from a dramatic soprano. Taruskin attributes its use here to Serov's early fascination with Italian opera and Giacometti's play.[47] The passages suggest a kind of ecstasy (p. 376; the note is barely audible on the recording, drowned out by the large chorus). The opera ends on a triumphant E-major chord heard in the large chorus, with Judith sustaining a G# (*g#"*).

Conclusion

This opera is in a class of itself, as the Russian language and hyper-dramatic style single it out. (Confession of this writer: I am very partial to Russian opera). This opera will satisfy the reader and listener eager to be swamped by melodrama and passion. In addition, the characters are well delineated, not only through their words and music, but also in how they modulate their voices to put across their outward or innermost thoughts. The original story is changed but not to excess. Lengthy choral and dance scenes in Holofernes's grand tent replace the intimate tête-à-tête between Judith and Holofernes in the original story. This is not historically inaccurate, as a general like Holofernes no doubt would have had access to such entertainers. It establishes a sense of place and time, thereby opening up the biblical book. These lengthy "party" scenes, found in most Judith musical settings, establish a striking contrast with the events that follow. The character of Judith's servant is much more developed here, as she is in many musical works discussed in this book. This adds to the drama in terms of both their relationship and the conflicts between the two women, which create greater interest. It is truly a pity this opera has virtually disappeared from the repertoire, as it ranks with some of the finest nineteenth-century Russian operas. But operas on biblical themes have simply fallen out of favor, and Serov's name is hardly known outside Russia. To those interested in a compelling musical retelling of Judith's story, this opera will be very satisfying.

Chapter Conclusion

There are more striking contrasts between the works discussed here than was true in other chapters, due to differences in the political and social climate as well as in opera traditions. One common link between the Italian and Russian operas is the use of parts of Giacometti's play, Marcello's libretto, or Hebbel's play. These were all influential texts that took significant liberties with the original story. But the music of these four operas brings those texts to brilliant, palpitating life. Exposure to these operas will forever change the reader's response to the book of Judith.

---

[47]   Taruskin, p. 75 (n. 105).

5

Twentieth-Century Operas: George Whitefield Chadwick, Emil von Reznicek, Sir Eugene Goossens, Siegfried Matthus

This chapter will include discussion of three early-twentieth-century operas, the first dating to the turn of the century and the other two from the 1920s; as well as a much more recent work dating to 1984. As would be expected, the style of the earliest (Chadwick, 1901) is rooted far more in the nineteenth than the twentieth century. Reznicek's and Goossens's operas recall the operas of Richard Strauss from only a few years earlier. Their music fell into Strauss's orbit of influence much as that of eighteenth-century opera composers' operas fell into Verdi's. The final work, by Siegfried Matthus, is atonal and thus less accessible and less expressive of character and mood than tonal music. The opera has not been favorably received by critics but is included here as an example of how far-reaching the inspiration from the book of Judith has carried even into the modern era. That opera's libretto, like parts of Reznicek's, is based on Friedrich Hebbel's 1840 play (see Chapter 3), which is a distortion of the original biblical story.

George Whitefield Chadwick (1854–1931)

George Whitefield Chadwick was a representative composer of what is known as the Second New England School of American composers of the late nineteenth century, along with Amy Beach, Arthur Foote, and Edward MacDowell. Chadwick was steeped in the traditions of German late Romanticism, as were most of his contemporaries. In 1877 he headed to Germany like many other composers of his generation. He studied in Leipzig at the Royal Conservatory of Music under Carl Reinecke (1824–1910).[1]

Chadwick is most well known for his long tenure as Director of the New England Conservatory of Music from 1897 to 1930. He was also Music Director of the Worcester

---

[1] "The Encyclopedia Americana (1920)/Chadwick, George Whitefield," *Wikisource*. Available online: https://en.wikisource.org/wiki/The_Encyclopedia_Americana_(1920)/Chadwick,_George_Whitefield (accessed October 22, 2020).

Music Festival from 1899 to 1901, and he himself conducted the premiere of his opera *Judith*, a "lyric drama," at this festival on September 26, 1901. This was Chadwick's largest score. The dramatic action as well as some of the orchestral sounds are clearly inspired by Camille Saint-Saëns's opera *Samson and Delilah*, which Chadwick had conducted only a year before writing *Judith*. The choral writing is also influenced by Felix Mendelssohn. In one critic's opinion, "The central scene of seduction and murder is one of the most expertly constructed and tautly lyrical passages in American dramatic music ... [even if] sections emphasizing the chorus ... are more like oratorio scenes." Many parts are clearly inspired by "French sonorities."[2]

The opera's success warranted a second performance a year later, plus one performance in Boston. It was given only one more complete performance in Chadwick's lifetime, in Philadelphia in 1911. The work is a hybrid between oratorio and opera, modeled after the French *drame lyrique* (one example is the 1877 work of Charles Lefebvre; see Chapter 4). It was never performed as an opera, as Chadwick had hoped, but in "tableaus" in concert form. Nonetheless, Chadwick marked the score with explicit stage directions, probably in hopes that someday it would be fully staged. A *New York Times* reviewer stated emphatically:

> Judith should be put on the stage; it would immediately acquire a definite meaning
> ... Judith belongs on the stage and can never be expressed in all its force until the
> music and the text are supported and enhanced by action and spectacle.[3]

There was also a feeling that the story of Judith was not well suited to the oratorio form—too much "sin, seduction and fanaticism."[4] Chadwick wrote his own scenario, which he sent to his librettist William Chauncy Langdon (1871–1947) in 1899. Langdon had previously written a libretto for an 1898 cantata, which brought him to Chadwick's attention. *Judith* was expanded into a reading play twice the length of the libretto. The libretto is in rhymed verse that unfortunately has a stilted, almost hokey sound. The "oriental flavor" in the music was partly achieved by "strange modal harmonies."[5] There is also a *leitmotif* throughout the work, first heard when Judith describes her "vision." The theme comprises triplets, symbolizing Holofernes's death. The text, and some of the music, are firmly grounded in the late nineteenth century, including the abundant use of archaic English (thee and thou). The music succeeds most wherever it surpasses the verses.

In 1977 the Handel Society performed this work at Dartmouth College under the direction of Steven Ledbetter. The archivists at the College kindly provided me with notes related to that performance. The advance publicity highlights the "Near Eastern ambience" showing the influence of Saint-Saëns's opera *Samson and Delilah* (which was also originally written as an oratorio). Apparently Chadwick knew that an opera

[2] Steven Ledbetter and Victor Fell Yellin in *New Grove Dictionary* (2001), vol. 5, p. 420.
[3] Frederick Burton, "The New Opera 'Judith,'" *New York Times*, September 29, 1901.
[4] Steven Ledbetter, program notes, 1977.
[5] Walter Lancaster, program notes for *Judith*, in *The Forty-Fourth Annual Worcester Music Festival, 1858–1901*, pp. 46–7.

by an American composer would never be performed in that period, so he called his work an opera-oratorio.

A very positive review in High Fidelity/Musical America calls the work's "sumptuous orchestral score … its most impressive feature." The reviewer comments on the mix of musical styles, including echoes of Mendelssohn, Giacomo Puccini, and Saint-Saëns, mixed with "Eastern evocations … and anthem-like music." The most effective moments, this critic observes, are when Chadwick "threw off his German-oriented learning and reverted to a simpler style."[6]

Judith (1901)

Text by Langdon after a scenario by Chadwick. Piano-vocal score: Schirmer, 1901.

> Judith: mezzo
> Achior: tenor
> Holofernes: baritone
> Ozias: bass or tenor

There is no role for the servant, unlike most works treated in this book.

The score is not available online but can be found in some libraries. There is no commercial recording; I acquired a private recording of the 1977 performance through Dartmouth College, on which my comments are based.

Act I

In Scene I, a mournful orchestral introduction opens the opera, followed by a Handelian chorus with a short *fugato* in the middle. Ozias sings a lyrical aria, opening with:

> Oh Israel, be not dismayed,
> For God will quickly bring you aid!

The aria includes a few dramatic octave leaps. The chorus repeats his tune to different text, concluding with the confident "If Thou, O God, art on our side, the victory is ours!" Unusually, Judith has been visible throughout this scene, though in the back and silent.

Scene II opens with Judith's prayer, "O God what bodings," a musical highlight of the score. Ranging in mood from pleading to hopeful, the music is intense and moving. She sings that she understands how weary her people are from the siege, and she fears they will soon fall. She begs God to protect her people:

> Protect her in this hour of sorest need!
> And for her sin, O let me, let me bleed!
> But spare them all!

---

6   M. Dickey Drysdale in High Fidelity/Musical America, May 1977.

On the word "sin," the key suddenly modulates from B-flat major to G major, although the music continually shifts and modulates. In more sustained passages, the orchestra shifts to quarter notes from steady eighth notes, as Judith sings in poignant, sweeping phrases (see Figure 5):

> O show me Lord, how I may save this land,
> Make Thou mine arm its duty understand,
> And keep me in the hollow of Thine hand
> By Thy great might, by Thy great might.

She reaches her highest note, $f\#"$ on "hand," after a steady *crescendo* leading up to it. This aria presents an appealing Judith who loves her people above all else and trusts God to help them.

Scene III opens with the entrance, to trumpet fanfares, of Achior and Assyrian soldiers. In a strange plot addition, Achior is in Bethulia (along with Assyrian soldiers, even stranger), warning the people to be wary of Holofernes. He tells them if they yield, Holofernes will grant life to all of them—men, women, and children of Bethulia. The soldiers briefly echo the same upbeat fanfare music, repeating "Yield, O Israel!" The music lacks pathos and seems inappropriately and inexplicably upbeat. When Achior sings "But his wrath will leave you ... bleaching bones and ashes," the key modulates from E-flat major to G# minor. His voice reaches a dramatic a' on "bones." When he repeats "Hark to Holofernes," the music is marked *più dolce* (sweeter) and returns to E-flat major. This section ends with the fanfare theme.

The key suddenly changes to E-flat minor, suggesting a darker mood, when Ozias enters. He sings: "Ye slaves of Asshur, go!" on which his voice leaps an octave from *e-flat* to *e-flat'*. He assures the enemy that they will not prevail because Jehovah is the Lord. Achior joins in the same key, warning the people that those who scorn the wrath of Asshur (the original capital of Assyria and also the name of the Assyrians' supreme god) shall see the blazing of their towers and the ashes of their town. On "see," there is an enharmonic shift from G flat to F# along with a switch to Achior's earlier key. After Ozias's defiant retort, the time changes from 2/4 to 6/8 and the key returns to E-flat minor. These constant harmonic shifts create a sense of instability and uncertainty.

Scene IV opens with a weeping, poignant theme. The chorus of Israelites is marked *Andante espressivo* and the sopranos open with a pleading motif, a descending half step (known as a *seufzer* or sigh). Like other works discussed here, the opening chorus shows the strong influence of Saint-Saëns's 1877 opera *Samson and Delilah*, which was very popular then. The tenors sing a different motif, a descending diminished fourth followed by a half-step rise. They sing of their lost hope, of the sky that "no pitying raindrop sheds" and plead with Ozias: "Water, water! Or we die!" All the choruses alternate between homophonic and *fugato* sections, in which they echo each other.

Ozias enters in a faster tempo and a sudden change from the previous B minor chord to a bright G major. He sings a lyrical *arioso* (brief aria), begging the people to trust in God, who watches over Israel and never sleeps. Then the tempo changes to *Allegro* and the time from 4/4 to 3/4, as excited dotted rhythms introduce an angry chorus. The people curse Ozias, calling him a "false priest" who is deceiving them.

Figure 5 George Whitefield Chadwick, "Judith's Prayer"

Ozias's response is in the same key and tempo but returns to the calmer time of 4/4 with no dotted rhythms. The chorus reenters to angrier music, singing that "Jehovah has left us to die!" and then calling out "Hail, Asshur, hail." Cymbals underline the drama of these words. The final chords under "Hail!" are open fifths, C-G, spanning two octaves—a modal and unsettled sound.

Scene V opens with Judith singing "Stay, ye cowards!" beginning unaccompanied, a signifier of her strength and dominant personality. The scene consists only of this lengthy aria, "The Vision of Judith." In the first part, Judith reminds the people that their God Jehovah has always been present to help them through troubles. In increasingly assertive and dramatic music, over steady *tremolos*, she then reminds the people that God brought them out of Egypt. These last words are sung very low in the mezzo register, on *g* below middle C, musically suggesting the descent into Egypt because of the unusually low range. Between sections, a rapid ascending scale is heard in the orchestra. Judith reminds the people of the manna God provided so they would not perish in the wilderness. After the next ascending scale, the *tremolos* become groups of hammering 8th notes under her words "Repent ye, repent ye" sung in strong phrases. In slower music, she assures the people that their Lord Jehovah will forgive and deliver them. A new section is introduced by a key change, from B-flat major to A-flat major and a broader tempo. Speaking more personally, in stately music recalling her earlier prayer (Scene II), she tells her people that she has cried out to God and he heard her prayer. Then the mood changes again as she recounts her "vision." The music modulates continually, creating a sense of instability. The next part is very lyrical, as she sings:

> With grief and lamentation, my lonely couch I sought,
> And as I lay in slumber, a wonder there was wrought.
> Behold, there came unto me from the dim world unseen
> A vision of my lost one, with calm and radiant mien.

This introduces Judith's account of her vision of Manasseh, her dead husband, speaking to her: a "mighty thrill" passed over her as her spirit rejoiced. On a sweet, descending line punctuated by rising chords in the harp (often a trope for "heavenly"), she relates what he said to her, in increasingly impassioned music:

> Fear not, O Judith, thou brave and faithful heart,
> To save and bless thy people, hast thou been set apart.

In faster, more rhythmic music including trumpet calls, she continues:

> For thou shalt slay the tyrant even with thy fair right arm,
> And the God who reigns above thee shall protect thee from all harm.

In very different music, marked *grazioso* (sweet or graceful) and very sinuous, in the broad time of 12/8 and with prominent chromaticism, Manasseh continues to address Judith, in her vision. He instructs her to dress in her finest clothes, wearing jewels and flowers, and to go alone to the enemy camp. Her courage should not fail her and dishonor will not harm her. Then the tempo picks up and dotted rhythms are heard together with repeated rapid ascending 32nd-note runs in the bass, as Manasseh describes the hour that will "sound the tyrant's knell." He assures Judith that his spirit will protect her, then bids her farewell.

The triumphant music that was heard at the opening of Manasseh's speech is reprised here, but in the brighter key of F major. To this soaring melody in the orchestra, Judith relates that the vision passed but it had given her soul strength and had uplifted her spirit. She no longer has any fear. In more rhythmic phrases, she tells the crowd that she is now doing as she was bidden, going to Asshur's camp. She says that they will not see her face again until Asshur is laid low. In very effective musical painting of a text, the last word is sung on a low F—*f* below middle C, near the bottom of a mezzo's range (it is optional; *f'* is also written in the score). The scene ends on a high F major chord, a sign of hope.

The blatant sexism of this scene is hard to overlook, but it reflects attitudes toward women in that era. The fact that Judith could only believe in herself if she got reassurances from her (dead) husband is an imagined scenario nowhere suggested in the original story. A more modern interpretation of this "dream" could be that Judith imagining such a scene was the only way she could find the strength to have faith in herself. But at the time it was written, the interpretation would surely have been that a woman can only do her husband's bidding and can know herself only through his image of her. Men of that time could not accept a woman conceiving and carrying out such an act entirely on her own. This aspect of Judith's original story troubled librettists and playwrights in that era, and indeed every era. But it did not seem to disturb the original writer of the story, interestingly enough for such an ancient document.

In the Finale of this act, the chorus and Ozias all try to dissuade Judith, in very dramatic music. The tempo is *Allegro molto agitato*, in cut time (twice as fast). They tell Judith that "vile dishonor" awaits her and beg her to stay, not to throw her life away or become a slave. They plead with her on their knees, reminding her that "lust digs every grave." Judith's responds "Unscath'd I pass them by," because she has heard God's word. She sings:

> The tyrant's end is nigh! Jehovah's wrath is stirred …
> Heavenly power shall guard me through Asshur's tents! Farewell!

She sings these phrases on broken descending chords, ending on a low A# (*a#*) under middle C. The low notes of the mezzo voice are very effectively used in this opera. On the mention of Jehovah's wrath, trumpets and horns sound. The next phrases open a new section, *Andante*, starting with *tremolos* in the orchestra. "When the hour cometh" echoes earlier phrases from her aria, featuring unusual intervals and some chromaticism. The word "Farewell" starts on *f#* below middle C, eventually ending on *b*, on a tonic B-major chord.

The chorus responds in a prayer, beginning *a cappella* but later joined by a few chords in the orchestra, sparser than elsewhere in the opera. The beginning sounds very hymnal but grows more complex and more richly orchestrated. After some dissonance, the ending is again in a tonic, this time E major. It concludes with Judith singing, accompanied only by *tremolos*: "Have you forgotten Moses' hymn of deliverance?" before she exhorts the people to pray for her.

Act II

In Scene I, the opening chorus includes soldiers, camp followers, and captive Hebrews. The presence of Hebrew slaves in the Assyrian camp is also a feature in Lefebvre's opera (see Chapter 4). Though not in the original story, it adds an interesting touch. It also mirrors similar onstage Hebrew slaves in such widely popular operas as Verdi's *Nabucco* (1841) and Saint-Saëns's *Samson and Delilah* (1877). The opening music has a very martial sound and includes prominent snare drums and trumpets. The two groups—Assyrian soldiers and Hebrew slaves—sing contrasting music to suggest their differing positions. This device was also used by Lefebvre in his *drame lyrique* of 1877 (see Chapter 4). The soldiers sing in a quick rhythm, mostly composed of 8th notes, while under them the slaves sing unison half notes, including "Woe" sung on descending octaves. The soldiers sing praises to their gods, including Baal and Nebuchadnezzar, as well as bloodthirsty lyrics about their many battles. For example: "Carnage is deepening, corpses full heaping … women shrieking, garments reeking … Then charge, ye men of blood!"; and more of the same. Meanwhile, the Hebrews sing of lying in the chains of slavery, awaiting death: "Woe, one by one we faint and die." The music underlines the polar differences in the character and sentiments of the two groups. A third group enters to much lighter music, including bells and triangle. These are the camp followers, who ridicule the captive Hebrews in such verses as "In shackles live forever, nor cease your plaintive wail! Ah, ha ha!" They end each phrase with the same laughter and conclude by hailing both Asshur and Holofernes, just as he makes his first appearance.

Scene II opens with Holofernes bragging about his might and victories. His music is marked by jagged and changing rhythms, and dramatic interval leaps for his voice. Each one of three stanzas becomes more dramatic and also changeable. When Holofernes sings of "Far Egypt's dry and breathless sands," the music becomes modal, suggesting an "oriental" or "exotic" setting. The final verses, sung to highly dramatic music, are:

Mine anger once awake … let earth in terror quake!
Naught can my power resist! Nor blood nor fire my wrath can slake …
Till round the charred impaling stake, grim death has fed full grist.

On the word "death," his voice reaches *f'*, quite high for a baritone, sung *fortissimo* to excited music in the orchestra, which also plays a dramatic postlude.

Scene III opens with Achior bowing before Holofernes. This is another plot addition: in the original story, Achior does not return to Holofernes's camp after being sent back to Bethulia. In this libretto, Holofernes asks Achior what he learned, returning from Bethulia, about those "who dare to resist." Achior's response, to very lyrical and tonic music, approximately matches his speech in an earlier chapter of the original story, before he was ever sent to Bethulia (Jdt 5). Achior talks about the Hebrews' worship of a God, Jehovah, "who never sleeps… as long as his chosen people keep his laws." The soldiers, outraged, wonder what he is talking about; after all, "Is not Asshur God?" Trumpets underline these words. Achior continues, explaining that Judah fell only when the people's hearts forsook this God, and that the Assyrians can never overcome Jehovah. The music begins as a plea and then grows increasingly complex, both tonally and rhythmically, a pattern typical of this score. The soldiers shout: "Traitor! Coward! Death to the craven coward!" Holofernes, equally furious, swears he will grind the Bethulian's insolence into the dust. He orders Achior chained and bound, with a log about his neck: "And he shall know that Asshur, he is God!" Achior pleads for mercy and pity, but Holofernes ignores him and orders that he be cast at Bethulia's gate. The music becomes more frenzied as the soldiers cry out: "Death to the Ammonite! Death, death!" while violently dragging him away. This is a dramatized version of Achior's expulsion in the original story.

Scene IV opens as the captives in the camp see Judith coming and recognize her. This plot addition was also found in Silveri's opera (see Chapter 4), and I commented there that it is hard to understand how these Hebrews, who presumably were captured in various areas of Judea, would recognize a widow who lived in seclusion in little Bethulia. The librettist and composer were not concerned about these anomalies. It is more likely that they were trying to emulate Verdi's chorus of Hebrew slaves in his well-known 1841 opera *Nabucco*. When the captives recognize Judith, they sing an *a cappella* hymnlike chorus of praise:

> 'Tis Judith, Alas! Ah, nobliest of Judah's women!
> The palm tree of mighty Judah.

They continue to wonder why she has come to the camp alone and predict that her beauty will wither, "ever in shame," and she will find no human pity there.

Judith sings "Peace, peace, Jehovah will protect me" very sweetly. It is not clear whom she is addressing. But Holofernes hears her and asks gruffly whose woman's voice that is. The sentinel (an invented character) tells him it is a Jewish woman who is "passing fair." The music accompanying this phrase is very sensual and chromatic, musical devices that suggest Judith's allure. Holofernes says she may approach, for "*Fair* Jewish women may my mercy gain" (italics in libretto). The chorus of extravagant praise that follows has become familiar in Judith operas:

> Behold, a goddess comes! What wealth of raven hair!
> For her who would not dare the war-god's wrath?
> How lithe, tall and straight!
> How goddess-like she walks, majestic is her mien!
> A queen, a very queen!

That is quite a buildup! Holofernes asks Judith: "Who art thou? For thou art beautiful." The use of archaic English in this (barely) twentieth-century libretto clearly is an attempt to sound more "ancient"/"biblical" (or Victorian). The implication of Holofernes's question is that he only cares who Judith is because she is beautiful. After she answers, he assures her that she shall find favor in the court of Nebuchadnezzar. On this word, the orchestra plays trills under Holofernes's sustained note, sounding almost like a satire of his pomposity. Judith boldly tells Holofernes that her Lord is great but adds that Holofernes is the mighty arm of Asshur. He responds by cursing all the tribes of Judah but also assures her that she will be exalted at his court because her beauty is incomparable. Then he cuts to the chase, not only inviting Judith to his feast that night, but adding that he loves her and wants to make her his. Judith prays in an aside: "Jehovah, save me! In my husband's love, pure and unstained!"

Judith's dead husband Manasseh has a greater presence in this work than in any other, excepting Hubert Parry's oratorio, which was not actually based on the book of Judith (see Chapter 2). The three-day interval between their first meeting and the banquet she attends is omitted. The mention of love, present in many librettos but not in the original version, comes much sooner in this opera than in other works.

Judith now asks Holofernes for permission to leave the camp in order to pray "at midnight and at noon." This is sung to a lovely, lyrical melody. As in many works, the music alters Judith's voice more effectively than a spoken tone could. When she mentions praying, the theme of her Act I prayer is reprised, though the end of the phrase is modified. She ends her plea on $a\#$, low in the register. Such low tones can suggest both seduction and hopelessness. The orchestra plays a bar of dotted rhythm leading to Holofernes's immediate agreement, though he implies that because he has granted her wish, she will also grant him his "heart's desire." Judith prays to God to strengthen her heart and save her from disgrace. On the word "strengthen," a modal sound is heard in the orchestra, a *Phrygian* interval strongly associated with Jewish music. There is no indication that Chadwick would have been familiar with this modality's Jewish roots, so he most likely used it here to suggest a general Middle Eastern, "exotic" sound. Holofernes orders the attendants to let Judith come and go freely. He adds: "Cursed and tortured be the Jewish God, if he refuse this beauteous woman's prayers!" which is original and possibly slightly comical. He continues raving that Judith's beauty surpasses even that of Ishtar and concludes by repeating "Tonight! Tonight!" These final words are sung lower and softer each time, a wonderful effect with some irony, considering what tonight will bring.

Scene V opens with sounds of revelry from Holofernes's tent. The orchestral introduction includes prominent bells to suggest a festive, "oriental" atmosphere. In an ensemble, Judith, outside the tent, expresses her thoughts simultaneously with the chorus inside the tent and with the sentinel. Judith expresses her revulsion at the revelries, calling them "an orgy at its height … the vile Assyrian lords and their ribald jests … the women's wanton laugh." At the same time, the revelers sing about flower wreaths, golden cups, dances, and ruby wine. The sentinel spots Judith outside the tent and asks whom she is looking for. She answers that the captain sent for her. In this retelling, there is no three-day wait, as Judith arrived earlier the same day as this banquet.

In Scene VI, the sentinel introduces Judith as she enters the tent, and Holofernes welcomes her elaborately. His music is sensual, filled with trills and chromaticism. He tells the slaves around him to kneel and salute their queen, which they happily do. Judith protests that this welcome is "too fervent" and will put her too much in Holofernes's debt. She adds: "Such honor for thy servant, thou surely will regret," an ambiguous phrase that she leaves for Holofernes to understand. She sings these lines with no emotion. Holofernes responds by insisting she is worthy of this honor and invites her to sit next to him and join the feast. The chorus asks Judith to join their party, with its wild dances, wine, and song, as tambourines are heard in the orchestra. Holofernes notices Judith is not eating, and she tells him that the strict law of her nation forbids Asshur's food (in other words, it's not kosher). Both their phrases are accompanied by short musical figures marked *capriccioso* (whimsical), a musical wink. This is one of the few librettos that includes even a passing reference to Judith's adherence to dietary laws. As the revelers leave one by one, the music gets softer and dies away. Holofernes asks Judith what she wishes, and she says she wants to serve him, alone. This is an addition to the original story, where she does not have to ask to be alone with him, since Holofernes invites her to join him after three days. Here, he interprets her request to mean that she is confessing to wanting him as much as he wants her. Holofernes orders everyone to leave.

In romantic, tonic, and lyrical music, Holofernes begins on a descending C major phrase, marked *Amoroso* (amorously), beginning the longest scene in the opera. Holofernes asks Judith to "yield to love's delight," telling her he loves her and wants to press her in his arms. She protests that she is a Hebrew, one of those whom he himself would kill. She adds: "Thy favor is too great for such as I," with blushing modesty clearly intended to put Holofernes off his guard. He insists again that her sheer beauty gives her the right to be a queen. She protests again, reminding him that she is only a Hebrew widow. He then asks why she has come. In a soft, sad, and simple melody, with a sinuous oboe solo (a poignant sound that can suggest sensuality), she describes the suffering of her people. She explains that the drought-induced famine has driven them to eat meat from the temple sacrifices and even to drink from the temple's wine jars. Because these items are sacred to their God, their doom has been sealed. Holofernes swears that he will worship "this meat-robbed Jewish God," one of the unintentionally more humorous lines in the libretto. He says that the sacrifice to this God will be His own Jewish dead. His words sound sarcastic and mocking. Holofernes's music here, with its strong rhythm and *staccato* (dry and broken) phrases, contrasts greatly with Judith's passionately lyrical singing.

They sing a duet in which they both express their own thoughts simultaneously. Holofernes seductively asks Judith to bind his temple with her hair and "wreathe thy snowy arms around me." At the same time, Judith, aside, sings: "What awful doom, O God! such blasphemy must bring!" To Holofernes, though, she sings only praise:

The wasted plains declare thy power …
Thy splendor and fame are gone forth,
I saw how the Israelites fear thee, the nations thy praises repeat.

She tells him she wants to be near him and has come to seek grace at his feet. There is no mention here of sharing a battle plan as in the original story. Holofernes echoes Judith's praise of him by repeating: "My splendor and fame go forth!" as the music begins building to greater excitement. Judith repeats that it is enough just to be near him and to find favor at his feet. Increasingly impassioned, he tells her to kiss him and drink his wine, singing with soft persuasiveness. She protests: "It is too much, my lord!" and he grows more impatient. He argues that no honor is too much and asks what can buy her lips. In a change of key and tempo, he offers her any jewelry she wants, showing her rings and jewels and singing sensuous music. Suddenly a "sword" motif is heard, high rippling 16th-note arpeggios, as Judith spots his sword and says "the sword" aloud. Holofernes hears—and he offers it to her. He tells her its jewels are priceless, yet she can take it, it is hers. It is an interesting twist to suggest the sword is jeweled and thus presumably appealing to a woman. Continuing to play her part, Judith comments disarmingly:

> A pretty thing! But where is wine to celebrate thy might?
> Thou needest thy sword no more!

Holofernes repeats that all his power is hers, including the sword—a comment pregnant with irony. He now grows more insistent, his request punctuated by *fortissimo* chords as he angrily insists again that she kiss him, that she has delayed for too long. Judith suggests they drink together first. She holds up her cup to toast him and encourages him to drink from his "bowl of wine" (ancient pottery includes many examples of such a vessel for drinking). The opening phrases are broad, suggesting a toast or salute. But chromaticism and more sensual music soon take over. Judith demurely suggests that he will cast her off soon, because his people scorn her. He denies that he will ever do that, and she asks him to repeat the denial again, as she kneels at his feet, still stalling for time. As he grows increasingly drunk, his response brings a musical shift into D-flat major, often called the "sensuous" key. In music marked *Andante amabile*, as well as *pianissimo* and *dolcissimo* (very soft and sweet) and in the broad time of 9/8, there is a rising pattern in both the orchestral and vocal lines. While Holofernes sings a melodic tune, the accompaniment is a subtext, filled with ominous dissonances. He nostalgically recalls an idyllic life "afar on the banks of the Tigris, where naught but the honey-bee roams." He drinks between stanzas. The final stanza, beginning "Far away," is sung very softly, in *mezza voce* ("half voice," almost whispered), and the time switches to 3/4. As in some other works, Holofernes's music makes him a somewhat sympathetic or at least very romantic character, who feels homesick. The composers' aim seems to be to make Holofernes appealing to the audience. Whether their intent was to cast some shadow on Judith's deed can only be conjectured. Perhaps there is a suggestion of even greater strength on Judith's part, since she must also resist an irresistible man.

Judith's encouragement to him to drink, "A single cup to crown the night!," is sung to the same accompaniment as the opening of Holofernes's aria, the only change being in the groups of 8th notes which here are *staccato*, suggesting a mocking tone. She continues urging him to drink, in chromatic music filled with unusual chords such as augmented fourths and sevenths. The contrast with Holofernes's more lighthearted music creates tension and suspense. He continues to drink, reprising stanzas from the "Far away" aria but to an altered accompaniment. In the lower parts, the same groups of 8th notes heard in the earlier melody are repeated. But in the higher parts, the accompaniment is groups of four 16th notes against three 8th notes, a lopsided beat evoking instability and drunkenness. When Holofernes sings "Far away" the last time, Judith echoes his words in a mocking and ironic aside, in which her last few notes descend chromatically:

> Aye, far away! Ere dawn of day, far from thy power may I be!
> From thy thick wine! Far from thee!

Singing together, they begin each phrase either a beat after or on the last note of each other's music, so the voices are both together and not together. They are each singing their own thoughts as the music begins to fade. When Holofernes falls asleep, Judith sings on a clear D-flat major chord: "The time is near," followed by a brief orchestral reprise of the "Far away" motif.

Judith's Prayer, which follows, is arguably the musical highlight of the opera. The music powerfully portrays Judith's changing moods, and Chadwick displays a brilliant use of orchestral colors to bring the well-known scene to vivid and harrowing life. The prayer opens very slowly, marked *Lento* and *sotto voce ad lib.* Judith sings the opening measures *a cappella*: "Jehovah, strengthen thou my fainting hand." Then the orchestra doubles the vocal line as she begs God for mercy, saying she can endure no more. As the tempo picks up, over *tremolos* and strong chords in the bass, she continues more dramatically: "His vile caresses and his loathsome smiles!" Then, singing *con passione* (score note, "with passion"), her voice rises to higher pitches and her melody is doubled in the orchestra. She starts the next passage on *e"* and in a few measures drops over an octave to *b*, suggesting great emotion. The passage after this one is similarly constructed. She sings:

> Have I not yet my people's sin atoned?
> Have I not yet their pardon fully gained?

The mood and rhythm change again as Judith recalls her earlier vision (in Act I). Groups of repeated 8th-note triplets, some with dotted rhythm, pound under her voice. She repeats what Manasseh told her in the vision, that "her fair arm would slay." The music grows quieter and more sustained as she repeats: "Thy hand shall save Judah: Now God, point the way." On the last word of this phrase, the music changes dramatically. The rhythm shifts from 4/4 to 3/4, the key from G major to G minor, and the tempo to *Allegro molto vivace*, very fast. Three groups of 8th-note chords play relentlessly in a very high range, often dissonantly. Judith sings a sustained line over the excited, almost shrill background: "His falchion gleams in the torches' red light" (a falchion is a slightly curved sword in use from roughly the thirteenth to the sixteenth century, so historically it makes no sense to include it here, but the librettist must have thought it sounded more dramatic than "sword," and it goes with the use of Elizabethan-era English). After she sings "light," rapid and harrowing descending and ascending arpeggios are heard in the orchestra, music that brilliantly evokes a gleaming sword. Then the pounding groups of 8th-notes immediately return. This pattern is repeated throughout this section of the aria. Both text and music suggest ecstasy and determination:

> He gave me the sword that shall slay him tonight!
> Come, falchion, come! Thou gleamest in my sight;
> Mine, thou are mine! And all Asshur's might!

The mood suddenly changes again, growing slower and calmer, with a menacing phrase repeated in every measure as Judith sings, more calmly: "At last let the price of the faithless be paid." The same phrase grows louder and higher and continues throughout this section. She prays again for mercy and aid. Then the excitement builds, as she sings: "Tyrant! Oppressor! Lie bare to my sword!" On "bare," she reaches one of her highest notes, *g''*, sustained for two full measures over the repetitive sinuous theme and *tremolos*. But she tops that with a *g#''* only a few measures later, on "Judah," which she will save when she slays him. After singing "O Lord" on a much lower pitch, she is quiet, while the orchestra continues to play continually building repetitions of the sinuous theme. Finally the orchestra reaches its climax: three repetitions of a rapidly rising passage, followed by a high trill and a precipitous descent. The final repetition takes the trill even higher and the descending passage is even faster. This is one of the most vivid musical depictions of the decapitation to be found in a musical setting. It is truly a pity that no one had the means to stage the scene utilizing this brilliant musical portrayal. There is a brief pause after the final passage, when obviously the head finally rolled off his body. Then very calmly and quietly, almost breathlessly, Judith sings *a cappella*: "Jehovah, Thy mercy … Judah … is free." This is followed by a very broad, triumphant theme in the orchestra (reminiscent of Parry's oratorio; see Chapter 2), played as Judith falls to her knees.

In a wonderfully ironic touch, immediately after the aria, the sentinel standing outside the tent announces, in soft martial music, that all is well and it is midnight. Judith quickly hides the head under her mantle. Since there is no servant in this libretto, there is no one to hold her food bag (never mentioned) while she put the head in it. The sentinel gives Judith permission to pass. To gradually fading martial music, the sentinel bids Judith to go and make her prayer to the God of her people, another ironic touch. He repeats "All's well" three times, twice in a B-minor cadence, finally resolving into D major. Three *ppp* chords (softer than the softest) end Act II.

Act III

Act III takes place outside the walls of Bethulia, beginning with an orchestral prelude. The dark music opens with very soft, mysterious chromatic passages. The music gradually gets faster and louder, ending on a *fff* (louder than the loudest) C-major *tremolo* when the curtain rises. Musically, this foretells a happy conclusion. Ozias, kneeling on the wall, sings a recitative and then a prayer, asking God to send relief and victory before the sun rises higher in the sky. This is the fifth day, and he had hoped to see Judith. His prayer ends in C major, musically suggesting hope. Judith's voice is heard calling to him in the distance, on descending octaves, a heraldic sound. She sings triumphal phrases while Ozias continues to comment joyfully on her arrival. The people rush in and swarm around Judith. Then the full chorus sings: "Awake, rejoice! Judith returns!" Judith tells them in a recitative, with only *tremolos* under her voice, that the Lord has sent deliverance and saved his chosen land. They sing: "What! Is the tyrant dead?" and the key changes to B-flat minor on the last word. When she responds, she echoes the closing measures of her earlier aria.

The aria that follows, "The monster wooed me," is rather conventional and tonic, sounding more nineteenth than twentieth century except for a few unexpected dissonances. It is also bouncier than would seem appropriate. In catchy verses, Judith relates how Holofernes wooed her but she filled his cup with wine, and "that wine with blood besmeared his fame, and kept disgrace from mine." The chorus responds in *a cappella*, chorale-like music in praise of God. Judith sings another refrain of her aria with more catchy lyrics:

> The monster lured me to disgrace,
> But boldly gazing on my face
> He soon forgot my haughty race
> And yonder now he lies.

After another chorus of praise, she sings a third stanza, this time describing the act itself after she took the jeweled sword: "across his drunken throat it went, and blood with wine was strangely blent [*sic*]," concluding this gory description with "Jehovah be adored!" The chorus now sings a virtual paean to Judith: "O noblest of Judah's women, the palm tree of mighty Judah!" It begins very softly, accompanied by four groups of 8th notes. The music become more and more hymnal (and nineteenth century). After this chorus, Judith sings in a tempo twice as slow (marked *Il doppio più lento*) and *Largamente*, very broadly: "Praise unto Jehovah's name!" She sings this to the melody heard at the conclusion of the beheading account. The chorus echoes her in a very triumphal and Elgar-like sound.

In the next scene, Achior appears in Israelite garb, announcing in very lyrical music that he now knows Jehovah is the Lord. Clearly, he has formally converted. Judith welcomes him into the fold in a duet where they sing their own texts but their voices are woven together. Ozias joins them to make a trio, adding that he knows Jehovah is God because he has seen "the gory head of their mighty host." The trio ends on a bright G major chord.

In the Finale, Judith sings in a recitative that they should hang Holofernes's head on their towers and let it swing there (a small but effective addition to the original version). There is no indication that she ever displays the head, possibly because this work was only performed as an oratorio, not staged. Her praise of Jehovah is very assertive and proclamatory, repeated in a square chorus in 4/4 time and D major, with not much dissonance in sight. Here too, the influence of Edward Elgar and Parry is unmistakable. When the chorus develops into a call to arms, the time switches to 3/4 and a more martial sound. All sing "To arms! To arms!" as the voices echo each other, then come together. The conclusion changes to a very broad 6/4 time (marked *Più animato ma maestoso*, faster but majestic), a loud and triumphant ending in D major. The opera ends not with praise for Judith or God but with a call to war punctuated by loud brass in the orchestra.

Conclusion

This hybrid opera-oratorio has many strong points in terms of what it adds to the story of Judith. First, Judith is cast as a dramatic mezzo-soprano, immediately establishing her as a powerful figure. As in other works, she modulates her voice to sound sweeter when addressing Holofernes, or praying to God, but expresses her strongest feelings in powerful notes, particularly some in a very low range (possibly a less female sound). The other strong point is the wonderfully rich orchestration. Chadwick uses instruments and techniques very imaginatively to evoke strong emotion as well as action. This music truly illuminates the text. His music inconsistently wavers between staid late-nineteenth-century traditional oratorio sound and dissonant twentieth-century opera. This makes the work patchy but still worth hearing. The libretto is probably the weakest part of the work and its greatest shortcoming in terms of creating a realistic drama. The addition of Manasseh as a figure urging Judith on, giving her strength and confidence (possibly replacing God's role in this), can only be excused as a product of its time. The idea of a woman acting completely alone was simply incomprehensible to men of that era, so the creators of this work explained that by imagining Manasseh's ghost being the guiding hand or force. Listeners at the time were probably comfortable with this interpretation. Another change was the expansion of Achior's role, making him Holofernes's messenger. The absence of Judith's servant may be due to Chadwick's strong focus only on Judith, who acts independently, her only guidance coming from her dead husband's words. There is a wonderfully ironic touch in Holofernes's offering Judith the jewel-encrusted sword as a gift—the same sword she later uses to kill him. In spite of its flaws, this opera would be well worth reviving, for its brilliant musical retelling of Judith's story.

Emil von Reznicek (1860–1945)

Emil von Reznicek was born in Vienna. He studied law and music together in Graz but ultimately settled on music. After his first wife died in 1897, he moved to Germany permanently in 1899, with his second wife.[7] When Hitler came to power in 1933, Reznicek (who was not Jewish) was already in his seventies and not only was his wife Jewish, but his daughter Felicitas worked in the Resistance. His wife retired from public life and died in 1939. He associated with Richard Strauss and as a result was accused of being a Nazi sympathizer after the war.[8]

Though Reznicek's music was rooted in late Romanticism, his work reached far into the twentieth century in style. With the decreasing popularity of avant-garde music after the Second World War, Reznicek's music increasingly fell into oblivion. Reznicek was friends with Strauss, but he himself claimed in 1933 that his greatest musical influence and inspiration was Gustav Mahler. He could not repeat this assertion when he wrote his self-published memoirs in 1941, however, because of Mahler being Jewish. His musical style changed over the years. His earliest success was with his first opera in 1894. He wrote his second opera, *Judith and Holofernes* (sometimes called *Holofernes*), based on Hebbel's 1840 play (see Chapter 3), in 1922. In a letter to a friend in 1921, he claimed to have modernized his style considerably. Though Reznicek never left

---

[7] David Wright, "Emil von Reznicek," https://www.wrightmusic.net/pdfs/emil-von-reznicek.pdf (accessed April 29, 2020).

[8] James Manheim, https://www.allmusic.com/artist/emil-von-reznicek-mn0001644569/biography (accessed April 29, 2020).

the realm of tonal composition, he often used bitonality (music played in two keys simultaneously). And in the dramaturgy of his operas he sometimes copied the silent-movie style of acting. Reznicek was skeptical about Arnold Schoenberg's concept of twelve-tone composition but not against atonalism per se. He greatly admired Alban Berg's operas *Wozzeck* (1922—the same year as *Judith and Holofernes*) and *Lulu* (1937, left incomplete). Reznicek also was open to all types of music as possible sources for his own compositions.[9]

In the late 1920s, Reznicek was respected as one of the most important German or Austrian composers of the generation born in the 1860s. But even then, his fame began to be surpassed by the modern music of younger composers. Like so many composers who had adhered to tonal music in the twentieth century and were still writing after the First World War, his music fell to oblivion after the Second World War with the rise of serialism or twelve-tone music. In the case of Reznicek, the situation was also aggravated by the false accusation that he had been a Nazi sympathizer.

The German libretto is online.[10]

The score (Vienna, Universal Edition, 1923) is available on IMSLP.[11]

Reznicek's *Judith und Holofernes* was performed in Bonn in June 2016 as *Holofernes*, the first time the work had been heard in ninety years. I obtained a private recording of this performance (which was broadcast), on which my analysis is based. The conductor of this performance, Jacques Lacombe, had been unfamiliar with Reznicek's work and found himself pleasantly surprised. He wrote extensive comments about the work on a blog:[12]

> What I discovered was an incredibly talented and imaginative composer who seems at home using so many different languages, styles and composition techniques. With such a wide pallet of expressions, he uses and mixes all these elements in a very personal way, with a clear intention to adapt each musical moment to the needs of the drama on stage … Because of Reznicek's great sense for theater, he didn't seem to fear at all to go back and forth (sometimes with absolutely no transition or "warning") between stylistically extremely contrasting elements that could be as far apart as the twelve-tone scale and the pure tonic/dominant relationship of a simple major key … There are so many passages in his opera where he manages to create incredible and beautiful atmospheres with his choices of instrumental combinations … this work [seems to be] written in many different languages, each one linked to a specific character, idea, emotion or situation.

[9] Dr. Michael Wittmann, "Errichtung des E.N. von Reznicek – Archives (Wedemark)," *MW-Musikverlag*, August 4, 2018. Available online: https://mwmusikverlag.wordpress.com/2018/08/04/errichtung-des-e-n-von-reznicek-archivs-wedemark/ (accessed May 24, 2019).

[10] https://imslp.org/wiki/Judith_und_Holofernes_(Reznicek%2C_Emil_von) (accessed October 23, 2020).

[11] https://imslp.org/wiki/Judith_und_Holofernes_(Reznicek%2C_Emil_von) (accessed October 23, 2020).

[12] Jacques Lacombe, "Reznicek: Polyglot," *Holofernes*, May 22, 2016. Available online: https://holofernesblog.wordpress.com/2016/05/22/reznicek-polyglot/ (accessed May 24, 2019).

Where Wagner would have taken thirty minutes to express and describe a situation, Reznicek takes thirty seconds. This amplifies the surprises created at first by so many contrasting elements throughout this work and gives us an 85-minute opera that takes you through an incredibly concise, rich and varied musical and theatrical experience.

A reviewer of this production, Matthew Rye, found the music far less appealing than conductor Lacombe did. Rye states:

> Reznicek doesn't seem able to sustain anything for long: the score sounds fragmentary, a sequence of short, unconnected moments, rather than the through-composed music drama it is presumably aiming to be.[13]

I can only add my own observation: One listener's "fragmentary" is another's "constantly shifting." For this listener, once the ear grows accustomed to the constant shifts, the music is riveting and exciting.

Judith und Holofernes (sometimes *Holofernes*; 1922)

The opera is in two acts, freely based on Hebbel (*frei nach Hebbel*).

Judith: Soprano   Abra: Mezzo   Osias: Bass   Holofernes: Bass-baritone
Achior (not listed in the score): tenor

In Act I, the very interesting overture—on the recording, not in the score—is based entirely on the melody of the Jewish prayer Kol Nidre. The overture features amazing variations on the theme. Reznicek was probably familiar with Max Bruch's arrangement of this melody for cello and orchestra, written in 1880.[14] The overture was later published separately (1929) as *Symphonic Variations on* Kol Nidre. This work has been recorded and can be heard on YouTube.[15]

---

[13] Matthew Rye, "Holofernes – Theater Bonn – 2 June 2016," *Ferneklang*, June 3, 2016. Available online: http://ferneklang.blogspot.com/2016/06/holofernes-theater-bonn-2-june-2016.html#comment-form (accessed May 24, 2019).

[14] Neil Levin, liner notes, at https://www.milkenarchive.org/music/volumes/view/masterworks-of-prayer/work/kol-nidre/ (accessed May 28, 2019). Nothing is known of Reznicek's second wife, but it is always possible that Reznicek may have attended a service with her where he heard the Kol Nidre chanted.

Bruch was a Protestant who became acquainted with the Kol Nidre melody when his Jewish teacher Ferdinand Hiller introduced him to Berlin's chief cantor Abraham Lichtenstein. Lichtenstein was known to have cordial relations with many Christian musicians and supported Bruch's interest in Jewish folk music. The original melody for the Kol Nidre prayer is the Ashkenazi musical version of this prayer, chanted on Yom Kippur. The tune belongs to a group of fixed seasonal *leitmotifs* and melodies that originated in medieval German communities. These melodies are "a bedrock layer of Ashkenazi custom" in Levin's words. Originally, other apparently unrelated melodies were also employed for this prayer, but the one known today was probably established as the sole intonation by the fifteenth century. This is confirmed by references in writings of the sixteenth century (Neil Levin, liner notes).

[15] https://www.youtube.com/watch?v=jKA30FrX4jU (accessed April 29, 2020).

The opera opens in Bethulia, unlike Hebbel's play which opens in Holofernes's camp. The five-act play has been reduced to a two-act opera, so Reznicek chose which parts to eliminate and shifted the chronology. The opening measures are very soft and modal. The opera starts with Osias praying to God to look upon their shame; his words are echoed by the people. Both Osias and the chorus sing *a cappella* in a very prayerful sound. Osias's phrases are dominated by the typically Jewish Phrygian mode. A plangent cor anglais plays sinuous phrases between the measures of singing. They sing to God who has abandoned them out of anger. A slow and rhythmic "religious dance" with a very "oriental sound" that was popular in an earlier era briefly interrupts the singing (p. 5). The people resume their prayers briefly before entering the temple. Another dance resumes (p. 6), soon dying down to nothing.

A sudden, dramatic change in the music, now marked *Allegro con brio*, introduces Judith. She appears alone, in sackcloth and ashes, and sings a lengthy prayer (p. 7). The introduction to this aria is a good example of Reznicek's constantly shifting musical styles. Lacombe comments:

> Her inner troubles are expressed by a very unstable "almost perfect" twelve-tone series that could have been written by Schoenberg, only to conclude in the most surprising way on a pure D-major chord on the word "Gott." This already gives us a hint of Reznicek's choices throughout the piece.[16]

The text and action are based on Act III of Hebbel's play (see Chapter 3):

> God! God! I did not want to pray, but I must pray. Why do you not incline unto me? I am too weak to ascend to you. Behold, here I lie as if out of the world and out of time. Anxiously I await a sign from you that will bid me arise and act.

Even though the orchestral part has elements of the twelve-tone system, Judith's emotional vocal line does not. It is quite tonic and accessible, in a clear A minor key. Her moods change constantly, reflected in the music: from pleading to anxious and fervent. She continues:

> I swore a sacred oath, never to rise, or only when you had shown me the way to Holofernes' heart.

To a halting, suspenseful rhythm, Judith sings "Holofernes" on a *g#"* over a *fortissimo* and dissonant chord group (p. 9). (She exclaims "Ah!" on the recording.) Over more suspenseful chords, Judith muses about a thought that keeps returning to her and suddenly realizes it came from God: the way to her deed leads through sin. After this revelation, she exults and thanks God for making her eyes clear. This last, dramatic phrase reaches *a"* over a clear F major chord, at the end of a harp *glissando*.

---

[16] Lacombe 2016.

The mood changes as the music grows softer and slower and Judith, "with fervor" (score note) sings: "You have made me beautiful; now I know why." Looking in a mirror, she greets her own image. The very lyrical, light music has echoes of Strauss. As she begins enumerating the features she will praise, the key changes to A-flat major and the music takes on an ecstatic, almost mystical quality (p. 11). Over almost continual high trills in the orchestra, Judith sings several rapid 32nd-note *melismas* (one syllable sung on several notes), imitated by a violin *obbligato* on increasingly higher pitches. When she sings "Poor mouth, I don't blame you for being pale—you must kiss horror" (*das Entsetzen*), her voice touches high C (*c'''*). These musical passages, not surprisingly considering the reference to a kiss of horror, powerfully echo Strauss's 1903 opera *Salome*.

The music is tranquil again, as Judith puts the mirror down. Over continual low, soft *tremolos*, she sings: "Holofernes, this is all yours; take it, but tremble when you have it." In every other measure of this declaration, a loud, quick, and high short phrase sounds like an eerie shriek (p. 12). In ominous, nervous music, Judith sings:

> I shall emerge at an hour when you do not expect it, like a sword
> from the scabbard, and pay myself with your life. If I must kiss you, I will
> imagine that it is with poisoned lips; if I embrace you, I will think that I am
> strangling you.

The music varies with each phrase: when she refers to being a sword, the music is briefly hysterical; when she sings of paying with his life, the line is sung freely and unaccompanied, and reaches *b* below middle C. Then the music builds to a frenzy again up to the climactic word "strangling" (*erwürge*), which is sung on a high B (*b''*). Judith remains standing in a sort of ecstasy (score note), then collapses and drags herself back to her corner, where she cowers (score notes, p. 14). The excited music, punctuated by horns, gradually quietens.

Abra (Mirza in Hebbel's play) worries about Judith. Her words are taken from Hebbel, where she spoke these lines before Judith's prayer rather than after it (see Chapter 3). In a sparsely accompanied, dry recitative, Abra comments that Judith has been sitting for three days and nights without eating, drinking, or speaking. She sings: "I believe she wants someone to pack her into a coffin, nail the lid over her, and carry her away" (p. 16). She asks Judith sarcastically if she should send for the gravedigger, and Judith waves her away. Expressing her loyalty to Judith, Abra sings in more agitated music:

> I forget the enemy and all our distress because of you. If an arrow were aimed at
> me, I should not notice it so long as I saw you sitting there like the living dead. At
> first you had so much courage that the men were ashamed, and now …

Judith interrupts Abra and in gentle music, marked *Allegretto con grazia*, orders her to adorn her.

Abra encourages Judith to eat, but she refuses and insists, in playful music, on being adorned (p. 18). A new section begins, marked *Molto tranquillo* and dense with inner voices. Judith describes a vision she has had (p. 19):

I saw it hover above the world like a dove which seeks a nest to brood upon, and the first soul which burst the bonds of its torpor must have conceived the thought of liberation!

This text is taken from the Hebbel play, but there it was in a different context. Judith says that because Abra looks so sad, she will go with her. Then in a return to the *Allegretto con grazia* music of before, she tells her that after they eat, Abra must adorn her as if for a wedding. Then she tells her not to smile (Abra squeals with delight on the recording), because "my beauty is now my duty" (p. 21), emphasizing the last word (*Pflicht*), which is sung on *a*". They leave together quickly.

The crowd is heard from behind the scene, singing "Woe, woe" in very dramatic and dissonant music, over hammering low chords. Speeding up to a hair-raising tempo, they shout that they do not want to wait any longer but want to open the gates: they want peace. The music vividly depicts their hysteria. On the last repeat of this word (*Friede*), the sopranos sustain a high B (*b*") over a dissonant chord (p. 26). They beat on the gates with their fists. The excited music abruptly stops, and the key and tempo change as Osias approaches with the priests and elders. The crowd retreats and makes room for them at the gates, as a bright light falls on them. Osias begins to tell them what the high priest Joachim said, but the crowd violently responds that they trust nothing unless it will lead them to a spring. Osias, in a recitative over sparse accompaniment, tells them they must remember Moses, servant of God, who struck Amalek not with a sword but with prayer. The crowd asks in very fast phrases and over a shrieking orchestra, each section of the chorus immediately following the previous: "Where is Moses, and where are the Prophets?" (*die Heiligen*, lit. "holy ones").[17]

The music stops again as Osias repeats in an *a cappella* recitative that they must have courage, because God's sanctity is threatened. Women approach, holding up their children, and in poignant, pleading music ask if a mother can be so sinful that her innocent child must die of thirst (p. 29). The people forcefully insist again that the gate be opened, threatening to do it themselves. (This text is all from Hebbel, where the scene is much lengthier.) In a side plot from Hebbel, a character named Assad incites the crowd to force the gates open, and another character named Daniel suddenly rises and in a "ringing voice" (score note; on the recording it is hoarse and muted) shouts: "Stone him!" (p. 30). This comes as a shock to everyone because Daniel had been deaf, dumb, and blind all his life—which is explained by Assad, his brother. Incited by Daniel, the crowd begins to stone Assad. These individual incidents are found throughout Hebbel's play and serve to make the "crowd" of Bethulians less anonymous and more like a group of individuals. They resume their calls to open the gates, threatening to do it themselves. The music is marked *Allegro tempestoso*. Osias calls out to them: "Deluded ones, stop!" and a melee breaks out, over increasingly

---

[17] Christians do not consider the prophets to be "holy men" but rather just part of a long lineage of such men. So the Christian writers were here referring to their own holy men rather than to those whom the Hebrews would have considered to be such men (Susanne Scholz, personal communication, May 31, 2019).

frenzied music (p. 33). (This scene is also represented in Matthus's opera, where the crowd burns Daniel to death, to prove he is not a prophet; see below).

Suddenly the mood changes, shifting from 3/4 to 4/4 time, much slower (marked *Adagio maestoso*), and to the unusual and very bright key of F# major. Over ecstatically strumming harps (often a trope for holiness), Judith suddenly appears, striding through the parting crowd, and sings: "Stop!" She confronts the people and asks, softly and somberly in lyrical phrases, if they remember the feeling of God's presence. The music then suddenly speeds up, switching abruptly to F major, as the constant *tremolos* stop. Over sparser accompaniment, Judith asks if the people want to now pretend their deepest feelings were a lie (p. 35; from Hebbel). The final word *Lüge* (lie) is sung on a sustained high A (*a"*). The people (a single woman in Hebbel's play) softly ask Judith, over a dry, *staccato* accompaniment, what she wants. Then they sing even more softly, and expressively: "Do you not know that we must despair, because we are people?" This phrase is sung *a cappella* and almost in a whisper. Their final chord is sung in a low range and ends in a clear F major key, sung *ppp*. To strumming harps, Judith asks if they want to dictate to God what path to follow. The people ask, more loudly and now with all four parts in unison, speaking as one, why God could not work a miracle in the heart of Holofernes and move him to retreat. Judith responds strongly: "Now could I seize the hand of Holofernes and lead him here, and even sharpen his sword before it had cut off all of your heads" (based on Hebbel's play; p. 38). The chorus sings in a very quick *fugato* with the voices following one another, marked *Allegro tempestoso*, that they don't want to hear any more "woman's prattle" (*Weibergeschwätz*; not in Hebbel's play).

The bickering continues until the crowd pushes toward the wall, where Judith throws herself before them. She pleads with them to wait for God's will and to determine how long they should wait. With "superhuman effort" (*übermenschlicher Anstrengung*), she stops the mob. She proclaims that they need wait only until the next dawn, and when they wonder if God might not need more time than that, she says he will not. The music for these passages is lyrical and flowing, with a violin *obbligato* (p. 40). To herself, Judith adds: "Thus tonight Holofernes must die." This, of course, differs entirely from the original story in which the people all agree to wait five days. That would give Judith enough time in Holofernes's camp to build up both trust and lust, leading to his beheading. This truncated and less realistic scenario also deviates from the Hebbel play, which retains the original timetable. The brief dialogue that follows is accompanied only by a single sustained note in the orchestra. Judith asks Osias to open the gates, telling him she has "business with Holofernes" (*ein Geschäft bei dem Holofernes*) and that no one can know except God. He agrees to do it, singing over a D major and then C major chord—striking tonic moments.

As the gates are opened, Judith steps forward into the moonlight and in very slow music, with a high violin *obbligato* to create an eerie, ominous mood, sings (text from Hebbel; p. 42):

Oh, rise up from your graves before me, you whom
he has put to death, that I may behold your wounds!

Come before me, you whom he has dishonored,
and open once more your eyes, now closed forever,
that I may read therein how guilty he was!
You shall all have reparation. But why do I think of you,
why not of the youths whom his sword can yet devour,
of the young women [or virgins: *Jungfrauen*]
whom he can yet crush in his arms?
I will avenge the dead and protect the living.

In this long recitative, the mood changes every few measures. On the word "reparation," the voice rises to a high A (*a"*). A few measures later, the end of the phrase "crush in his arms" descends to B below middle C. This wide range reflects the depth of her feeling, ranging from anger to compassion. Occasional solo *obbligato* passages are heard, in violin, oboe, and flute, adding poignancy. The people are now kneeling before Judith. The final line, after a high trill and loud rapid ascending passage in the orchestra, is sung to a new tempo, *Alla marcia, lento e maestoso* (march tempo, very slow and majestic), with a very triumphant sound (p. 44). Judith then asks the people (only Achior in the play) if she is beautiful enough for an offering (*Opfer*) and they respond quietly and reverently: "No one has seen your equal." Judith addresses all the people and tells them to pray for her as for one who is dying, to teach the children her name and let them pray for her. She repeats a phrase from earlier, "I will avenge the dead and protect the living," which all the people repeat. Tonal music in this work, generally in a major key, suggests the idea of the divine and the concept of redemption through God, in conductor Lacombe's view. This triumphant hymn at the end of Act I is a good example.[18] Judith, singing high above the chorus, goes through the gate into full moonlight as the curtain falls. Though much of the text is taken from Hebbel's play, a great deal of the play's dialogue was omitted from this scene, making the drama more concise and realistic. And the constantly changing, always exciting music adds many layers to the text.

Act II takes place in Holofernes's "palatial tent" (*Prunkzelt*). The text and action are based on Act IV of Hebbel's play. The extended musical introduction is marked *alla marcia*, march music, opening with drumrolls and trumpet calls, which are played on the stage throughout the interlude (score note, p. 46). Trills in a very high register played by piccolos are later added. The music grows increasingly more dramatic, leading up to several *fff* and dissonant measures, during which the curtain is to be raised "as quickly as possible" (score note, p. 49). Just before the curtain comes up, the unusual sound of a bull horn (*Stierhorn*) is heard, probably representing a call to arms. The action and text for this scene are based on Act I of Hebbel's play. Holofernes opens the scene singing toward the back of the stage, in a "terrifying" voice (*fürchterlicher*) and proclamatory tone: "There is no god but Nebuchadnezzar." Voices behind the scene echo the phrase. Holofernes then orders the Priests: "Go and smash Baal," which they agree to do. They exit and the rear tent wall is closed. Holofernes, alone now, curses Nebuchadnezzar

---

[18] Lacombe 2016.

in powerful phrases, marked *Agitato*, saying he had a great idea that he failed to carry out. The music is very gruff and blustery, softening a little as Holofernes continues over sustained chords:

> I have known it for a long time: mankind has only one great purpose, to bring forth a god, who will show that it is he by setting himself in eternal strife against them, grinding them into the dust and even in the hour of death, compelling them to sing an exultant song.

The final word, *Jubelruf*, is sung exultantly on a sustained F (*f'*), a fairly high and dramatic note for a bass-baritone (p. 52). A captain announces ambassadors from Mesopotamia, who beg for Holofernes's favor. The music is suddenly very "oriental," with exotic percussion and a pompous rhythm. He tells them they are late, but they insist that they are not the last to submit, because the Hebrews are still defying him. Holofernes tells him that in that case, he accepts their subjugation, and laughs heartily. The exotic "Mesopotamian" music returns.

A captain enters to announce that a Hebrew woman is outside, asking for him. (In the Hebbel play, the rest of this scene is found in Act IV). The music is slightly eerie, fluttering with "oriental" percussion sounds. Holofernes asks what kind of woman she is. The response, to suspenseful music of repetitive high pitches, is: "Master, every moment that you are not looking at her, is a lost moment. Were she not so beautiful, I would not have brought her to you." This is followed in the play by a lengthy account of finding Judith by a fountain, which adds more dimensions to her portrayal (see Chapter 3). One of the main themes of the opera is seduction and feminine beauty, which Lacombe points out is commonly expressed in chromaticism. This is found not only in Judith's music but also in Holofernes's aria in which he speaks about his own not so beloved mother (see below).[19] Holofernes, testing the captain, asks in a snarl if he "tried Judith out" (*Hast du sie versucht?*), and the captain, abashed, answers that she is beautiful but also demure (*spröde*). Holofernes is enraged that he would have approached her knowing she would please Holofernes, and he almost yells his next lines. He strikes the captain down, accompanied by terrifying music: a loud slide (almost a *glissando*) in the horns interrupted by a high and dissonant chord, followed by another *glissando* (p. 56). (This action is from Hebbel's play but occurs later in the scene there.)

Holofernes orders his soldiers to take the body out and bring in the woman, manifesting his ruthless nature. This is followed by a long monologue (from Hebbel's play) sung to lyrical music in a broad 9/8 time. Holofernes opens by proclaiming he is happy to see any woman in the world, except his own mother. He proclaims that a mother is a "mirror of her son's powerlessness." He says he never knew his mother because he was abandoned in a lion's den and suckled by a lioness; later he once crushed a lion in his arms. This pseudo-mythological account turns Holofernes into an almost superhuman hero, although it is not usually the hero who cites his own mythological

[19] Lacombe 2016.

origins. An aria follows in which he expresses his disturbing philosophies about conquering women (from Hebbel's play; pp. 59–63):

> A woman is a woman and yet one imagines that there is a difference. Truly a man feels his worth nowhere so much as on a woman's breast. Ha! when they strive, trembling, against his embraces, in a struggle between lust and shame; when they make feints at flight, and then, suddenly mastered by their nature, hurl themselves upon his neck; when their desire, awakened in every drop of blood by treacherous kisses, vies with the desire of the man … —yes, that is life; then one learns why the gods took the pains to make men. And it is complete, if their little souls were filled but a moment before with hate and cowardly rancor, if the hand that now caresses would gladly have mixed poison with his wine! That is the triumph of triumphs, and often have I celebrated it.

This aria contains the least tonal sections of the opera. The music is rambling and chaotic, with occasional outbursts. After the words "a woman's breast," the tempo increases and the next section, beginning with "Ha!," grows increasingly more excited. There is a climactic moment as Holofernes sings about conquering women's resistance on a long sustained *d'* over rapid descending passages in the orchestra, suggesting submission. The music becomes increasingly wild and abrasive. Near the end, the word "men" (*Menschen*) is sustained on *e'* for four measures (p. 62). The final word is sung on a *c#'*, also sustained for four measures, as drums and other timpani join in what sounds like celebratory music. This may rate as one of the ugliest portrayals of Holofernes in any opera, since it is based on Hebbel's play and magnified. The playwright's and composer's motive may have been to portray a repugnant Holofernes, which would put Judith's act in a positive light, since she is ridding the world of a monster. Yet it also shifts her motive from one of saving her own people to simply killing a violent and abusive man (particularly after he has raped her).

The music suddenly dies down as Judith enters, with Abra (p. 63). The music is soft and highlighted by short plangent solos in clarinet and oboe, in sharp contrast with the long and frenzied music of Holofernes's preceding aria. Judith is initially confused, but soon grasps the situation and throws herself at Holofernes's feet (score notes, p. 64). She sings: "ou are the one I was looking for, Holofernes," in a simple line over tonal chords. Holofernes makes the oft-quoted comment (in the original story) that a people who have such women are not to be despised (Jdt 10:19, there said by a group of Assyrian soldiers). This phrase is sung to highly expressive music, with high violin *obbligatos*. In still more ecstatic music, he comments that looking at Judith is like taking an expensive bath. He adds, in a simple recitative, that only the blind are miserable and he swears never again to have anyone blinded (p. 65). Such throwaway phrases suggest a level of heartless evil far surpassing the biblical portrayal of Holofernes.

The dialogue that follows stays close to both the original story and Hebbel play. In a simple, sparsely accompanied recitative, Holofernes asks Judith why she has come. She answers that she knows that none can escape him, because her own God will deliver her people into his hands. Holofernes, laughing, says in playful music: "Because you are a woman, because you know that Holofernes has eyes in his head" (p. 67). The music for these phrases is marked *scherzando* or playful. Judith tells Holofernes that "the wrath of our God is kindled against us. Long has He made known through his prophets that He will punish my people for their sin." The music, filled with octave leaps, starts lightly and becomes increasingly urgent. Judith falls to her knees. Holofernes tells Judith that he had sworn to destroy these people, but that now he needs to take back that oath. Judith, laughing shrilly, proclaims that she was foolish. In excited music, she says she knows her people have brought on their own death. She adds (p. 69):

> I know that the Lord my God has appointed you His avenger,
> yet I throw myself, overpowered by mercy and pity, between them and you.
> Happy for me that your hand held fast its sword,
> that you did not let it fall to dry a woman's tears!

The last two phrases are sung over clear tonic chords, always a marker of clarity in this opera. In very quick music, Holofernes responds: "Woman, I feel that you are playing with me … But no, I insult myself when I think that possible." This dialogue is a distillation of a far longer dialogue in Hebbel's play. Holofernes orders a servant to set the table and to bring much wine and dancers. The goal is presumably to awaken Judith's sensuality with exotic dances. After he has ordered the dancers, Holofernes and Judith stand apart, looking at each other with increasing interest (score note), over rhapsodic passages. Abruptly breaking the mood, Holofernes brusquely says they will meet again after the feast and rushes off to his sleeping chamber.

Alone now, Judith prays to God (in the score, not in the libretto). Singing unaccompanied between rapid 16th-note phrases, Judith wonders what is happening and questions what she is feeling (p. 70). In slower and softer phrases, she sings: "I must not hate him or curse him—him, the executioner of my people!" She ruminates that she has come to kill him and yet has "this feeling." Her voice reaches *a*" on this phrase, projecting passion. There is a suggestion here, as in Hebbel's play, that Judith has feelings for Holofernes. This idea, a betrayal of the original biblical story, is a misogynist intimation that no woman could resist a man like Holofernes. Judith then begs God, in slower and very heartfelt music, not to leave her in this difficult hour (p. 71). She also pleads for strength and to not be led into temptation. She asks that her heart not betray her before the deed she has sworn to do—to save her people from annihilation. The tempo shifts to *Andante religioso fanatico* and a broad 12/8 time, with a soaring vocal line. Judith sings: "The Lord is my light and my salvation, and I should fear Him" (based on Ps 27) and similar biblically based verses. Each phrase takes the voice higher, up to *a*", to project her increasing desperation. In the conclusion, she simply asks God to hear her plea and be gracious to her, ending in a lower register.

The music abruptly shifts to a sweet and gracious tune in 4/4 time, to accompany the servants who are preparing the tables. A group of captains enters, among whom Achior is seen (score note; he has not yet appeared in the opera). An exchange between Holofernes's servants is inserted here before the dance (not in the libretto), based on text from the opening of Act IV of Hebbel's play. One of the captains says that Holofernes "looks like a fire about to go out." A second captain responds: "One must beware of such a fire. It devours all that comes near it, to nourish itself." They are quiet as Holofernes approaches, without weapons and dressed in a tunic, lost in thought as reflected in the slow and plodding music (p. 76). He sits at the table and makes a sign to begin the banquet (score notes, p. 76). The dancers rush in to excited music.

The dance is an addition to the play; dances are frequently a part of operas and one was included in the Goossens opera of only several years after Reznicek's (discussed below). A good example of Reznicek's instrumental combinations is found in this dance music. The sinuous music prominently features cor anglais and oboe, both sensual sounds, and exotic percussion. Other instruments are added for a fuller sound as the dance progresses. The dancers are virtually naked but covered in veils (libretto note). The role described in the score as "a female voice" sings an *arietta* in B-flat minor accompanied by harp and cymbals, with some melodic interjections from woodwinds (p. 80). At the same time, in a totally different key, some punctuated chords from the strings play harmonics doubled by the celesta. This creates an amazing and mysterious effect using bitonality[20] (two keys played simultaneously).

After the dance reaches it wildest point, it dies down gradually, with very effective use of rests of increasing lengths, suggesting exhaustion. The dancers stagger out, while Holofernes sits brooding (score note, p. 84). The scene that follows is not in the libretto, so Reznicek clearly added it later. The text is from Hebbel's play and is a dialogue between Holofernes and Achior, completely out of sequence. Achior has not been introduced in the opera before this point, and this dialogue is taken from the first act of Hebbel's play. (His presence in the opera was previously only mentioned in a score note; see above.) The music remains calm throughout the duet. Holofernes asks Achior about the Hebrews, and Achior responds: "Lord, I know them well, these people, and I will tell you about them." The musical theme introducing this text is none other than Kol Nidre, heard predominantly in the overture but nowhere else before now. This prayer apparently is treated a *leitmotif* for the Hebrews. Presumably the melody would only be familiar to Jewish members of the audience. Achior continues, weaving in themes from the Kol Nidre melodies in the opening phrases:

> They are contemptible when they go forth with spears and swords, which their own god breaks in pieces, for he does not want them to fight and stain themselves with blood. He alone will undo their enemies. But these people are frightful when they humble themselves before their god as he demands; when they fall upon their knees and cover their heads with ashes; when they cry out in lamentation and curse themselves. Then it seems as if nature forgets her own laws.

On the text "these people are frightful," the music is more agitated and the accompaniment is mostly rapid *tremolos*, initially low and then high. Achior continues in the same vein, elaborating that the sea divides itself and bread falls from the heavens—clearly describing scenes from Exodus. The music for these descriptions vividly describes the scenes with very suggestive rippling harp arpeggios (p. 87).

---

[20] Lacombe 2016.

This music stops as Achior tells Holofernes the name of the Hebrew God, "Jahweh." (In Hebbel's play, Achior says the name cannot be pronounced aloud.) The last part of Achior's speech is based on Hebbel's play as well as on the original story (Jdt 5:20–21), in which he tells Holofernes it will only be safe to attack the Hebrews if they have sinned against their God. Achior proclaims those words in strong, accented phrases. He also explains that if they have not sinned, their God will protect them, being more powerful than Holofernes. Holofernes, furious, orders Achior bound and taken to Bethulia, to share the Hebrews' fate. In strong and heavily accented music, Holofernes proclaims that whoever finds Achior in Bethulia the next day during the battle and brings him his head will be rewarded its weight in gold (from Hebbel's play; p. 90).

That entire scene belongs early in the story, before the appearance of Judith. Reznicek has inserted it in the middle of the banquet scene, a very puzzling choice. After Holofernes has had Achior dragged away, he sings lightly: "Now let's drink and be happy, and hear how I will deal with the Hebrew God." Cutting short a lengthy scene from the play, Reznicek leads directly into Holofernes's "drinking song" (p. 91). This too is not in the original libretto.[21] This drinking song is heavier and more ominous in mood than traditional operatic drinking songs. Heavy, dissonant chords crash loudly in the bass, accented by cymbals and bass drum. High trills shrieking in the winds provide contrast and add to the foreboding mood. The accompaniment is marked *sempre pesante* (always heavy). The opening words are "Wine, ha ha, blood red, sparkling wine, ho ho," echoed by the chorus. After these opening bars, the tempo doubles and switches to 6/8 time for several measures, "with dithyrambic momentum" (score note, p. 91; a dithyramb is a wild choral hymn of ancient Greece, usually dedicated to Dionysus). To excited music dominated by constant high *tremolos*, he sings: "Wine loosens the tongue, opens the heart, and swells the breast."

Returning to the original tempo, he continues:

> It takes me to dizzy heights, to the thrones of gods, gives strength without measure. So, Jahweh, hear my oath: Surrender Bethulia, lay it at my feet, and you, Jahweh, will be my God. I drink to you!

Holofernes's promise to the Hebrew God is based on a passage in the original story, but there he says it to Judith: if she does as she says she will, her God will be his God (Jdt 11:23). But that is different than making the same oath directly to God. After a repeat of the first verse of the drinking song, Holofernes again addresses God directly, "oath against oath": "If Bethulia does not surrender, I will scourge you, level the city and destroy the Hebrews." After each promise, the soldiers laugh heartily and cheer him lustily after the final phrase. He sings this oath as a recitative, accompanied only by sustained chords, which gives it more power. He raises his glass to Yahweh one final time (p. 95). Some of the text of this section is based on Act V of Hebbel's play, but the

---

[21] Conductor Lacombe (2016) comments: "The hard and merciless personality of Holofernes is described by the use of a scale where there is no tonal pole or harmonic attraction and where all relationships between each note of the scale are equal: the whole-tone scale. This leads to one of the most original 'drinking songs' ever written."

direct address to Yahweh is original to the opera. The music throughout this section is violent and dissonant, in sharp contrast to Holofernes's drinking song in other, earlier operas. The drinking song is usually a vehicle for Holofernes to proclaim his love for women, in particular Judith, and for wine. His character is much darker in this opera, as in Hebbel's play.

A very dramatic orchestral interlude, including predominant brass, depicts muffled thunder. Judith is seen in the background, standing in a humble pose. The pale light creates an eerie mood. Holofernes spots Judith and sends the servants away (p. 97) and over ominous rumbling in the orchestra warns them that whoever disturbs him tonight will pay with his head. The music is marked "tranquil" as he approaches Judith. Following Hebbel's text, he tells her to sit and comments that she is pale and her "bosom is fluttering." This last phrase is accentuated with a sinuous, "fluttering" clarinet passage. He asks if he terrifies her, and she says he has been gracious to her. He shouts, insisting she be honest, but when she tries to answer he silences her, saying she dares too much. Then he grabs the "barely reluctant" Judith toward the bed and, over ecstatic chromatic music, tells her to give him the first kiss, which she does. Then, as in Hebbel, she says to herself: "Oh, why am I a woman?" (p 98). A modern reader would interpret that as an expression of anger at being helpless and taken advantage of. But the music suggests a different subtext: that Judith is succumbing to her own arousal or attraction, as she believes women are expected to do. The subtext of the music makes more obvious what the play's text only suggested. The rest of the scene, though condensed, is all text from Hebbel's play. Holofernes looks at Judith and exults, in appropriately ecstatic music (p. 99):

> How she glows! Like a meteor that I once saw in the dark sky ... Welcome, lust heated on the flames of hate. Kiss me, Judith! Your lips bore like leeches and yet are cold. Drink wine, Judith. In wine is all we lack.

He sings "Kiss me, Judith" on a descending passage (p. 100). After the kiss, the music becomes very loud and dissonant, with loud horn passages and opening with a *tremolo* on *A* against a loud *B flat*—a harsh dissonance. Just after the kiss, on the recording Judith utters a sound of distress.

There is no more suggestion of ecstasy for this second kiss. After kissing him, she responds: "Yes, in wine there is courage!" Then she throws down her glass of wine and begins to weep, asking forgiveness. Holofernes tells her he can see into her heart and knows she hates him. Rising, in music now marked *Agitato*, she admits that she hates him, that he must know how much she hates and curses him if she is not to go mad. (Holofernes can be heard chuckling on the recording during these lines.) The first two phrases are sung on descending major seventh intervals: *ich* (I) is sung on *c'* followed by *hasse dich* (hate you) on *d-flat'* and *du sollst es wissen* (you must know) starts on *d"* and makes the same descent. The next line builds quickly up to *wahnsinnig* (mad), which is sung *fortissimo* on *a"*, followed by a loud and rapid scale in the orchestra descending over two octaves. After an eerie and suspenseful measure, Judith sings "Now kill me" *a cappella* on middle C (almost spoken, on the recording). The wide range and large interval leaps in these passages suggest frenzy. After a long pause,

Holofernes answers "ironically": "Kill you? Maybe tomorrow; tonight you will serve my desire" (*Heute dienst du meiner Lust*). This is followed by a suspenseful passage leading to a very expressive section. Judith says to herself: "I must kill him, if I'm not to kneel to him." Holofernes continues in faster and heavier music, in the broad time of 6/4 over hammering repetitive notes in the orchestra. The relentlessness of the music combined with the text builds suspense and terror: "Behold, woman, these arms of mine have been plunged to the elbows in blood; my every thought brings forth horror and devastation; my word is death."

Their voices come together briefly in rhythmical, strongly accented phrases (p. 103), as Judith sings: "God of my fathers, save me from myself, that I may not honor what I abhor!" At the same time, Holofernes sings: "Let him come who will oppose me, who will overthrow me! I long for him." There are rare moments of tonality in the duet. Then Holofernes continues alone, singing of his own glory to very dramatic storm music including shrieking piccolos and powerful horn passages: "The hurricane passes through the air, but it uproots the oak trees that seem to defy him. He overturns the towers and lifts the globe off its hinges." After the climactic conclusion, with loud descending horn passages, Judith, trembling, sings softly: "And if the Lord hurls the lightning at you to dash you to pieces?" This is sung as an *a capella* recitative with only a low sustained chord under her voice, a dramatic contrast to the previous passages (p. 105). He vaingloriously responds that he would then stretch out his own hand and "the flash of Death will clothe me in somber majesty." This last word is sung on f', quite high in the bass-baritone range, and is followed by a very loud, dramatic group of dissonant chords (p. 106). The next two measures are unaccompanied.

Judith, appalled, calls him a horrible monster, in a phrase that leaps down a tenth from f' to d'. (On the recording, it is half spoken, in breathless tones.) In contrast, Holofernes sings on a single note, as he commands her to fall on her knees and beg (p. 106). Her strong response, sung "with dignity" is: "Learn to respect women! A woman stands before you to murder you, and she tells you!" The last words are sung very low in the range, down to b. (These words are spoken, very effectively, on the recording, followed by a shouted *Ja!* ("Yes!") not in the score. Also on the recording, Holofernes chuckles when she says this.) Of course, this plot completely distorts the original story, in which Judith succeeds in killing Holofernes through stealth, not laying out all her cards.

Holofernes comments to himself how desirable Judith is, in two ominous-sounding measures marked *Lento misterioso* (very slow and mysterious) in the very broad 6/4 time. Then switching back to 4/4 time and singing *a cappella*, he tells her he wants to "know" her (*kennen lernen*), a euphemism she surely understood (as would the audience). He downs another glass of wine and grabs the reluctant Judith. In faster ascending and descending passages to an excited dotted rhythm, they wrestle and then he asks her to straighten herself out. She wriggles free again and runs to the other side of the bed. Their voices sometimes come together, or follow on the heels of one another, creating the feeling of a wild chase. The music vividly depicts anxiety and quick movements. Out of breath, Judith says: "I must ... I will ... shame on me if I cannot," an ambivalent phrase suggesting either that she is giving in or working up the courage to kill him (p. 107). The time signature changes constantly throughout this scene, creating instability.

Another duet follows. Judith sings: "My senses and my thoughts whirl like dry leaves," while Holofernes sings that he knows she wants to kill him, but: "To extinguish the lightning that threatens the world fire—oh that may be tempting! I could be seduced by that myself, if I were not who I am." While he is still singing those lines, Judith sings in a high range: "Man, monster!" (*Entsetzlicher*), reaching a *b-flat*" on that word (p. 108). She continues to sing, together with his voice, that he is forcing himself between her and her God, that she needs to pray but cannot. At the same time, he asks Judith to show him the fire that can both extinguish and nourish itself. To steady and heavy repeated chords, he sings that the answer is power:

> I bore deeper and deeper with my sword. Judith, no one dwells in your heart except God, and I want to now drive him out. I want to destroy you. You must die before me through the betrayal of your senses.

At the same time, Judith sings that she sees more clearly now, that Holofernes trusts in his power but does not realize it has gone astray and left him, that it has become his enemy: "Tremble, Holofernes, the avenger is near!" This final line is an addition by Reznicek. The first word, *Zittre*, is sung on high C (*c*" with an optional lower note written in), with a clear C major chord under her voice. In a sea of dissonance, this moment of clarity and purpose stands out. The final word, *Rächer* (p. 110), is sung on a sustained *a*". Only in music, albeit very fast and chaotic in this case, can two characters be simultaneously expressing such opposing thoughts.

As the duet concludes, fast and "frenetic" music (score note, p. 111) begins as Holofernes lifts Judith and carries her to the bedchamber. Voices are heard from far away, singing in lyrical phrases "Always yearning, never sated, eternally longing" over strumming harp—echoes of the earlier dance. Abra creeps into the tent to eerie music, marked *Lento misterioso* (very slow and mysterious). Under this music, she sings: "Quiet!" (*Still*) twice, first on a low *b* and after a few more measures of the eerie music, while listening at the entrance to the bedchamber, again on *b'*. Pointing toward the bedchamber, she sings very hesitantly in broken phrases: "I believe that there, someone is being murdered" (deleting from Hebbel's play "whether Judith or Holofernes I do not know"). She expresses her fear and anxiety, relating this story to faster and anxious music (p. 113):

> I once stood upon the shore and watched a man who was drowning. Anxiety urged me to jump in after him. Then I screamed as loud as I could, screaming only in order not to hear his screams. So I speak now! O Judith, Judith! I have no courage; I am very afraid. But it is not fear speaking now, not a dread of failure.

The music shifts from one mood to another during this short section, reflecting the many moods Abra is experiencing. Loud and very dissonant measures precede her line: "A woman should bear men, never should she kill them" (p. 115).

Judith, her hair disheveled, comes crashing into the room now, to agitated music with strong rhythms (marked *Agitato*). She cries out that it is too bright and tells Abra to extinguish the candles because they are brazen (or shameless: *unverschämt*). Accompanied by several measures marked *Espressivo, lamentoso* (expressive and lamenting), with descending chromatic passages in the bass and harsh minor seconds above them, Abra comments on Judith's glowing cheeks. Judith cries out that Abra should not look at her. More dramatically, she sings that no one should see her. That phrase starts on *g#"* and rapidly descends through a C#-minor cadence to *e'*. The opening chord is in C# minor with an intrusive dissonant F double sharp (enharmonic G). Abra sympathetically tells Judith to lean on her and to leave with her. Judith relates her horrifying story, in music marked *Allegro tempestoso*, fast and tempestuous (p. 117):

> He dragged me off, he pulled me down upon his shameful couch, can you endure all this? And now I must be repaid for the annihilation which I suffered in his arms; now I will wash off with his heart's blood the degrading kisses which still burn upon my lips.

In softer and calmer music, Judith asks Abra if she does not blush to take her away from there. Abra asks Judith what she is thinking. Judith, surprised, calls Abra "miserable creature," wondering that her heart has not told her. (A loud percussive sound during these words, on the recording, suggests Judith is banging on the floor for emphasis.) She continues her account, to a furious and turbulent accompaniment (text based on Hebbel but very condensed):

> He tore off my neck scarf and praised my breasts. Then something bright glittered before my eyes! It was his sword. Upon that sword my reeling senses seized. Pray for me; now will I do it.

Judith's last phrase reaches a sustained *a"* while Abra sings under her "Awaken him, God," ending on the same note and holding it longer than Judith. There is an interesting suggestion that Abra does not want Holofernes killed. Judith rushes into the chamber and snatches down the sword. Overcome by horror, Abra remains rooted to the spot. The offstage beheading is vividly suggested by the music. A rapid ascending figure ends in a high *tremolo* followed by two low thumping notes played *fff*. The same exact group of phrases is repeated three times (p. 120). The music abruptly calms and soon becomes triumphant, as Judith slowly walks out of the bedchamber, pale but upright. She stops at the entrance, the sword in her right hand, Holofernes's head in her left. An unearthly light shines above her (score notes). There is far more dialogue and the action is described much more fully in Hebbel's play. But the abruptness here has a stunning effect.

In faster, "jubilant" music, Judith brusquely tells Abra to hurry to the city and announce to her people: "Let rejoicing be heard in cymbals and drums. Holofernes is dead!" The music is lively and upbeat, and clearly tonal, in great contrast to the immediately preceding scene. Judith then tears the rear tent wall apart and the watchman can be seen sleeping. In a completely original twist, Judith exits the tent and confronts the Assyrians, holding Holofernes's head high: "See here, the head of Holofernes! Flee, or Jehovah's revenge will shatter all of you!" The word "Jehovah" is sung on a high B (*b*"). Judith flings the head under the horrified soldiers, who all cry out "Flee! Flee!" in quick and excited music. This confrontation presents a bolder Judith than other retellings, or even than the original story. The soldiers, horrified, scatter in all directions as the curtain quickly falls.

After an interlude of martial music, including trumpets on the stage and very exuberant yet dissonant music, the curtain rises to an initially empty stage, in early morning light. Judith appears at the front of the stage, looking shattered. The music is marked *Animato jubiloso* and is clearly tonic, in D major (p. 124). The Hebrews run in from all sides, waving flags and weapons, the women with palm fronds. As Osias, the priests, and elders all appear, the morning sky is red. Everyone sings "Hosanna! Hail!" in jubilant, triumphant music. Osias tells Judith to demand her reward, and she asks if he is mocking her. In simple, sparsely accompanied music, she asks: "If it hadn't been a sacred duty, was it then arrogance or sacrilege?" Her next words are in the score only, not in Hebbel or Reznicek's libretto. To very slow and broad music, in 12/8 time, she sings:

> I must bear my deed and it crushes me. Yes, I have killed the first and last man on earth … my heart is like a mortal wound. I must, and want, to die. God, give me strength for the final consummation (*Vollendung*). My task is completed, my people are free.

In still brighter and more majestic music, she praises God, accompanied by harp (p. 130).

Then she tells the people that she will demand her reward, but they must vow to honor it. They swear in the name of all of Israel. She tells them abruptly to kill her, over a quick, very dissonant orchestral figure. The final phrase reaches *a*" sung over a sharply dissonant chord. The people remain frozen in place, and then in breathless, broken phrases repeat her words and say: "Never!" So, Judith says, she will do it herself, stabbing herself. Furious music is heard as the chorus sings out "Judith! Stop!" The same low two-note "thumping" phrase heard when Holofernes was killed is repeated here, after a harshly dissonant chord. Then in very slow and calm music, as she is dying in Abra's arms, she sings breathlessly in a very low range: "I do not want to bear Holofernes' son." On these last two words, the key shifts to a bright B major and the tempo to *Adagio* (very slow). Judith dies to peaceful, almost heavenly music, with a high violin *obbligato* and a long high trill on F# that continues to the very end, as a *ppp* B-major chord ends the opera. Light floods the stage and the curtain falls quickly. It is not clear if her final words are heard by the crowd.

The music following Judith's suicide initially seems surprisingly peaceful for such a dramatic situation. Conductor Lacombe comments:

> Reznicek doesn't waste any time in telling us this story (she's dead, rest in peace … all of that in less than 12 bars!!!) … The sudden appearance of a perfectly tonal musical moment here gives an impression of purity and total release of any sort of

harmonic tensions that have built up to this point. This is the main idea/principle inspiring Reznicek both musically and dramatically for his entire opera.[22]

Conclusion

The opera's conclusion, like Hebbel's play on which it was based, obviously goes against the central thesis of the biblical story: that Judith remained untouched and that she spent the remainder of her days cloistered, honored by all of Israel. Hebbel's play reduces and distorts the story (see Chapter 3) to make it personal, and turns the beheading into a kind of rape revenge. In the play, Judith's demand is that the people will kill her when she asks them to. She privately tells her maid that they should pray that her womb will be unfruitful, in which case she can live. But Reznicek took it a step further and not only provided no glimmer of hope but also had Judith commit suicide in front of the whole town. The suggestion of martyrdom for Judith is a very Christian concept. Suicide is antithetical to Jewish history and practice,[23] as well as being a betrayal and corruption of the original story. It is upsetting to think that audiences who saw this opera—whether in 1923 or 2016—might be led to think this opera is true to the biblical story. Like the Hebbel play on which the opera is based, it is not so much a retelling of the story as a perversion. Yet as offensive as it is to modern readers and listeners—particularly biblical scholars—it is nonetheless important to understand how the original story has been used (and misused) in our time. The music is dramatic, interesting, and compelling, and this makes the opera worth listening to.

Sir Eugene Goossens (1893–1962)

Sir Eugene Goossens was a prominent British conductor and composer. Both his father, Eugène Goossens (1867–1958), and grandfather, Eugène Goossens (1845–1906), were noted conductors. Goossens conducted several orchestras in the UK, Australia, and the United States and he was knighted in 1955. His early compositions were influenced by Impressionism, but he later developed a polyphonic style, using impressionistic, chromatic, and sometimes almost atonal harmonies. In 1907, Goossens's skilled violin playing earned him a scholarship to the Royal College of Music in London (RCM), where his composition professor was the noted composer Sir Charles Villiers Stanford. After quickly gaining a reputation for his stylish compositions, Goossens was made an associate of the RCM in 1912. At the short-notice request of (Sir) Thomas Beecham, in 1916 Goossens conducted *The Critic*, an opera by Stanford. Goossens's success at his formal debut encouraged Beecham to use him as his unofficial deputy, and this arrangement lasted almost ten years. The collaboration led to prominent engagements such as directing Sergei Diaghilev's Les Ballets Russes and the Carl Rosa Opera

---

[22] Lacombe 2016.

[23] Suicide is not explicitly forbidden in any Jewish text but it is considered antithetical to Jewish laws and values. The only exceptions are in the case of martyrdom (such as at Masada).

Company at Covent Garden.[24] Goossens became a world-famous conductor and composer, a friend of Pablo Picasso and Igor Stravinsky. His friend Noel Coward once said: "My heart just loosens when I listen to Goossens."[25]

In 1921 Goossens assembled a virtuoso orchestra under his own name to give concerts of contemporary music in London. These included a critically acclaimed first concert performance in England of Stravinsky's *Le Sacre du Printemps*, with the approving composer in attendance. The *Evening News* referred to the young conductor as "London's Music Wizard."[26] He wrote the first of his two operas, *Judith*, in 1927 and it premiered at Covent Garden in 1929.[27] Goossens was upset that many reviews compared it to Richard Strauss's opera *Salome*. But Roger Covell, a preeminent Australian musicologist, states:

> A comparison could hardly have been avoided, since both works treat a biblical story in which the ideas of kissing and beheading are juxtaposed. Both works employ large orchestras. In Goossens' opera, the weight, colour and pungency of [the] orchestra, with two harps, triple wind and elaborate percussion, is used to emphasize the physical elements of the story with a kind of refined savagery. Goossens' sovereign command of orchestral color and texture can be heard in its most sustained form in [this] opera.[28]

In 1931 Goossens succeeded Fritz Reiner as permanent conductor of the Cincinnati Symphony Orchestra, and he held that position for fifteen years. By now a prominent figure in international music, he was appointed to the Légion d'honneur in 1934. Goossens used his authority as a conductor to champion new music in his programs. Salter describes Goossens as "a tall, handsome and immaculately dressed figure with thinning, swept-back hair, [who] conducted in the grand charismatic manner with a long baton and large beat." After a well-received tour of Australia that year, Goossens was appointed the first permanent conductor of the Sydney Symphony Orchestra (SSO). In addition, he was offered the directorship of the New South Wales State Conservatorium of Music. The combined salaries from those two posts reportedly provided him a combined income greater than that of the prime minister's.[29]

Goossens was determined to make the SSO "one of the six best orchestras in the world," starting by culling its weaker members and promoting younger players. Both the orchestra and the public responded enthusiastically to Goossens's musicianship and skill leading to the point where subscriptions soon doubled, and the Australian

[24] David Salter, "Goossens, Sir Eugene Aynsley (1893–1962)," *Australian Dictionary of Biography* 14 (1996). Available online: http://adb.anu.edu.au/biography/goossens-sir-eugene-aynsley-10329 (accessed April 30, 2020).

[25] Shane Maloney and Chris Grosz, "Eugene Goossens & the Witch of Kings Cross," *The Monthly*, March 2009. Available online: https://www.themonthly.com.au/issue/2009/february/1290492531/shane-maloney/eugene-goossens-witch-kings-cross (accessed April 30, 2020).

[26] Salter 1996.

[27] "Sir Eugene Goossens: British Conductor," *Britannica*. Available online: https://www.britannica.com/biography/Eugene-Goossens (accessed April 30, 2020).

[28] Roger Covell, liner notes for sound recording, 1984.

[29] Salter 1996.

Broadcasting Commission was able to attract top-ranking soloists and conductors to perform with its orchestras. Goossens introduced Australian audiences to more than fifty major works that had previously been considered too difficult or inaccessible. At the Conservatorium, Goossens insisted on an immediate improvement in standards, leading him to fail whole classes, dismiss staff, and use his reputation in Europe to recruit new teachers. He also staged a series of ambitious opera performance. Those included his own *Judith* for which he selected a little-known local 25-year-old dramatic soprano, (Dame) Joan Sutherland, to make her operatic debut in the title role, in 1951. (This is certainly a little-known fact! Sutherland had in fact previously made her stage, but not opera, debut in Henry Purcell's *Dido and Aeneas* in 1947.) Goossens continued to teach many classes, and his students included Richard Bonynge (who married Sutherland a few years later) and Geoffrey Parsons, who became an internationally renowned accompanist.[30]

The music of Goossens's 1927 opera *Judith* is dramatic and changeable. The strongest influence, in this listener's view (and of other critics: see above), is Strauss. Both his operas *Salome* (1905) and *Der Rosenkavalier* (1913) must have been well known and studied by Goossens. The predominant use of bells and glockenspiel along with other less common percussion instruments has powerful echoes of those two Strauss operas. In fact, several reviews of the Covent Garden premiere commented on the similarities between the two works (see above).

Arnold Bennett (1867–1931), the librettist for *Judith*, based the libretto on his own play of 1919. (The two collaborated on another opera in 1935.) The two men first met at a friend's house in 1911, where Goossens was playing in a string quartet and Bennett, a great lover of music, was attending. Bennett was impressed by Goossens's talent and musicianship and kept an eye on him, considering him a kind of protégé. When Goossens returned from a tour in America in 1924, he persuaded Bennett to turn his *Judith* play into a one-act opera. The only change Goossens made (in the part of the play he used) was the addition of a dance sequence, which he added much later.[31]

The libretto is a very abridged version of the play, which, in George Simmers's words, "was largely written in what was then called the Wardour Street style (because Wardour Street was then London's center for second-hand furniture). It is full of archaisms, and sentences whose rhythm is clunkily reminiscent of the King James Bible."[32] The playwright and composer were close collaborators. Bennett wrote to their publisher about the requirements for the sets and costumes for the opera:

> In my opinion the set should be simple, except as regards the large tent in the centre, which should be elaborate. The more attention is concentrated on the tent the better. The text of the opera gives all necessary indications. I think that the

---

[30] Salter 1996.

[31] Covell, liner notes.

[32] George Simmers, "Arnold Bennet's 'Judith,'" *George Simmers's Research Blog.* Available online: https://greatwarfiction.wordpress.com/2011/01/08/arnold-bennetts-judith/ (accessed April 30, 2020). Go there for a longer discussion of the play and a photo of the leading actress playing Judith.

costumes, especially Judith's, Holofernes' and Bagoas', are more important than the set. The first and last ought to be very rich. In the play Miss Lilah McCarthy (Lady Keble) wore as little as propriety and the censor would allow—that is after she had removed her travelling garment. It is to be remembered that she came prepared to fascinate Holofernes.[33]

Because the playwright also wrote the libretto, I am going to discuss some action in the play (including the entire third act) that was left out of the much shorter libretto. The opera is in one act, the play in three. The first act of the play takes place in Bethulia; the second in Holofernes'a camp and tent, where the entire opera takes place; and the third act is back in Bethulia. This play is well worth exploring and is widely available for purchase or downloading. It is available as an e-book.[34] I will discuss Acts I and III of the play. Any comments on Act II of the play that are interspersed with the discussion of the opera will be bracketed to avoid (and hopefully not increase) confusion.

Judith, a Play in Three Acts Founded on the Apocryphal Book of Judith (1919)

The first act of the play features extensive bantering and philosophizing between the elders of Bethulia, conversations filled with insights, humor, and pathos. In this scene, the plot of the original story is related quite accurately through the mouth of Ozias, depicted as a self-righteous and pompous leader. In a completely original twist, he is in love with Judith and hopes to marry her. After Judith has entered, Achior is found bound outside the walls. The people drag him in, calling him an Assyrian and calling out to slay, stone, and whip him. Judith's response is "nobly scornful": "Oh, brave men of courage and high valour!" The sarcasm adds a new and appealing element to her personality. The people question Achior, who explains how he angered Holofernes and was taken to the foothills of Bethulia. Ozias and Judith, in a battle of wills, argue about whether they can trust Achior. Ozias wants him chained, but Judith says she knows he is telling the truth by looking in his eyes. In the original story, there was no such argument: all the people accepted Achior's story. Bennett has created a conflict between Ozias and Judith that highlights her wisdom and strength contrasted with his concern only for himself.

A lengthy dialogue between Judith and Ozias is followed by a scene between Haggith (Judith's servant) and a soldier.[35] She is seen bringing sacks from the house and confesses that she and her mistress are going on a journey. Judith kneels and offers her prayer, using the biblical text (Jdt 9) but here offering the prayer publicly rather

---

[33] James Hepburn, ed., *Letters of Arnold Bennett, Volume I: Letters to J.B. Pinker* (London: Oxford University Press, 1966), p. 387. [There is a footnote to the page: "Eugene Goossens remarks in his book *Overtures and Beginners* that 'apart from Shaw, I doubt whether any writer of this period had read or acquired more knowledge about the subject of music than Arnold Bennett.'"] My thanks to the Arnold Bennett Society for providing me with copies of these documents.

[34] http://www.gutenberg.org/ebooks/12794 (accessed May 17, 2019).

[35] Haggith was one of David's wives; her name means "festive." She is mentioned in 2 Sam 3:4, 1 Kgs 1–2, and 1 Chr 3:2. It is not clear why the writer chose this name for Judith's servant. Haggith is mentioned in the Bible only as Adonijah's mother; she has no independent role in David's story.

than in private. A small gesture crucial to the plot is Haggith retrieving a knife from Judith's house and handing it to Judith, who conceals it in her dress. This undercuts one of the main themes of the biblical account, the fact that Judith leaves without a weapon or a plan, while the play includes both.

Act II of the play opens with an interesting scene between Haggith and an Assyrian guard. She is portrayed as clever, charming, and manipulative. In no other work discussed here does Judith's servant have these qualities or this much personality. But it does not contradict the original story, where the servant never speaks. Her paving the way for their entrance into the camp with a charm offensive is not an implausible notion. She tells the guard that she has come from Bethulia in search of water, because they have none. She seduces him with her words to gain an ally in the camp and then tells him she is with her mistress. Suddenly the guard is alarmed at the approach of Bagoas. The guard tells Haggith that Bagoas is chief eunuch of the Prince, in charge of all the women of the Prince's tents. Haggith is startled to learn of the presence of multiple wives, concubines, and virgins. When Bagoas approaches, the guard introduces Haggith as a woman of the Hebrews. Bagoas scornfully says to her: "Rise, scum, and let me behold thy deformity." When told that her mistress, Judith, is also there, he says the name "is fit only for a cat!" and wonders suspiciously why she has come, what her "detestable purpose" is. From this point on, the opera libretto follows the play very closely. Some action is omitted from the opera, but the text is taken almost verbatim from the play.

Judith, an Opera in One Act, Opus 55 (1927)

> Judith: dramatic soprano
> Haggith, her servant: mezzo
> Holofernes: bass-baritone
> Bagoas, chief eunuch: tenor
> Achior: baritone

The score is available in some libraries.

A sound recording is stored at the National Library of Australia; I obtained a private copy of an LP recording, on which I based my analysis.

The opera takes place entirely in Holofernes's camp (as in one other work discussed: Hillemacher's 1876 *scène lyrique*, which is only one scene, like this one-act opera; see Chapter 2). The time is "towards evening." The slow and ominous opening features loud horns, heavy winds and lower strings playing a chromatic theme in octaves. A gong is also heard, all of which creates a foreboding and dark atmosphere. This music introduces the voice of Achior, heard from behind the curtain. He is proclaiming to Holofernes that the God of Israel is great and has given power and strength to his people. Singing over *tremolos* and drums, he warns Holofernes to attack only if the Bethulians commit an error against God; otherwise, he should pass them by. This section is taken directly from Scene 1 of the play, though there it is in the context of his confrontation with Holofernes. After this proclamation, the curtain rises (p. 4). Achior is chained at the center of the stage, in Holofernes's camp, before being sent to Bethulia.

Highly dramatic music ensues, in cut time (twice as fast as previously), as Achior is dragged in by Holofernes's guards and bound to a stake with ropes. This is a deviation from the original story (and the play), in which Achior was taken back to Bethulia and left outside the gates. Since the action in this opera all takes place in Holofernes's camp, the plot was altered. A frenzied orchestral section describes the action. When the guards exit, the music slows by half as Haggith enters, carrying a sack (score note, p.5). She is startled to see Achior bound and asks him why he is there. She tells him that she is a Hebrew from Bethulia. He acknowledges that this is the city besieged by his lord Holofernes, which of course Haggith knows already. She says she left to find water for her thirst, since in Bethulia, men are dying of thirst in the streets. Then she tells him she escaped "into the plain" with her mistress. (If Haggith is seeking water, the obvious question is why she is holding only a sack.) She indicates Judith's approach, for which the tempo and mood change abruptly and dramatically (p. 8).

Haggith introduces Achior to Judith as "an Assyrian, an evildoer" (in the play, they met in the first act). Judith imperiously tells Haggith to stand aside as she looks at Achior. As she does so, the music suddenly becomes very expressive. Achior is impressed by Judith's beauty and tells her so, also warning her, over shimmering *tremolos*, that she is in danger because she is standing in front of the tent of Holofernes which no one dare approach. Haggith is alarmed, which suggests that in this plot Judith never told her servant where they were going, only that they were seeking water (perhaps the knife was for self-defense?). Judith tells Achior, in very simple music, that this is whom she is seeking. Achior warns her that "the terrible Bagoas" will appear at sunset and that he has great power, since he is in charge of all the women of Holofernes's tent. Judith responds, echoing the same musical phrase she sang before: "I will speak with him," and when told Holofernes will also come, she says she will speak with him too, repeating the same musical phrase. To more anxious music, Achior tells her again that she is in danger, but Judith insists that she is not. Repeated trumpet calls sound, like an alarm, as Judith decides to confide in Achior the reason for her visit (score note, p. 13).

Judith assertively announces that she has come to save Bethulia from the hand of Holofernes. Achior tells her Holofernes's hand is too almighty to be overcome. But Judith explains that she has come by the will of God to save her people. As she says this, a half-veiled Assyrian woman appears briefly behind the tent, looks at them, and disappears (score note, p. 15; one or more of these figures appears randomly throughout the play). Judith realizes that Achior is not an "evil-doer" and asks him who he really is. He explains that he is the Captain of the Ammonites in the army of Holofernes. He tells her his story, which hews closely to the original, summing up the account in Jdt 5. His music opens to a strong and steady beat, but the time signature shifts in every measure, giving the music almost a conversational feeling (p. 16). This changes completely when he talks about the Hebrews, and the music grows very lyrical, particularly when Achior mentions God; it is much more dramatic when he talks of the "forsaken' people" (p. 19). The mood shifts continually, corresponding to the text. Judith, enthralled by Achior's narrative, urges him to continue, while Achior is "lost in admiration of her beauty" (score note, p. 20). This alters and amplifies the relationship between Judith and Achior, which was never romantic in the original story. In his conclusion, Achior repeats the words heard at the opening of the opera. In more threatening music, he tells Judith how Holofernes's face darkened, and he relays what he said. In this case the words are taken straight from the book of Judith (5:2–4), but in the original story they are never related to Judith by Achior or anyone else.

Judith is "deeply moved" by Achior's story and after a few measures of highly charged music, representing her indecision, she decides to free him. She orders Haggith to take the knife from the sack and uses it to cut his bonds. Introducing a knife—in Judith's possession, no less—at this point in the story is somewhat anticlimactic. In the play's first act, she is seen leaving Bethulia with the knife (see above). She tells Achior that because he speaks with the voice of their God, she is freeing him. He warns her again of her danger, and again she insists she is not the one in danger. As Achior exits, he blesses Judith. Trumpets are heard onstage (score note). Judith and Haggith are alone on the stage. Judith hands the knife to Haggith, who puts it in the sack. Judith now recites a prayer, based on the text of the original story, 9:2–14. (She recites this prayer before leaving Bethulia in the play; see above). This is some of the strongest music in the opera, though the mood is more frenzied than pleading (see Figure 6). The prayer was often a highlight in English oratorios of the late nineteenth century (see Chapter 2). Unlike most other retellings, this version does not eliminate the reference to "deceitful lips" (Jdt 9:10, 12); in fact, it includes both verses containing this text. Judith sings dramatically high notes on crucial words: "by the hand of a woman: reaches *b*" (p. 30) and on "God" she sings *a*". After her triumphant conclusion on *f#*" to be sung *fff* and sustained for three full measures, the orchestra plays a strong postlude that dies down as "onfused sounds offstage" are heard (score note). Haggith tells Judith someone is approaching and warns her to beware.

Following a few measures of alarming music, Bagoas enters, "with a train of attendants, soldiers, servants, slaves, etc." (score note, p. 32). Both the playwright and composer greatly expanded the role of Holofernes's eunuch slave. The scherzo-like music accompanying his pompous entrance suddenly grows very agitated as he is startled to see Judith and Haggith. They immediately bow and then rise. The scene between Bagoas and Judith that follows is completely invented. (In the play, it is preceded by a brief dialogue between Bagoas and Haggith). Bagoas asks Judith who she is and she responds in light and simple music, over sustained chords (p. 34). Then he asks who Haggith is, and when Judith answers "my serving woman," Bagoas sharply orders his attendants to "take the slut away from my face." After Haggith is taken away, Bagoas looks at Judith and tells her "blandly" (score note) that she is very beautiful. Though the composer indicated "blandly," the music belies that indication, since it is soaring, filled with bells and high strings. Judith answers: "There are beautiful women in Judea but no man there looks twice at such as me, a shrunken widow like dried fish!" Judith never utters such a self-deprecating remark in either the original story or any retelling. It may be intended to be a form of manipulation, to hide her self-confidence from Bagoas. He asks what her errand is, and she tells him in almost monotone phrases that it is "to have speech with the illustrious Prince and mighty conqueror Holofernes."

Stage trumpets are heard again, as Bagoas decides, after his initial surprise, to grant Judith's request (score notes, p. 36). He sings pompously, to music marked *Allegro giocoso* (fast and cheerful), over regular groups of 8th notes, that they are well matched, since he is the "chief eunuch of the almighty Holofernes." (He orders an

Figure 6 Eugene Goossens, "Judith's Prayer"

attendant to bring a box of veils for Judith at this moment in the play.) Then in an aside, he says to an attendant: "If this be a pattern of the women of Bethulia I shall have momentous employment when the city falls," obviously implying that many women of the conquered city will enter the harem. Though he is making light of it, to the modern reader it is a terrible reminder of the fate that awaited captive women in that world. He adds: "This dried fish by her damnable beauty will attain great power in Assyria" and comments that he has to tread lightly to stay on her good side (pp. 37–8).

These bitter but amusing lines add an interesting touch to the story, one that does not contradict the original meaning but adds a lighthearted moment while also displaying the heartless realities of war in that (and every) era.

Bagoas asserts his power by insisting Judith tell him why she has come to see Holofernes, because she can only have access to the Prince through him. She refuses, insisting she will only talk of her errand to Holofernes. Over a series of quick dissonant chord groups (p. 40), an infuriated Bagoas calls Judith a series of insulting names—minx, shameless wrench, and in the play, the archaic terms of insult "chit" and "mopsy." He warns her that if she does not obey him, chief eunuch of all the camps of Assyria, he will make her the slave of his slaves. He continues with his threats in dissonant but subdued music (p. 41), concluding that she will learn how much power Bagoas possesses. Judith, singing softly and sweetly and "smiling soothingly" (score note), addresses him as "Mightiness, mightiness," this salutation reaching a high B flat (*b-flat"*). She agrees that she is Bagoas's servant, yet also insists that it was determined by Heaven that she will speak with "the illustrious Holofernes alone." A few measures of lyrical music, marked *Tranquillo ma espressivo*, follow. Bagoas, "under the spell of Judith's beauty, begins to relent" (score note, p. 42). In an aside, he sings: "The sweetness of her glance dissolves my backbone," a wonderfully descriptive phrase set to soaring music, including bells and glockenspiel.

The music slows to half the tempo as Bagoas agrees that if it was appointed by Heaven, it must be, and he apologizes for testing her. In an aside, very softly under continual high *tremolos*, he says he will lead her away, for if the Prince even just sees her before taking Bethulia, Bagoas fears it will never be conquered, and they will all be her slaves. As he leads Judith away, a theme is heard in trumpets and then cellos as Judith momentarily recoils, but as the music grows more resolute, she recalls her purpose and her courage returns (score notes). As loud and pompous music is heard, highlighted by many trumpet fanfares, the heralds of Holofernes appear. Bagoas, realizing his master is close, quickly orders the attendants to hide Judith, "or Assyria is undone this day" (p. 45). Bagoas's remarks add an interesting twist to the plot. He has a much smaller role in the original story and in most, but not all, musical retellings. His attendants stand in front of Judith, trying to block her.

Holofernes's entrance is marked by a series of rapid and long ascending chromatic passages in the orchestra, growing steadily faster and louder: a vivid buildup to this climactic moment in the opera. Loud, Wagnerian-sounding brass introduces Holofernes; this will become almost a *leitmotif*. He enters blustering "Where is this woman?" and when Bagoas feigns ignorance, Holofernes tells him "This Hebrew woman," rumors of whose appearance have "spread like a plague" through the camps. He wonders why he has not yet seen her, whose beauty "exceeds all the beauty of the East and ravishes the eye" (p. 48). This phrase is sung to romantic music with a hint of melancholy, a high oboe *obbligato* underlining this mood. Bagoas, affecting surprise (score note), lightly says: "Ah! It is Judith … I have caught her, but she hides in shame from the glances of my Lord." Then he brusquely tells his attendants: "Stand aside, dogs!" Judith is revealed; she prostrates herself and then rises. Holofernes is entranced (score note), as suggested in music that echoes Wagner's *Tristan und Isolde*.

His first words to her follow the biblical text very closely (Jdt 11:1–2). But right after he reassures Judith, Bagoas tells Holofernes in an aside not to trust her, that she is full of guile and must have a hidden purpose against them. Holofernes warns him to be quiet before he is overthrown and insists that Judith's face has no guile. When he asks Judith her purpose, she says she must speak with him alone. Bagoas whispers to Holofernes that it is a device against him. Holofernes apparently ignores both this remark and Judith's request, and now commands Judith to speak.

She explains, in a dramatic opening, that her message concerns the fate of Bethulia, the Assyrians, and her Lord, this last word sung on *a*" (p. 52). The vocal line is very simple, with many repeated notes over sustained chords. Unlike in other retellings, Judith does not relate a long story but simply tells Holofernes that she has communed with God. Holofernes challenges her to say which God—hers or his? The next part of this dialogue is an *a cappella* recitative. Judith responds calmly that there is only one God, to which Holofernes immediately cuts in with "And he is Nebuchadnezzar." Then he asks Judith to continue, to speak from the heart and quickly. She says resolutely (score note), singing *a cappella* to indicate her strength and resolve: "I will speak to my Lord in his tent." This is followed by a measure of harsh chords as Holofernes menacingly responds: "In my tent?!" He asks who she is that she can defy him and defile his tent. In a deviation from the play, Holofernes warns Judith that his anger has already struck down the insolent Achior who provoked him "with cackling of this Hebrew God." Then he looks around and asks where Achior is, since he wants to show him to Judith as an example. He looks to Bagoas for an answer, but Bagoas, frightened, says that his role does not include taking charge of captives. The music reflects Holofernes's fury as he continues to ask where Achior is. Judith assertively responds (p. 56) that she had spoken with Achior and because he feared the God of Israel, she cut his cords with her knife, this last word sung on a dramatic *b-flat*". This plot conflicts with the original story (and with the play), in which Holofernes ordered Achior taken back to Bethulia, where he would presumably be slaughtered with his "kinsmen" in the next day's battle. Another inconsistency is Judith revealing to Holofernes that she is in possession of a knife. Obviously it would have been taken from her immediately, before she ever reached Holofernes's tent.

Holofernes completely gives in to his fury (score note) and in frenzied, raging music orders Judith bound and taken away. This twist delays the eventual "seduction scene" and at this point seems to even derail it. Holofernes orders the attendants to twist the cords around Judith's neck and when she is choked, to "cast her insolence into the lake" (score note, p. 57). But as they begin dragging her away, Holofernes hesitates and repents, and tells them to wait. In sweet, lyrical phrases, Bagoas whispers a warning to Holofernes:

Prince, beware of the benevolence of thy heart,
for in the beauty of her face is cunning and great peril.
All my days have I lived among the trickeries of women,
and my Lord also knows something of their craft,
which brings ruin to the carnal.

These comments are a very interesting addition to the original story. No character there plays advisor to Holofernes or tries to help him avoid an encounter with Judith. This adds interest and conflict to the story. Holofernes's response is a paraphrase of a verse in the original story, spoken by one of the Assyrians in the camp when he saw Judith (Jdt 10:19):

> Who can despise these people, when they have such women among them? It is not right to leave one man of then alive for if we let them go they will be able to beguile the whole earth.

Judith now displays her powers of deceit and manipulation, asking Holofernes in her sweetest voice: "Will the wise man cast away a pearl ... and in anger lose his servant forever?" She sings in calm phrases with descending dissonant chords continuing under her voice (p. 59). Bagoas, more perceptive than his master, again warns Holofernes not to speak alone in his tent with Judith. But Judith continues to insist: "I will speak alone with the prince in his tent ... or never!" This line is sung *a cappella*, suggesting both Judith's strength and also vulnerability. There is a pause before the last two words. (In the play, Judith agrees to talk to Holofernes with Bagoas present, with a sly smile.) The music quickens and Holofernes cries out that he cannot lose Judith forever, almost "resenting his passion for Judith" (score note: also "he wavers between two powerful impulses"). After more frenzied music, Holofernes shouts: "Unbind her!" Bagoas again repeats that this woman is against them, but Holofernes ignores him and orders that Judith be veiled. He wants her to not be seen by anyone, "for she is mine tonight." She submits to a veiling ceremony in which she is "elaborately veiled" as night falls and torches are lit. The high rippling music vividly evokes flickering lights. (In the play, the slave who captured Haggith asks Bagoas to reward him with her, and Bagoas agrees. This will be important in the last act.)

A lengthy musical interval (pp. 64–7) describes the preparation of the tent for Judith's arrival. In the play, before Holofernes's arrival there is a dialogue between Judith and Bagoas, in which she explains to him that her God commanded her to speak with Holofernes alone, with no one else present. But, she says, the God of Israel addressed her again and gave her permission to also speak to Bagoas. Bagoas comments that her god is wise and discerning.

In an interesting scene from the play that was omitted from the libretto and opera, Judith confirms that there is now peace between them and Bagoas claims that the two of them could rule over the rulers of all of Assyria. This exchange is another indicator of Judith's cunning intelligence and Bagoas's gullibility. Holofernes then questions Judith about Achior: whether he reached Bethulia, and what her are thoughts about him. She bravely tells Holofernes that he should heed Achior's words, because he will not prevail against the Israelites unless or until they sin against their God. Holofernes is impatient to attack right away, but now considers just leaving the Hebrews to be killed by their God when they sin. Judith tells him to realize that the world would see that instead of attacking, he waited passively. Holofernes agrees but is still eager to attack. Judith tells him to wait until God has informed her that her people have sinned, because then they will have no protection. Clearly as gullible as Bagoas when it comes to beliefs about God's power, Holofernes agrees to wait. There is a moment of humor when Holofernes exclaims in an aside to Bagoas that there is no woman from one end of the earth to the other like Judith, for beauty and wisdom. Bagoas replies: "It may well be so, but I have not seen the whole earth."

Attendants are waiting on Holofernes, who orders the tent flaps to be opened because it is hot and lamps to be lit against the darkness (p. 67). Judith remains standing, motionless. (Her veils are removed at the scene's opening, in the play.) Introduced again by loud trombones, Holofernes orders her to go to the inner chamber, and she obeys. Then he orders Bagoas to prepare meat and wine for Judith. This is the rare opera that goes directly to the scene between the two main characters, skipping the lengthy party and banquet scenes found in most works. The text here is based very closely on the original story: in her sweetest voice, Judith refuses the food and drink, hoping not to offend. She explains that she has brought her own provisions and knows they will last until she accomplishes what she came for (Jdt 12:1–4). She does not explain her refusal of his food, but dietary rules are usually left out of musical retellings. In another plot twist, Bagoas is sent to fetch Haggith for Judith, and he reminds Holofernes of a council of the captains meeting. Bagoas worries Judith will escape, but Holofernes assures him that he has ordered guards all around the tent—only not too close, since he intends to be alone with her later that night. These plot twists are all a form of delaying tactics. Judith, in dulcet tones, assures Holofernes that she has no intention of fleeing. As Holofernes exits, he says "cynically" to Bagoas: "She is moved towards me" followed by a "somber" laugh (p. 72). Bagoas dismisses all the attendants with a wave of his hand. Judith is now alone.

Haggith enters timidly with the sack. With a sense of wonder, she exclaims: "Can this be in truth the tent of the monster?" Then she also notes how unclean it is, wondering that they have no besoms (brooms made from twigs around a stick). Judith tells her to stop her prattle. Judith's servant in this portrayal is a sweet and chatty country girl, very different from her portrayal in other works.

The play enlarges her role still further. She tells Judith that she has been spending time with Ingur, the soldier with whom she had flirted. She refers to an earlier command by Judith to "delude and tangle with wiles" any Assyrian she meets, so the idea came from Judith. But Haggith has accomplished the task very well, commenting:

> Either all men are simpletons and besotted with self-conceit, or Ingur exceeds greatly in folly. I have been given to him for his slave, but he is mine and knows it not.

This exchange is not in the opera, where Haggith immediately encourages Judith to eat the food she has brought in (in the play, Haggith confesses that she ate of Ingur's provisions, and Judith scolds her, telling her it is a sin and offense for her as an Israelite). The ethnicity of Judith's slave has never been established, but some scholars believe she was a Hebrew. Her response to Judith, however, is very interesting. She says it would be an offense only for the high-born, while a handmaid "can eat as she can, and the Lord turneth away his glance until she has finished her platter." This implies that she identifies as a Hebrew. She also reminds Judith that her command was to beguile Ingur, as she has done.

Judith is too distracted to eat, "on fire with expectation and suspense" (p. 75). Judith tells Haggith to remain while she goes out to commune with her God. She cannot do that in a heathen place. In the opera, not the play, she orders Haggith to give her the knife, as the knife *leitmotif* is heard. She takes the knife with her, and once outside, gazes at it and "with a sweeping gesture holds it aloft" (score note). After a rapid *crescendo* and terrifying long *glissando* in the orchestra, she conceals the knife in her dress and heads back to the tent. This focus on a knife Judith is carrying is a complete change from the original text. Logically, Judith could not easily have gotten past numerous guards and soldiers in Holofernes's camp with a concealed knife (even without X-ray scanners). And part of her heroism is venturing forth into an enemy camp with no weapon but her beauty (and her faith). This aspect of the original plot has been erased.

Holofernes enters the tent and is frantic and furious to find Judith missing. Haggith emerges from the shadows and when Holofernes asks Bagoas who she is, he calls her Judith's "waiting wench." She tells them, almost stuttering, that her mistress has gone out to pray, and Bagoas imperiously tells Haggith to fetch her: "Her God may wait, but not his royal Highness the Prince Holofernes." On the final word, his voice reaches and sustains a'', quite a high pitch, heightening the force of his words.

In the play, Holofernes urges Bagoas to persuade Judith to come eat and drink with them that night (Jdt 12:11 in the original story). Then he recites a verse, also from the original story (12:12), which has been translated in a wide variety of ways over time. The gist is that it would be a disgrace to let such a woman go without enjoying her company (or: having sex with her) that they would be mocked. This was not included in the opera.

As Haggith exits, Holofernes starts drinking, "lost in reverie" (score note, p. 79), as reflected in the music. A wind starts blowing, as seen by the billowing tent, causing Holofernes to spill his wine. Gloomily, Holofernes reflects on his situation, calling love a calamity, moaning that "no slave is so trodden down as the one that is the slave to desire." In a change of mood, he shares with Bagoas his fear that Judith has fled back to her own people. In an aside, Bagoas says: "I would she had!" but he reassures Holofernes that the guards would have stopped her. Holofernes replies: "What guard could restrain such a woman?" (p. 81). When Bagoas repeats this line, Holofernes angrily accuses him of echoing all he says and tells him to leave. Bagoas moves to the back of the tent and raises the curtain to reveal Judith there, fully veiled. Bagoas remains in the background as Judith approaches Holofernes.

The orchestral music for the next few minutes seems to describe ecstasy, its soaring and passionate music recalling Strauss. (Covell calls it "music of luxuriant texture and caressing tenderness."[36]) The score notes indicate that the two look at each other intently, "Judith inscrutable, Holofernes fascinated." While they are staring at each other, moonlight floods the room. As this light increases, the music grows increasingly louder and faster. It is an interesting choice to include a wordless scene, dependent only on the music and the facial expressions of the two singers to create a mood. Holofernes suddenly notices Bagoas and orders him out, and no less than five hundred paces away.

---

[36] Covell, liner notes.

After he leaves, Judith kneels with her forehead to the ground, while Holofernes paces. The music builds and becomes more ominous. Suddenly he runs toward her and rips the veil away, saying: "Arise, sorceress!," ordering her to come closer (p. 86). Grabbing her arms, he calls her "Hebrew sorceress" and says she knows her power. She responds that she has no power except what is given her from on high. Freeing herself, Judith calmly asks if his council of the captains is already over. He says brusquely that it is over, then angrily adds that he cares nothing for the captains and left them "drunken with wine and with their pride." But, he sings in a suddenly melting tone, the feast between the two of them has not yet begun (p. 88).

The accompaniment is now steady and calm, as Holofernes tells Judith that his heart "thirsts horribly" for her and that he is full of a "great madness." She says enigmatically: "I am here." Smiling seductively, she tells Holofernes that when he feared that she had fled, she had only gone out to commune with her God, the God of Israel. Holofernes asks what her God had to say to her. She says God told her about Holofernes's vast army. These passages are filled with bell and glockenspiel sounds, possibly to create an otherworldly effect and powerfully evoking Strauss's orchestrations. Flattered, he boasts that he has 132,000 men who bow to him and who without his leadership would be rabble. Judith comments: "But my lord lives," adding to herself "yet," to which he replies: "I live in thee" to soaring tonic music. Then she tells him that her God informed her that the Bethulians have sinned by drinking the holy wine reserved for priests. She adds that because of this sin, she heard, the Assyrians will be victorious the next day against Bethulia. Overjoyed, he promises Judith, in gratitude, that her God shall now be his God. This line is taken from the original story (Jdt 11:23) where it was stated as a conditional. There, after Judith has told him about his upcoming victory, he makes that pledge on condition it happens. In this retelling, he has no doubts about her prediction. Judith does not reply in the original story, but here she states: "In truth thou art set apart to be his," a rather oblique phrase that may be referring to his forthcoming death.

Holofernes approaches Judith and notes that she is trembling. She says she had been afraid for him but now is sure of his fate as decreed in heaven. She then goes further than in any other musical setting: She proclaims that she will remain at his side as he conquers Judea, all the way to Jerusalem, where she will set his throne, and no one will speak against the Prince. Then, she continues in more lyrical phrases over a swelling orchestra: "In my great boldness I will dare to sit beside thee" (p. 95). She continues to foresee that they will live side by side for many years. In ecstatic music, she proclaims that it will be known to generations that there is none to compare with Holofernes, "neither in power nor in bliss" (pp. 97–8). In conclusion, she says these things were foretold to her in Heaven and she was sent to relate them. These words would have certainly encouraged and enflamed Holofernes. Judith in the original story and in numerous retellings does not go this far to persuade Holofernes of her loyalty, but it is a convincing scenario, nonetheless. These words are in the libretto only, not in the play, so it would seem that Goossens wanted to depict Judith as even bolder and more manipulative than she was in the play.

Holofernes, of course, is enraptured and passionately declares that he will triumph tomorrow but also tonight. He reminds Judith that they are alone and suggests they eat and drink. Judith gaily says: "Let us feast" (p. 99). In seductive music, marked

Molto legato ed espressivo (smooth and expressive), Holofernes coaxes Judith to take off her tunic, for she is in her own house. She declines and moves further away from him, saying he will now be her slave and singing lyrically "Pour out the wine, mighty slave!" which reaches an exciting *a*". This scenario borders on a dominatrix fantasy, quite far from the intent of the original story. While Holofernes is busy pouring out the wine, Judith removes the knife from her garment and carefully places it behind the couch. In this retelling, Judith's violent act is fully planned, contrary to the suggestion of a sudden impulse in the original story. She then slowly removes her tunic (a short-sleeved pull-on garment worn over clothes in antiquity) and takes the wine from Holofernes. Orchestral passages of ecstatic drinking music follow. Then Holofernes remarks that he thought Judith's "Hebrew scruples" would not allow her to drink his wine. This is one of the rare librettos that refers to dietary rules. Judith replies that she will drink more.

Holofernes suddenly summons Bagoas and asks him to bring his dancing women—an odd request considering he is in the throes of seducing Judith (p. 105). But it would seem that this was expected at any banquet, and the two settle down to watch the dancers perform. A dance was frequently performed in operas; it is not found in the play. This dance music was a late addition to the score. The first part of the dance is very lively, and features some of the most interesting music in the opera. In fact, a recording of the dance sequence was released long before the full opera was ever recorded. There is fascinating use of unusual percussion sounds combined with harp. When it becomes languorous, Holofernes is clearly bored and calls Bagoas over. He says he is experiencing strange fears, suggesting a sense of foreboding. Then he brusquely orders "wilder" music, and at a signal from Bagoas, the dancers begin an "orgiastic" dance (p.112) to much faster music, eventually growing frenzied at a *Presto* tempo (p.118). Pounding drums predominate and call to mind Stravinsky's ballets. The two composers were friends early in Goossens's career (see above) and Goossens was very familiar with Stravinsky's music, which he had also conducted. Throughout the dance, Judith has been continually serving wine to Holofernes, while she has only simulated drinking (score note). It is somewhat unusual to include a lengthy dance in a one-act opera, but it creates suspense and mood. Most earlier operas include a lengthy banquet scene with dancing. After a final *Prestissimo* measure, Holofernes suddenly shouts "Enough!" as he rises quickly and unsteadily in much slower music. The dancers remain frozen in their final position and then quickly exit, as does Bagoas.

Depicted by a harp *glissando*, the moonlight begins to wane (p. 119). Holofernes asks Judith in long sustained lines over ominous loud horns if she truly knows her power and her dominion, as he continues to drink. She replies that she knows it better than he does. He argues that she does not, and proclaims his love in flowery verses (the opening line recalling Song of Songs 8:6):

Thou hast set thy seal upon me for evermore.
My heart cannot hold thee, for thou hast filled it to overflowing.
Thy glance is my joy and my sorrow, according to thy whim.

He asks Judith to command him to do something and not to be afraid, because he is very powerful. Judith responds "tenderly" that she commands him only to be happy, referring to herself as his captive in highly lyrical passages. He corrects her and says that it is he who is her prisoner. Then he tells her that he will set her on a throne and they will reign together in Assyria. This idea is found in other librettos and is based on a single phrase from the original story: "…you shall live in the house of King Nebuchadnezzar" (Jdt 11:23b). There, Holofernes makes this promise during their first meeting, long before the banquet. Judith replies solemnly in a puzzling and equivocal statement: "There is no requisition in the grave, whether you have lived a hundred or a thousand years" (from the play; p. 124). She follows this with a statement of faith that "the God of Israel is a shield." Holofernes immediately reminds Judith that he said her God is also his God and adds that she herself is his God, his voice reaching *e'*. "He gazes into her eyes with passionate longing" (score note, p. 124). Judith changes the mood as she coyly asks Holofernes about his other wives, and the innumerable concubines she has heard about. This dialogue is a recitative accompanied only by a long sustained note. Holofernes replies that it is a lie, because from this day on, he is pushing aside all women but her, and none of them can compare. On this phrase, the music begins to soar. Holofernes asks Judith if she agrees that since God wrought a miracle this night, it proves that God has appointed them for each other. Judith responds simply that she will not deny that "God is in this thing." Then she offers to tell him something he does not know.

Judith presses his shoulders down to sit on the couch and leans over him. The bell and glockenspiel sounds that have been featured at key points in the opera are heard again. She begins by relating that when she was in Bethulia lying on her bed at night, a vision came to her. This seems to be a nod to Chadwick's opera (see above; it is possible that that American work would have been known to Goossens), in which Judith had a vision of her dead husband Manasseh. Anyone familiar with that earlier work would be surprised to find Manasseh's name replaced here by Holofernes, whom she saw "in the likeness of his majesty and his might" (p. 128). In Chadwick's account of a vision, Manasseh inspires Judith to take action. Here, she says that it was this vision that spurred her to come to meet Holofernes in person. She tells him that she could not reveal this secret to anyone else. He is overcome with emotion. From this point on, "the music steadily grows in passionate intensity" (score note). He says he will kiss her lips and make her his. She bends lower and sings: "Kiss my lips," the first word on a sustained *g"*. This the only work treated here in which Judith initiates a kiss. They kiss and he falls backward, lying on the couch now, his head not visible. Judith struggles to free herself of his grasp. (In the play, as they kiss, the mysterious figure of a half-veiled Assyrian woman appears again, but this time she is seen by Bagoas and killed. No explanation is ever offered, and this action is not included in the opera.)

After some moments of frenzied music, with echoes of Strauss's 1903 opera *Elektra*, Judith rises and stealthily retrieves her knife to slower, heavy music. The only light now is the lamp in the tent. Judith sings tenderly to Holofernes:

O mighty child, where is thy strength? And where thy terribleness?
Rest thee a moment on the couch, and thy soul's captive will tend thee.

She is holding the knife in her right hand while caressing Holofernes with her left. Distant trumpets are suddenly heard and Holofernes briefly awakens and mumbles in a drunken stupor: "My great joy has overthrown me!" This dramatic device of Holofernes waking up from his stupor was used by several librettists in previous centuries. Still caressing Holofernes with her left hand, she kills him with her right, the haunting sound of a bass clarinet solo the only indication of the violent act. The fundamental change in this opera is the use of a knife rather than a sword to behead Holofernes. It is hard to imagine a knife small enough to conceal that is long enough to behead a man with only one hand. But opera always involves a suspension of disbelief.

As Judith stands up, "her repressed scorn, loathing and disgust are now plainly evident" (score note, p. 132). (In the play, she expresses her fury by "murmuring" the lines below while she is killing Holofernes. In the opera, she recites them after the act.) Feeling free to now express her feelings, she sings these harrowing phrases addressed to the corpse, on a repeated *f#"* over continual high *tremolos*:

Thou that wouldst go against the God of Israel
Thou that wouldst defile Judea!
Thou that hast dishonoured with thy kiss the widow of Manasseh.
Thou that hast compelled me to lie and deceit and much lying
So that I might perform the will of God: The grave shall be thy house!

The orchestra flares up, briefly recapping the opening motif of the opera. No other libretto explored here portrays Judith expressing her fury and her regrets. The word "grave" is sung on a highly dramatic sustained high C (*c"*), on a clear C minor chord. Over a single sustained note, she calmly tells Haggith, who has just entered, that she has done what she had to do and that Assyria has fallen. She tells Haggith to put the head into the sack, which she does without a word or reaction. (In the play, she more specifically orders her to "take the head by the beard.") They exit as the curtain falls quickly. The final measures of the opera are two rapid and very high *glissando* passages, ending on a *fff* high B-flat major chord.

Conclusion

The abrupt ending of this opera differs from almost all other works, which end with a triumphant victory chorus in Bethulia. It is the same in this regard as the one-scene work of 1876 by Paul Hillemacher, which was also based on a play. The single-scene format puts the spotlight entirely on the Judith-Holofernes encounter and develops that in greater depth. Goossens's music underlines the constantly shifting moods as the encounter between the two characters steadily builds in intensity up to the end. It is a gripping presentation of this central scene of the original story. Goossens has created a vivid representation of the Holofernes-Judith encounter and both a Judith and her slave as multidimensional, appealing characters.

Conclusion of the Play

The lengthy Act III of the play, which Goossens chose not to include, is worth recapping here for its unusual retelling of the original story. Haggith arrives at the gates of Bethulia ahead of Judith, bearing water. She is also bringing Ingur, who is now her "bondman" whom she has tamed. She announces that there are another ten Assyrians outside the gates, carrying gourds of water for her, chained together by their necks. She tells the people that they are out of danger because the camps of the Assyrians are broken. Ozias is impatient and skeptical. Haggith shows him Holofernes's head in the sack and Ozias proclaims: "Great is the Lord of Israel!" Haggith announces that her mistress "is the right hand of the Lord," but Ozias repeats his praise only of the Lord. Haggith relays Judith's order to display Holofernes's head on a high wall, as well as to send men out to attack the fleeing Assyrians. All these commands come from Judith in the original story, so this is an unusual change. In yet another twist, Haggith explains that Judith is hidden in the valley, since Bagoas has sworn an oath to kill her. But Haggith knows that God is watching and protecting Judith.

Elders and others approach Ozias to inquire about the "miracle" they have heard about, and Ozias blandly informs them that there is no miracle, only "that which I planned with the lady Judith has come to pass ... and the wells are delivered into my hands." It is astounding that a male playwright would present such a negative portrayal of a man, but the playwright Bennett was very active all his life in women's rights. This is quite evident. Ozias also wants to chain Ingur to Achior but Haggith does not allow it, repeating that he is her slave. In an additional plot line, a messenger arrives from Jerusalem to offer aid to Bethulia. Ozias informs him that they no longer need aid, because "the Lord has delivered Bethulia from the Assyrians by the subtlety of his servant Ozias." When pressed for details, he explains that he knew the weakness of Holofernes and therefore secretly sent a woman to him, known as Judith, and with his counsel, by her wiles she brought about Holofernes's death. He concludes: "The God of Israel hath saved Israel—by my hand." When Judith appears, verses from the final Song of Praise in the book of Judith are recited. But after this nod to origins, the play swerves wildly into imagination.

Achior has apparently won Judith's heart. Ozias, who had hoped to marry Judith, is insanely jealous of him. He also questions if Judith sinned with Holofernes. Then he praises her for her act, and she sarcastically responds that she has done nothing, that the Lord saved Israel by the hand of Ozias. She recounts that she met the messenger who had just spoken with Ozias, and he shared this view with her. She reminds Ozias that he never knew of her plan. In an interesting dialogue, he shares how he feels torn between a hunger for "glory and dominion" and for Judith. She accuses him of deception, and he reminds her that she too used deceit. But she counters that her use of deceit was for Israel, not for herself, while his is only for power and advancement. In spite of these criticisms, Ozias persists and begs Judith to marry him. She announces that she has chosen Achior, who came to them for a sign from God and will be "joined into the house of Israel" that very day. After their marriage, she will submit herself to him. This statement runs counter to every portrayal of Judith, both the original and all the retellings. For the crowning touch, Haggith announces that Ingur will also be received into Israel and marry her. She however adds: "He shall be my husband, yet shall not rule me," in sharp contrast to Judith's statement accepting submission. Ozias continues with his self-promotion, announcing that he has been called to higher office in Jerusalem because he delivered Israel. Judith says: "The lord Ozias is called to greatness. Peace be with him." Hopefully this line is said with sarcasm.

Conclusion

The conclusion of the play betrays the original meaning of the story. Judith performed her deed for God and her people, not for herself. She then withdrew and never sought glory or attention again. Part of her appeal and strength is her non-reliance on any man or on the convention of marriage. After so many feminist sentiments throughout the play, Bennett ultimately betrays that ideal. It seems he had an agenda of his own, or needed to give his audience what they expected. Whether Goossens's decision to draw only from the second act for his opera was based on the content of the other acts, or the appeal of the Holofernes-Judith scene, will never be known.

Siegfried Matthus (b. 1934)

Siegfried Matthus, a German composer and opera director, was made the youngest composer in residence in the history of the Komische Oper Berlin by Walter Felsenstein. Matthus has written more than a dozen stage works. His opera *Judith* (1982–4) was performed in 1985 by the Komische Oper Berlin.[37] It was recorded on the label Ars Vivendi in 1986 and reissued on Berlin Classics in 1998. Both recordings feature the original cast, but the Ars Vivendi includes notes and libretto in German, English, and French, while the Berlin Classics recording includes notes only in German. The original performance can be seen on YouTube.[38]

Its American premiere was at Santa Fe Opera in 1990. The reviews were not kind:

> Alas, in the performance heard Friday night, the East German composer's retelling of the Old Testament tale proved a relentlessly overwrought, ultimately tiresome neo-expressionist horror show. While David Alden's production managed to rub the audience's collective nose in a variety of effective theatrical shocks—most of them of the Grand Guignol variety—neither the stage direction nor the valiant performers could save "Judith" from ending up a bloody bore.[39]

---

[37] http://www.musicassociatesofamerica.com/roster/matthus/matthus_biography.html (accessed April 30, 20200.

[38] Full performance: https://www.youtube.com/watch?v=GJMvTvIFn1g; Act 1, audio only: https://www.youtube.com/watch?v=pPdS4ZNnBSQ (both accessed April 30, 2020).

[39] John van Rhein, "Despite Brave Effort, 'Judith' Ends Up a Bloody Bore," *Chicago Tribune*, August 12, 1990. Available online: https://www.chicagotribune.com/news/ct-xpm-1990-08-12-9003070596-story.html (accessed April 30, 2020).

The *New York Times* was no kinder:

> As soon as the lights go up on the set of "Judith" we know where we are, and it definitely is not Israel in Biblical times. We are in the grim land known as German Expressionism, and any doubt as to where the composer, Siegfried Matthus, and the director, Davis Alden, have brought us is erased at the appearance of a black-faced executioner who busies himself hacking off the heads of prisoners with a meat cleaver. We are not in for a night of fun.[40]

The reviewer continues:

> For two seemingly endless hours [the soprano] and everyone else involved were restricted to the drably atonal declamation that passes for singing in this once-experimental but now dated genre ... No melodic line was allowed to live beyond a moment, let alone blossom. Encountered once again are those self-defeating ensembles in which orchestra, chorus and solo voice try to scream one another into submission ... the score seldom offered the instruments any role more grateful than that of background to a horror film.[41]

Another critic discussed the opera:

> Matthus based his libretto on the Bible and on Friedrich Hebbel's 19th-century drama on this theme but added his own twists. Chief among them is the ending, wherein Ephraim, a Jewish weakling whom Judith has rejected, drunkenly enters Holofernes's tent, cries, "Hail, whore of Israel," rips off her clothes and rapes her "with the participation of everyone in the cast," according to the stage directions, as the chorus prays for forgiveness.

"I thought that made a more operatic ending," Mr. Matthus explained.[42]

This ending, thankfully, was not used in the staged production. A reviewer, Michael Oliver, describes the ending in this production:

> In a stunning coup de theatre the chorus then marches into the auditorium to sing a powerful but despairing passacaglia while, on stage, all the characters of the drama present a nightmarish dumb-show of Judith's destruction.[43]

---

[40] Donal Henahan, "Tale of Judith, Updated," special to the *New York Times*, August 3, 1990. Available online: https://www.nytimes.com/1990/08/03/arts/review-opera-tale-of-judith-updated.html (accessed April 30, 2020).

[41] Henahan 1990.

[42] John Rockwell, "Siegfried Who? The Limits of Fame," *New York Times*, July 22, 1990. Available online: https://www.nytimes.com/1990/07/22/arts/music-siegfried-who-the-limits-of-fame.html (accessed April 30, 2020).

[43] Michael Oliver, "Maathus Judith," *Gramophone*, April 1999. Available online: https://www.gramophone.co.uk/review/matthus-judith (accessed July 17, 2019). As of May 2020, this article is no longer accessible without registering with Gramophone magazine.

One of the few reviewers who writes favorably of the opera, Oliver finds the music powerful:

> The word-setting is frequently jagged, the orchestra harshly violent, but brief melodic motifs are often repeated obsessively, with pounding rhythms owing something to the later Carl Orff … after the killing Judith sings as though in a trance, accompanied by a glittering "continuo" of harp, piano, cymbals and tuned percussion.[44]

In the CD liner notes, commentator Eberhard Schmidt offers some debatable ideas: for example, that "the opera essentially relates the story of two great individuals."[45] This is certainly the only reference to Holofernes as a great individual that I have seen in any commentary. Schmidt continues to display his admiration for Holofernes: "Judith may have killed him, but he lives on inside her as the most impressive and most important human being she has ever encountered. And that is her tragedy."[46]

Judith (1984) (Based on Hebbel)

Most of the libretto is taken directly from Hebbel's play,[47] discussed in Chapter 3.
    I will make references to page numbers in that document throughout, to avoid repeating too much text.

Judith: soprano
Holofernes: baritone
Ephraim: tenor
Achior: baritone
Mirza (maid): contralto
Ozias: bass

The effect of the music is amplified by watching the very controversial production (YouTube link above), and I chose to listen to it while watching. This is the only available visual presentation of any Judith work discussed in this book, which makes it uniquely appealing.

Act One

If the audience did not know they were watching an opera based on Judith, they would not guess it. The opening scene, only 10 minutes long, is a very abbreviated adaptation of the same scene in Hebbel's play (Act I, pp. 258–9). In this production, a balding

[44] Oliver 1999.
[45] Eberhard Schmidt, CD liner notes (Ars Vivendi recording).
[46] Schmidt, CD liner notes.
[47] https://quod.lib.umich.edu/g/genpub/AJD8469.0025.001?rgn=main;view=fulltext (accessed April 30, 2020).

Holofernes in glasses and garbed in black leather, and the surrounding army, all suggest stormtroopers. This imagery evokes a modern dictator far more than a warlord of biblical times. Sacrifices are offered to large, futuristic machines belching smoke, probably meant to represent crematoria. This Holocaust, inferno-like imagery is as terrifying as the music.

The opening scene is set in two places at the same time: Bethulia, located on a hilltop; and the Babylonians' camp at the foot of the hill. The plot unfolds in both places simultaneously. Thus, the Bethulians are singing of their misfortune and misery at the same time as the Babylonian soldiers sing of wine and gluttony. The simultaneous choruses employ conflicting rhythms to highlight the opposition between besiegers and besieged (this device was also found in Lefebvre's opera; see Chapter 4). The quality of the music, although it is not accessible or pleasing, is also contrasted in the two choruses. Holofernes appears and confers briefly with the Babylonian high priest about which god they should sacrifice to. During the sacrifice, the Babylonians sing about their gods as the Bethulians sing of their agony and their need to pray. The sacrifices are placed in what look like giant incinerators.

The next scene is between Judith and Mirza, her servant (Hebbel, Act II, pp. 265–6). In this production, she is dressed completely in white—wedding white, perhaps?—with a white turban, gown, and shoes. In flowing cantilenas (smooth, lyrical melodies) with dramatic moments, Judith relates a dream she has just had. In more muted music, Judith relates her wedding night with Manasseh, acting almost mad and treating Mirza roughly. In an interesting staging idea, Holofernes sings his next monologue simultaneously with Judith singing hers, though they are clearly in different places. Judith's image is seen as a projection, as if floating. Holofernes sings a monologue about how he loves to conquer women, while Judith simultaneously sings paraphrased verses from Song of Songs (an addition by Matthus, not in the Hebbel play).

The action shifts back to only Holofernes's camp again as emissaries are announced (Hebbel, p. 261). The messenger is characterized as almost grotesquely obsequious, singing exaggerated modal music in a falsetto voice. The effect is somewhat comical and certainly meant to be mocking. When it is decided that all the gods should be destroyed, leaving only Nebuchadnezzar, their destruction in the "incinerators" has a very futuristic look.

Two scenes now occur simultaneously: in Holofernes's camp, the soldiers sing about their gods, while in Bethulia, the people moan about their thirst. An invented character named Ammon (Assad in Hebbel) demands that the gates be opened, while his brother Daniel (considered a prophet) begins shouting "Stone him!" (Hebbel, Act III, p. 282). The crowd becomes more worked up, singing in almost a whispered moan over a pounding rhythm.

Holofernes now sings a monologue, philosophizing about Nebuchadnezzar and the role of gods (Hebbel, Act I, p. 262). There is no melodic line in this very proclamatory music, over a colorful orchestra. The spotlight shifts to a scene with Judith, Mirza, and Ephraim (Hebbel, Act II, pp. 269–71). Mirza encourages Judith to trust in her beauty. Ephraim tries to warn Judith of the danger of Holofernes, but she dismissively says she would like to meet him. Ephraim shows her a knife he made and she grabs it, mocking him for pulling away. In rare measures of lyrical, pleading music, accompanied by harp, Ephraim proclaims his love for Judith. They continue to bicker about who should kill Holofernes, until Judith finally proclaims she will do it herself (Hebbel, Act III, pp. 272–3).

The scene shifts back to Holofernes's camp, where he greets emissaries (Hebbel, Act I, pp. 263–5). Their music, as earlier, is comically "oriental." Holofernes asks the envoy from Edom about the Hebrews (strangely misspelled in the libretto as "Ebrus" in the CD's English translation). In a very abbreviated scene from the play, Achior warns Holofernes about the Hebrews and he is seized and taken away. The scene shifts back to Judith, praying desperately for a sign from God (Hebbel, Act III, p. 274). At the same time, Holofernes is conferring with his captains about Bethulia (Hebbel, Act IV, p. 299) while Judith continues her prayer (Hebbel, Act III, p. 275), with winds prominently woven into the orchestra. The climactic moment of the prayer is her realization that "the road to my deed passes through sin." After this, she greets her own image in the mirror triumphantly, now full of confidence. (The libretto states that she puts on a new dress and adorns herself, but this does not happen on stage.)

In the next section, several scenes occur simultaneously: the Bethulians continue to argue (Hebbel, Act III, p. 282), Judith concludes her prayer (Hebbel, Act III, p. 275), and Holofernes compares himself to a storm (Hebbel, Act IV, p. 293). Each section can be heard even though most of the singing is simultaneous. The sense of chaos and cacophony is powerful and probably deliberate. The climax of the multiple scenes occurs in Bethulia, where the people, angered that Daniel had incited them to stone his brother Ammon to death, urge each other on to tie Daniel to the stake and burn him. They proceed to do that, vividly depicted onstage. This was an addition to Hebbel's play and possibly an excuse to write an updated version of Wagner's "Magic Fire Music" from his opera *Die Walküre*. The music is as effective as the scene is horrible to watch. The depiction of the Hebrews as a barbaric mob, in Hebbel and even more in this opera, could justifiably be labeled anti-Semitic (although no critic has suggested this, to my knowledge).

Achior encourages the people to set a time after which they will open the gates (Hebbel, Act III, p. 286). Judith then questions Achior about Holofernes (Hebbel, p. 288–9) in very suspenseful music. In some of the most powerful lines from the Hebbel play, Judith addresses all those whom Holofernes has killed and defiled (Hebbel, p. 289) in lyrical lines over a light strumming accompaniment. This is one of the most accessible moments in the opera, rising to the demands of the emotionally charged text. As she continues singing this text, Holofernes counters her words with his own, at the same time:

> Come here all whom I hurt, you whom I crippled,
> You whose wives I tore from their arms ... come and devise tortures for me ...
> Kneel down before me, for I am your God.

As Holofernes is singing these lines, the Bethulians are praying for a miracle, the Babylonian soldiers are toasting wine, and Judith is demanding the gates be opened, so she can go to Holofernes.

Act Two

The act opens in Holofernes's tent, where he has woken from a dream and philosophizes at length about the meaning of death (Hebbel, Act IV, pp. 293–4). His attendants tell him a Hebrew woman they have captured is standing by his door and they describe her. Judith enters, now dressed entirely in black. The dialogue that follows is all from Hebbel (pp. 295–8). Once Judith has prostrated herself in front of Holofernes, she remains on the floor and sings sinuous music. In the course of their conversation, Judith rises and slowly changes from her black garments to a red gown—not a particularly subtle touch. The text for the remainder of the opera is all from Hebbel's Act 5, pp. 303–19, very abbreviated.

Judith and Holofernes sing their monologues simultaneously, as elsewhere in this opera. Judith's monologue beginning with "Oh, why am I a woman?" (p. 304) is accompanied by music with powerful echoes of Strauss, which were also noted in Reznicek's 1922 opera (see above). Judith sings the line "Yes, I hate you, I curse you" in passionate music. After Holofernes sings "Lie down and worship me!" he drags Judith to his bed. A tent with diaphanous walls is center stage, so the two can be seen in silhouette on the bed. The denouement is delayed by a brief encounter between Mirza and Holofernes's "Chamberlain," who disparages Mirza, calling her a "Hebrew spider" who should crawl back unto her corner. Left alone, over nervous bass clarinet passages, Mirza muses about what she is hearing from the tent. A striking line from Hebbel, "A woman should give birth to men, never should she kill men," is sung very slowly over the accompaniment of bells. Judith rushes out of the tent, now in a black slip, raving. Then she returns to carry out the deed. The beheading is very effectively almost visible through the diaphanous tent. Mirza faints when she sees it.

Judith prays after the killing, holding both the head and the sword and accompanied only by high strings. This is one of two texts in the opera written by Matthus, roughly paraphrasing Psalms:

> It is a heroic deed! Help me, God, and bring me justice through your power. Let the mountains bring peace and the hills bring justice. Let wells gush in the earth … Let the times flourish and peace reign throughout the land.

Judith seems to be invoking a utopia that God must now make Bethulia—an Eden of peace and happiness. But this is not the end of the opera. The music between the killing and the arrival of the plundering Bethulians includes celesta, cymbals, glockenspiel, vibraphone, piano, and harp, which combine to create an uncanny sound. Mirza questions Judith about what she has done (pp. 313–14), and Judith, her foot on Holofernes's head, confesses that ultimately she did this for herself, to find "reconciliation" with herself. This of course goes counter to the message of the original biblical story. This is followed by an operatic mad scene for Judith (pp. 314–15) in which she rants about what she has done, about the finality or non-finality of death, and about what she should do now.

The plot jumps ahead to Judith's return to Bethulia (p. 319), where Achior and the Bethulians greet Judith and hail her, and God, as their savior. But unlike other operas and oratorios, there is no simple hymn of praise. Instead, because the two locales of Bethulia and the Babylonian camp have been separated throughout, here they merge as the Bethulians are seen plundering and killing the enemy soldiers, with only a few stopping to praise Judith. This negative portrayal of the Hebrews is another display of an anti-Semitic slant. Ephraim adds his voice: "Hail Judith, savior of our people! Hail the whore of Israel!" In the libretto,"he tears Judith's clothes from her body." In other settings of Hebbel's play, she kills herself or asks her people to kill her, so she will never bear Holofernes's child. Matthus did not include that; instead, his stage instructions were:

> Depiction in mime of Judith's destruction involving all characters in the plot and employing previous depicted and reported episodes in an unreal time and sensory dimension.

Since this is a rather vague description, in this production, Judith enters a kind of cage which rises to the top of the stage, from where a rope is dropped and she hangs herself. The music of the closing chorus, a passacaglia (a set of variations over a bass ostinato), in the words of one critic is "a prayer for salvation from profound misery. It neither consoles nor reconciles but articulates despair and a cry for help."[48] The Bethulians roam the stage like zombies, mouths agape, as they sing one of the most despairing and least triumphant choruses of any Judith opera (Matthus wrote this text):

> Lord, save me! Hear my prayer and let my screams reach you ... Deliver me. You know my suffering and my shame ... I wait for consolation but find none ... I am wretched and in fear. Lord, save me, save me!

The opera ends on this nihilistic and hopeless note. There is no logical reason for the people's hopelessness, since they have just been saved from their oppressor and have conquered the enemy. Yet their savior, Judith, has clearly gone mad and hanged herself publicly. This would have dampened their spirit of triumphant exaltation, to say the least. Why the composer chose to take the already tragic ending in the Hebbel play and double the tragedy is not clear. The idea of suicide, also found in Reznicek's opera, is anathema to Jewish law and practice. It is also a terrible distortion of the meaning and message behind the original story. But this is how the composer heard and wanted to transmit the story. It is his interpretation, and a musically powerful one. Yet it can only be hoped that audiences who encounter this opera are aware of how far this retelling strays from the essence of the original biblical book. Both Hebbel and Matthus used the book of Judith merely as a frame on which, in my estimation, they built their own twisted, misguided interpretation.

---

[48] Schmidt, CD liner notes.

Chapter Conclusion

There are vast musical differences between the earliest work treated here, Chadwick's opera of 1901, the two operas of the 1920s (Reznicek and Goossens), and the much later Matthus work of 1984. The earliest work is rooted more in the nineteenth than the twentieth century, the two middle works both show the influence of Richard Strauss, while the last is atonal and musically challenging. The main link between the last three is that all are based on a play, in two cases on Hebbel's influential play of 1840, which was also incorporated into nineteenth-century operas (see Chapter 4); and in Goossens's case, on a play by a popular contemporary playwright. As has been mentioned before, plays offer wide-ranging and creative additions to the original story. Music set to plays also tends to be more inventive and dynamic to meet the challenges posed by the new text. In all cases, though, these works will challenge the listener to read the book of Judith in a new light and with a different understanding. Music fills in the gaps between the lines in much the same way as midrash, perpetually stimulating the reader and listener to ask "What if? "and "Why not?"

Conclusions

This journey through three centuries has examined composers and writers drawn to the drama of Judith's story who use their art to delineate real people, filling in many gaps in the original story while creatively and provocatively responding to the questions of "Why?," "How?," and, most of all, "What if?" The varied responses to these questions will challenge readers' and listeners' prior assumptions. These new interpretations of an old story offer exciting ways of reading the book of Judith, which has continued to draw in readers for almost two thousand years and continues up to this day.

I offer here a review of the various plot variations found in musical works, musical portrayals of the three central characters, and a discussion of voice types as an essential part of these musical portrayals.

Plots: Opening and Closing Scenes, Plot Additions or Twists

All but three of the works open in Bethulia, with those three opening in the Assyrian camp: Vivaldi, Hillemacher, and Goossens. These last two contain only a single scene, that between Judith and Holofernes. Those are also the only two works that do not conclude in Bethulia with a victory chorus. The last opera discussed, Matthus, opens and closes in both Bethulia and the Assyrian camp, on a split stage.

Major plot additions or twists (all a form of midrash) are first found in nineteenth-century Judith plays (see Chapter 3). These changes were incorporated into librettos for several operas in both the nineteenth and twentieth centuries. They include Judith's finding a spring outside Bethulia to which the people run, only to discover later that the water had been poisoned by the Assyrians. Another twist is the addition of a love interest for Judith in the form of a tenor, who pursues her but whom she ultimately rejects. Some commentators have seen this as a device to weaken Judith, but I see it as the opposite: a woman who rejects a suitor is strong and self-confident. A common plot addition is first seen in the earliest work treated here, Scarlatti's Naples *Giuditta*: Holofernes mumbles and calls out in his drunken sleep, causing Judith to hesitate and doubt herself. This dramatic device, found in many operas, adds suspense to that pivotal scene, while not contradicting anything in the original story. Virtually every work elaborates on the banquet scene, including lengthy choruses, solos, and dances to create a milieu barely described (but easily imagined) in the original book. Readers of earlier periods might have assumed this background. In the operatic orgy scenes, a sense of intimacy is missing. But when eventually the revelers are dismissed, the intimacy between only Judith and Holofernes is more striking in contrast.

To add even more drama, a few works include storm music during the beheading scene. This was a favorite device of nineteenth-century Italian opera, where it appears here, as well as in a twentieth-century work, by Reznicek (see Chapters 4 and 5). The sword of Holofernes inspired several differing plot twists: in some works, Holofernes hands Judith the sword to show off his strength and her weakness; in others, she notices it because it is jewelled; and most realistically, she has trouble holding on to it with one hand because of its weight. These ideas add realism and tension to the original plot. The description of the aftermath of the beheading, missing from the original story, is often bloody and vivid.

Judith and Holofernes

Judith's portrayal is more nuanced than the original story in many works. In some instances, she displays a self-confidence not particularly evident in the original. On the other hand, she also admits to doubting herself, her beauty, and her power. This self-doubt adds a new element to Judith's portrayal that rounds her out as a person. In resisting Holofernes, she is variably shown as clever, manipulative, sarcastic, and determined, through both textual and musical devices. But the singing voice often holds within it a subtext: when Judith sounds soothing and seductive, it is clear that she has a plan in mind but is distracting Holofernes. She is most truly expressing her real feelings in duets with her servant and in prayers. How she feels after committing the murder is never explored in the biblical book and only rarely in musical works. The standout is one of Honegger's versions, in which she expresses deep remorse for her act and explains that as the motive for retiring into seclusion for the remainder of her life (which is never explained in the biblical book). The notion of her feeling guilty is taken further in Hebbel's play, which, however, goes well beyond retelling by including a rape. In this scenario, Judith's primary motive for killing Holofernes is revenge for that rape. At the end, she asks her servant to kill her if she carries his child to term. This theme is picked up by librettists for two twentieth-century operas: Reznicek and Matthus. In both, Judith commits suicide at the end, a total corruption of the original story, in my view.

It has been shown how librettos and especially music have the ability to greatly amplify and add dimensions to characters' personalities. The positive depictions of Holofernes in every era challenge the reader's assumptions about his evil nature. After all, the story was written by the victors. Had the Assyrians prevailed, Holofernes would certainly have been portrayed as a martyred hero and Judith as a villain. Holofernes's feelings for Judith are described at great length in most works. He uses the word "love" repeatedly in many works, which is not found in the original story. In fact, the only works in which he does *not* proclaim his love for Judith are those based on Hebbel's 1840 play, in which Holofernes is a megalomaniac obsessed with his power. Even where he sings of his love for Judith, it is hard to separate his feelings of love from lust, since his soaring and passionate music evokes both. In some works, he is portrayed as more clever than his biblical counterpart (the Cambridge Scarlatti, for example), while in others he is disturbed by his own feelings for Judith and tries to fight them. Some portrayals are very nuanced and complex, which adds interest to the story. Absent from much of Holofernes's music is any undercurrent, or subtext, of menace. Such undercurrents are often heard in the buildup to the beheading, with common musical devices such as low *tremolos* and unexpected dissonance. But Holofernes sings music that is appealing and sentimental, which can almost convince the listener that he truly has feelings for Judith. And what if he did? That would make Judith's violent act both more difficult to carry out and more abhorrent, seeming almost like a betrayal. Yet interestingly, even where Holofernes is portrayed sympathetically, Judith is in no way censured for her act.

"Abra" the Servant

Judith's servant/slave also has an important voice in many works. Her complete silence in the original story was clearly seen as a gap in need of filling by later writers and composers, as well as artists, who invariably included her in paintings of Judith during and after the beheading. She actively gives Judith advice, comfort, and support. Her character is given an interesting backstory in some musical works: for example, she was taken captive as a girl and kept in Holofernes's harem; or she was Judith's nursemaid and has therefore been with her for her entire life. These stories give new meaning to the relationship between the two women. And musically, they often sing in harmony to express their closeness, in works of every era.

Voice Types and What They Mean

The voice type for a character immediately suggests certain characteristics, such as age, power, confidence, and others. This choice is an important facet of music's power to surpass the spoken word.

As seen in Table 1, Judith is sung by a soprano in a majority of both oratorios and operas. She is a soprano in both Scarlatti's and Arne's oratorios of the eighteenth century, as well as in two nineteenth-century oratorios, Parry's and Hillemacher's. A soprano Judith is even more prevalent in opera, represented by that voice in six of the eight operas discussed here, both in the nineteenth and twentieth centuries. A soprano voice has a higher range and more power than a mezzo, which explains the choice in most of these cases. A light soprano, which is the casting in earlier works such as Scarlatti and Arne, generally represents youth more than power. However,

Table 1 Voice Types

	Judith	Holofernes	"Abra"
Oratorios			
17–18th Centuries			
Scarlatti (Naples)	Soprano	Tenor/bass	X
(Cambridge)	Soprano	Countertenor	Alto
Vivaldi	Contralto	Contralto	Soprano
Arne	Soprano	Tenor	Soprano
Mozart	Alto	X	X
19th Century			
Leslie	Mezzo	Baritone	Soprano
Parry	Soprano	X	X
Hillemacher	Soprano	Bass	Mezzo
Operas			
19th Century			
Peri	Mezzo	Baritone	Alto
Silveri	Soprano	Baritone	Mezzo
Lefebvre	Soprano	Baritone	X
Serov	Soprano	Bass	Mezzo
20th Century			
Chadwick	Mezzo	Baritone	X
Reznicek	Soprano	Bass-baritone	Mezzo
Goossens	Soprano	Bass-baritone	Mezzo
Matthus	Soprano	Baritone	Contralto

X: This character is not a sung role in this work

the dramatic soprano voice was not common in seventeenth- or eighteenth-century oratorios, so it would have been an unusual choice for that period.

The choice of a mezzo or alto voice for a heroine, on the other hand, was more unexpected. Mozart, Leslie, and Honegger, whose oratorios represent different periods and styles, all made this choice and thereby created a powerful portrayal of Judith. In opera, only Peri in the nineteenth and Chadwick in the twentieth century cast Judith as a mezzo. In opera, a mezzo is not usually cast as the heroine, but the voice represents maturity and often seduction (the most well-known operatic examples are Carmen and Delilah). Though Vivaldi uniquely cast Judith as a contralto, his work was written for a cast of female singers, and this is the lowest voice. In sound and timbre, the contralto can imitate a counter-tenor, a voice that in that era represented power. Holofernes is also sung by a contralto in Vivaldi's work, so both characters are represented as powerful. This casting is usually altered in modern performances.

Holofernes is cast almost universally as a baritone, bass-baritone, or bass. There is little distinction between these voices, which are all low and have a dark timbre. A bass's range is the lowest, and that voice's lowest notes can be very effective. The only works that cast Holofernes as a tenor are early—Scarlatti, Vivaldi, and Arne. But that casting was fluid and not rigidly adhered to. Holofernes is variably portrayed as powerful, evil, passionate, and seductive. The baritone voice can suggest all of those qualities. Holofernes is not portrayed at all in two works: Mozart and Parry, where his role is relayed second-hand.

Judith's servant (or slave) has no singing role in five works: oratorios by Scarlatti (Naples version), Mozart, and Parry; and operas by Lefebvre and Chadwick. This is not entirely surprising considering she has no speaking role in the original story. Where she does appear, she is variably and creatively named (she has no name in the original story), and is cast most often as a mezzo or alto. In this case, it would seem to stand for maturity, as she is sometimes called Judith's "nurse" or "mother." This is true in two oratorios: Scarlatti (Cambridge version) and Hillemacher (there named Zillah). In the six operas that include her, of both the nineteenth and twentieth centuries, she is an alto or mezzo, variously named Abramia, Avra, Abra, Haggith, and Mirza. She is a soprano, suggesting youth and innocence, in only four oratorios spanning the eigtheenth through the twentieth centuries: Vivaldi, Arne, Leslie, and Honegger, variously called Abra, Amital, and Servant.

Personal Postscript

On a personal note, I have been exploring Judith and her story for close to two years, living every day with her words, actions, fears, and hope. As a classically trained singer, I have been lucky to be able to sing some of the music created for her by the composers featured in this book. When I sing her fervent prayers, she seems to be stirring to life again, through me. The power and magic of music bring this fictional, fascinating female character to vivid life. I hope the reader will listen to some of the operas and oratorios discussed here, and will thus be able to truly experience Judith's story in a new light.

Bibliography of Musical Works

(chronological order)

Middle Ages

1143   *Piyyut, Mi Khamokha Addir Ayom ve-Nora,* song sung on the Sabbath of
    Hanukkah.
n.d. "Canticle of Judith": *Hymnum cantemus Domino,* Catholic (based on Jdt 16:15–21) for
    Laudes (dawn service).

Sixteenth Century: Miscellaneous Formats

Judith and Holyfemes, 1566–7. Lost ballad, printed by William Pekerynge.
Ballade intytuled the moste famous historye of Judith and (H)Olofernes, 1588.
    London: Sampson Clerk.
Drayton, Michael. 1591. *Praier of Judith* and *Song of Judith* in *Harmonie of the Church.*
    London: R. Ihones.

Seventeenth-Century Oratorios

Foerster, Caspar. 1667. *Dialogus de Holoferne.*
Draghi, Antonio. 1668. *La Giuditta.*
Cazzati, Maurizio. 1668. *La Giuditta.*
Ziani, Marc Antonio. 1686. *Giuditta.* Vienna.
Colonna, Giovanni Paolo. 1690. *Bettuglia liberate.*
Biber, Henricus. 1691. *Faustus Confusus seu a Juditha fusus Holofernus.* Salzburg.

Eighteenth-Century Oratorios

Charpentier, Marc-Antoine. *c.* 1700. *Judith sive Bethulia liberate.*
Lotti, Antonio. 1701. *La Giuditta a 3 voci.* Vienna.
Zacher, J. J. 1704. *Die Heldenmüthige Judith.* Vienna.
Carlo Badia. 1704. *La Giuditta.* Vienna.
Marcello, Benedetto (to his own libretto). 1709. *La Giuditta.*
Almeida, Antonio. 1726. *La Giuditta* (Portugal).
de Fesch, Wilhelm. 1733. *Judith* (English libretto).
Reutter, Georg, 1734. *Betulia liberata* (first setting of Metastasio's libretto; Vienna).

Sehling, Joseph Anton. 1741. *Firma in Deum jiducia…in Judith Israelis Amazone*. Prague.
Jomelli, Niccolò. 1743. Betulia liberata (Metastasio's text; Venice).
Bernasconi, Antonio. 1754. *Betulia liberata* (Metastasio's text).
Holzbauer, Ignaz. 1760. *Betulia liberata* (Metastasio's text).
Smith, John Christopher. 1760. *Judith* ("scenic oratorio"; never performed).
Gassmann, Florian. 1771. *Betulia liberata* (Metastisio's text; Vienna).
Koželuch, Leopold Anton. c. 1780. *La Giuditta* and *Judith und Holofernes* (after
    Metastasio; as opera, *c.* 1779; as oratorio, 1799)

Nineteenth-Century Oratorios

Emmert, Joseph. 1800. *Judith*. Würzburg.
Strauss, Joseph. *c.* 1830. *Judith*. Karlsruhe.
Eckert, K. 1841. *Judith*. Berlin.

Seventeenth- and Eighteenth-Century Operas

da Gagliano, Marco. 1626. *La Giuditta*, three-act opera (lost), libretto Andrea Salvadori.
Opitz, Martin. 1635. *Judith, Singspiel* (from Italian source). Breslau.
Porsile, Giuseppe. 1723. *Il trionfo di Giuditta*.
Haman, J.G. 1732. *Judith* (written for the Hamburg Theatre).
Cimarosa, Domenico. 1770. *Giuditta* (*opera sacra* or sacred opera, an opera-oratorio).
Fuss, Johann (János Fusz). 1798. *Judith*.

Nineteenth-Century Operas

Levi, Samuele.1844. *Giuditta*. Venice.
Naumann, Emil. 1858. *Judith*. Dresden.
Meyerbeer, Giacomo. 1864. *Judith* (operatic fragment, unpublished).
Doppler, Albert Franz. 1870. *Judith*.
Goetze, Carl, 1887. *Judith*.

Nineteenth-Century Song

Concone, Giuseppe. 1887. *Judith, Scène et Air*. Boston: White, Smith.
    This lengthy concert song/aria is composed of several sections of changing moods,
    all highly melodic in the best *bel canto* tradition. Concone was mostly noted for his
    collections of vocal exercises. This song was performed at the London Proms in both
    1896 and 1898. The text is in French, probably because Concone lived and taught
    in Paris for many years. The score is available on IMSLP at https://imslp.org/wiki/
    Judith_(Concone%2C_Giuseppe).

Twentieth-Century Opera

Ettinger, Max. 1920. *Judith*: *musikalische Tragoedie in 3 Akten* (eight editions published in 1922 in three languages).

Grad, Gabriel. 1931, 1939. *Judith and Holofernes* (opera in Hebrew; only parts published).

Berg, Carl Nathanael. 1935. *Judith*.

Parac, Frano. 2000. *Judita* (Croatian; premiered July 14, 2000, in HNK Split, Croatian National Theater).

Bibliography

Ackerman, Susan. 1998. *Warrior Dancer Seductress Queen*. New York: Doubleday.

Bernardini, Paolo. 2010. "Judith in the Italian Unification Process," chap. 22, pp. 398–409, in *The Sword of Judith: Judith Studies Across the Disciplines*, ed. Kevin R. Brine. Cambridge: Open Book. Available online: http://books.openedition.org/obp/972 (ISBN: 9781906924171).

Brenner, Athalya. 2015. "Clothing Seduces," chap. 12, pp. 212–25, in *A Feminist Companion to Tobit and Judith*, ed. Athalya Brenner-Idan. London: Bloomsbury T&T Clark.

Brine, Kevin. 2010. "The Judith Project," chap. 1, pp. 3–21, in *The Sword of Judith*.

Brison, Ora. 2015. "Judith: A Pious Widow Turned Femme Fatale, or More?" pp. 175–99 in *A Feminist Companion to Tobit and Judith*.

Craven, Toni. 1983. *Artistry and Faith in the Book of Judith*, SBL Dissertation Series 70. Chico, CA: Scholars Press.

Craven, Toni. 2001. "Judith 2," pp. 104–6 in Carol Meyers, ed., *Women in Scripture*. Grand Rapids, MI: William Eerdmans.

De Luca, Maria Rosa. 2012. "Giuditta versus Oloferne. Un percorso didattico sull'oratorio musicale," *Musica Docta, Rivista Digitale di Pedagogia e Didattica della Musica* 2: pp. 107–21.

Efthimiadis-Keith, Helen. 2015. "Judith, Feminist Ethics and Feminist…Interpretation," chap. 8, pp. 141–63, in *A Feminist Companion to Tobit and Judith*.

Frymer-Kensky, Tikva. 1992. *In the Wake of the Goddesses*. New York: Fawcett Columbine.

Gera, Deborah Levine. 2010. "The Jewish Textual Traditions," chap. 2, pp. 23–39, in *The Sword of Judith*.

Glancy, Jennifer A. 2015. "Judith the Slaveholder," pp. 200–11 in *A Feminist Companion to Tobit and Judith*.

Harness, Kelley. 2010. "Judith, Music, and Female Patrons in Early Modern Italy," chap. 20, pp. 371–83, in *The Sword of Judith*.

Levine, Amy-Jill. 1995. "Sacrifice and Salvation," pp. 208–23 in *A Feminist Companion to Esther, Judith, and Susanna*, ed. Athalya Brenner. Sheffield: Sheffield Academic Press.

Lhaa, Alexandre. 2010. "Marcello and Peri's *Giuditta*," chap. 23, pp. 412–30, in *The Sword of Judith*.

Marsh, David. 2010. "Judith in Baroque Oratorio," chap. 21, pp. 386–96, in *The Sword of Judith*.

Milne, Pamela. 2015. "What Would I Do with Judith Now?" chap. 7a, pp. 137–40, in *A Feminist Companion to Tobit and Judith*.

Moore, Carey A. 1985. *Judith: A New Translation*, The Anchor Bible, vol. 40. New York: Doubleday.

Pasler, Jann. 2010. "Politics, Biblical debates, and French Dramatic Music on Judith after 1870," chap. 24, pp. 432–52, in *The Sword of Judith*.

Sadie, Stanley. 2001. *The New Grove Dictionary of Music and Musicians*. 2nd ed. 29 vols. New York: Grove.

Schmitz, Barbara. 2015. "The Function of the Speeches and Prayers in the Book of Judith," chap. 9, pp. 164–74, in *A Feminist Companion to Tobit and Judith*.

Sheaffer, Andrea. 2013. "Images of the Indentured," pp. 75–96 in *Biblical Reception 2*, ed. Cheryl Exum and David Clines. Sheffield: Sheffield Phoenix Press.

Smither, Howard E. 2000. *A History of the Oratorio vol. 4, The Oratorio in the Nineteenth and Twentieth Centuries*. Chapel Hill: University of North Carolina Press.

Stocker, Margarita. 1998. *Judith: Sexual Warrior*. New Haven, CT: Yale University Press.

Taruskin, Richard. 1982. "The Case of Serov's Judith," pp. 33–77 in *Opera and Drama in Russia*. Ann Arbor: University of Michigan Research Press.

Vanderkam, James. 1992. *No One Spoke Ill of Her*. Atlanta, GA: Scholars Press.

Biblical References

Index

Lightning Source UK Ltd.
Milton Keynes UK
UKHW020612110123
415155UK00006B/173